Rebecca Brandewyne
Shannon Drake
Kasey Michaels
Christina Skye

Four of the brightest stars in romantic fiction now display their extraordinary talents in boldly original ways. Here are haunting, unforgettable tales of passions that transcend the boundaries of our world, love that conquers time . . . and death. Glorious, sensuous dreams, hitherto unimagined, come alive within these pages— flights of romantic fancy that will beguile and bewitch . . . and fill your heart with the poignant and unparalleled ecstasy of supernatural love.

Bewitching
Love Stories

Avon Books Presents

Bewitching Love Stories

**REBECCA BRANDEWYNE • SHANNON DRAKE
KASEY MICHAELS • CHRISTINA SKYE**

AVON BOOKS ◆ NEW YORK

AVON BOOKS PRESENTS: BEWITCHING LOVE STORIES is an original publication of Avon Books. This work, as well as each individual story, has never before appeared in print. This work is a collection of fiction. Any similarity to actual persons or events is purely coincidental.

AVON BOOKS
A division of
The Hearst Corporation
1350 Avenue of the Americas
New York, New York 10019

Devil's Keep copyright © 1992 by Rebecca Brandewyne
Vanquish the Night copyright © 1992 by Heather Graham Pozzessere
My Aunt Grizelda copyright © 1992 by Kathie Seidick
What Dreams May Come copyright © 1992 by Roberta Helmer

Published by arrangement with the authors
Library of Congress Catalog Card Number: 92-93062
ISBN: 0-380-76832-1

First Avon Books Printing: September 1992

AVON TRADEMARK REG. U.S. PAT. OFF. AND IN OTHER COUNTRIES, MARCA REGISTRADA, HECHO EN U.S.A.

Printed in the U.S.A.

RA 10 9 8 7 6 5 4 3 2 1

Contents

Avon Books Presents

Bewitching Love Stories

Devil's Keep

Rebecca Brandewyne

Devil's Keep

I fled him—down the nights and down the days,
I fled him, down the arches of the years,
I fled him, down the labyrinthine ways
Of my own mind's fancies and flame that sears
To the very soul, burning dark, unquenched.
Up feverish dreams, I sped;
And shot, precipitated
Adown diabolic glooms of shadowed fears,
From those strong feet that followed, my heart wrenched
And torn apart, bedeviled,
All my thoughts and hopes disheveled,
Wind-tossed senses scattered far and wide
By glittering eyes and honeyed voice—.
At its low murmur, I did rejoice
That there was no place at Devil's Keep to hide.
All that he took from me, he did but take
Not for my harms,
But just that I might'st seek it in his arms;
And when, on the horizon, dawn did break,
The night had cast its splendorous spell,
Lo, triumphant was he I loved full well!

—Adapted from *The Hound of Heaven*,
by Francis Thompson

1

Cornwall, England, 1813

I WAS caught fast in the grip of the nightmare I had suffered since I was a child—except that this wild, primeval night was no nightmare at all, but a terrifying reality from which there was no escape. Like flotsam upon the frothy waves of the roiling sea I could hear breaking against the scarred black cliffs that edged the jagged coast, I was powerless against it, a helpless victim of capricious fate. Shivering both with fright and from the brutal elements of the raging storm outside, I could do naught but huddle amid the plump squabs of the plush red-velvet coach seat, clutching the strap as tight as I could to keep from being flung violently about the vehicle traveling at such a reckless pace, on such a savage night.

Surely, the coachman was mad, I thought fearfully for the hundredth time since I had first beheld him in Launceton—a cockroach of a man, stooped, grizzled, and ill-kempt, his garments such that even a ragpicker would have scorned them, his eyes sly and shifting, unable to meet mine as he had scuttled to fetch my trunk containing all my worldly belongings and heave it up onto the top of the well-sprung carriage. Only this last, with its imposing although unfamiliar coat of arms upon the door, had reassured me, however slightly, that

Renfrew was who and what he had claimed—coachman to Count Drogo von Reicher, my reclusive, unknown employer, to whose manor on the desolate northern coast of Cornwall I was currently en route on a night not fit for man or beast.

Not for the first time did I doubt my own sanity, as well as that of the coachman; for surely, only a woman as mad—or as desperate as I—would have responded to that distinctly peculiar advertisement in the London *Times*, which, despite my lamentable lack of testimonials, had nevertheless resulted in my being retained as governess to Count von Reicher's seven-year-old son and was the cause of my long journey from London to Launceton, and thence to the isolated manor that was to be my new home. Despite my wretched circumstances, that I had been hired without benefit of referral or interview had given me pause; almost, I had withdrawn my application for the post.

What kind of a man committed the care and education of his only child to a governess without recommendation and sight unseen? It did not speak well of him or of his son, I had reflected soberly. Still, beggars could not be choosers; and I, destitute, having been ignominiously turned off without a reference from my previous place of employment—though for no fault of my own—had known with certainty that I was highly unlikely to find another position. Weeks of fruitless searching had made me all too aware of that. At the orphanage in which I had been reared, all the knowledge I had so diligently acquired, and that I had so blindly and foolishly trusted would stand me in good stead by ensuring me a secure future, had availed me naught in the end. For God, in His infinite wisdom, had seen fit not only to bless me with an intelligent mind, but to curse me with a striking beauty that, had my situation been different, would easily have captured me a rich, handsome, titled husband, but that, in concert with my poor and indisputably common background, was instead the bane of my existence.

I was painfully cognizant of my station in life and made no attempt to rise above it; indeed, I went to great lengths to render my suitability for it unimpeachable. Still, no matter how severe and firmly pinned my long hair, how plain and unprepossessing my outmoded gowns, how proper and demure my reserved demeanor, I inevitably attracted the unsought, unwelcome attentions of unscrupulous men and the spiteful jealousy of the vigilant women to whom they belonged. That my maidenhead was yet my own was a testament to both my character and my strength; my dire straits were witness to the fact that I would rather be thrown out on the streets by the wives and mothers of the households in which I had served than surrender my virtue to their husbands and older sons in order to maintain my job. Nevertheless, conviction did not fill my belly, nor courage keep the wolf from my door.

Thus it happened that I now perched precariously in the coach of a man about whom I knew little and suspected worse with each passing mile. Clearly, if Renfrew and I were any example, Count von Reicher had scant care about his servants. For all I knew, the coachman was a lunatic escaped from some asylum; certainly, he drove as though the hounds of hell harried our heels. This would have been ill-advised under even the best of conditions; in the face of the barbarous storm, it was sheer folly. The silver moon that gleamed sporadically amid the seething black thunderclouds massed in the night sky did nothing to illuminate the winding road that stretched before us across the sodden moors. Nor did the dimly glowing flames of the brass lanterns bolted to the vehicle, flickering wildly with each rough jolt, penetrate the darkness and the pelting rain. Still, Renfrew pressed on frenziedly, his shouted epithets and the harsh lash of his whip as fierce and discordant as the shrieking wind, goading the four galloping black horses furiously onward. Specks of white foam flew from their wet, lathered coats; clumps of mud churned up by their pounding hooves spattered the underbelly of the carriage. The coach wheels clattered and lurched, and the springs convulsed beneath me, as though at any moment the strain upon the axles would prove too great and one or both of them would snap into splinters, hurling the vehicle to its doom. Lightning split the firmament; thunder roared as though God shouted at the devil, and the wind howled like a legion of vociferous demons. Rain pummeled the windows, poured down the panes as, like the pictures of a magic lantern, my nightmare unfolded before my eyes, its images erratic, disjointed.

In my mind, somehow, it was my father's carriage careening crazily down the road, in a vain attempt to outrun the storm that all too quickly overtook us—for no man or beast can outstrip the wind—and Renfrew's curses were those of our own coachman, Sykes, the hand that wielded the snaking whip Sykes's, as well. I was a seven-year-old child again, the ghost of my mother sitting anxiously across from me, cringing as the foul imprecations and the sharp cracks of the lash reached her ears, the ghost of my father beside her, grim-faced and angrily leaning forward to hammer with his cane upon the box just before, without warning, there came from beneath us a sound like a bomb bursting that was the axle shattering; and then the coach pitched heavily to one side and toppled over to begin the ghastly, lethal tumble that crushed my mother's chest and broke my father's neck.

To this day, I do not know how or why I was spared. I remember only my parents' stricken faces, my father's reaching out in a loving but futile gesture to protect my mother before I hit my head hard and a merciful blackness swirled up to engulf me. I knew nothing more until I awoke in an infirmary bed to learn that my parents were dead and that I was totally alone in all the world. My heart ached at the memory, even as my dread and panic increased at the thought that now, thirteen long, lonely years later, I should follow my parents to the grave, as I might have done that fateful, fatal night.

But just as I believed I should give way at last to my terror, the vehicle bounced through the open wrought-iron gates of the manor, past the darkened lodge, and, weaving its way along the serpentine drive beneath the canopy of tall, twisted Cornish elms that lined the verge, came to a bone-jarring halt before the front porch of the manor. Then, eerily, for Renfrew had not yet dismounted from the box above, the handle of the carriage door turned; the door itself swung slowly open on its brass hinges, and the steps were lowered as though of their own accord. From the depths of the wind- and rain-swept portico, a seemingly disembodied hand reached out to me.

"Fraulein Blakeley, I presume," drawled a low, throaty, foreign-accented voice whose timbre was both so dulcet and so delusory that it prickled the fine hairs on my nape. "Welcome to Devil's Keep."

The words echoed strangely beneath the cavernous roof of the portico, faintly mocking, and somehow menacing, as well. My heart still thrumming, my nerves stretched as taut as the strings of a harp, I hesitated to alight from the coach, some primordial instinct warning me of a sudden that danger lurked beyond, within the walls of the foreboding manor that rose before me like the dark, imprisoning tower of some evil legend, and in the shape of the man whose touch sent a shudder through my body, as though a goose had just walked over my grave. Rattled, I involuntarily tried to snatch my hand away, but the fingers that closed tight around mine, while long and slender, were strong as an iron band, inexorably drawing me from the vehicle—and toward my fate. I had again that fleeting impression of looming gray stone walls as bleak and mysterious as some castle aeons spellbound, and then, as he stepped from the shadows into the fitful light of the torches blazing on either side of the massive oak portal, I had a fearsome glimpse of him who was surely master here, and no other.

Has he not a rogue's face? . . . a hanging-look to me . . . has a damn'd Tyburn-face, without the benefit o' the Clergy . . .

Unbidden, Congreve's words rang in my mind at the sight of my unknown employer, Count Drogo von Reicher. Unwittingly, my breath caught in my throat. Never in my life had I seen a man so dark, so demonic, so unutterably handsome that he was proud Lucifer personified, at once so wicked and yet so irresistibly tempting that in a blinding moment of revelation, I understood absolutely why God had cast that unrepentant archangel from heaven's realm. For even God, had He continued to gaze upon it, must have denied that face nothing.

It was a face wild and bold, beautiful and brutal and breathtaking to behold. His shaggy, disheveled hair was blacker than the smoke of the infernal abyss, glistening as though frosted by an unholy light where the wavering flames of the torches kissed the rain-damp strands. His skin was darker than the sweet-flowing honey of the promised land. Thick black brows that each swooped like a terrible, two-edged sword cut a startling oblique across his noble brow; his dark, burning eyes glowed hotter than the sacrificial fire of an altar. Beneath his chiseled Roman nose, his mouth curved as sensual and dissolute as that of the whore of Babylon; his teeth shone whiter than the proverbial pearls cast before swine. Tall and powerfully built, as lean and hard-muscled as the predatory beast loosed by the breaking of the seven seals, he was a creature fashioned to rule in hell, not to serve in heaven . . .

Had he not held my hand captive, I should have fled from him, lest I willingly offered up my body and soul to him, such was his diabolically potent effect upon me, the manner in which his dark eyes smoldered like twin embers as, slowly, deliberately, he appraised me. I could not guess his thoughts, for he hooded his eyes against me; but as though he had read my own mind, he did not release me. Instead, with a sudden, snapping spread of his black, many-caped greatcoat, his free arm came up like a giant bat's wing to encircle my trembling shoulders, pulling me so near to him that I could feel the strength and warmth of his hard body against my own soft one. As though they formed a shroud, the folds of his cloak swirled about me, shielding me from the wind and rain as, without another word, he ushered me across the threshold into the manor, then slammed shut the ponderous door and locked and barred it tight against the night.

2

By the faint, unsteady light of a tarnished silver candelabrum, I saw that I stood in a great hall that must once have been very grand but now showed time's unmistakable neglect. The hard oak floor was dull and dark with age, the wood scarred; the planks were pulling away from one another; the red carpet upon the long, sweeping staircase that curved up to the second-story landing was shabby and frayed. The furniture, although magnificent, was dry and brittle from lack of polish; layers of dust swathed the rickety cabinets and tables, soiled the faded damasks and brocades of gilded settees and chairs, the bedraggled yarn of threadbare tapestries. A murky shield reflected not only the gloomy candle-light, but also the corroded weapons arrayed upon the walls; at the foot of the stairs, a suit of armor stood, its visor rusted shut. Gossamer cobwebs draped the cracked corners of the high ceiling and laced the ropes of prisms that encrusted the cloudy crystal chandelier. The drafty air was pungent with the musty scents of dust and disuse and decay. Over everything, there hung a pall of desolation, as though no human foot had trodden within the manor for many a long year.

Yet oddly enough, it seemed the perfect setting for him who was master here; for he himself, I fancied, was not quite human, not quite real, but some pagan god— or demon—of yore.

Turning, he hung his greatcoat upon a nearby hall tree, revealing how his exquisitely tailored black silk jacket clung to his broad shoulders, how the frothy lace jabot of his crisp white cambric shirt spilled down his massive chest. This tapered to a belly firm and flat beneath his waistcoat, from which hung a plain but superior gold watch chain adorned with a single fob and seal. His black silk breeches hugged thick, cord-ed thighs, and calves encased in black leather boots. He was, by far, not only the handsomest, but also the most elegant man I had ever seen. Even so, I sensed that beneath his civilized veneer lay the dark, elemental magnetism and menace of an animal. He moved with the sinewy, hypnotic grace of a panther on the prowl; his black eyes were equally mesmerizing, holding me fast where I stood, as those of a predator rivet its prey an interminable heartbeat before the kill. Fluidly, as one motion, he clicked his heels together and bowed low over my hand; lingeringly, his lips brushed its back. The sensation of his carnal mouth pressed against my skin was such that another tremor, even more violent than the first, swept over me; I felt dizzy and breathless, as though I had run a long way and now was nigh to swooning. At the core of my being, a slow-burning heat I had never before known ignited and spread like a fever through my blood. Surely, I must be growing ill, I thought, coming down with an ague; for what other explanation could there be for my faintness? That there might be one, I determinedly thrust from my mind.

"Permit me to introduce myself, Fraulein Blakeley," he murmured, in that voice that flowed like sweet summer wine. "I am Count Drogo von Reicher, late of Prussia and . . . other places. I trust that your journey, however unpleasant due to the inclement weather, at least proved comfortable and not too fatiguing?" One devilish black brow lifted inquiringly, a gesture I was to come to know well but that now unnerved me.

"Y-y-yes, my lord—" I blushed to hear myself stammer like a silly schoolgirl, wishing he would release my hand so I could collect my composure, which seemed, wretchedly, to have quite deserted me. "—though the pace was perhaps swifter than was wise on such an inauspicious night."

"Hardly that, Fraulein Blakeley," he rejoined softly, the pressure of his hand about mine increasing ever so slightly, "for fortuitously, haste—at least, in your case— did not make waste."

His eyes raked me in a way that deepened the rosy bloom upon my cheeks and made my heart beat fast with both trepidation and an odd, perverse excitement as I realized he did not find me displeasing. Still, though excessively flattered, I was not so young and foolish as to suppose that despite his being a widower, Count von Reicher would ever perceive me as a woman to be both bedded *and* wedded; such had not been my experience with men of his rank and riches. Remembering that, I coolly drew my hand from his, so he would know that although I had come to him without testimonials, I was a chaste woman.

Although provocation had not been my intent, his eyes flared with more than a passing interest; a sardonic smile curved his lips. I suspected he felt I had flung down between us the proverbial gauntlet and he was more than up to the challenge. The notion sent a shiver down my spine, leaving me as unsettled as before; for belatedly, it occurred to me that with the exception of Renfrew, I had as yet to spy any servants. Given the state of the manor, I supposed that however bizarre and unlikely this appeared, it was just possible I was alone here with the master of Devil's Keep, with none but a lunatic and a child to defend me. Or perhaps there was no child at all, I thought suddenly, stricken, my imagination running wild. Perhaps Count von Reicher's peculiar advertisement in the *Times* had been no more than a vile ruse to lure gullible or desperate young women such as I into his wicked clutches.

"You are shaking, Fraulein Blakeley," he observed, his voice holding a trace of amusement, I fancied, indignant at the idea and yearning to give him a smart set-down. "You must be chilled to the bone. How churlish of me to have kept you standing here in the great hall. Come. Let me lead you in to the fire, where you may get warm. The hour is late, but I am certain some hot tea and a light repast can be managed; and then, no doubt, you will be longing for bed . . . ?"

"Yes, my lord," I said, feigning ignorance of the double entendre he had surely intended with his last words. I allowed him to slip my pelisse from my shoulders. "I am accustomed to an early night and am more worn out by my journey than I had supposed. Alas, I am poor company, I fear."

"You underrate yourself, Fraulein Blakeley; still, your modesty is refreshing," he declared as he turned from hanging my cloak upon the hall tree. "I do not recall when I was last so captivated by a woman."

"I am a mere governess, my lord, with neither charming coquetry nor clever conversation to entertain you. I am afraid you are making a mock of me."

"To the contrary, I am making you my compliments. I am a man infinitely jaded; nevertheless, you have succeeded in piquing my interest. I confess you are not at all what I expected in a governess."

"Nor you I in my employer, so it seems we are quits, then, my lord."

"Not at all, Fraulein Blakeley. We have only just begun."

At that, taking up the candelabrum to light our way, he led me into the drawing room and bade me be seated in a chair before the hearth, where a fire burned. Gratefully, I sat and held my hands out to the blaze to warm them, for I was, in truth, chilly, and the manor, centuries old and built of stone, was drafty and cold. It groaned and shuddered and strained so as the wind whipped and whined about it that I marveled it had stood for so many years against the elements of the wild northern Cornish coast.

As I gazed about, I saw that the opulent drawing room—hung with sumptuous draperies and priceless paintings, filled with lavish furniture and exotic curios— suffered from the same disrepair as the great hall, not a sight to inspire my confidence. Now, more than ever after the brief dialogue I had exchanged with Count von Reicher, I heartily wished I had followed my instincts and withdrawn my application for the post of governess at Devil's Keep. That many among the gentry were accustomed to engaging in such dual-edged repartee and found it neither shocking nor improper, but a skill to be honed to its utmost sharpness, I knew. Still, for all my heavy mass of copper hair, my sloe green eyes, my porcelain skin, my hourglass figure, I was not a woman to be flirted with by a gentleman for purposes other than mere dalliance. I feared that the dire straits that had driven me to reply to Count von Reicher's unconventional advertisement in the *Times* had perhaps placed me in an even more untenable position than I had been in before; for surely, I was at the utter mercy of my strange, enigmatic, saturnine employer.

No servants but Renfrew did, in fact, seem to exist. From the great hall, I had heard the crunch of the carriage wheels upon the gravel as he had driven away, presumably to the stables, and then, from the shadowy, as yet unknown depths of the manor, the muffled sounds of his dragging my trunk inside. But my ears had discerned no voice save that of his own, muttering and babbling to himself. Now, as he sidled subserviently into the drawing room to receive his master's orders that food and drink be brought to me straightaway, I knew with a sinking heart that however queer and alarming the manor's lack of staff, Renfrew alone must serve the household. I thought of how my employer had locked and barred the front door tight, slipping the iron key into the pocket of his waistcoat; doubtless, the remainder of the portals were similarly secured. Further, even if I *were* able to flee from the manor, the storm outside yet raged, its fury undiminished. On foot, without conveyance, I should be exposed to its full force; I should surely lose my way upon the dark, deceptive moors, perhaps even drown in one of the treacherous peat bogs with which they were riddled. Flight was not a realistic choice.

I did not suppose that Renfrew would be of any help to me. Sane or mad, he appeared to behold his master with as much dread and suspicion as I did; for Count von Reicher's coolly voiced demands were met with much obsequious jabber and bowing and scraping on the cowering servant's part, and he scurried away not a moment later than was necessary.

"Poor fellow," Count von Reicher intoned after Renfrew had left us. " 'Twas a blow to his head that addled his wits. Still, he is harmless and serves me well enough."

From the side pocket of his jacket, he produced a baroque gold snuffbox and, after shaking back one ruffled cuff, with a flick of his wrist sprang open the lid. The strong, fragrant scent of the tobacco he favored permeated the air as, taking a generous pinch, he inhaled it up first one nostril and then the other. As he did so, my attention was drawn to the large, unusual, bejeweled gold ring upon his right hand; it was, surely, the kind of ring in which a small portion of pills or powder might be kept, I thought. Troubled by the notion, I wondered what, if anything, it contained; but I could not bring myself to ask. Instead, more disturbed by the fact that I did indeed appear to be virtually all alone at the manor with my employer, I inquired:

"Have you—have you no other staff, my lord?"

"Seldom, Fraulein Blakeley. As I believe I made clear in my advertisement, I am something of a recluse, and Devil's Keep is quite isolated; it is thought by many to be haunted, as well, a superstition that does not lend itself to the acquiring of servants locally, even if I wished for them, which I do not. Thus my advertisement in the *Times*. Even so, I had little hope, actually, of finding a governess for Nikolaus; your letter of application for the post came as an agreeable surprise, I'll admit."

His eyes, hypnotically compelling, invited me to confide in him; somehow, I resisted the nearly overpowering impulse, thinking it best not to reveal to my employer that I was not only penniless, but without family or friends. Instead, I asked:

"Nikolaus? Is that your son?"

"Yes. You shall meet him on the morrow."

"You mentioned in your advertisement that he is 'a difficult, sickly boy, with special needs'? I believe that was how you phrased it," I said, somewhat relieved that there evidently really *was* a child, for if so, it seemed much less likely that Count von Reicher had enticed me here under false pretenses, for some villainous aim of his own.

"Yes. Unfortunately, my son suffers from an as yet undiagnosed illness, which the physicians are unable to treat or cure, a lingering complaint that manifests itself in periodic bouts of . . . weakness and depression, occasional fits of . . . violence and mania, migraines and an . . . aversion to strong light. Some . . . time ago, he lost his mother, as well, a terrible tragedy. My wife—" Did I imagine it, or did his mouth tighten as though soured by those two words? "—Stephanine, died a particularly singular and gruesome death, and Nikki was much affected by it. He was always a shy, solitary boy; now, I fear, he has withdrawn even more into his own private self. He does not take easily to strangers. That's why I thought a governess rather than a tutor— He so needs a woman's gentle touch and devotion, you see."

"Yes, of course," I replied, feeling a sudden, warm rush of sympathy for both father and son; for how could I, who had lost my own loving parents in that catastrophic carriage accident when I was no older than young Lord Nikolaus von Reicher, fail to comprehend his pain and devastation, or the obvious love his father bore him?

Plainly, it had been difficult for Count von Reicher to speak of his son's illness, bitterly unpleasant for him to be reminded of his dead wife. The marriage had been troubled, I suspected; perhaps Count von Reicher had been relieved by his countess's dying, a feeling that must surely have engendered guilt in him, as well. That he cherished his son was evident. But how much of his

tender regard was born of love, and how much of pity
for the mysteriously ailing boy, how much of blame and
regret for the child's lack of a mother? I wondered. It
could not be easy for Count von Reicher, so strong and
vital, to cope with a son—and his only heir—frail and
listless, who perhaps might not survive to grow into
manhood.

"You spoke of Nikolaus's being prone to occasional
fits of—of violence and mania. Is the boy . . . dangerous,
my lord?"

"I will not deceive you, Fraulein Blakeley. There
may be times when it will be necessary for me, and
no other, to handle my son. Mercifully, however, such
periods are rare. For the most part, you will find him
biddable enough, so you need have no fear on that
account. His manners, when he chooses, are faultless,
and he is not without his own particular charm and
appeal."

Count von Reicher's words reassured me—for indeed,
I found it difficult to imagine that a mere seven-year-old
child, no matter his disposition, could do me any real
harm—and no more was said on the subject, I resolv-
ing that I owed my employer the courtesy of meeting
his son before determining whether I was capable of
undertaking the care and education of the boy, and
Count von Reicher feeling perhaps as though he had
said all that was required. And indeed, he had. I now
had a much clearer picture, I believed, of why things
stood as they did at Devil's Keep. I could more easily
understand why my employer was so reclusive. Proud
and arrogant, he would welcome neither pity nor prying,
I suspected; thus, like his son, he had withdrawn from
the world. For all his title and fortune, his life was
scarcely ideal. I was now half ashamed that earlier, I
had supposed him wicked and depraved. In truth, it was
far more likely that he was as lonely as I. Viewing him
in this kinder, most hospitable light, I felt my fear of

him dissipate. Surely, he was without evil designs upon me; for if such were his intent, would he not already— knowing I was totally in his power, helpless against his every whim and desire—have made them plain, perhaps even acted upon them?

Renfrew materialized, bearing an extravagant sterling-silver tray ladened with a matching teapot and a cold collation consisting of a selection of meats, cheeses, and dried fruits, as well as slabs of thick, crusty bread generously spread with butter. Carefully, he placed the tray upon the satinwood tea table between his employer and me. Then, ascertaining that his services were not further required, he hurried from the drawing room, doubtless off to bed. Count von Reicher, playing the perfect host, leaned forward in his chair to fill a plate for me and pour out the tea.

"Milk or lemon, Fraulein Blakeley? Honey or sugar?"

Deftly, he prepared the tea as I liked it, then handed me the Sèvres china teacup and saucer, so costly and fragile that I was half afraid they would shatter at my touch. The tea was very strong and sweet and had a strange, exotic flavor, a special blend of Count von Reicher's own devising, he told me when I commented upon the unique taste. Because of his son's cryptic affliction, he was, he explained, much interested in the healing properties of herbs and spices and other aromatics, as well as those of crystals and metals. Having traveled widely abroad from his native Prussia and studied extensively over the years, particularly in the Orient, he was, in fact, an adept alchemist. He had, since his son had been stricken, devoted his life's work to finding not just a treatment, but a cure for the boy.

Not only because, famished, I ate as my employer spoke, but also because I was growing increasingly dazed with fatigue, I contributed little to our conversation. My head felt light and dizzy; the drawing room seemed suddenly, strangely, to spin about me, as though I were drunk or dreaming. I was mortified to hear how my teacup clattered as I gingerly lowered it to my saucer, accidentally knocking the spoon to the floor.

"Fraulein Blakeley, you are exhausted." Count von Reicher rose swiftly and smoothly rescued the teacup and saucer that, much to my chagrin, were somehow slipping from my weakening grasp. "The hour is late, and despite my knowing how long and wearisome your journey here to Devil's Keep was, I have boorishly kept you from your bed. Please accept my humble apologies, and allow me to escort you upstairs to your chamber."

Dumbly, I nodded, my mind clouded by confusion, my limbs becoming more numb and leaden with each passing minute, despite how I struggled against the burgeoning lethargy that assailed me. I felt abruptly as though I were going to swoon; and I was only too glad, after he had once more taken up the candelabrum, holding it aloft to light our path, of my employer's free hand firmly at my elbow, conducting me from the drawing room and supporting me up the grand staircase.

The bedchamber that was to be mine was located in the west wing, the east wing's, Count von Reicher informed me, being closed off. Like the rest of the manor, my room was almost overwhelming in its luxuriance, dominated by a massive rococo canopy bed hung with heavy, forest-green velvet curtains trimmed with fringed gold braid, and piled high with plump gold satin pillows. The remainder of the furnishings were equally elaborate; and here, at least, a halfhearted attempt had been made to sweep away the cobwebs and dust. Somewhat to my surprise, the bed had already been turned down for the night, and a brass warming pan leaned against the blazing hearth, so neither my sheets nor I should be cold. My leather-bound trunk sat at the foot of the bed, unopened.

"I'll bid you good night, Fraulein Blakeley," Count von Reicher murmured as he once more raised my hand to his lips. "Pleasant dreams."

"Good night, my lord."

After shutting the door and firmly turning the key in the lock, it was all I could do to unfasten the straps of my trunk and withdraw my white flannel night rail, which I donned as quickly as possible after stripping off my gown and petticoats. I took the pins from my long hair, too tired even to brush it, much less braid it, as was my custom at night. After that, with the warming pan, I heated the sheets, then climbed into bed and pulled the curtains about me, burrowing gratefully into the soft feather mattress beneath the layers of warm wool blankets and the lush green-velvet counterpane. I slept as soon as my head touched the pillow; but for all that my slumber was deep, it was restless, disturbed by a morbid, chilling dream.

I dreamed that sometime in the night, the key revolved in the lock of my door and the door itself creaked slowly open to reveal Count von Reicher poised upon the threshold, the tarnished silver candelabrum in his hand and a small, pale, handsome boy at his side. Like specters, their footfalls making no sound, the man and boy seemed to float into my chamber, coming to rest beside my bed. Noiselessly, the rings mysteriously making no scrape against the rods, my bed curtains were parted. Then my employer and his son drew near to stand there staring down at me, their eyes burning like hot coals, on their faces equally sinister expressions of such avid, animalistic hunger that it was as though they intended to spring like beasts upon my sleeping body and, rending me limb from limb, devour me.

"She's lovely, isn't she, Father?" the boy observed softly, in a voice that was a higher, childish echo of Count von Reicher's own—euphonious, beguiling, making gooseflesh prickle my body. "Her hair is as scarlet as blood in the firelight, her skin as white as death."

"Yes, she is the most beautiful woman I have ever seen."

"Is she the one, then, Father? Is she?"

"Yes, Nikki, she is the one. The moment I saw her, I felt in my bones that it was so."

"Then she will belong to us forever, Father, won't she? You'll see to that, won't you? You won't let her go away as you did all the others?"

"No, son. I won't let her go away, I promise. She will be ours until the end of time, and beyond, for she will never leave Devil's Keep alive . . ."

Hearing that, I cringed and cried out in terror. But in my dream, no matter how long and loud I screamed and screamed, no sound emanated from my throat; not even the merest of whispers issued from my lips. I was as voiceless as a mute. Desperately, I tried to rise from my bed, to flee. But my body was as heavy as though weighted down by massive stones and would not obey my mind. I could not awake, could not move, but lay there like a prisoner stretched upon a dungeon rack, my heart pounding so frantically that it was as though it would burst from my breast.

For I knew with horrific certainty that the hard, hot mouth that brushed my tremulous lips, the strong, possessive hand that caressed my unbound hair, the low, hoarse voice that muttered, "Lenore . . . sweet Lenore," against my bare, vulnerable throat belonged to Death.

3

I AWOKE to darkness, bewildered as to how that could be; for it seemed that like the fabled Briar Rose, who had pricked her finger on a spindle and fallen into a deep, unnatural trance, I had slept a hundred years. I knew instinctively that dawn should long since have broken. Yet dark it was, and disorienting; gazing at the closed curtains of the unfamiliar bed in which I lay, I did not at first know where I was. It was only gradually that hearing the pitter-patter of light rain against the windows, I realized that the continuing drizzle was responsible for the gray, dreary day; and the events of the previous evening returned to me, along with vague, incoherent images from my terrifying dream. For surely, it *had* been a dream, I told myself, a hideous nightmare.

Sluggishly, I folded back the covers and rose from the bed, my head throbbing, my mouth as dry as though I had drunk wine, not tea, last night—and far too much of it. I did not know what ailed me; perhaps I was, indeed, suffering from the onslaught of some ague. Yet of a sudden did I remember Count von Reicher's distinctive gold ring, his knowledge of medicinals, the strange lethargy that had so swiftly come upon me; and dwelling on my nightmare, I could not help but wonder, gnawingly disquieted, if my employer had drugged me with some soporific elixir so he could slip into my chamber and take advantage of me while I lay sleeping. Still, the idea seemed preposterous, fantastic, the product of my vivid imagination and agitation. I had no evidence that I had actually been physically violated and would have laughed at the notion had I not been so afraid that my hilarity would hold a hysterical note. For despite how staunchly I tried to reassure myself, I could not refrain from shivering as I recalled the vibrant feel of my dream-lover's hungry mouth upon mine, his hand tangled roughly in my hair, his voice huskily muttering my name. He had seemed so very real that even now, it was difficult to believe he had been no more than an illusion.

She will never leave Devil's Keep alive . . .

Unbidden, the macabre words rang in my mind, haunting me, horrifying me, despite that common sense dictated they could only have been spoken in a nightmare—and that itself born of my exhaustion, my overwrought nerves. My weeks of spiraling anxiety that I should be cast into a workhouse or forced to take to the streets to earn my living, my upsetting journey, the harrowing carriage ride that had resurrected memories of my parents' tragic deaths, the barbarous storm, the decadent manor, my dark employer . . . all had been too much for me, culminating in the eerie, grotesque dream that had troubled my slumber. That was all; there was no more to it than that. I would not be so foolish and fanciful as to believe otherwise, I resolved.

I was inordinately glad of my sensibility when, a few minutes later, there came a knock at my door and a young, pretty maid timidly poked her blonde head into my chamber. In fact, I was so happy to see her that I did not think to wonder how my door had come to be unlocked.

"Oh, miss, yer awake at last," she said, smiling shyly as she stepped inside, a stack of folded linens and a kettle of steaming water in her hands. "I was beginnin' ta think thee meant ta stay abed all day, though t' master said as how thee'd had a wearisome journey, an' so thee was ta sleep as late as 'ee liked, that I was not ta disturb 'ee. I be Sarah, miss, Sarah Tremaine, Renfrew's granddaughter," she announced, hanging the towels on the washstand and filling the porcelain basin with the hot water from the kettle, then turning to stoke up the fire that smoldered in the grate and to make up the bed. "Grandfather fetched me from t' village this mornin', claimin' as how t' master said 'tweren't fittin' that thee had no woman ta wait upon 'ee. So here I be, miss— an' there be my husband, Dickon, ta help out, as well, in t' house an' in t' yard," she added.

"But I thought . . . that is, last night, Count von Reicher informed me that the villagers are afraid to come to the manor, that they believe that it is haunted," I rejoined slowly, puzzled though greatly relieved by Sarah's presence; for I simply could not envision my employer's hiring her if he was plotting and planning to murder me.

"Oh, aye, miss, that be true enough," she confirmed, her blue eyes wide with awe and superstition. "There be few among us villagers who care ta set foot upon t' place, even in broad daylight, much less after sundown. Sold a bill of goods, t' master were, if thee ask me; fer 'tis not just a shambles t' manor be, but haunted indeed. Till Count von Reicher arrived here a few months ago, t' manor had not been lived in fer so long as I can remember. But before that, when t' old master were in residence, an' t' master before him, an' so on down through t' years, there be strange an' evil goin's-on here, miss. On nights when t' mist hung low over t' moors an' t' wind an' t' sea were high, there be unearthly lights spied a-flickerin' on t' grounds an' at t' windows of Divvil's Keep, an' horrible voices heard, a-howlin' like wild dogs or wolves a-bayin' at t' moon. Oh, miss, 'twas sights an' sounds fair ta curl yer hair, I'm told. Grandfather were witness ta many of t' frightful happenin's—an' he saw some of t' bodies, too, of them what was most foully murdered here, set upon by t' like of what surely nivver were any man nor beast, miss, but some monstrous, unnatural creature what ripped out t' throats of all them brave or foolish enough ta trespass here at t' manor—may t' poor, lost souls rest in peace." Sarah crossed herself quickly, then continued.

"Because of that, there's them what swear t' place, in truth, belongs ta no man, miss, but ta t' divvil himself. That's how it come over t' years ta be known as Divvil's Keep. 'Tis rumored that whenever there be a man so bold as ta call himself master here, t' divvil steals his body an' soul, an' in t' shape of him so possessed walks t' earth ta stake his claim on all those he would have serve him in hell. They do say—" Here, she lowered her voice and glanced about apprehensively. "—that all of them what died here, miss, come back ta life afterward, undead, ta prey upon t' livin', that they could not rest easy in their graves until their heads was severed from their corpses an' their hearts cut clean out of their breasts!" She shuddered visibly at her own gruesome announcement, then after a moment went on to confide:

"Were it not fer t' money t' master offered Dickon an' me, we'd not have agreed ta come here, miss, nay, not on yer life. But I don't mind admittin' we're poor, plain folk, so a bit of coin will be more than welcome, an' with what t' master be payin' us, why, we'll soon have enough put by fer a new roof on our cottage— which we badly need, fer t' water comes in summat fierce when it rains." Briskly, Sarah plumped up the pillows on the bed and gave the counterpane a final twitch, settling it into place. "Well, then, that's done, isn't it?" She nodded with satisfaction as she looked about the tidied room. "Shall I lay out yer clothes, then, miss, an' help 'ee ta dress?"

"Yes, the dove-grey gown, Sarah, if you please," I directed absently, lost in contemplation of her lurid tale.

That murder had been done here over the ages, I could easily believe. Yet that it had been committed in a fashion so grisly as to give rise to Sarah's morbid story seemed incredible, as wild and bizarre as my own dreadful nightmare.

By nature, the Cornish—descendants, for the most part, of the Celts—were a clannish and superstitious lot, I knew, given to believing in such mythical creatures as kelpies and piskies. Further, the northern coast of Cornwall was a savage and desolate place, home to smugglers and, worse, wreckers—the latter villainous men who, by means of a false signal light, would lure ships into crashing on the coast, after which the wreckers would kill all those aboard and rob the vessels of their cargoes. Such was the place to which I had come. Was it any wonder, then, that over the years equally grim and ghastly tales should have sprung up about Devil's Keep? The isolated manor clung like an aerie to the cliffs overlooking the sea, towering grey and daunting over the land. It was a natural setting, surely, for the kind of story Sarah had recounted.

Since my arrival last night, even my own imagination had run unchecked, and that there was a grain of truth in Sarah's narrative, I did not doubt. Yet inventive as I was, even I could not credit the existence of such a creature as she had described. So, the remainder of her account I compelled myself to disregard as mere superstition, thrusting to the back of my mind the thought of Count von Reicher's uncannily devilish visage and demeanor.

Moving to the window, I drew back the heavy draperies and was startled to grasp how late the hour must be. The morning was long gone; it was afternoon, surely. A glance at the small clock ticking upon the mantel confirmed that it was after two. I was overcome with anxiety at the realization. What would my employer think at my tardy appearance my first day at work? That I was a slugabed and therefore no fit governess for his son? Despite how deeply Count von Reicher and Devil's Keep both had unsettled me, I had no wish to lose my job. Hurriedly, then, with Sarah's deft assistance, I washed, dressed, and pinned up my long red hair, silently bewailing the fact that, oddly, neither the washstand nor the dresser nor any wall in my chamber contained a mirror, by which I might examine myself to be certain I was properly attired. After that, flushed from my haste and perturbation, I found my way with some difficulty through the maze of long, narrow corridors of the west wing to the staircase that descended to the shadowy great hall. There, I drew up short, my heart catching in my throat as I saw that my employer stood at the foot of the steps, as though awaiting me.

"My lord," I began, treading downward so nervously and rapidly that I nearly stumbled, "I am terribly sorry I overslept. I can assure you 'twill not happen again—"

With an elegant motion of one hand, Count von Reicher waved away my apology.

" 'Tis of no importance, Fraulein Blakeley," he asserted, shuttering his black eyes against me, so his thoughts were unfathomable and I could not discern whether he had, in truth, drugged me for some sinister purpose of his own last evening or whether it had indeed been only in my nightmare that he had kissed and caressed me and muttered my name. "Since both my son and I are, unfortunately, cursed by . . . insomnia and neither of us is therefore an early riser, sleeping well past noon is the rule rather than the exception in this house. Naturally, as I expect you will adjust your own schedule accordingly, I trust that you will soon grow accustomed to our . . . unusual hours. Indeed, I daresay you will find the experience of sleeping late a not unpleasant indulgence."

"Yes, my lord. Still," I continued doubtfully, for my years of dull routine at the austere orphanage had instilled in me a strict sense of orderliness, "it nevertheless seems sinful to waste the greater part of the day—"

"The night is not without its own particular attractions, Fraulein Blakeley," he interrupted me smoothly, "all of which you will discover, in time." He paused, his eyes sweeping over me in a manner that would have brought a blush to my cheeks had his mouth not abruptly tightened with disapproval. "Fraulein Blakeley—" He spoke with a touch of asperity. "—am I to understand that that outmoded gown you are currently wearing and the similar one you had on upon your arrival last night are indicative of your entire wardrobe?"

"My—my lord, they—they *are* my entire wardrobe," I stated stiffly, mortified. "I regret that they are not the latest fashion, but they are suitable for my station and—and all I have. I am sorry if they displease you."

"They do," he rejoined bluntly, "for mine is an aesthetic nature, as is my son's. His life is dismal enough as 'tis, I fear, without his being subjected to the sight of a governess so depressingly garbed, nor does such drab raiment . . . become you. Since 'tis I who find your wardrobe objectionable, however, I will, of course, assume complete responsibility for its replacement."

"My—my lord, I—I don't know what to say. I fear that your offer is far too generous and—and—"

"Improper, besides?" Lifting one brow demonically, Count von Reicher smiled with mocking amusement at me. "Fraulein Blakeley, I feel certain that like all good mothers, yours adjured you never to accept anything other than flowers and candy from a man who is neither your fiancé nor your husband. Rules, however, were made to be broken; and as we come to know each other better, you will learn there are a great many to which I do not adhere and would hope a young woman of your apparent intelligence and common sense would not slavishly follow, either."

"Even so, my lord, I simply cannot permit—"

"You can. You *will*, Fraulein Blakeley. I insist . . . and must warn you: one way or another, I invariably get what I want. So, please, let me hear no further protest from you on the matter."

"As you—as you wish, then, my lord."

I swallowed hard as I descended the remaining few steps, for briefly, I had seen upon my employer's face an expression of such fierceness and determination that it had been frightening. In that moment, I could well believe that he was a man accustomed to demanding—and getting— what he wanted and would brook no thwarting of his desires; that he would, in fact, prove quite merciless to whatever—or whoever—dared to stand in his way. I was not so bold as to make myself an obstacle in his path. Besides, however inappropriate his intention to purchase me a new wardrobe, I knew deep down inside that I was not wholly averse to the prospect of having some modish clothes. In truth, my plain, serviceable garments were due as much to my inability to afford anything more stylish as to my idea of what was seemly for a spinster governess.

"You will find a late breakfast waiting for you on the sideboard in the dining room, Fraulein Blakeley," Count von Reicher informed me, his mien and tone now so cordial that almost, I could believe I had imagined his earlier saturnine behavior. Yet I knew I had not, and I marveled at his mercurial changes of mood. "My son and I have already dined, so we will not be joining you. When you have finished, I shall expect you in my study, where we will discuss the requirements for

Nikki's care and education. After that, I will take you to the schoolroom to meet him."

"Very well. I shall be with you shortly, then, my lord." Relieved that this particular interview, at least, had ended, I started toward the dining room, located to one side of the great hall. Then, suddenly recalling the lack of a looking glass in my chamber, I reluctantly turned back to my employer. "My lord, a minute more of your time, if you please, for a small matter of little importance, except perhaps to a woman: I noted this morning that there is no mirror in my room, and I was wondering . . ." My voice trailed away as he quirked one brow upward in that diabolical fashion I was beginning to recognize.

"Fraulein Blakeley," he drawled, "one would presume, given the . . . vintage of your gowns, that vanity is not one of your vices. It would surely be a disservice of me, then, would it not, to encourage you to acquire it?"

"Yes, of course, my lord," I said coolly after a moment, taken aback by his response.

I was exceedingly confused that he should be willing to furnish me with a new wardrobe but would refuse me a simple looking glass. Really, it was, I thought, not only a puzzle, but also most provoking. It was unlikely after all these years that I should grow vain about the beauty that had proved the bane of my existence, so what real harm could there be in my having a mirror? None of which I was aware. Still, it was clear that for some strange, unfathomable reason, Count von Reicher did not intend to cause one to be hung in my chamber.

What sort of reflection of his character was that? I wondered curiously—and, quite unknown to me at the time, most ironically; for even then, the answer was within my sight.

I just did not see it.

4

I SUFFERED such a dreadful shock at my first sight of young Lord Nikolaus von Reicher that I nearly swooned—for he was, incredibly, the boy of my nightmare.

Realizing this, I had to reassess my determined conclusion that my slumber last evening had been troubled by naught save a bad dream; and I shivered at the notion that perhaps Count von Reicher and his son really *had* visited my room and stood beside my bed, conspiring to kill me. Still, even as I inwardly shrank with horror at the idea, my common sense was once more struggling to assert itself, pointing out the ludicrousness of my thoughts. For what possible motive could my employer and his son have for murdering me? They had naught to gain by my death.

Still, it *had* been Nikki I had seen last night, if not in the flesh, then in what had been some—however dark and distorted—undeniably precognitive dream. I had never before experienced such; but as a teacher, I prided myself on having an open mind and so did not readily dismiss the idea that knowledge might be gained from sources other than the five senses. Yet even so, that I might possess some small amount of clairvoyant aptitude disturbed me, for all that is not understood is frightening, and I feared that the ability to glimpse the future might prove not a gift, but a curse.

Bowing with the same flourish his father had exhibited upon our first meeting, the boy addressed me politely, his voice sending another involuntary chill up my spine, for it was an eerie echo of the childish voice I had heard in my nightmare.

"How do you do, Fraulein Blakeley?" he said solemnly, his face grave as, stepping forward from the shadows of the schoolroom to greet me, he took my hand in his own small, slender, but nevertheless curiously strong one.

Young Lord Nikolaus von Reicher was a diminutive, much paler replica of his father, indisputably handsome, his tousled black hair contrasting with his fair skin. Still, his head seemed too big and heavy for his thin little body, as though its weight would snap his delicate neck; and his black eyes, far too large for his finely chiseled countenance, wrenched my heart, for they were unbelievably haunting, filled with a world of knowledge and sorrow that should not have belonged to one of his tender years. His were terribly old eyes that had witnessed things, I somehow knew, no one ought ever to have seen and survived.

"Hallo, Lord Nikolaus." I spoke gently, kneeling down so I would be at his level. "I hope we are going to become good friends."

" 'Twould be nice to have a friend, *fraulein*," he replied wistfully, such a pathetic mixture of wariness and eagerness transforming his sober little face that I was filled with pity for him.

Poor, sad, lonely boy! I thought, and felt a deep sense of unmitigated shame that I should ever have suspected him of creeping into my chamber last evening, of scheming with his father to kill me. Truly, I must have been more overwrought by my weeks of indigence and my journey to Devil's Keep than I had realized.

After a short while, evidently satisfied that Nikki and I had got off on the right, however reserved, foot together, Count von Reicher left us; and I turned my attention from his son to the schoolroom. Here, as in my own chamber, some effort had been made to clear away the cobwebs and dust. A fire burned cozily in the grate; candles had been lighted all around, and even a bouquet of early fall flowers had been arranged in a vase upon the mantel. Still, it was, I reflected, a lugubrious place. As at all the windows of the manor, the heavy draperies were uncompromisingly pulled shut—my employer had earlier, in his study, explained to me that none were to be opened to permit in light, due to the weakness of his son's eyes. The result was an atmosphere of such gloom that even I found it dispiriting.

The realization that this was the extent of the brightness of Nikki's world, that he could not stand before a window with light streaming in, that he could not venture outside to feel the sun upon his face, strengthened my compassion for the boy; and I resolved that I would do whatever I could to cheer up his life in all other aspects.

To that end, I chose from among the books lining the shelves of the well-stocked schoolroom several novels that had been my favorites when I was a child; and rather than instruct Nikki to take his place at the small desk that was clearly meant for him, I drew two chairs near to the hearth and motioned for him to sit beside me.

"Let us begin by discovering what you already know, my lord," I told him, opening one of the slender volumes to its first page. "If you will read aloud this story, it will give me some idea of how far you have progressed in your studies, and then we can decide what needs work."

Obediently, although unenthusiastically, he started to read; and although I had deliberately selected one of the easier books, I was nevertheless surprised to hear how fluently and without hesitation the words came to his lips. Plainly, he was considerably more advanced than I had been at his age. I handed him several more volumes to read aloud, as well as a number of primers on various subjects; and as the afternoon wore on, I was astonished to grasp that, incredibly, his level of academic erudition was such that were he not only seven years old, he could easily have qualified for enrollment at Oxford or Cambridge University. The child was, it appeared, a prodigy.

"In truth, the boy has no real need of me, my lord," I dutifully and, with much distress, reported to Count von Reicher much later that evening.

"To the contrary, Fraulein Blakeley," my employer rejoined coolly, unruffled, as he glanced up from the paperwork strewn across his desk. "I think Nikki has great need of you. Surely, it did not escape your notice how quiet and withdrawn he is? How much he requires a caring companion to coax him from his solitude?"

"No, my lord. But . . . my lord, I am a governess, not a nurse—"

"You are first and foremost a woman, are you not? And not without motherly instincts, I trust," he shot back, rather sharply.

"Yes, my lord. No, my lord. But—"

"But . . . what, Fraulein Blakeley? Are you saying that you cannot be as a mother to the boy, that you cannot teach him all that a devoted mother would teach her son—of love, of life, of the lightness of being? For you must have realized Nikki knows only the darkness of the world; and unfortunately, however much I long to, I cannot show him any more than that. In my time, I have grown far too jaded and cynical and ruthless for that."

"Surely not, my lord."

"Your opinion of me is flattering, Fraulein Blakeley," Count von Reicher declared dryly, "but far too charitable, I fear. I do not deceive myself about my failings . . . nor should you," he warned me softly, his tone such that it prickled the fine hairs on my nape, for once more I had caught a glimpse of the savagery that lurked just beneath his civilized veneer, and it unnerved me. "The world has not treated me kindly, you see, and over the years, I have learned to strike back with a vengeance. But my son . . . my son is of a gentler nature, and I would not see the remaining vestiges of that gentleness destroyed." Urgently, he leaned forward across his desk; I could see his handsome visage clearly then, drawn with bitterness and pain and self-mockery, his intense eyes haunted by shadows. When he again spoke, there was such an ache in his voice that it was hurtful to hear. "You are my last hope, Fraulein Blakeley. Will you not help me to help Nikki?"

Thus appealed to, what could I do but agree? I had not thought to see my proud employer humble himself so by revealing to me the dark depths of his private emotions, his knowledge of and derision for his own harsh character, his inability to teach his son aught but cynicism and contempt for the world. Yet I thought, even so, that Count von Reicher was not so cold and unfeeling as he would have us both believe, for if so, he would not have wanted to spare Nikki from his own biting disillusionment with life. Somewhere deep inside my employer, I suspected, were the remnants of the man he had once been—before time and the world had changed him into what he now was. Like his son, he had withdrawn into seclusion. Perhaps his fervent plea had been as much for himself as for Nikki, I reflected soberly, and in that moment, my heart went out to the man, as it had to the boy.

The world had not treated Count von Reicher kindly, he had said. I wondered what it had done to make him so severe, so sardonic. But I did not ask—and he did not volunteer to tell me.

My days at the manor soon settled into a pattern, however irregular and bizarre. Though, before coming to Devil's Keep, I had been wont to rise at six o'clock, I did not now get up until noon or later. After I had washed and dressed, I took my breakfast in the dining room, almost always alone, for invariably, Count von Reicher and Nikki had either dined before me, intended to dine after me, or were not hungry; and though I fretted over Nikki's lack of appetite, my employer explained that it was a product of the boy's illness and no real cause for alarm. With that, I had to be content, as I myself had no clue as to what afflicted the child or how best to treat it.

Sometime between two and three o'clock most afternoons, if Nikki were up and feeling well enough, I joined him in the schoolroom for his lessons. These were as unusual as our schedule, for plainly, he needed no further formal education in reading, writing, and ciphering, and he already spoke many more foreign languages than I. He enjoyed both music and art, and was proficient at the pianoforte, although his paintings, while they clearly demonstrated natural talent, disturbed me with their darkness. More often than not, his landscapes were of cemeteries, abounding with grimacing ghosts and other ghoulish, decaying creatures rising from yawning graves, and his seascapes were of ships wrecking upon brutal shores, the foam upon the angry waves cleverly but gruesomely fashioned of weird, elongated phantoms and grossly contorted specters. He appeared to be obsessed with death and fascinated by the supernatural—macabre interests reflected not only in his paintings, but also in our discourse. For most of our hours were taken up with theological, philosophical, and historical debate, during which I was continually amazed by the extent of Nikki's sagacity and scholarship. My own hard-earned knowledge seemed woefully inadequate in comparison to his; as a result, I spent many long hours in the manor's musty but bountiful library, diligently poring over tomes so ancient that the fragile, yellowed pages were prone to crumble at my touch, no matter how carefully I handled them.

During these forays, I was startled to discover that several of the volumes were personally inscribed to Count von Reicher, and I did not understand how that could be. The authors of the books were scores, even centuries dead, hardly my employer's contemporaries.

"My line is a very old one, Fraulein Blakeley," he elucidated, his mouth curving in that derisive smile when, one evening in his laboratory—where, obsessed with his life's work of finding a cure for his son's affliction, he spent most of his nights, seldom retiring before dawn—I mentioned to him my curiosity regarding the inscriptions. "I am by no means the first of my house to bear the name Drogo von Reicher—or did you truly think me over two hundred years old?"

"No, of course not, my lord. How silly of me. I ought to have realized . . ." Under his mocking scrutiny, my voice trailed away, and I flushed with embarrassment at my stupidity.

Of course, he had inherited the books from some ancestor, whose name he bore. I did not know why that obvious conclusion should not have occurred to me. Perhaps it was because he and Nikki both appeared to have a peculiarly strong affinity with the distant past, almost as though they themselves had actually lived it. They often spoke of famous, historical personages, places, and events as though they were intimately acquainted with them, and made reference to things that were so obscure that only a historian could have been expected to know them or that I could find no record of at all, despite hours of searching through the tomes in the manor's library. I was puzzled as to how my employer and his son could have come by such detailed knowledge of happenings so far removed from the present.

"As I have told you before, in my time I have traveled widely abroad, Fraulein Blakeley," Count von Reicher avowed as he proceeded with his work, which, to my untrained eyes, appeared most involved. The laboratory was cluttered with an array of tightly corked bottles containing herbs, spices, aromatics, and unknown liquids; untold crystals and metals shone in the candlelight, and the wooden shelves and tables were strewn with a profusion of complicated apparatus that hissed and steamed and gurgled. "Over the years, I have met many whose wisdom and learning were the culmination of erudition acquired and preserved over centuries by others of like acumen; I have trodden the narrow streets and dark alleys of ancient cities, and I have had access to many more books than are here at Devil's Keep. Would it not, then, be reasonable to assume that my education, and therefore my son's, also, is surpassing?"

"Yes, it would, my lord," I replied somewhat stiffly, for it was clear to me that I was being put in my proper place. "I apologize if my questions were presumptuous—"

"Not at all, Fraulein Blakeley. It's one of the things I admire most about you . . . your intelligent, inquisitive mind. I confess I did not realize until you came here how lonely I had grown for stimulating conversation and companionship. You are a challenge to me, Fraulein Blakeley."

His eyes surveyed me brazenly, making me blush and my heart beat fast; for having no looking glass in which to view myself in my new wardrobe, which had recently arrived at the manor, I must permit Count von Reicher to serve as my mirror, and the expression upon his face told me he admired my beauty as much as my mind. The frock Sarah had laid out for me this day was the color of dark, old gold, which I knew must make my red hair gleam like burnished copper and my green eyes glitter like emeralds in the dim-glowing light of the candles that burned all around us. The gown was fashioned in the latest style, being sashed beneath my breasts and cut in flowing folds that clung to my body when I moved;

and while there was nothing in the least improper about it, it did reveal the length of my throat and a modest portion of my bosom in a manner that made the depths of my employer's eyes flicker like twin flames as he boldly assessed me.

I flushed all the more scarlet at the unwitting thought that even the sinfully silken undergarments I was wearing, he had chosen; perhaps he had even imagined me in them, had imagined himself slowly removing them, one by one. Unbidden in my mind rose a picture of myself sprawled shamelessly beneath him in my canopy bed upstairs as he inexorably stripped me naked, then crushed me to him; and I was beset again by that slow-burning heat I had felt like a fever in my blood when I had first beheld him.

As the sweet, gilded fire spread through me, I shuddered, though only half with fear, despite that these were dangerous thoughts for a woman such as I. They could lead only to my ruin, as well I knew. But somehow, it was difficult to remember that with Count von Reicher's eyes holding mine, as though he gazed into my very soul, claiming it for his own. At the thought, I suddenly recalled Sarah's words about the devil's taking possession of the master of the manor and walking the earth to stake his claim on all those he would have serve him in hell; and an involuntary grue chased up my spine. Blinking my eyes as though I were awaking from a trance, I took a step back from my employer, my hands held before me as though to ward off whatever spell he had seemed to cast upon me. That I was strongly attracted to him, I could no longer deny. But even so, I dared not permit myself to become his victim, which was surely all I would be in the end. The disparity between our stations in life was a chasm too great for me to cross safely.

"My lord, we were speaking of your library and of your son's education," I reminded him, my breath coming far more shallowly and rapidly than I would have liked.

"Were we? I rather fancied otherwise. But please do go on, Fraulein Blakeley."

"Yes, I will, my lord." Briefly, I paused, trying to regain my composure and choosing my next words carefully. "My lord, I have noticed over the passing days that Nikki seems to be inordinately preoccupied with . . . death."

At that, Count von Reicher, in the midst of crushing with a pestle some dark leaves in a mortar, suddenly went very still. After a moment, he smoothly finished the process and, after examining the resultant powder, shook it carefully into a beaker of liquid boiling over a flame. Then, laying aside the mortar and pestle, he began with a long spoon to stir the bubbling mixture.

"Does he? But then, I suppose that's natural, isn't it, for a boy who may never grow to manhood?" His face tightened grimly at the thought; and though I longed to reach out to him, to offer him some reassurance, I knew that there was little I could do or say to comfort him, and that he would scorn my pity, besides.

"Perhaps, my lord," I conceded slowly. "However, I have noticed that in your library, there are a number of volumes devoted to that specific subject, as well as to the . . . supernatural, in which Nikki also appears to have a consuming interest; and I thought . . . that is— My lord, I know he is extraordinarily advanced for his age. Nevertheless, do you think it wise to encourage him in what are surely . . . unhealthy obsessions, especially for a child?"

"Does the thought of death, then, of things beyond our ken . . . disturb you, Fraulein Blakeley?"

"I—I don't know, my lord. I suppose I never really thought much about them before coming to Devil's Keep. My parents died when I was no older than Nikki; they were killed in a carriage accident. However, I was too badly injured in that same accident to attend their funerals, so truly, I've little experience of death, or of the supernatural, either. I know only the deep sense of loss engendered by the former, the awe and mystification born of the latter."

"But even so, you think we should not explore such things, so they may be understood rather than feared?"

"I'm—I'm not sure, my lord."

"Then consider that I am a better judge of what is appropriate material for my son's studies, Fraulein Blakeley. As you said, Nikki is extraordinarily advanced for his age. If these particular topics, however unsuitable in your opinion, interest him, test him, then by all means they should be pursued. That is the whole point of a challenge, Fraulein Blakeley, is it not?"

"Perhaps, my lord," I answered, unsettled by the under-tones of our conversation, all too aware that we were again no longer speaking of his son. "However, it has been my experience that oftentimes, a greater challenge may be found in not pursuing a challenge rather than in taking it up."

"An observation worthy of note, a road worthy of travel, no doubt—though I myself have invariably found such a course of action far too . . . tame for my liking. You see, Fraulein Blakeley, man is by nature a predatory beast, given to the thrill of the chase, the triumph of the conquest."

"Which results in a mere, fleeting moment of ecstasy for the victor, my lord, and, far too often, in a lifetime of agony for the defeated, does it not? A cruelty, surely, unworthy of the chivalrous and of the civilized."

"But then, my dear Fraulein Blakeley—" Count von Reicher spoke lightly, with amusement, favoring me with that sarcastic smile of his. "—man is, unfortunately, so very seldom either, is he? Oh, I grant you, he may appear so, superficially at least, for evidence of his supposed gentility and progress surrounds us daily, does it not? But in reality, underneath his skin man is the same savage animal he has been since the beginning of time—and doubtless will remain until its bitter end; for 'tis a brutal world we live in, Fraulein Blakeley, one in which only the strong survive."

"You are a pessimist, my lord," I remarked coolly.

"No, I am a realist, while you, I suspect, are very much a romantic at heart."

"And what is wrong with that?"

"Nothing . . . except that such a disposition renders one susceptible to emotions—when, in the end, a lack of them inevitably serves one far better."

"Are you, then, always ruled by your head instead of your heart, my lord?"

"Always, Fraulein Blakeley."

"Then I feel sorry for you, my lord. For if you have no heart, you have no soul, either, and yours is a brutal world, indeed, without hope, without joy, and without love—but not, I think, without despair or sadness or pain."

In my desire to protect myself from what my employer had surely intended as advances, however honeyed and adroit, I had gone too far, I knew. For at my words, his hands clenched at his sides, and there came upon his face such a dark, murderous expression that I half feared he would strike me, and I cowered from him.

"I do not want your pity, Fraulein Blakeley!" he growled, sounding so like some wolfish animal that for a horrifying instant, I wildly imagined he was not, in truth, human.

Of a sudden, the air seemed as dark and threatening as before a rising storm; and in that moment, I could have sworn that his eyes glowed red, that his upper lip curled in a feral snarl, revealing his teeth, gleaming oddly in the half-light. He took a menacing step toward me, then abruptly paused, his entire body shuddering as though he fought some violent battle within himself. Then, apparently regaining some semblance of control, he gave a low, jeering laugh, and whatever had seized him dissipated so quickly that I was left wondering if it had not been my imagination and some trick of the flickering candles that had made him appear so sinister.

"It seems you are, indeed, an opponent worthy of my steel, Fraulein Blakeley. *Touché.*" As though I had, in truth, dealt him a mortal blow, Count von Reicher pressed one hand lightly to his breast. But there was a harsh edge to his mockery, nevertheless; and I saw by the shadows that now haunted his fathomless eyes that I had, in fact, wounded him deeply, however much he sought to conceal it. "When you strike, you strike hard and true—and to the heart. I had not thought so, but you could prove deadly, Fraulein Blakeley, most deadly, indeed. I shall have to remember that," he said softly.

Then, sketching me an elegant but insolent bow, he deliberately turned his back on me and, picking up his pen and dipping it into the inkwell, bent over the copious notes he kept with regard to his experiments. I stood there dumbly, shivering and staring at him, not quite understanding why, despite the iciness that pervaded my body, my eyes should suddenly be blinded by tears. After a moment, when it became clear that he intended to ignore me, I slipped from the laboratory as quietly as my tears streaked my cheeks.

5

I T was several days later that I awoke to find Sarah agog
with an appalling tale of how Count von Reicher's
small herd of dairy cattle, which roamed the pastures
beyond the park that surrounded the manor, had been
ferociously slaughtered during the night. All the beasts'
throats had been ripped open wide, as though the herd
had been set upon by a pack of savage animals. Renfrew
had made the awful discovery that morning.

"Oh, miss, 'tis begun again, I tell 'ee!" Sarah exclaimed,
her eyes as big as saucers in her face. "Just like before,
when t' old master were in residence. T' divvil has
come among us, to seize possession of our souls! First
t' cattle—an' then us, miss! Fer mark my words, we'll
be next, aye, that we will. There'll be none what will
be safe—not here at t' manor, nor in t' village, either.
Grandfather has warned me so an' given me this ta
protect me. Look." From beneath the collar of her
gown, she drew forth a slender pewter chain, from
which dangled a tiny pewter cross. "He told me that
I mustn't nivver take it off fer nowt, that I must wear
it always."

I was shocked by Sarah's story. Nevertheless, common
sense dictated that whatever had killed the cattle, it had
not been the devil or any other creature so monstrous
and unnatural. For late last evening at supper, there had
reached my ears the echo of eerie, horrendous baying far
off in the distance, and although it had been like nothing

46

I had ever before heard, Count von Reicher had assured me that it was only wild dogs or wolves—though I had thought there were none of the latter left in England.

"You have naught to fear, Fraulein Blakeley," he had told me, as I had shuddered at the spine-chilling sound. "The manor is perfectly secure."

Still, as he had toyed with the wineglass from which I had rarely, if ever, seen him drink, I had noticed that for all his reassurances, he held his head cocked a trifle, listening intently as the baying continued. Oddly, it had seemed to me that he was beset by some tumultuous emotion at the clamor, some perverse excitement coupled with what I should have said, however bewildering to me, was an enormous rage. After a time, as though no longer able to contain himself, he had stood.

"I must go out, Fraulein Blakeley," he had announced curtly.

I had been somewhat startled by this, for to the best of my knowledge, he had no previous engagement. He was not given to socializing. He was so driven by his desire to find a cure for his son's illness that most nights, he labored until dawn in his laboratory or study, his life's work consuming him utterly. I had never before known him to abandon his experiments and note-taking, however temporarily, to go out.

"Shall I—shall I put Nikki to bed, then, my lord?" I had asked, for this was not one of my duties, my employer having made known to me from the start that he preferred to take care of this himself.

"No, I will do it when I return," he had said, and left me.

Now, reflecting upon Sarah's narrative, I supposed it likely that Count von Reicher, hearing the baying, had been concerned for the safety of his stock—and rightly so, it now appeared. That a pack of ravenous beasts could commit such carnage was dreadful. Doubtless, the animals would have to be hunted down and destroyed. That would surely be a wiser course of action than trusting that a cross would protect one, I thought, both amused by Sarah's superstitions and touched by her simple faith.

However disturbing the slaughter of the cattle, I did not long dwell upon the incident; for later that day, something far worse occurred.

Nikolaus attacked me.

I had never before witnessed anything like it. It was as though he suddenly went berserk as a rabid dog, turned into some kind of diminutive demon fashioned of naught but teeth and talons.

I had known from the start that it was not one of the child's better days, for he had looked extremely pale and weak when I had joined him in the schoolroom; and though he had insisted on continuing our lessons, he had been unusually withdrawn all afternoon, to the point of being surly and difficult. Over the passing weeks, we had managed to establish between us a rapport that, while yet restrained, held promise of deepening into real friendship; and I had sensed that however slowly, I was nevertheless making headway at winning Nikki's trust and liking. It was clear to me that he enjoyed our debates, during which he had grown increasingly apt to forget himself so far as to behave almost like any other normal seven-year-old boy. Several times, I had glimpsed a spark of mischievousness in his eyes when he had asked me something I had felt certain he had known full well I could not answer; and once or twice, I had actually even coaxed a laugh from him when I had stumbled into some verbal trap he had laid for me and found myself defeated by his cleverness. I never minded in the least being outwitted by him, for it always gladdened my heart to see his small, somber face light up with some semblance of gaiety; he had so little of it in his young, dark life.

That I was moved to pity and caring by his plight, by his suffering from such a strange, debilitating illness, was only natural; and so, to have him suddenly turn on me was deeply shocking and painful.

As was usual for us, given the irregular hours we kept at the manor, Sarah came to the schoolroom shortly after five o'clock, bearing a heavy, sterling-silver tray ladened with a substantial high tea. Also as was usual, Nikki partook of little. Yet as always, when he thought I was not looking, I spied him staring with such a peculiar mixture of avidity and revulsion at the array of sandwiches and scones, the cakes and bonbons Sarah had prepared that I was beset by confusion and concern. Plainly, the boy hungered for the repast; yet it was equally clear to me that for some unknown reason, he could hardly bring himself to consume a single morsel of it. He managed no more than a few strangled swallows of tea, a few choked mouthfuls of food before, without warning, he vehemently threw down his napkin and, flinging out his arm, dashed against the hearth the fragile china dishes arrayed upon the serving tray, shattering them. I, in the midst of buttering a slice of bread, was so startled by his unexpected action that I jumped, causing the butter knife to slip, cutting my hand. The wound was not deep, but bled more freely than one might have supposed. I had no chance to treat it, however, for it was then that Nikki uttered a terrible, guttural cry from deep in his throat and sprang upon me, knocking me from my chair.

Dimly, I realized that one of the fits of mania about which my employer had warned me must have seized the child, and terrified, I began to scream, even as I struggled to free myself from his incredibly strong grip. Though I knew that it was not possible, he seemed to have metamorphosed into some kind of monster, for his eyes were dreadful to behold, like two red-hot pokers stabbing me to the core, and his teeth shone uncannily

like fangs in the candlelight. Dully, I was aware of
his hands tearing at me, of his fingernails raking my
tender skin; and then, suddenly, to my everlasting relief,
Count von Reicher was there, dragging Nikki from my
cringing form as easily as though the boy had weighed
no more than a puff of smoke. My employer did not
pause, but, shouting furiously for Renfrew, strode from
the schoolroom, carrying the fiendish child with him.

I do not know what happened after that. I suppose I
must have fainted, for when next I opened my eyes, it
was to discover that I reclined upon the settee in the
sitting room adjoining my bedchamber, and that Count
von Reicher was bending over me, his face dark with
emotion, his voice low but sharp as he addressed me.

"Lenore! Lenore!"

"M-m-my lord?" I whispered weakly.

Dazed, disoriented, I attempted to rise, but immediately, his hands were upon my bare shoulders, pressing me
back down upon the pillows arranged beneath me. His
touch was like flame against my flesh, scorching me,
making me tremble with more than just the dizziness
that assailed me. For the first time, I became aware of
my dishevelment, of how my long red hair had tumbled
from its pins, of how the sleeves of my gown had been
ripped down and shredded, revealing a risqué amount
of my bosom and back, of how my shoulder had been
bitten and my arms scratched, as though I had been
savaged by some animal; and of a sudden, in an awful
rush, I remembered what had taken place in the
schoolroom.

"Nikki!" I cried out softly, hurt and horrified, not
wanting to believe he had actually attacked me, trying
to tell myself I must have dreamed or imagined it. But I
knew with a sinking feeling that it was not so. "Nikki! Is
he—is he . . . all right, my lord?" I asked, blushing with
mortification that I should be half naked before him and
self-consciously folding my arms across my chest and

fumbling at my dress, trying to draw up my tattered sleeves.

"Yes. I've administered him a sedative, and he's resting quietly now. He shall be much recovered tomorrow." My employer paused for a moment, as though carefully considering his next words. "Fraulein Blakeley, I want you to know how deeply I regret Nikki's . . . act of aggression toward you this evening. Although I did warn you that he was subject to fits of violence and . . . mania, naturally I did not expect that you would be the victim of such. I do most earnestly assure you that it will not happen again, and I beg that you will not hold it against him."

"Oh, my lord, how could I? The poor child! He didn't—he didn't really mean to harm me. I feel certain of it!"

"No . . . no, of course not." Abruptly, Count von Reicher rose and strode to a small, nearby cupboard, upon which sat a number of crystal decanters. He unstoppered a bottle of French brandy and splashed a generous measure into a snifter. Then, rejoining me upon the settee, he pressed the goblet into my hands, commanding, "Drink this, Fraulein Blakeley. It will make you feel better."

"My lord, I am—I am not used to strong spirits—"

"Nevertheless, I'm afraid I must insist. You have suffered a bad shock, I fear—and sustained some minor injuries, besides." His uncompromising tone warned me that further protests would avail me naught. I at last drank obediently, while he turned to the satinwood table before the settee, upon which were a basin of water, some fresh linens, a bar of soap, and various powders and potions. "The scratches are of little concern to me," he announced, as, taking up one of the cloths, he began meticulously to cleanse my wounds, "but a . . . human bite can be . . . most virulent if left untreated."

I could not read his thoughts, for he had hooded his eyes against me. Still, it seemed to me that he was filled with some turbulent emotion as he silently tended my hurts, for his hand clenched almost convulsively around the rag with which he wiped away the blood that encrusted my skin, and once or twice, he inhaled sharply, as though it were only with the greatest of difficulty that he held himself in check. No doubt, under other circumstances, I should have been unnerved by his strange, seething mood. But the considerable amount of brandy I had consumed now blazed like a fire in my belly, spreading its heat throughout my body, making me feel as though I were floating on a cloud of flame; and I was aware only of his strong hands, seeming to move with slow, loverlike sensuality over my flesh as he rubbed upon my injuries some soothing ointment he had prepared from his store of medicinals. Perhaps I only imagined it, but I thought he lingered over the bite mark inflicted upon me, his fingers tracing the small curve, his breath coming harsh and fast.

His handsome countenance was bent very close to mine. So close that I could see my face reflected in the glittering black depths of his eyes. I could smell the faint, sharp fragrance of sandalwood and some other earthy scent, like that of rich loam after a pouring rain, that emanated from his skin. I could feel his breath, warm against my bare shoulders and throat. Of a sudden, I was swept with unbearable longing. In some dim corner of my mind, I realized I wished he would come even nearer. I wished he would kiss me. I wanted urgently to know what it would feel like to have that carnal mouth possess mine. I had wanted to know since the first moment I had beheld him. I just had not wanted to admit it—until now.

As though he had read my mind, Count von Reicher's eyes locked on mine, mesmerizing me. His hands flowed like molten ore against my skin, sliding up my arms to my shoulders, one thumb beginning once more to caress the tiny teeth imprints. At his touch, a curious languor seeped through me; I was torpid with brandy and passion. I was a candle, aflame, melting ever so slowly in his arms, warmth trickling like hot wax through my body. Somewhere in my dulled brain, an alarm rang, warning me of my foolishness. But I ignored its reverberation; I did not want to hear it. My eyes closed; my lips parted; of its own volition, my tongue darted out to moisten them.

"Lenore . . . sweet Lenore," he muttered—his voice the low, throaty voice of my nightmare.

The alarm in my mind pealed again urgently, but I did not hear it. Count von Reicher's mouth had claimed mine—hot, hard, hungry, devouring me. My head reeled like a Catherine wheel; sparks of blazing light danced before my shuttered eyes; a shower of fire erupted inside me. No man had ever kissed me so. Violently, demandingly, brutally waking within me emotions and sensations I had never dreamed existed, emotions and sensations so fierce and exhilarating that they were like the savage storm I could hear now brewing outside, unleashing something wild and wanton inside me, ruthlessly catching me up and bearing me aloft to some shadowy, unknown destiny. His hands tangled roughly in my unbound hair as he crushed me to him, bruising my lips with his kisses, swallowing my breath. Slowly, erotically, his tongue traced the outline of my mouth before forcing it to yield beneath his merciless onslaught upon my senses. Deep, his tongue plunged between my lips, and deeper still. The world dropped from beneath my feet, spun away into nothingness. I was falling . . . falling . . .

Down—

Down—

Down—

Into a place barbarous and primeval, black and hellish as the infernal abyss. The devil's mouth moved on mine, searing me to the core; his tongue stabbed me with its red-hot flame. I was lost . . . lost. But it did not matter,

I thought, muddled and maddened with passion. It was only a dream, as it had been before. In some small, dark cranny of my mind, I knew otherwise. But I did not care. As his lips burned ardently across my cheek, to my temple, the sweat-dampened strands of my hair, my arms crept up as though with a will of their own to twine about his neck, my fingers tightening in his silky black hair. At that, however, startling me, he suddenly wrenched himself away, one hand ensnaring my tresses and jerking my head back so he could see my face. His visage smoldered with a dark and dangerous desire; his eyes glowed intensely with a strange, feral light, boring intensely, hypnotically, into mine.

"Lenore . . . *liebchen*, be sure. Be very sure that this is what you want," he whispered hoarsely, his breath warm and exciting against my skin.

Outside, without warning, the wind rose with a roar, shrieking across the moors to whip and whine about the manor, banging the shutters and rattling the lead-glass panes of the windows. Again and yet again, great tridents of lightning cast by some titanic hand shattered the heavens, and in response, like the vociferous growling of an unholy pack of hell hounds, thunder rumbled across the night sky.

"Drogo . . ." I moaned low in my throat—and drew him down to me.

6

THE following day when I awoke, I was faint and dazed, initially unsure whether Count von Reicher had truly made love to me so brazenly, so barbarously, so gloriously, last night, or if I had only imagined it in a brandy-soaked stupor, dreamed it in a vividly concupiscent dream. I remembered it all as though through a glass darkly, shadowed memories that moved in slow motion in my mind—of his sweeping me up in his arms, carrying me into my bedchamber, and laying me upon my bed. There, he had pressed me down and possessed me absolutely, and at last, crying out, I had known the sharp, sweet pain that makes of a maid, a woman, and of a man, a conqueror. Had it all taken place nowhere but in my own mind?

Dizzily, lethargically, I attempted to rise; and as the coverlet slipped down about me, I realized I was utterly naked and my body marked by faint bruises, where Count von Reicher's mouth and hands had laid claim to me, had had their fierce, exquisite will of me. I became aware then of how I ached at the secret heart of me, and of the traces of virgin's blood that stained my pale white thighs. It had truly happened, then. I was a maid no longer.

Abruptly, the full import of what I had done swept over me, shaming and sickening me. I had lain with Count von Reicher; I had given myself foolishly—willingly!—to him. Aghast, I recoiled in fright and revulsion as the consequences of my action struck me. What had I done? Should there ever prove a decent man in the offing, it would not matter; he would not have me now. There could be naught ahead for me in the future save heartache and dishonor and abandonment. What had last night felt so wildly passionate and rapturous now seemed vilely vulgar and degrading. I was no better than a whore—Count von Reicher's mistress. I wept bitterly at the thought. That no one need ever know, that I could succeed at concealing my disgrace, I did not even consider. Though it was well past noon, nearly two o'clock, in fact, Sarah had not come to wait upon me as she usually did. There could be only one explanation—that Count von Reicher had told her that she need not attend me this day; and I knew that even if he had proved chivalrous enough to phrase his words delicately, there was but one conclusion she would draw from them.

I must get up, I told myself frantically. I must get dressed. I must get away. Once more, I struggled to rise, still strangely giddy and weak, as though I were ill or drunk or drugged, I thought, recalling Count von Reicher's distinctive gold ring, his store of medicinals. I fell back amid the pillows, and it was then that I spied the single, perfect bloodred rose that lay beside me, fresh and dewy, as though newly cut. *He* had left it there, I knew. But . . . how? No rose bloomed at this time of year. As I continued to stare at it, some dark and disturbing memory stirred deep in my brain, a fleeting image that slipped like quicksilver through my grasp. Unbidden, my trembling hand stole slowly to my throat, to the two small wounds I felt there. I had lain upon the rose while I had slept, I thought dimly; its sharp thorns had pierced me, drawing blood . . .

A soft rapping upon my door roused me from my troubled reverie, and then the door itself swung open to reveal Count von Reicher standing there, his bold black eyes raking me in a way that recalled vividly our shared intimacy. I had never seen him look so handsome, so magnetic, so menacing, like some lethal animal on the prowl. As though I dreamed, I watched him stalk me, his gaze never leaving my pale face.

"I hunger for you, *liebchen*," he murmured, his low voice like sweet-flowing honey in my ears, seductive, treacherous, "and I cannot stay away from you. Not now. Not after last night. But you have naught to fear from me. Surely, you know that."

One strong, slender hand was at his cravat, untying it. To my shock and horror, I realized he meant to make love to me again; and despite my dread, to my utter shame a thrill of perverse, perfidious, perilous excitement and exultation shot through me, making my heart beat fast, my body shudder with an agonizing desire. As though mesmerized, I stared at him wordlessly, stricken, my eyes helplessly pleading as he stripped away his jacket and waistcoat and shirt, revealing his massively muscled chest matted with dark hair. But my silent beseeching availed me nothing. The expression upon his visage told me that I was his now, and that he would have me as he pleased. Dully, belatedly, I tried to gather my wits, to flee, and then, finally, to fight him as he bent over me, determinedly pressing me down upon the bed.

"No, Drogo, please, no," I whimpered brokenly as his lips sought mine.

"Don't fight me, *liebchen*. You know that you want me just as much as I want you."

"No, it's not true—"

"Isn't it?"

To my shame, I knew that it was. Yet I would not make his taking of me easy. I *could* not! Desperately calling up my last ounce of strength, I twisted and turned like a wild thing beneath him. But my struggles seemed only to amuse and arouse him, for he laughed

softly, mockingly, as he easily grabbed my wrists and
pinioned my arms above my head, throwing one leg
across my body to imprison me yet more firmly and
deliberately leaning his weight upon me, expelling all
the air from my lungs and making me acutely aware of
the hard essence of him throbbing against my naked
thighs.

"Have it your way, then, *liebchen*," he growled against
my mouth, one hand entwined roughly in my hair to hold
me still as he kissed me deeply, sensuously, his tongue
shooting deep between my lips, sensuously wreathing
and teasing my own tongue. "Fight me all you please.
It will not change the fact that you are mine now, that
I will not permit you to deny me."

Gasping, exhausted by my futile contention, I was
forced to lie helpless beneath him, even the sounds of
my entreaties and demurring stifled by his hot, exact-
ing mouth that swooped down again to claim mine
savagely, his tongue compelling my resisting lips to
part, invading me, pillaging me, leaving me faint and
breathless, filled with trepidation and a terrible, thrilling tantalization that shocked and shamed me, even
as it ignited a wildly burning fire of passion in my
blood.

I prayed he would soon be done with me, but to my
despair, he was not so inclined. It was as though the
clock of time had stopped ticking, as though the sun
would never again rise on the horizon and he had all
the time in the world to kiss me, and to go on kissing
me. His tongue darted forth to follow the lush curves
of my mouth, as though my lips were a scarlet riband,
a love knot, tying about him a spell of bewitchment
he sought to loose so it would unravel and ensnare
us both in its silken skein. He opened my mouth, and
his tongue wove deep, binding mine, making of it a
magicked captive, even as he taunted it with the false
possibility of escape.

I tried to turn my head away, to speak. But goaded by his desire, he would allow neither, his fingers snarling in my hair to prevent my eluding him, his lips silencing mine insistently until, finally, despite myself, I was kissing him back, yielding to him and to my inevitable fate, knowing he was far stronger than I, as powerful as the wind that swept across the moors, bending and breaking the stems of the dying heather and bracken, as he bent and broke me, scattering my senses so I could not think, could only feel. Like rich, dark wine, he intoxicated me. The black hair that matted his chest was like silk beneath my palms and against the sensitive peaks of my breasts; his broad back was as smooth as satin, rippling and quivering with muscle as he clasped me to him, his mouth and tongue and hands everywhere upon me, mapping each line and every curve of my body, as I mapped his; for though I were to be damned for it, some dark, primitive part of me wanted him, had wanted him since the beginning. I could no longer deny it—and Drogo's face told me that he knew it.

He cast away the remainder of his clothing, shocking me, enticing me; for until last night, I had never before seen a man naked—or been naked myself before a man. The red heat of him seared me like an unending flame as he once more covered my body with his own. He was bathed in sweat, as was I; our bodies glistened in the diffuse light of my shadowy bedchamber, he dark, I pale, as he slid ruthlessly across me, his turgid sex both a threat and a promise, making me shiver uncontrollably in his unrelenting embrace. His hands cupped my breasts, swollen and aching with passion, molded them to fit his palms, glided erotically across my nipples, taunting them into taut buds bursting to unfurl. His mouth drank long and deep of their nectar.

"Sweet," he muttered huskily, his lips moving lower still. "Sweet . . ."

Then, in a moment so intimate that I wanted to die, he suddenly spread my thighs wide to encroach upon the secret heart of me, tasting the engorged folds of me that quivered and opened to him of their own eager accord. My breath caught in my throat, for I had not known that such a thing could be done to me, and I reveled in it, moaned like a wounded animal and writhed helplessly beneath him, my hands tangled in his hair to draw him even nearer as he intensified his onslaught upon me by plunging his fingers full length into my softness. Then, slowly, tortuously, he withdrew them, only to dip deep into me again and yet again. And all the while, his tongue flicked the pulsing fount of me, until I was mad with desire for him, aching unbearably to be filled to overflowing with him.

I strained against him, and on steely arms, he rose, poising himself above me, dark and naked and pagan, his saturnine features making him appear strangely like some unearthly, unholy beast in the half-light. His black eyes were rapacious, glimmering with hunger and triumph as he stared down at me, his bold shaft hard and heavy with desire, so huge that I feared he would split me in twain. Instinctively, I shrank from him, and as I did, a sardonic smile twisted his lips. There was between us then a moment as highly charged as a storm; and then, snarling low in his throat, he flung himself upon me, impaling me so suddenly, so savagely, that it took my breath away. I gasped and cried out, taking him deep, deep into me, spurred to frantic want and need as he surged into me again and again, faster and faster, his hands tightening upon my hips, arching my body against his to meet each brazen, barbarous thrust, his head buried against my shoulder, his harsh, labored breath hot against my throat as, fiercely, exquisitely, he kissed me there, his mouth seeming to drain the very life and soul from my body. Feverishly, I enwrapped him, enfolded him, clung to him as waves of ecstatic fire assailed me, blazing higher and higher, until I was blinded by a thousand, shimmering bloodred flames that consumed me utterly, burning me to ashes as he crushed me to him, shuddering long and hard against me as he spilled his seed inside me.

There was blood upon his lips when he at last withdrew from me; in his passion, he had kissed me so hard upon my throat that he had opened the tiny punctures where the thorns of the rose he had given me last night had pricked me. His breath still coming in uneven rasps, he slowly lowered his mouth to mine, and I tasted the blood that stained his lips, bittersweet upon my tongue.

"You are mine, *liebchen*," he grated against my parted mouth, stroking the two small wounds at my throat before his fingers tightened there possessively. "You shall be mine until the end of time, for I shall never let you go, I swear it!"

Despite myself, I shivered at his words; for he was like an animal, and I recognized that some equally dark, wild, earthy thing inside my own self wanted him on that primitive level. He both frightened and excited me. I was a fool, I knew, to think perhaps he did care for me, to believe he wanted anything more from me than what he had already had—and would have again. For I did not deceive myself that he would permit me to leave him; I had been stupid to believe earlier that I could. It was too late now for that, far too late.

As though he had read my mind, Drogo wrapped his hands in my unbound hair and, tilting my face up to his, claimed my lips deeply once more, his naked body moving inexorably to cover mine, making me cry out in surrender as he took me again and then yet again before his hunger for me was finally sated.

And when he was done, I knew he had taken not only my body, but my heart—and perhaps even my very soul.

7

YEARS afterward, whenever I remembered those nebulous, mysterious, darkly halcyon days of that autumn at Devil's Keep, when Drogo made me his absolutely, I was to see them as though through a dusky vignette, misty with shadows all around, at their heart a kaleidoscope of red-hot fire and brilliant colors pulsating with passion and intensity. I seemed to live those days in a daze, a dream, a nightmare, an interlude out of time, in twilight and moving in slow motion.

Only Drogo was real.

By day and by night, he came to me, for hours on end, hungry as though he could not get enough of me. Time and time again, he pressed me down upon my canopy bed to weave his dark, wicked, splendorous spell upon me, until I knew every plane and angle of his hard, powerful body as well as I knew the soft, vulnerable ones of my own. We mated like animals, savagely, passionately; where we were was a place without light, a place without gentleness, as wild and violent and breathtaking as the earth's beginning. In his arms, I trembled with both fear and exultation. Despite that some part of me continued to struggle against him, he dominated me unequivocally. There was nothing he did not know, did not teach me, initiating me utterly in the rites of lovemaking. There were drowsy, prolonged afternoons when he tormented me slowly, erotically, almost cruelly, until, despite myself, I begged him to take me; and fierce, unbridled nights when, long after I had fallen asleep, he came to force himself upon me, urgently, barbarously, without any preliminaries. Inevitably, in the end, I was lost, helpless against him, his to shape and to mold and to do with as he willed, swept away by whatever dark thing he loosed inside me, setting me aflame with a fire only he could quench. Afterward, always, he left a single, perfect bloodred rose upon my pillow; and afterward, always, while I slept as though drugged and dreamed of lying in the arms of the devil, I awoke to find that the thorns had pierced my throat and that the taste of blood was upon my lips.

And then, at last, there came the day when I awoke with a lucid mind to find Sarah bending over me, her pretty face knitted with a frown of concern as she pressed a cool, damp cloth to my brow.

"Oh, miss, yer awake at last—an' in yer right mind!" Her blue eyes lighted with a smile at the realization. "I must let Count von Reicher know at once. 'Tis most anxious he's been fer yer welfare; day an' night, he has sat by yer bedside, carin' fer 'ee an' treatin' 'ee with his medicinals, fer he be a man learned in t' healin' arts. Nay, miss, don't try ta get up just yet. Thee be weak as a newborn kitten yet, I'll wager. Thee've been ill, ever so ill with some strange fever."

"F-f-fever?" I managed to say feebly, my head beginning to throb with the utter confusion that suddenly assailed me.

"Aye, miss, 'tis out of yer head with it, thee've been— fer over a fortnight now."

"A fortnight!"

"Aye, miss." She nodded gravely as she bustled about, stoking up the fire that burned in the grate and tidying up the disordered room, gathering up the basin of tepid water and the used cloths upon the nightstand. "Now, thee stay put in that bed, miss, while I fetch 'ee a cuppa hot tea an' a nice, steamin' bowl of barley broth. 'Twill be just what yer needin'.''

Sarah scurried away, leaving me abed, for indeed, I was too frail to rise. My head spun at her tale, for I could not credit what she had told me. It was not true! I thought. Though my memories of the past two weeks were dim and, deep down inside, deeply disquieting in some inexplicable fashion, nevertheless I could recall the feel of Drogo's hungry mouth and possessive hands upon me all too vividly for it to have happened in a dream. I had lost my virginity to him; I had been his mistress for a fortnight. Why should Sarah tell me I had been ill instead? Did she seek to spare my feelings, to pretend she was unaware of my shame? Did she honestly not know that the master of Devil's Keep had also mastered me? Or had Drogo somehow bedeviled her as he had me? Perhaps she was in league with him and whatever dark enchantment he had worked upon me! My imagination ran wild with conjecture; I did not know what to think. Nor was there time for reflection; for just then, without warning, Drogo appeared in the doorway of my bedchamber—looking so like he had that first day after we had become lovers that I shuddered with both apprehension and desire.

"Fraulein Blakeley," he greeted me formally as he advanced into my room, bewildering me further. Why did he address me so, as though I were naught to him but his son's governess? Had I not been Lenore . . . *liebchen* these past two weeks in his embrace? "How are you feeling? Sarah informs me that you are much improved this day. I was very glad to hear it."

I was so stunned by his polite but dispassionate words that I could only stare at him mutely, thinking I must somehow have gone mad. Surely, only that would explain why he was behaving toward me as though I had not surrendered to him my virtue, as though I had not lain in his arms, beneath the hard-muscled length of him, and known him as deeply and intimately as a woman could know a man. His eyes appraised me intently—familiar desire flickering in their depths—before his lids swept down to conceal his thoughts. From the side pocket of his jacket, he drew forth his snuffbox, concentrating on the ritual of inhaling the tobacco before turning his attention back to me and continuing.

"Still, you are a trifle pale yet." He sat beside me on the bed, stretching out one hand to cup my face, his eyes searching mine, as though he could see into my mind, my soul. I quivered at his touch. I had felt it before, knew that it was a prelude to a dark rhapsody. Involuntarily, I shrank from him, even as my heart began to pound hard and fast in my breast, my body to tingle with passion and longing. "Now that the fever with which you were stricken appears to have run its course, you must rest and regain your strength." Turning to the bottles of medicinals that strewed my nightstand, he carefully prepared in a silver goblet some unknown potion for me, which he then handed to me and bade me drink. "A mixture of certain herbs and spices," he told me, "with which I have treated you these past few weeks. You will find the taste . . . not unpleasant."

Though frightened, dazed, and suspicious, I seemed to have no will of my own as his eyes riveted mine. Obediently, I drank. The elixir had a strange but sweet taste and, like brandy, warmed me to my toes as I drained the goblet to the dregs.

"You will sleep now," Drogo murmured.

Even as he spoke the words, my lids were fluttering shut. When next I awoke, he was gone—nor did that single, perfect bloodred rose lie upon my pillow.

For the first time since my arrival at Devil's Keep, I had the afternoon to myself. Though I had recuperated from the apparent fever that had so mysteriously beset me,

Drogo had nevertheless judged me too wan to resume my lessons with Nikki and had prescribed fresh air, a stroll through the park and gardens, to restore the bloom to my cheeks. In truth, I was grateful for the opportunity to explore the grounds, which I had had little chance to examine and enjoy, due to Nikki's being unable to venture outside. Now, eager to get away, glad to have some time alone to reflect, I wrapped my pelisse tight about me against the brisk autumn wind and slipped out through a side door to make my way across the lawn. Dickon, Sarah's husband, was at work in the flower beds, and I stopped to chat with him a moment; but he was inclined toward a wary and taciturn bent, so I did not linger.

The gardens were abloom with fall flowers and greenery that had turned scarlet or gold with the season. In one hand, I carried a large wooden trug and a pair of garden shears; recalling the flowers arranged in the vase in the schoolroom, I had thought to cut a bouquet for Nikki, to cheer him, and now and then as I meandered along, I clipped a particularly fine stem or two and laid them in my basket. He had quite recovered from the fit of mania that had driven him to attack me and, when he had come to visit me in my room while I had lain abed, had been so pathetically anxious for my forgiveness that my heart had ached for him. I had known then that I cared for him far too much, that he was a large part of why I did not run away from the manor, wherein, since the beginning, my days and nights had proved so strangely dreamlike that I felt I must be losing all hold on reality. That Drogo, too, even more strongly than Nikki, kept me at Devil's Keep, I did not want to admit. It still seemed incredible to me that in my delirium, I had built up such a fantasy about him; and even now, I could not shake the persistent feeling that it had all really happened just as I remembered, that Drogo had claimed me as his, had taken me ruthlessly again and again in some dark, wild interlude of animalistic hunger and lust.

Had he, in truth, shown me relentlessly during those days and nights of my reputed fever what it was to love a man—to love him? If so, I knew I should go away from here before it was too late—if, indeed, it were not already. Still, despite how wild and desolate the northern Cornish coast, how gloomy and isolated the manor, how bizarre and trancelike my life within its walls, how strained my sanity, I could not bring myself to leave. Every time I thought to go, I seemed to lack the strength or will to do so. It was as though some strange spell had been cast upon me, as though some unknown force held me at Devil's Keep, preventing my departure.

It was as I was returning to the manor that I noticed a young man. He was crouched in a thicket, hiding, it appeared to me, and spying on Devil's Keep in the distance, for he held a pair of opera glasses in one hand; it was the dull glint of the leaden autumn sun upon the lenses that had attracted my attention to him. My heart leaped to my throat at the sight of him, for while I had lain abed, convalescing, Sarah had regaled me with a horrifying tale of how, during my fever, two young women had been murdered in the village. Just as with Drogo's herd of dairy cattle, deep, massive, inhuman wounds had been found upon the dead women's throats, and every single last ounce of blood had been drained from their bodies. That was not all, however. According to Sarah, the nights after their respective funerals, the women had been seen again in the village, alive as though they had never died but now transmogrified into demons who had attacked their bereaved husbands. The villagers were utterly terrified. Yesterday, they had gone to the cemetery to lay garlic about the women's graves—which was supposed to keep them from rising from the dead, Sarah had claimed—and there, the villagers had discovered that the women's coffins had been dug up.

"Aye, miss,'tis true!" she had breathed, her blue eyes wide with horror. "An' what's more, somebody had cut off their heads an' driven stakes straight through their hearts!"

Now, as I peered at the stranger concealed in the bushes, I could not help but wonder if he were the crazed man who had killed the two young women. Yet he hardly seemed capable of the deed; he was of but medium height and slight build, and he wore a pair of wire-rimmed spectacles that contrived to give him a studious rather than a threatening appearance. As I timidly advanced upon him, I realized he was a foreigner, for his somber clothing was of a fashion unfamiliar to me, and his English, when I finally worked up courage enough to speak to him, was broken and inflected with an accent similar to but much more pronounced than Drogo's.

" 'Tis illegal to trespass," I said, startling him, for he was so intent on his apparent espionage that he had not observed my approach.

At the sound of my voice, he jumped and whirled about so quickly that he not only dropped his opera glasses, but also lost his balance and, stumbling, fell back into the bramble, where he thrashed about for a minute before at last managing to scramble to his feet. Upon doing so, he at once grasped the plain wooden cross he wore about his neck and, with a trembling hand, held it out toward me, as though I were a spell he hoped to ward off. In his other hand, he clutched a Bible, and this, he shook at me as though to invoke the very wrath of God while, closing his eyes, he began to chant some litany I could not understand. Clearly, he was far more afraid of me than I was of him, something that mitigated my own fear so, it was all I could do not to burst out laughing at his ludicrous appearance—

although I suspected that the sound would have held a hysterical note.

"Plainly, you are not a poacher, but a preacher," I declared, dryly and rather more bravely than I had spoken before, "however unlikely that would appear, given your cowering in that thicket."

"*J-j-ja. N-n-nein*," he stammered, abruptly opening his eyes and breaking off his chanting. "Dat is, I am . . . professor, teacher of theology and—and history at university. Permit I introduce myself. I am Dr. Eli Morgenstern. Does dat—does dat name mean anyt'ing to you, *fraulein*?" His tone was stern, his demeanor alert; his dark, intelligent eyes pierced me as he awaited my reply.

"No, should it?"

"Perhaps. Perhaps not. It all depends."

"On what?"

"On you, *fraulein*, and vhether you are vun who hunts de night."

"One who hunts the night? What is that?" I was beginning to grow alarmed once more, thinking perhaps the professor was an escapee from a lunatic asylum. He was acting most peculiar, standing there quaking in his boots, continuing to thrust his cross and Bible toward me. He stared at me like an owl from behind his spectacles, as though he were attempting to mesmerize me, to place me under his control. "Look here—" I spoke sharply when he made no response. "—what are you doing creeping around here, spying on the manor?"

He started to say something, then broke off abruptly, evidently considering better of it. For upon his not unpleasant young face, there came an expression of shrewdness and watchfulness. His voice, when he finally answered, was forceful, as though he dared me to disbelieve him.

"I vas not spying! I am—I am . . . bat vatcher. *Ja*, dat is it," he insisted, tucking his Bible into his coat pocket and bending to retrieve his opera glasses, which he held up triumphantly. "You see, you see!" he cried. "Here are my opera glasses, vhich I dropped vhen you sneaked up on me. I vas hoping to catch glimpse of—of rare bat I haf heard about in de village."

"Don't you mean bird?" I inquired, frowning at him suspiciously, which to my secret astonishment made him take a hasty step back from me, so he nearly toppled into the bramble again. At his obvious confusion regarding my meaning, I uttered, "Never mind! Bat, bird, whatever . . . if it is so dangerous a creature that you require a cross and a Bible for protection during your stalking of it, I should think you would be wise to pursue some other variety." My words were clipped, my tone forbidding; for I was beginning to believe that Dr. Morgenstern was a curiosity seeker. Doubtless, he had heard about the slaughter of Drogo's dairy cattle, the murders of the two young women in the village; surely, the wicked legends about the Devil's Keep— never having truly died—had been revived with a vengeance. Rumors and horror stories about the manor must even now be spreading far and wide. The professor was probably but the first of those who would prove brave enough to encroach upon the manor's grounds. "Take my advice, Professor, and do your . . . bat watching someplace else. Count von Reicher does not take lightly the invasion of his property and privacy."

"*Nein*, of that I feel certain, *fraulein*. If you are not vun of his own kind, you vould be vise to take *my* advice and leave dis hellish place of haunting and death at vunce!"

Despite myself, a frisson of fear shot through me at his words, at the fervor of his eyes. I could not doubt that his warning was earnestly meant, for plainly, Dr. Morgenstern sincerely believed what he had told me. Such was his zeal that he looked fanatical in the diffuse light that—barely infiltrating the shadowy canopy formed by the interlaced branches of the trees—dappled the earth where we stood. The hour had grown late, I suddenly realized; sundown was upon us. Soon, it would be dark, for twilight was fleeting this time of year. I shivered at the thought, for despite my determination to be ruled by intelligence and common sense rather than fright and superstition, still I was not eager to roam the manor's grounds after the sun had set. All at once, it seemed that the wind was no longer a gentle sigh, but the eerie, mounting moan of a ghost swirling about us, shaking the ancient trees. Decaying debris blown up from the moist earth whorled about us, a dance of malevolent piskies. The rustling of the leaves was like the rattle of bones, the creaking of the boughs like the rasp of coffin lids being raised on rusty hinges. Even as I turned to go, the light faded, evanescing into darkness, leaving in its wake something that reeked of menace, of death. From the sea, on cat's paws, the mist drifted across the moors, settling in the hollows of the land. Within moments, the air was so thick as to be almost tangible, heavy and oppressive with portent. Of a sudden, a horrific howling echoed on the rising wind, the strange, savage baying I had heard before, and a terrible crashing resounded in the woods, as though some gargantuan animal charged, swift and deadly, through the tangle of trees and thickets.

"Run, *fraulein!*" Dr. Morgenstern shouted, his breath coming in hard rasps, sweat beading his panic-stricken face. "If you are not de devil's own, run!"

Even as he spoke, he was racing away toward the gates of the manor, his cross and Bible held before him as though they were a sharp sword and stout shield to defend him. I needed no further urging. Heedlessly dropping my trug and shears as I grabbed up my skirts, I ran. I ran as though the hounds of hell harried me, spurred on by the professor's terror, by whatever monstrous, unknown thing was moving with seemingly impossible speed through the park, like a giant bat on the wing, an immense dark shadow I sensed at my back as I fled; for it was I, not Dr. Morgenstern, it chose to pursue, leaving the professor to make good his escape.

The wind gusted and roared, shrieking through the trees, buffeting the mist, tearing at my skirts and ripping the pins from my hair. My long tresses whipped about me wildly, blinding me, so I tripped over a rotten log in my path and fell. I was so frightened that I did not even feel the scrape of pain upon my hands and knees. Crying out, my heart drumming as though it would burst inside my breast, I staggered to my feet and lurched on, terrified of the thing that chased me, whose hot breath I imagined I could feel even now on my nape. My skirts hampered me, catching on knotted brambles and sharp thorns that gouged me, drawing blood. The scent of both it and my fear filled the air, seeming to frenzy the thing behind me. Faster it came, and faster. Chilled to the very marrow of my bones, I knew I would never outrun it. I had a stitch in my side; my breath came in labored gasps, my legs moved as though weighted down by heavy stones. Tears stung my eyes, streamed down my cheeks. I would never reach the manor in time.

And then, suddenly, the thing loomed up from nowhere before me, huge black bat wings spread wide, swooping toward me in a rush from which there was no escape, enveloping me in a cloud of darkness. I screamed and then screamed again, struggling hysterically to free myself, to no avail. I was wrapped tight in the folds of a cloak, imprisoned by arms as strong and unrelenting as the iron bars of a gaol, crushed against a massively muscled chest and thick, corded thighs that surged powerfully against me. I knew that body; I knew it as well as I knew my own.

"Lenore," a low, familiar voice grated against my throat.

"Drogo!" I sobbed with relief. "Oh, Drogo! Thank God, 'tis you!"

I was filled to overflowing with gladness until, as the night clouds passed from the face of the early moon, I caught a glimpse of his handsome visage, dark, unholy, unnatural, twisted with some terrible, murderous emotion that made me cry out in horror. Desperately, I tried to flee, but he yanked me to him savagely, whirling me about, and then, to my utter bewilderment, placing himself before me, as though to shield me. It was then that I heard it, saw it, the thing I had feared and run from, growling ferociously and bursting from the mist-cloaked trees, as big and black and amorphous as a shroud billowing in the wind, such was the effect of the black, many-caped greatcoat that swirled about it. It was Death who stood there. I knew in my bones that it was so. In moments, it would be upon us.

Hissing and snarling like some feral beast, Drogo sprang forward to meet it; and at that, incredibly, I heard the thing speak.

"Drogo!" it spat, in a voice that rasped like rusty nails pulling loose from a casket.

And then it vanished.

8

'T WAS a *man!*" I gasped, stunned and appalled, my heart still pounding at an alarming rate, my breath still coming unevenly. "A *man* chasing me! Even now, I can hardly believe it! I thought—I thought that it was—it was some huge, wild beast, so fast did it run, almost as though it—as though it flew on the wings of the night . . . Oh, I know that sounds crazy, my lord, but 'tis true! But it can't have been an animal. It must have been *him!*—that queer young man I met in the woods! Yes! He wore a black cloak and peculiar hat, and he behaved so oddly, as though he were unbalanced, a madman . . . He lied to me. He said he was a bat watcher, but he was spying on the manor, my lord. He said that it was a place of—of haunting and—and death. He tried—he tried to—to frighten me, to—to scare me away from Devil's Keep—When the wind rose, 'twas *he* who told me to run. But now, I see that 'twas just a ruse to terrify me, for he chased me—It *must* have been him who chased me— Oh, my lord, he meant to kill me; I'm sure of it! Just as he must have murdered those two poor women in the village—"

"Who?" Drogo's voice was sharp as he turned to me, his hands grasping my arms so tightly that I winced. "Who, Lenore?"

"I'm—I'm trying to tell you, my lord. Dr. Morgenstern. He told me that his name was Dr. Morgenstern; he said he was a professor, a—a teacher of theology and history. He—he seemed to know you, my lord; and that man . . . that man who chased me, he—he knew your name. I heard him call you—call you Drogo, my lord. *Was* it Dr. Morgenstern?"

"He is indeed mad," Drogo muttered, almost as though he had not heard me. "A fanatic, a maniac. He must have followed me here from Prussia. He believes I did him a great wrong once, and he has hunted me for years, to destroy me." He was staring off into the distance, as though lost in his unpleasant memories of the professor; yet as he spoke, I had the strangest feeling he was not talking of Dr. Morgenstern at all. Indeed, the more I dwelled on what had happened, the more unlikely it seemed to me that the professor could have been that brutal, bestial thing who had melted like a phantom into the darkness. "Come, Fraulein Blakeley." Drogo took my hand firmly in his, interrupting my musings and leading me toward the manor. "You have had another bad shock, I fear, and you are marked by several scratches from bramble thorns, as well."

We went inside, upstairs to my bedchamber, where his bottles of medicinals still sat upon my nightstand. There, he treated my wounds, as he had before; and as before, he seemed to tremble with some violent, inexplicable emotion as he carefully cleansed the bloody gouges. His face was bent very near to mine. I wondered if he would kiss me again. But much to my disappointment—for I would surely then have learned the truth of what had taken place the past fortnight, I thought—he did not; and because of that, I was reluctantly forced to conclude that I had either lain delirious with a fever or was indeed losing my mind.

After Drogo had finished with my injuries, he left me alone, requesting that I join him downstairs when I had changed from my torn garments. A short time later, I found him waiting in the drawing room, standing before the fire that blazed in the hearth. In one hand, he held a silver goblet of dark-red wine, which he pressed upon me, saying that it would calm me.

"I fear that the past two weeks have been a sore trial to you, Fraulein Blakeley," he remarked as I drank deeply from the goblet. "You must allow me to make them up to you. 'Twould not suit me at all for you to grow unhappy and leave . . . Devil's Keep."

With that, he set out deliberately to cheer me, to charm me, to captivate me. He instructed that supper be served to us in the drawing room; and in that intimate setting—so different from the long, formal table in the dining room, where he sat at one end and I at the other— he entertained me as though I were a titled lady, to whom he paid court, rather than a mere governess. He was more handsome and fascinating than any man I had ever known, and now that he intentionally wooed me,

I was devastated, all my defenses tumbling before his rapier-sharp wit, his smoothly seductive compliments. More than once, he made me blush, but he also made me laugh; and though I tried to fight my feelings, I was increasingly attracted to him. Despite our differences in station, we had much in common, both emotionally and intellectually, a shared passion for the same books and art and music, a mutual interest in traveling and learning of the world, for although I had never been beyond the shores of England, I longed to see the exotic places he described to me, to experience the cultures of which he spoke.

When I had eaten—for Drogo himself partook of little—he led me into the ballroom, insisting I must have some divertissement to delight me. Here, the candles in the crystal chandeliers had been lighted, though only enough to provide dim illumination, so there were shadows all around, giving the ballroom a surreal quality. Through the French doors that opened onto the terrace, the moonlight streamed in, silver and radiant, making the dust motes we stirred glitter like tiny fairies weaving about us a gossamer spell. The doors themselves stood open, and with each sigh of the cool night wind, the mist from the sea drifted in to swath the floor, so it seemed that we floated upon clouds; but I was not cold, for Drogo's gaze warmed me to my toes. There was a musical box in one corner and, setting it to playing some slow, haunting melody, he held out his hand to me, saying:

"Will you dance, Fraulein Blakeley?"

And so we danced; and though I told myself I was breathless from my recent illness and giddy from the wine, in my heart I knew that it was Drogo who made me feel so as he whirled me about the mystical ballroom and then swept me through the French doors, along the length of the terrace. I was a fool, I thought. I had fallen in love with him, desperately—and there could be nothing for me in that but heartbreak. But I did not care. I loved him. My feet were wings with which I soared in his arms to dizzying heights. If I looked down, I would surely fall . . . .

Then don't look down, liebchen.

His voice echoed inside my mind—or did I only imagine it? It did not matter. If this were a dream, I did not want to awake. From beneath his languorous lids, his fathomless black eyes gleamed as he stared down at me, his silent appraisal telling me more eloquently than words how beautiful and desirable he found me. For the first time in my life, I was glad a man should find me so. I wanted him to make love to me, so I would know that it was truly happening, that it was real. As though he had read my thoughts, Drogo slowly lowered his mouth to mine, and as he kissed me hungrily, his tongue compelling my lips to part, shooting deep, I knew that I could not be wrong, that I had tasted him countless times before.

From somewhere in the distance, that terrible sound I had heard in the woods, like the baying of wild dogs or wolves, but stronger, wilder, fiercer, rang on the night wind, making me shiver and breaking the magic that held me locked in Drogo's arms. Releasing me, he drew away.

"Forgive me, Fraulein Blakeley," he murmured, his head cocked, listening intently to the far-off wailing, even as he spoke to me. "You are cold, and I have taken advantage. The music, the mist, the moonlight— My apologies. Let us go inside. The hour is late, and I still have work that must be done."

Somehow, I knew that he lied to me, that he intended to go out. Yet I said nothing, merely nodding, such was the lump in my throat that he should behave to me as though he had never kissed me before, embraced me passionately, made love to me with a ferocity as erotic and rapturous as it had been dark and frightening, thrilling me to the depths of my very soul. Did I mean nothing to him, then? I could not bear it if that were true.

That night, after he had gone, I cried myself to sleep— and for the first time since coming to the manor, I did not dream.

After that night, I became obsessed with learning what had really happened to me during that feverish fortnight. Deep down inside, I was now convinced that the story of my illness was a lie, but what was behind it, I did not know.

The next morning, I discovered from Sarah that there had been two more vicious murders in the village late last evening, committed in the same grisly fashion as before; and as I remembered the howling in the distance and Drogo's abruptly leaving the manor, I, like Sarah, began uneasily to think that these killings were in some way tied to Devil's Keep and even to Drogo. Rising from my bed, I quickly dressed and hurried from the manor. I would search out young Dr. Morgenstern, I decided; no matter what he had said to me yesterday, I knew that he had been spying on Devil's Keep. I wanted to learn why. It seemed as good a place to start as any; and despite my misgivings about his bizarre behavior toward me and Drogo's believing him a madman, I sensed that the professor was not responsible for the murders. Remembering clearly now, my memories uncolored by shock, I felt he had been as terrified as I of whatever had come as swift as sundown in the park, as powerful as the wind.

To my disappointment, I did not find Dr. Morgenstern that day. But I felt that the walk in the brisk autumn air did me good; and thereafter, it became my practice to rise earlier than I had been wont at Devil's Keep, so I might venture outside to clear the cobwebs from my brain, to convince myself that I was not losing my mind.

Neither Drogo nor Nikki was ever awake at that hour, though I always saw them later and, of course, spent afternoons and early evenings in the schoolroom, where Nikki and I continued our lessons, growing closer. At night, after the boy had retired to his bedchamber, Drogo supped with me, and we talked as we had that evening in the drawing room. Afterward, we read aloud to each other from books of poetry or played cards or chess; and now and then, we danced in the ballroom, to the musical box, and he kissed me. Yet though it seemed he courted me, there was a reserve in his manner, a restraint of some powerful but indefinable emotion I could not understand. It was as though he wished to make love to me, I thought, but refrained; and this both perplexed and perturbed me deeply, for if he had already taken me, why should he hesitate to do so again?

And then, at last, there came the morning when I saw the professor in the park once more, spying on the manor as he had been before, and I learned the answers to my questions. Even then, such was the state of my heart and soul that I did not believe him, did not want to believe him.

"De hour is early, *fraulein*," he greeted me, startling me, for I had not spied him standing in the shadows cast by the tall, twisted trees. "Still, you are up and abroad. It seems you are not yet vun who hunts de night."

"You used that phrase before, Dr. Morgenstern. Yet I know no more what it means now than I did then."

"Haf you never heard, then, *fraulein*, of de *nosferatu*, de undead?" I shook my head, and at the puzzled expression upon my face, he continued. "It is a creature dat in eastern Europe is more commonly referred to as a *dracul*—devil—or a *vampir*—vampire. It is a monster, *fraulein*, a vile t'ing dat vunce vas human but is no longer. Dead, it rises from de grave to prey upon de living, to suck de blood from deir bodies so dat it can sustain its unnatural life and create more of its foul kind."

"Why . . . that's—that's preposterous, Professor! No more than a wicked legend, surely. Come now. You cannot honestly expect me to believe—to believe that such a creature truly exists!"

"But I do, *fraulein*, for it is here—at Devil's Keep and in de village."

"What—what do you mean?" Despite myself, of a sudden I was as cold as the sea that lapped the jagged coast in the distance. An icy tingle of ominous portent and fear chased up my spine; for somehow, deep in my bones, I sensed what was coming.

"De murders, *fraulein*. De terrible murders in de village. Surely, you haf heard about dem? Dey are de vork of de devil, de vork of a vampire, de vork of Count von Reicher and—"

"No!" I cried, stricken to the heart. "No! 'Tisn't true! 'Tisn't true, I tell you! I don't believe you, do you hear? I don't!"

"But you must, *fraulein*, you must! For as I tried to varn you before, you are in de gravest danger if you remain at de manor. Not only your life, but your immortal soul is imperiled!"

"No! 'Tis a lie! 'Tis a lie! A trick to deceive me—"

"No, *fraulein*. Please, you *must* believe me—"

But I did not want to hear any more, and gathering up my skirts, I fled blindly from the young professor, my eyes blurred by tears. To my panic, he gave chase; and in my haste to escape from him, I tripped upon a trailing vine and sprawled headlong onto the earth. Instantly, he was upon me, and in that moment, I felt in my heart that I had made a hideously fatal mistake, that it *was* him who was guilty of the killings and that now, he intended also to murder me. Crying out, I struggled wildly against him. But he was surprisingly strong for one so slight; and presently, he succeeded in pinning my arms to my sides, whereupon he held me fast but gently, stroking my hair tumbled loose from its pins and crooning to me soothingly in the language of his homeland until, realizing I did not understand him, he spoke to me in English.

"Hush, hush, you haf not'ing to fear from me. I am not going to hurt you, *fraulein*. Dis I swear. I am trying to help you, to save your life, your soul. Come vith me now, and you vill learn dat it is so!"

So saying, Dr. Morgenstern tugged me to my feet, his hand closed tight about my wrist to prevent my wresting free of him as he began to drag my resisting figure at a vigorous, determined pace through the park. Weeping with fright, I begged him to let me go. But he paid no heed to my sobs or entreaties, fervently rattling on instead, like a zealot, about the characteristics of vampires and how he must rid Devil's Keep and the village of the great evil that enshrouded them. It was him, I grasped from his mutterings, who had dug up the corpses of the murder victims and had cut off their heads and driven stakes through their hearts; for only in this way could a vampire be killed. Best of all, he informed me, to ensure that such a creature was truly dead, was to remove its heart from its breast and to burn its body until only ashes remained, which should then be scattered to the four winds.

"You vill see, *fraulein!* You vill see dat I speak de truth!" the professor kept insisting, over and over.

It was only, however, as he continued to haul me, stumbling, behind him and I realized to my horror where he was taking me, that I began to have some dim inkling of what he intended; for he was leading me toward the manor's family cemetery, which lay not far from its ancient chapel, in the midst of the grounds. For the first time, I noticed the satchel he had slung over one shoulder; and as I guessed apprehensively at its contents, it came to me at last that he meant to perform—upon a corpse in one of the grey stone sepulchers—the ghastly ritual he had described. No sooner had the thought occurred to me than we drew to an abrupt halt before one of the tombs. Taking the plain wooden cross from about his neck, Dr. Morgenstern, his hands shaking with fear and excitement, draped it around my own neck, saying, "To protect you, *fraulein*." Then, despite how I hung back, he yanked me down the crumbling, moss-rimed steps of the vault and slowly pushed open the arched portal that barred our ingress. Creaking on rusty hinges, the massive wooden door swung open ponderously to reveal the gloomy interior of the sepulcher, and motioning for me to be quiet, the professor cautiously led me inside.

"Dis is de resting place of one of de vampires," he whispered triumphantly. "I am certain of it!"

I was so stricken by his words and manner that at first, I did not completely comprehend. It was only after my initial shock had passed that I understood the full import of what he had said.

One of the vampires . . .

If, despite how desperately I wanted to believe otherwise, he were right and Drogo were indeed such a dark, inhuman creature as Dr. Morgenstern had claimed, then, surely, it followed that Nikolaus, too . . .

"*No*," I moaned softly, thinking of the child I had come to love as my own. "No."

"Be silent, *fraulein*!" the professor hissed, agitated. "Ve do not vant to vake de undead."

As he spoke, he moved deeper into the shadows of the tomb, pulling me with him. Their tiny claws raking the stone floor, tails slithering, rats skittered away at our approach, making me shudder. By the diffuse light that filtered in through the open door, I could see the old granite crypts that surrounded us and make out dimly some of the names and dates chiseled upon the long grey slabs. Layers of cobwebs and dust encrusted the vaults, and the mausoleum itself was rank with the scents of death and decay, dank with mold and moisture. Warily, we edged toward what appeared to be a large wooden shipping crate lying upon the floor of the sepulcher, and as we neared it, I saw that it was stamped with bold black letters that read: PROPERTY OF ARCHDUCHESS ANASTASIE HOCHHAUSEN-OBERSTDORF, followed by the name of the manor's village and then CORNWALL, ENGLAND.

"Der. Do you see, *fraulein*?" Dr. Morgenstern asked softly, excitedly, pointing at the words. "Dat is de name of de grandaunt of Count von Reicher's deceased vife, de Countess Stephanine. Tell me, *fraulein*, how does de body of a noblewoman who died and vas buried in her native Prussia nearly three hundred years ago come to be lying here, in dis tomb? You cannot answer, because even now, you do not vant to believe dat such a creature as a vampire exists. But it is true. De Archduchess Anastasie is one. I know. For over a decade, I have hunted her—who hunts de night—as my grandfather hunted her, and his grandfather before him. Come. Der is much vork to be done, and you must help me, *fraulein*."

With that, releasing me, he lowered to the ground the pack he carried and, kneeling beside it, opened it to withdraw a crowbar, a small mirror, a hammer and wooden stake, some sort of surgical knife, a Bible, a rosary, and a holy wafer. The rosary he hung about his neck. Then, taking up the first of his tools, he started carefully to pry open the top of the shipping crate. Despite that I had now regained my freedom, I stood rooted to the floor of the vault, spellbound with dread and morbid fascination. Very slowly, as he eased up the lid of the makeshift casket, I spied the corpse within. It was that of a woman, in her early forties, I judged, and beautiful—for this, I could see clearly. The woman's body was as though newly dead, free of the black lines of rot and the slippage of flesh that are the cruel results of putrefaction and decay when life has been extinguished. She was blonde and, though pale, upon her cheeks bloomed the pink of a fresh, dusky rose. She looked alive, as though she were merely sleeping, not dead. Yet dead she was, surely, to be in this place, lying in an improvised coffin filled with rich, dark soil, in a peculiar mimicry of a grave.

Laying aside the crowbar, the professor held the looking glass up to the archduchess's face. At first, I thought he was attempting to determine whether she breathed. But then he indicated that I should draw near, and as I timidly stepped forward, I saw to my shock that the archduchess's image was not reflected by the mirror. At the sight, something dark and sinister stirred in my brain, a memory of myself at the foot of the stairs in the great hall of the manor, asking Drogo for a looking glass for my bedchamber. We had stood before the shield that hung upon the wall, and now, I realized that although I could remember seeing myself reflected in the murky metal, I could not recall Drogo's own image beside me. No, it could not be true!

"Now, do you believe me, *fraulein*?" Dr. Morgenstern's young countenance was filled with pity for me. "You have lived with—and perhaps loved, *ja?*— a monster! Come. Help me."

Handing me the Bible, he asked me to read from the scriptures, while he unbuttoned the front of the archduchess's gown to expose her throat and a modest portion of her bosom. Then, positioning the wooden stake at her heart, he picked up the hammer and struck the stake a violent blow, driving it in deep. To my utter terror, as he did so, the archduchess came suddenly and wildly alive, her lids snapping open to reveal red-glowing eyes, her face gruesomely distorted by the feral snarl upon her lips. Her bared teeth seemed to gleam like fangs in the half-light of the sepulcher. Pinned to the dirt in the shipping crate, she thrashed about maniacally, wailing and growling like some terrible, crazed beast as she attempted to free herself. Determinedly, the professor grappled with her frenzied form, his fear giving him the strength to hold her down as he hit the stake again and again, pounding it into her, while I stood there quaking, petrified, unable to move, though every nerve in my body screamed for me to run.

Abruptly casting away the hammer and grabbing the rosary that hung about his neck, Dr. Morgenstern pressed its silver cross to the unnatural creature's forehead. She shrieked as though delivered a fatal wound as the metal burned into her skin, sizzling and charring it; the smell of roasting flesh permeating the air, nauseating me so, I thought I should retch.

And then, without warning, a horrific, maddened roar like nothing I had ever heard before resounded through the tomb, and from nowhere, a huge, malignant blackness swooped down upon the professor, grasping him in a savage, murderous grip, plucking him up as easily as though he weighed no more than a child, and viciously hurling him across the vault. He smashed with such force against the far wall that I felt certain his neck or back must have broken. He seemed to hang suspended there for an eternity before, limply, he slid down the wall to fall forward, facedown, upon one of the stone crypts, his body hideously twisted and twitching spasmodically until, finally, it was still. Surely, he was dead, I thought, feeling sick.

Frozen where I stood, I screamed and screamed again as the evil, perverted thing that had seized Dr. Morgenstern turned toward me, teeth flashing white and ominous in the half-light, eyes smoldering like hot coals, burning into mine, as though to mesmerize me. Lifting its hand, it beckoned me forward, clearly expecting me to obey. As it did so, however, within me there rose a force I had not known I possessed, strong and resistant. As though sensing it, the creature snarled with rage and advanced toward me. Dimly, I registered surprise that what I felt when I saw its face was, in those first moments, not sheer terror, but an overwhelming relief that it was not

Drogo, but a man—if such a vampire could be called—unknown to me. He was Drogo's equal in height and build and muscle, but was as light as Drogo was dark, with hair as golden as the sun and eyes as blue as the sky, his once-handsome face heavily lined and dissipated and, at the moment, distorted with such malevolence that it was terrifying.

"*He* has had you!" he spat, in the rasping voice of the thing that had chased me through the woods. "It is *his* power I feel connecting him to you, combating me!—though he has not yet made you his bride. . . ."

Strangely enough, his words acted as a link for me to reality, to sanity; for with certainty, I knew that he spoke of Drogo, that my instincts had been right, that I had spent my feverish fortnight locked in Drogo's arms. Hard upon the heels of this understanding came the sure realization that whatever Drogo was, he had never intended for me the harm that this diabolic creature most certainly did. Remembering the poor professor's words to me earlier, I knew I must gain the door, the sunlight, to escape from the menace that confronted me.

Gathering my wits, I turned to the portal, only to watch in horror as it slammed shut at a flick of the vampire's eyes in its direction, leaving us in a darkness that chilled me to the depths of my very soul. With a jeering laugh, the profane thing swept toward me; blindly, instinctively, I fumbled for the surgical knife Dr. Morgenstern had brought into the sepulcher. With all my might, I threw it at the creature, even as I rushed frantically toward the door. I did not know if I had struck him or not, only that, suddenly, reaching out, he caught me in a grip of iron, tangling one hand agonizingly in my hair and cruelly jerking my head back, nearly breaking my neck, to expose my vulnerable throat. I could feel his fetid breath, hot and harsh against my flesh. I knew I was but a heartbeat from death.

And then, somehow, the door was abruptly ripped open again by another equally potent force, and a stream of muted sunbeams poured in where we stood. Hissing and growling, the creature spun about, his black, many-caped greatcoat swirling around him like a shroud as he flung up his arm to ward himself from the light.

I did not wait to see more, but fled as though the devil himself pursued me.

9

B Y the time I reached the manor, I had a stitch in my side and was gasping for breath. Hurrying inside, I staggered up the staircase in the great hall, drawn by some overpowering sense of urgency, a desperate need to know all the dark secrets of Devil's Keep. The door to Drogo's bedchamber was not locked; pushing it open, I stepped inside and carefully advanced toward the center of the room. As at all the windows in the manor, the heavy draperies were closed, shrouding the chamber. Even so, I could see the casket-like shipping crate that reposed upon the floor, at the foot of the massive canopy bed. Slowly, my heart pounding, I drew near to the makeshift coffin and, kneeling beside it, stretched out a trembling hand to gently ease open the lid. Instantly, my nostrils were assailed by the fragrance of rich, dark earth, damp as though after a rain. But the shipping crate itself was . . . empty!

Behind me, with a whisper, the door swung firmly shut; and as I whirled about, my pulse racing, I spied

Drogo standing before it, his eyes glittering with desire, his mouth curved in that faint, mocking smile.

"So now you know what I am, Lenore—" He spoke softly. "—and you fear me, do you not? In your eyes, I have become a monster, a foul, inhuman creature who hunts the night; and you would run from me. No, do not deny it, for I know your thoughts as well as my own. But I am no different now from when you lay in my arms and I made love to you, *liebchen*. For 'twas in no dream, no delirium that I came to you, but during those days and nights when I claimed you as mine. Yet despite how I hungered for you, did I not but taste of you, never draining you to the dregs? You cannot know what torture that was for me, Lenore! To take only so much of you as would open your mind to me so I could protect you from Karl Wilhelm, but not enough to make you my bride forever."

"K-K-Karl Wilhelm?"

I was shocked, appalled by Drogo's revelations; yet there rose within me, too, another emotion—sudden, strong, and sweet—as I unwillingly remembered being locked in his embrace. Determinedly, I thrust the image away. I had to keep him talking while I formulated a plan to escape, I thought, then realized, panicked, that he could read my mind—as the sudden flaring of his nostrils warned me. Mercifully, however, he chose to ignore my contemplation of how best to outwit him and flee—doubtless because he knew how futile it was. There was only one door, and he was blocking it.

"Karl Wilhelm, Baron Frankenburg, my wife's cousin and my most bitter enemy for over two hundred years." He paused, allowing me to absorb the incredibility of his age. Then he continued, seeming content for the moment to talk, as though to give me time to collect myself—or to lull me into a false sense of security. "You find it difficult to believe I am so old, *liebchen*, I know. But 'tis true. I was born in Prussia in 1543, to the noble house of Von

Reicher, and at my birth betrothed to the Lady Stephanine, of the equally noble house of Hochhausen-Oberstdorf. Our marriage was arranged for the usual reasons— property, politics, power—and in 1566, we were wed. But it did not answer, for Stephanine despised me. She wanted Karl Wilhelm, you see, her cousin, her lover." His face grew harsh at the memory; his mouth tightened.

"Was it—was it him who chased me through the woods that night, and who attacked me in the tomb this morning?" I asked timidly.

"Yes. It has enraged him to think that I might take a bride, that I might .have a chance after all these long years at the happiness of which he and Stephanine robbed me. For she was never truly mine, but his— and she lies dead and buried in her grave, while you are quick and vibrant with the life's blood flowing through you. Even now, I can taste it, warm and sweet upon my tongue, as it was when you trembled beneath me. You were not so afraid of me then, were you, Lenore? For did I not warn you to be sure, very sure that you wanted me? And was it not you who drew me down and of your own accord opened yourself to me?"

"Yes," I whispered, stricken and ashamed, sickened by the knowledge—and, worse, by my memories of those dark, wild days and nights when I had lain in his arms and let him do as he willed with me and gloried in it. "But I—but I did not know then what you—what you were . . . are— Oh, Drogo! How came you to be so?"

"Through Karl Wilhelm and Stephanine's shared grand-aunt, the Archduchess Anastasie. 'Twas she who, in search of immortal youth, was the first of their house to become a vampire. In time, she preyed upon Karl Wilhelm; and he, cruel to begin with, exulted in his new, unnatural power. Despite that she was my wife, Stephanine and he had continued as lovers; and he readily initiated her into the ranks of the *nosferatu*, the undead. Like him, she reveled in her newfound power and determined to use it to hurt me, for she had come with time utterly to abhor me. Knowing that I loved above all our son and my heir, Nikki, who had been born a year after our marriage, Stephanine—who had never wanted the boy— fed upon him and turned him into a creature such as she."

"No! Her own child! How could she? That's terrible!" I cried, horrified.

"Yes, terrible . . . terrible to be forever trapped in a boy's body, never to grow physically to manhood, despite how mentally and emotionally he matured. But Stephanine did not think of that, only of how she would injure me. When I learned of her betrayal, of the monster she had become, of the great evil she had done to our son, I willingly offered myself as her victim, in order to try to help Nikki; and then, when it was done, I killed her!"

"No! Oh, no!" I sobbed; but lost in his dreadful memories, Drogo did not hear me.

"She looked so beautiful lying there, sleeping, in the bed to which she had so seldom deigned to admit me; it was hard to believe that her loveliness could conceal so much ugliness, so much cruelty, so much hatred. But I knew that it did. She thought me too weakened from loss of blood to do her any harm. Still, somehow, I found the strength to rise and to pick up the fireplace poker and then—God help me, *liebchen*—to plunge it straight through her black heart! Afterward, I took my sword and cut off her head, then burned her body in the hearth. She was my wife," he uttered bleakly, "and I murdered her." He was silent for a moment, remembering. Then he went on with his grim, horrific, heartrending tale.

"For this, and because they want Nikki—whom they obsessively but quite mistakenly believe is Karl Wilhelm's own son, the product of his affair with

Stephanine and thus the heir to the house of Hochhausen-Oberstdorf—Anastasie and Karl Wilhelm have sought ever since to kidnap Nikki and to destroy me. For over two hundred years and across three continents, we four have played our deadly cat-and-mouse game, pursuing one another, even as we ourselves have been pursued, first by the original Dr. Morgenstern—whose daughter fell prey to Karl Wilhelm—and then, later, by the professor's descendants. For all that time, I have searched for a cure for Nikki and myself so we can become human again and lead normal lives; and I feel I am growing ever closer to finding it, Lenore. But that Anastasie and Karl Wilhelm cannot permit, for they know that if ever I were able to move about in broad daylight, nothing would stop me from hunting them down and destroying them. I am stronger than Anastasie, as strong as Karl Wilhelm—which is why he and I do not choose to battle face-to-face; for we would surely rend each other limb from limb. None of us knows if I discover a cure if that strength will remain to me, but the two of them dare not take the chance that it will."

"I—I believe that the Archduchess Anastasie is dead, Drogo, that Dr. Morgenstern killed her—as Baron Frankenburg would have killed me . . . .'Twas—'twas you who opened the door to the tomb, wasn't it, letting the sunlight in?"

"Yes, the bond between us permits me to channel a portion of my power through you, protecting you, if necessary. Can you not feel my mind touching yours? Yes, it is time, my chosen one. I have wanted you, hungered for you, since the first moment I beheld you, and have prepared you for this hour. Come to me, *liebchen!*" he demanded softly, holding out his hand to me. "Be my bride—for I *do* love you—and we will hunt the night together until the end of time!"

"And—and if I will not?"

"There is the door—" With a flick of his wrist, he indicated the portal, and slowly, it opened. "—and however much I will long to, I swear I will not prevent you from walking through it if that is what you wish. That is why I did not make you my bride before; I wanted you to be free to choose. Such is the depth of my love for you, Lenore . . . sweet Lenore."

His eyes kissed mine, speaking to me silently, eloquently; his thoughts became my thoughts, and I knew the truth of his words, felt the waves of his pain and loneliness, his desire and need. Despite myself, I had been deeply moved by his story. Now, his wordless outpouring of emotion overwhelmed me, tore at my heart. That he loved me with every fiber of his being, that he would indeed sacrifice his own happiness so my choice would be mine alone, I could no longer doubt. I could walk through the door, and he would not stop me. Yet despite what he was, I found I could not bring myself to leave him. I was as alone as he. I had no family, no friends; in my life, there was only Drogo. Unbidden in my mind came the thought that if all in the world should perish tomorrow and only he remain, I should be glad beyond my wildest imaginings; and I knew then that my love for him was stronger than my fear.

"Yes!" he breathed jubilantly, understanding—and closed the door.

The muscles in his powerful, lithe body rippling with savage grace, he stalked me; and when he swept me up into his arms and laid me upon the bed, I knew no will but his. Bending over me, he pressed me down upon the bed, his handsome visage darkening as he spied the professor's gift of protection at my throat. Growling, he grabbed hold of the plain wooden cross and, brutally snapping the simple thong from which it was suspended, flung it away before falling on me blindly, his hands tangled in my unbound hair, his mouth swooping down to claim mine possessively, his insistent tongue tracing the outline of my lips before arrogantly insinuating itself inside, piercing me, plundering me. Pliantly, I yielded to his lustful, overpowering invasion, drank him in like potent summer wine, my tongue meeting and wreathing his. He taunted, he teased, mouth and tongue and hands roaming over me greedily, covetously, working their devilish spell upon me, insidious as curls of perditious smoke, inciting as forks of infernal flame, making me moan and writhe beneath him as, feverishly, he tore at my garments, stripping me naked before casting away his own clothes.

Soft and silken as a gauzy cobweb, my long red hair enwrapped us as we slid and strained against each other, my arms twining a love knot about his neck, my fingers weaving like ribands through his glossy black hair, drawing him down to me. He was a pagan, a demon, both exalting and desecrating me, and I rejoiced at his barbarous idolatry, reveled in his blasphemous assault. His body was as hard as horn, in sharp contrast to the gossamer feel of the fine hair that matted his chest, where, fervidly compelled by him, I pressed my face and palms, my lips and tongue, touching him everywhere I could reach, feeling the thick cord of his powerful muscles, tasting the earthiness of his skin, while he buried his face in the fire of my tresses and scorched my throat and breasts with kisses, ravishing me with his mouth, his tongue, his hands. His breath was like sacrificial flame against my flesh, searing me, burning me, the words he muttered hoarsely in my ear and against my throat sounding like some lyrical, arcane chant.

"Lenore . . . *liebchen*."

I was drunk, drugged by him, as though his lips were a silver goblet from which I had drained to the dregs some honey-sweet, mind-numbing potion that had left me stupored and floating in a primeval place of mist and smoke and shadow. Time turned—and kept on turning. I did not know how much as I lay in his arms and let him do as he wished with me. I knew nothing, was oblivious to all save Drogo and the place to which he carried me, a place magical and mystical, where dark, hollow hills hove up from an ancient, mysterious, distant shore, looming and defiant beneath the gloaming heavens and in the face of an underworldly firestorm that maddened on the far horizon. A formidable, amorphous blaze, it gathered force and substance to hurtle forward relentlessly in a swirling scourge of berserk wind and riotous flames that smote the earth apocalyptically. Down into caverns fitfully illuminated by the sudden, harsh flare of erupting fire born of wild, sorcerous summoning and, in its wake, echoing with a fearsome, deafening roar that was the violent rending of some diaphanous veil between the planes of existence, he took me. There, he pressed me down upon shifting sands and sharp shingle that edged a churning pool of molten ore—source of all that had ever been or ever would be, a flickering gate unto all time, all places, all things—while beyond the gloomed, gaping mouths of the murky caves and serpentine catacombs, the wind bayed with the collective voice of a thousand hounds of hell and the fiendish firestorm quickened and raged against a black sky streaked bloodred with unnatural umbrage.

We were lost in the conflagration, devoured by the ferocious, feral passion that had, with carnivorous teeth and ripping talons, seized us both, bedeviling us, enthralling us, garlanding us with sinuous smoke, consuming us with tongues of flame. We wanted, we needed. Without warning, Drogo shoved my thighs wide apart and, snarling, drove down into me, his hard, questing manhood stabbing swift and deep and true into the secret heart of me, making me gasp and then cry out, a low wail of surrender that he smothered with his triumphant mouth as, blindly, he impaled me, again and again, his hands crushing me to him ruthlessly, arching my hips to meet each unbridled, throbbing thrust as dark flesh melted urgently into pale. His mouth burned red-hot against my throat, teeth sinking into me with an exquisite eroticism so ecstatic as to be unbearable. In a rapturous, heated rush, my blood and life flowed from me into him, and I burst into blaze, an inferno, unholy, eternally damned and defiled.

Raising his head, he raked his fingernails viciously across his breast, gashing himself above his heart; and the taste of his blood was sweeter than nectar upon my tongue as I pressed my lips to the wounds, tasting him, drinking long and deep. Rasping for breath, he threw back his head and howled exultantly, a wolfish ululation as, with a slow, seemingly interminable shudder that violently racked the length of his hard-muscled body, he spilled himself inside me.

Afterward, we lay still together, naked and entwined; and I slept the sleep of the dead, only to awake in his arms, as hungry as he. Making love once more, we feasted on each other; and when it was done, the sun had set, and I knew I should never again see another dawn.

When at last we rose, Drogo moved swiftly to prepare for our leaving England; for we knew that Karl Wilhelm, Baron Frankenburg, would stop at nothing to destroy us, and I was not yet strong enough to defend myself against him. Drogo feared to lose either me or his son while shielding the other. A ship bound for the Continent lay off the coast, and he was determined that we should be on it.

I learned that he and Nikki possessed numerous shipping crates each, which served as their coffins, and since Drogo's were large enough for he and I to share, he simply added several shovelfuls of Cornish earth to them, mingling it with his own

Prussian soil; for a vampire's casket must be lined with dirt from his native land to help protect him. We would take nothing else with us; for in addition to Devil's Keep, which he had acquired years ago, Drogo owned several other estates on three continents. He lived in each manor only a short while before moving on to the next, not only so people would not become suspicious about why Nikki never grew any older, but also to make the Archduchess Anastasie and Baron Frankenburg's pursuit of him and Nikki more time-consuming and difficult. Invariably, Drogo handled his travel arrangements as he did now, quickly and secretively, so that always uncertain as to where he and Nikki had fled, the Archduchess Anastasie and Baron Frankenburg must waste valuable time and effort tracking them down. Whenever he took up residence at another estate, Drogo either assumed a new identity or pretended to be some descendant of his own and simply transferred all his properties and bank accounts to himself accordingly. Having inherited his family's riches, he had over the centuries, through careful investments in various business ventures, increased his considerable fortune tenfold; and as a result, each manor was adequately furnished with all we would require.

If I had had any remaining doubts about having given myself into Drogo's keeping, the last vestiges of them were swept away when Nikki saw me and realized his father and I were one.

"Oh, Fraulein Blakeley!" he cried, flinging himself into my arms and hugging me tight. "I am so happy that you chose to stay with us, that you will never leave us! Father has been so lonely, and now, he will never be alone again!"

As I met Drogo's anguished eyes, my own filled with tears that Nikki's concern should be all for his father, when the boy's own life was so solitary, without friends and without hope that he would ever grow to manhood unless Drogo should find a cure for the curse that afflicted us. Yet in over two hundred years, he had not, and though he felt he was growing closer to its end, I knew he despaired at the thought that his quest might never prove successful.

Through Renfrew, he made arrangements to have the shipping crates taken by wagons to the coast, all of them traveling by different routes to ensure that at least some of the improvised coffins would safely arrive at their destination. It was not until they were securely loaded in the dark hold of the vessel that we would seek refuge in the shipping crates; for before that, it was possible they might be opened for cargo inspection. Thus we ourselves would journey on horseback to the coast, Drogo not liking to entrust our trip to a carriage that might break down upon the rough roads of the moors, stranding us far from the shelter of our makeshift caskets and thereby fatally exposing us to the light of day.

At last, we were ready, and saddling up, the three of us set off down the winding drive that led away from Devil's Keep, Nikki riding ahead of us, Drogo and I following behind, mounted together on his huge black stallion, his arm tight about my waist, I leaning against him, resting my head against his shoulder, still faint from loss of blood. Neither Drogo nor Nikki, I had thankfully discovered, preyed upon humans; it was only upon animals they fed, and even then drawing only as much blood as they required for sustenance, never killing the beasts. It had been the Archduchess Anastasie and Baron Frankenburg who had committed the murders in the village and who also had slaughtered Drogo's small herd of dairy cattle, so he and Nikki should have no readily available source of blood. That was why Nikki had attacked me that day in the schoolroom; the child had been ravenous, frenzied by his hunger. Though Drogo had immediately replaced the herd and had earlier taken blood from one of the cattle for me, I had not been able to drink much, so new and thus still offensive was the shock to my senses, the taste to my palate.

"Nikki and I felt the same way, too, at first, Lenore," Drogo had told me. "You will get over it soon enough; soon, it will be like a fever in your blood, a craving for a drug, almost as great as your need for me, and mine for you, *liebchen*."

We were halfway down the narrow, serpentine drive when, from behind us, there rose that dreadful sound that was like the baying of wild dogs or wolves; and then there reached our ears the thud of approaching hoofbeats, coming hard and swift through the trees. Glancing back, I saw that it was Baron Frankenburg in hot pursuit of us, viciously roweling the sides of his mount, cruelly and recklessly spurring the lathered horse forward. To my relief, by now Nikki was through the wrought-iron gates of the manor and safely away. Drogo and I were not far behind. But when next I looked ahead, I realized to my horror that at Baron Frankenburg's command, the portals were slowly swinging shut to bar our path. Despite his great strength, there was no time for Drogo to draw up the steed we rode; it was galloping far too fast and furious for that. My breath caught in my throat as I felt his arm tighten about me, the beast's powerful haunches bunch, surging and rippling beneath us as it prepared to plunge through the shrinking gap between the gates. We were not going to make it, I thought frantically. We were going to crash into the closed portals, be flung from the stallion onto the wicked, foot-long spikes that topped them . . . .

"No!" I wailed, stricken. "*No!*"

And then we were soaring on the wind, through the gates, to come down roughly on the other side just as they clanged shut behind us. Hard on our heels came

Baron Frankenburg, his own horse snorting and wild-eyed, flecks of foam flying from its glistening coat as it thundered forward relentlessly in response to his pitiless, lashing whip and sharp spurs. He was so hubristic and egotistical that I suppose he thought that no matter how humanly impossible the leap, he could through his own unnatural power vest his steed with strength enough to successfully fly over the closed portals; and perhaps he could have done so. I shall never know.

For suddenly hearing behind us a terrible cry of anger and torment, Drogo drew our own mount up short; and incredibly, as we glanced back, we saw Dr. Morgenstern staggering from the edge of the trees. I did not know how he had survived, how he had managed to make his way from the cemetery to the road; for clearly, he was gripped by great physical agony and mental anguish. Still, he stumbled on, his cloak flapping wildly in the wind. His eyes gleamed fanatically as he reached the gates; he seemed not to care that in seconds, he would be crushed beneath the churning hooves of Baron Frankenburg's stallion. Without warning, as the horse bore down upon him, the professor snatched something from his pocket and thrust it out high before him; and as a shower of moonbeams illuminated the object, I realized that it was his rosary. Its silver cross glowed in the dim, swirling light, momentarily blinding both the horse and Baron Frankenburg. In midair, the beast refused the jump, coming down hard upon the road, trampling Dr. Morgenstern to death and hurling Baron Frankenburg from the saddle, sending him sailing so suddenly and violently that he could not halt his horrible impetus. He landed atop the closed gates, and their spikes drove deep, stabbing him through the heart, pinning him fast, so he dangled there grotesquely, bellowing and thrashing about dementedly, plainly unable to escape.

Somehow, I knew he was still hanging there when the sun rose in the sky.

*   *   *

And now, I am come at last to the end of my story. As
men count time, I am grown old, though because I hunt
the night, my youth and beauty remain to me, as fresh
as a perfect bloodred rose. I have traveled the world; but
of all the splendorous sights I have beheld, I know that
none have been lovelier to my eyes than would be the
vision once more of dawn breaking on an eastern horizon.
This Drogo knows and laments, for my sake—though if
I could go back to what I was before, I would not, not
without him who is the half that makes me whole.

In the stillness of our shared coffin, our hearts beat
as one, and he holds at bay the shadows when they are
too haunting to be borne. At night, we work side by
side in his laboratory, he conducting his experiments, I
taking notes, both of us certain that someday, Nikki and
we will lead normal lives and die—though even death
shall not separate Drogo and me, I think. For through
the years, our love for each other has grown deeper than
ever, transcending our bodies and minds, entwining our
very souls, exalting us. It is like the stars in the night sky,
lighting up the darkness: unbounded, radiant, eternal.

I do not ask for more. I have no regrets.

10

Cornwall, England, 1913

THE long, narrow, serpentine drive—overgrown with
grasses and weeds and vines—twisted and turned so,

the manor in the distance appeared to be playing hide-and-seek with him as he wound his motorcar beneath the tightly woven canopy formed by the interlaced branches of the tall, ancient trees that lined the verge. Sometimes, he lost his way; for often, the drive vanished entirely beneath the spread of soft green moss and lichen, trailing vines, tangled ferns, and climbing ivy that, unchecked, had proliferated wildly over the years, clamoring up the rough bark of the elms and rowans, the beeches and yews, enveloping the woods, engulfing the lawns, and encroaching upon the manor. And then, suddenly—for time had played tricks with his memory, and he had forgotten how quick came the bend that would bring the manor itself into view—Devil's Keep loomed before him, a desolate ruin, more secretive and mysterious than even he, who had lived here once, recalled.

Drawing the long, low-slung black motorcar to a halt before the front door of the manor, he slowly got out, his being filled to overflowing with joy.

At long last, he had come home.

Tall, dark, and handsome, there was something earthy and exotic and foreign-looking about him as he stood there beneath the portico, staring intently at the manor, lost in reverie. His clothes were exquisite, expensive, clinging to broad shoulders, a massive chest, a firm, flat belly, and thick, corded thighs; his habits were those of a man accustomed to fine things, as well. From the pocket of his well-tailored jacket, he withdrew a cheroot, which he lighted and dragged on deeply as he continued to contemplate Devil's Keep, remembering.

" 'Tis haunted, people claim . . . the manor, I mean."

He moved with the sinewy, hypnotic grace of a panther on the prowl as he turned to the young woman who had slipped like a fairy from the gardens to address him; his black eyes were equally mesmerizing, holding her fast where she now stood, a few feet away from him. He was not startled, for he had sensed her presence and knew who she was; he had heard in the village of both her and her strange, fey affinity for the manor where her people had once worked.

Still, he had not expected her to be so ethereal, so beautiful. But she was, he thought as he gazed at her standing there in the streaming sunlight, her long red-gold hair like gilded flame and her sloe green eyes wide with sudden, breathless wonder as they met his own dark ones. She reminded him of his dearly beloved stepmother, with whom he and his father had been happy here at Devil's Keep, long ago. Tossing away his cheroot, he reached into the motorcar to withdraw an ornate golden urn, which he then opened and upended, pouring a fine trickle of ashes upon the ground.

"Somehow, I don't think that the manor is haunted anymore," he murmured as he smiled enigmatically at the young woman, knowing in that moment how much he would love her, that she would be his so long as they both should live. "Somehow, I think that all its ghosts have been laid to rest at last."

At his words, the ashes Count Nikolaus von Reicher had scattered from the urn gently billowed up from the earth and, like lovers dancing to the strains of some faint, forgotten melody, whirled away, eternally entwined, dust in the wind.

Rebecca Brandewyne

REBECCA BRANDEWYNE was born in Tennessee, but she has lived most of her life in Kansas, from where she has traveled widely, visiting many of the places about which she has written.

She was graduated *cum laude* with departmental honors from The Wichita State University, and holds a bachelor's degree in journalism, with minors in music and history, and a master's degree in communications. Before becoming a writer, she taught interpersonal communication at the university level.

She is a *New York Times* best-selling author of thirteen novels: nine historical romances, two gothics, and two fantasies. *Devil's Keep* is her first novella. She has received numerous awards for her work, has millions of books in print, and is published worldwide. She is a founder and member of Novelists, Inc., a charter member of Romance Writers of America, and a member of Science Fiction Writers of America, Western Writers of America, and Mensa.

She resides with her husband and son in the Midwest, from where, she says, Frank Langella's Dracula may summon her to Carfax Abbey any night he wishes.

Vanquish the Night

Shannon Drake

Prologue

1870, West Texas

THERE was a curious breeze that night.

Michael Johnston felt it first when the night shadows were just beginning to give way to the pink streaks of dawn. It was the breeze, in fact, that woke him.

Anne's window was open to the night. The breeze entered, seemed to touched him, swirl around him. His eyes opened, and for several long moments, he tensed, listening. He had become accustomed to waking quickly, alert to the first whisper of danger.

But there was no sound, just the breeze.

He slipped the covers from himself and crawled naked from Anne's bed, striding silently to the window. He looked out. The sun hadn't risen yet; the moon was still visible in the sky. Even as he stared at it, it seemed that a dark shadow passed over it. Quickly. So quickly that if he had blinked then, he'd never have seen it . . . sensed it.

He paused, still and silent by the window, for a long time. Listening. Searching the landscape beyond the ranch house. There was nothing unusual to be seen. A tumbleweed flew a few feet, bounced, flew again. Just outside from where he stood, a shutter broke loose, banged against the house, and went still. Cursing softly beneath his breath, he thrust the window further open, leaned out, and re-latched the shutter.

Then . . . silence.

The breeze vanished. The tumbleweed hung suspended in midair, then fell. All around him, there was nothing. Just the silence in the stillness of the night.

He wondered how a man who had survived sword-fights, cannon fire, and Indian arrows could feel such a strange unease over something so natural as a breeze.

But it had carried a chill with it . . .

"Michael?"

Her voice was soft, feminine. He knew it so very well, loved it so very deeply.

He walked back to the bed on his bare feet.

Her eyes were only halfway open. In the shadows, he could not see their color, but he knew it. They were amber. Not really brown, not hazel either. Framed by jet lashes, they were large, wide-set, intelligent, beautiful eyes. Just as Anne was beautiful, with her ivory skin, delicate features, flashing smile, and look of never-ending wisdom.

The heavy skeins of her ebony hair were tousled and wild, an indication of the way things had gone earlier in the evening. She held the pastel-yellow bedsheets to her breasts, and the way her gaze fell upon him, the way her hair curled so enticingly, aroused all the hunger within his body and soul. He smiled as he stroked her cheek.

"It's all right," he said softly.

"What are you doing up?" she whispered. Her eyes widened and focused upon him. "Did you hear anything? There hasn't been an attack anywhere?"

He couldn't guarantee that there hadn't been an attack somewhere, but not near them, he was certain. The citizens of Green Valley had banded tight and close against the possibility of an Indian attack. The alarm would have sounded, they would have heard shouts and screams.

Sometimes, Apaches were silent, stealthy when they came upon their victims. But once they had them . . .

Well, then they were anything but silent.

The Apaches in this area had been fairly bloodthirsty the first few years following the war. The town always had to keep an eye open to the threat of attack. But recently, a number of the tribes and the citizens of Green Valley had reached an agreement. Walks Tall, an important chief among the Apache, kept his word, and at the moment the white citizens were at peace with him.

Michael wasn't expecting an attack. Still, the members of the militia he headed were always on alert, each man devoting one night a month to guard duty. Most of them, like him, were old war-horses—quick to respond to the slightest hint of conflict. They were a close-knit community, all of them licking battle wounds in one way or another.

"No attack," he said.

Anne caught his hand, holding his palm to her cheek. He thought he felt a shudder rip through her body.

"It's all right. I swear it," he told her softly.

She nodded. A lock of her hair tumbled down over his fingers, soft as silk. It stroked his flesh. Fragrant, it seemed to send the scent of roses sweeping around the room.

It was amazing to him how such a thing, such a little thing, could be so sensual, creating such a swift and urgent desire within him.

Maybe it was just Anne.

Maybe it was love . . .

They'd both arrived in Green Valley at about the same time. She'd lost her home to Sherman's fires and her husband to a bullet at Sharpsburg. He'd lost his home to a cannonball and his fiancée to a triumphant Yank. Just as he'd lost a little bit of the ability to run, to dance gracefully, and even to mount a horse with his accustomed ease. A saber wound in his knee had never quite healed properly and now he walked with a limp.

But he wasn't bitter. He knew a number of the Yanks at the fort over the hills, and they were all-right fellows. He'd traded with a few downriver during the long years of the war. No, he wasn't bitter.

He just wanted his life to take a new direction.

From the time Anne Pemberton had first stepped off the stage at Green Valley station, he had known that he wanted her. That had been early in 1868. Then there had been a full year when they hadn't had a decent thing to say to each other. Maybe it had been good that they'd spent that year keeping a distance between them. Back then, they'd both still needed time to get over the war.

Then there had been the months when he had hated her for being so damned superior, and she'd hated him for being so right all the time. Then those flying sparks had finally ignited, and there had been one fantastic night when she'd forgotten the past, forgotten all other loves, and fallen prey to the wildness and fury of his seduction. Right in her front parlor. She'd been telling him that he'd no right to chew out her friend Billy over the way he had handled an Apache situation, and he'd been yelling right back that she should be thanking her lucky stars she wasn't staked out on an Apache plain that very moment. The next thing he knew, every longing, every flicker of desire that had been growing over the years had suddenly exploded.

And she'd been in his arms, and he'd been kissing her, and to his amazement, she'd suddenly kissed him back, and he had become tangled in her clothing as he struggled to free her from it. He never did strip her completely. But that hadn't altered either the passion or the tenderness with which he had made love to her.

Funny what war and circumstance could do to people. It hadn't bothered Anne that she had turned her back on propriety and made love with him. But she hadn't been ready to give everything to him either. She didn't like the idea that he was the leader of the militia and dedicated to solving conflicts with the Indians and that was something that he really couldn't change. She'd lost one husband to warfare, and she wasn't willing to risk another.

Sometimes, the townspeople managed all right with the Indians—sometimes, they didn't. But he knew the Mescalero Apache as well as it was possible for any white man to know them. He respected them, appreciated their way of life, and greatly admired their courage and their commitment to their tribes. They were a proud people.

And a warlike one.

Well, things did take time. And though he and Anne rather danced around each other, both expecting the other to give in, there was something strong between them. One day, she was going to be his wife. And in the meantime, he loved her. More and more deeply every day.

He knew that Anne loved him, too. If she just weren't quite so stubborn . . .

The amber of her eyes was like gold in the room's pale light. She reached out and touched his cheek.

"How odd!" she whispered. "Something . . . woke me."

"It was the breeze," he told her. He grinned, drew back the covers, and slid in beside her. Jesu, it was easy to forget that curious breeze now. Her skin was like silk, sensual and sleek against his. And warm, so deliciously warm.

She was shivering, though.

He swept his arms around her, covering the length of her naked body with his own. She was incredibly sensual, her body all curves, her breasts full and firm, the hardened pink nipples taunting against his chest. He kissed her lips softly, feeling the pulse of his arousal become a thunder. "It's all right," he assured her, his lips raised just a breath above hers.

Her eyes shone into his. "I was just dreaming, I think. The strangest dreams, Michael! Something dark had flown across the moon, like a huge black bird of prey. Then there was the most curious yellow light. It beckoned, and I started following it and then . . ." She shivered again.

"And then?" he persisted.

She shook her head. "I don't know. Then . . ." Her eyes widened. "I felt the breeze!"

"It's all right, I swear it!" he told her.

"I was so afraid, and I reached for you, and you were gone."

"I'm here now."

She smiled slowly. "I know." Her voice was husky, sweet. "I can feel you."

"The breeze is gone," he assured her.

"It is," she agreed. "Right now it feels like a very hot night."

"Burning."

He smiled, encompassing her in his arms. The power of his body gently forced hers to open, and he allowed his throbbing erection to tease against the soft, sensual flesh of her inner thigh. Then higher . . . a bit higher. She shifted beneath him, her eyes still on his. A wicked gleam shone within them, teasing and seducing.

"It's getting hotter and hotter," she whispered.

"You just don't know how hot!" he warned. His lips found hers again. Seared them. Then abruptly he rose above her, cupped a breast, lowered his head, laved and tweaked a hardened tip with his tongue. Her fingers dug into his shoulders. He moved lower against her. Lower and lower still. Suddenly, a desperate passion seemed to burst within him. He wanted to make love to her more fiercely than he ever had before. He wanted to make love in a way that somehow . . .

Somehow left a little part of him imprinted on her. As if he could own her . . .

No, as if he could protect her.

The thought burst in his mind, then faded with the strength of his desire. He touched her, kissed her, caressed her. When she rose against him, determined to love him in return, he pressed her back. Inch by silky, luxurious inch, he caressed her flesh, then flipped her to lie face-down and pressed hot fire at her nape, with the touch of his lips and tongue. He moved down her spine, again bit by bit until he came to the small of her back. His hands circled the curves of her hip, flipped her once again. His caress found the most tender and intimate erotic places. His fingers stroked and parted. His tongue explored.

He was like a tempest with her that night, hot and wild, giving and demanding. In all the times that he had made love to a woman, he had never felt like this. When the end came, it was a sweet explosion, a climax so violent that he held her, shaking with her, lost in blackness, then seeing the startling twinkle of stars against that blackness and finally feeling sweet shudders seize him again and again as they drifted back to an awareness of lying in her bed in her room.

Now dawn was beginning to break in earnest. Beautiful rays of color were filtering into the room. Reds and magentas, pinks and yellows and oranges. The colors of day were coming, sweeping away the shadows of the night.

His arms tightened around her. The strange uneasiness that had swept through him was melting with the shadows. Still, other feelings seemed to take over. The feel of Anne next to him stole into his heart, and for a moment, he felt that desperate urge to protect her again.

Soft, beautiful, entirely sensual, she lay against him, her damp flesh touching his. In any darkness, he could see her, the shape of her, the beautiful curves that were hers, the color of her eyes, of her hair. He didn't want to leave her. He wanted to wake every morning with her naked and replete beside him.

Yes, he wanted to be with her in the darkness, when the night breeze turned cold.

"Marry me," he urged her.

He felt, more than heard, her little sigh.

"Quit the militia," she responded softly. She'd said it before. Dozens of times.

"Anne, I can't! I'm our most experienced man. I'm also our best hope for peace. You know that."

"All I know is that you ride out all the time. And I never know if you'll ride back," she told him very softly. "And I won't wear widow's weeds again."

"Anne!" he whispered, pulling her close. "How can you say that when life is tenuous at best? Lightning strikes, accidents happen—"

"And I have to deal with them the very best I can," she responded. "I can't add to it the fact that you lead men into a hail of arrows."

"I don't *try* to get killed!" he said angrily.

She touched his cheek tenderly. "No, I won't marry you," she insisted. "Not now."

"When?"

She shook her head. "I don't know."

He pushed back the covers, rising above her. "So if I were killed now, Anne, it wouldn't hurt? It wouldn't cut into your heart just the same?"

"Michael—"

"Anne?"

Her eyes glittered in the darkness. And then it seemed that there was just a hint of tears within them. "Yes! Yes, it would rip me to pieces! Slash my heart, cast me into ungodly desolation! There, is that what you wanted to hear?"

"No, go on."

She stared at him, naked, so very beautiful. So defiant. "All right, I do love you, Michael. Very much."

A trembling seized him. He twisted his jaw to fight it. "Then marry me."

"I can't!"

He let out a long cry of torment. She reached up, long delicate fingers stroking his face. She pulled him down to her. Her tongue teased his lips, entered his mouth, hot, wet, promising.

"I can't marry you. But I can love you!" she whispered.

He groaned again, his frustration palpable on the air. "Anne, this is insane. We're both adults, but you force me to arrive through the back door and exit through the window to avoid any disrespect to your uncle. There's no reason—"

He broke off. Her hands were moving down his body. She knew how to distract a man.

"Anne—"

"I love you!" she whispered.

He sighed. The conversation was over.

Later, he wound his arms around her. She was an incredibly stubborn woman. Maybe she didn't feel the fear that had suddenly stolen upon him tonight.

It lingered.

He sighed. So she wouldn't marry him. Not yet. Maybe he could still hold her, make love to her . . .

Protect her.

He looked out the window. Light had almost chased away the last of the shadows. Almost.

Then he realized that he wasn't going to get any sleep, not until it was full light. It seemed as if the darkness out there had eyes, and only daylight could close them. Anne was sleeping at last. He felt the smooth rise and fall of her breathing. He held her more tightly.

Down the hallway, old Jem Turner, Anne's mother's eldest brother, was standing at his bedroom window. He rubbed his grizzled chin, his hazel eyes hard and alert.

There wasn't anything unusual to be seen. But then, Jem knew that the things you couldn't see were often the ones you should most fear.

Well, Anne was all right for now, no matter what the night wind brought in. She and Michael thought they were meeting behind his back, of course, but he knew darned well every time Michael silently entered the house. He didn't judge them. They'd all lived through too much. Actually, he just wished that stubborn niece of his would marry the fellow.

He felt the breeze again. Soon, he thought, soon.

He'd tried hard to ignore it. Tried to say that legend was legend, and superstition was just plain silly!

But it wasn't, was it?

And how damned odd that he could feel it, just feel it, in a breeze, and know that it was near.

Evil.

Don't leave her, Johnston! Jem thought. *Don't leave her. I'm old and I'm worn, and it's going to be damned hard to make you believe, but he's out there. Watching her. Wanting her.*

Stay. Help me . . .

Not far away, David Drago stood on a rise that overlooked the tiny town of Green Valley. He looked down at the cluster of small farms and ranches, and smiled slowly. It was so good, the night was so good. He could feel the pulse of life within him so strongly. He could feel it, almost taste it.

Soon . . .

He was a tall man, well-built, striking, with dark hair and golden eyes. Eyes that carried a hint of another color, but few people could ever really see that color, or guess at it, until it was too late. As he stood on the rise, a passerby might have thought him very attractive indeed. There was a European sophistication about him that was fascinating. He was a man of the world, accustomed to dealing with any circumstance that might arise. Of course, the world might best him at times, but in the end . . .

Well, he always bested the world.

Green Valley. How quaint a place when compared with London, Paris, Madrid. And what interesting people. These rough Americans, and the curious red savages.

It was a playground—a playground, indeed.

He'd already found it immensely satisfying.

And down there in one particular farmhouse . . . she waited.

He smiled, concentrating, and knew that she was with someone. That didn't matter. He could take care of it. He had plenty of time.

He turned and lifted his arms, raising his black cape to the breeze.

Not far away, stone angels and crosses decorated a cluster of gravestones. But where he stood was unhallowed ground. Without Christian adornment. Indigents were buried here. Heathens. The refuse of humanity.

The earth was rich with suffering . . . just as the night seemed rich with evil.

His smile deepened.

Dawn was breaking. He was weary. But the shadows would come again.

They always did.

1

Two weeks later

"ANNE Pemberton!" Cissy McAllistair exclaimed. "You just can't mean to tell me that you have yet to meet David Drago!"

Anne smiled patiently, biting the thread she'd been using to mend Uncle Jem's good winter jacket. She tied a quit knot before answering Cissy. She really did hate to put a damper on Cissy's excitement. Cissy was young, barely twenty. She'd grown up out here in the wild west of Texas, and although she'd learned plenty about the Apaches, she was innocent of the ways of the world. She'd never had to watch white men killing white men, like they had back East.

"Cissy, I'm sorry, but no, I haven't yet met this paragon of virtue. I've heard people whispering about him, though. They say he's having a big house built on some acreage he bought on the edge of town. Apparently, he intends to stay in Green Valley."

"Oh, I hope so! I hope so!" Cissy said. She was a pretty girl, with cornflower-blue eyes and the kind of white-blonde hair men seemed to go crazy over. Not that Anne felt any jealousy for the girl. Sometimes, she felt very old and worn—in just three years, she'd be thirty! Then again, Uncle Jem was always telling her that it wasn't the years, it was the experience that counted,

118

and she'd certainly chalked up some experience; they all had. But she was comfortable with herself. Michael thought that she was beautiful—at least, he said so fairly often—and for her, that was enough.

In any case, it didn't really matter how perfect this new fellow, David Drago, was. She might be as stubborn as Uncle Jem said she was, but she was in love with Michael. And Michael was pretty close to being perfect himself. He had wonderful deep-gray eyes and sandy hair that he let grow too long. He had a rugged face— a really fine one, with handsome features—and there was something indefinably masculine about those hard features that made him a very sexy man.

She had once been certain that only a truly bad woman could possibly share such intimacies as she shared with Michael and not be married. But the woman she was now was very different from the innocent girl she had once been. Besides, she was going to marry him, one day soon.

Just as soon as she managed to twist him around to her way of thinking.

Of course, that might not happen. Michael was damned stubborn, too. And he was responsible, and honorable, and all those other things.

He was a lot like Joe Pemberton had been. And she had loved Joe very much. Maybe not as deeply as she loved Michael, even though she had been married to Joe. But she and Joe had scarcely wed before a bullet had severed the ties between them.

She *was* going to marry Michael. Soon. Her heart started to beat a little more quickly at the thought. How odd that after all his constant urgings, she was going to say yes. She was going to have to, for the sake of the child she had realized yesterday she was carrying.

But she wasn't going to tell him just yet. Not until she had tried every way she could think of to get him to quit the militia!

"You don't understand because you haven't met him yet," Cissy told her, with wide-eyed eagerness. She wagged a finger at Anne. "But you will. Mrs. Simmons has invited him to her dinner party tonight, and you *are* coming, right?"

Anne shrugged with a slight frown. "I suppose so. But Michael hasn't returned from his trip out to Mescalero country. I won't have an escort."

Cissy smiled. "Then you can join the rest of us whose little hearts are fluttering for David Drago."

"Cissy—" Anne began with a touch of impatience.

Cissy waved a hand in the air. "Oh, Michael is handsome, I'll give you that. And he's tall and rugged, and everyone has always envied you, the way he's so determined to have you—even if you are a widow just a shade past your first youth—"

"Thank you, Cissy," Anne managed to interject.

"Michael is wonderful. Why haven't you married him? Really, Anne, perhaps you should, before you—"

"Dry up completely?" Anne finished for her.

Cissy blushed crimson. "Oh, Anne, you're beautiful, and you know it! But you are getting on!"

"Well, I probably will marry Michael. Sometime soon."

"My father says you don't like him belonging to the militia," Cissy said. "But if he were to leave it, what would happen to the rest of us? Think about it, Anne. He isn't making any demands on you. What manner of man would he be if he let you push him around—especially when Green Valley needs him so much!"

Anne smiled. Cissy did have a point. But then, Cissy didn't know what it was like to read in the newspaper that someone you loved very much was lying dead on a distant battlefield.

"Well, it's too bad you're not married to Michael. Then you'd be out of the running for David Drago."

"I'm not going to be *in* the running," Anne assured her.

"But you have yet to meet him!"

"As you say, I will meet him tonight," Anne said with a wry grin. "But I won't join your panting crowd of girls—still in the flower of their first youth! I'll have Uncle Jem take me. Then I'll observe this Drago character from the side!"

Cissy bounded up, very smug. "You'll see!" she promised. "Wear something absolutely fetching! You'll be glad you did!"

Anne sighed as she rose to see Cissy out. She leaned against the door frame as she watched Cissy go, her full calico skirt bouncing behind her. Cissy was so full of life, so sweet, so generous, so warm. She was like a lot of the inhabitants of Green Valley, and it was one of the reasons Anne liked the place so very much. People didn't ask a lot of questions about the past here. A new town, it gave people new chances in life.

"Well, Cissy," she murmured aloud, "I hope your David Drago falls absolutely in love with you. I hope you love him in return and you both live in his big new house happily ever after!"

Cissy turned a corner. Anne's gaze moved up the street. Far beyond it, she could see the rise on which the cemetery was located. There was the graveyard with its wrought-iron sign swinging slightly in the breeze. GREEN VALLEY CEMETERY it read. To the right of the fenced-in area, there were more graves. Years ago, the folks in Green Valley hadn't been quite so generous and open-minded as they were now. Back then, as in much of Texas, lawlessness had abounded here. Rapists, thieves, murderers, and general riffraff had passed through and called the town home. And when they had died, or killed themselves, they had been buried in the section to the right of the fenced-in area. On unhallowed ground.

Their graves were marked not with handsome angels

shipped in from the East, as in the more holy section of the cemetery. But with crosses crudely formed from tree branches tied together and thrust hard into the ground.

It just went to show, Anne thought, how far Green Valley had come along since those early times. Much of the West was still wild and lawless. Gradually, though, Green Valley had begun to appeal to a gentler variety of folk. Nothing terrible had happened here in years now.

Then again, maybe the war had exhausted a lot of the men, and they had just been seeking peace since then. Whatever the reason, a time of quiet had come to Green Valley.

But as Anne stared at the cemetery she had seen every day since she had first come to this town, she felt a strange uneasiness creep along her spine. She gave herself a shake, but the feeling persisted. It was like the other night . . .

The night when she had awakened and Michael had been gone; she had felt the most awful chill encircle her. She'd remembered her dream about a dark shape obliterating the light of the moon.

But then Michael had come back to her, and held her, and the fear had gone away. Strange, how it was back now . . .

Good grief! She was too old to be getting shivers in broad daylight. Maybe she was afraid because he wasn't back yet. He should be back. He and the militia should have met up with the Apache chief, talked and vowed their peace promises, and returned this morning.

The later he was, the more convinced Anne grew that something was dreadfully wrong.

All kinds of things might have happened. They might have been invited to a special ceremony. They might have met with some inclement weather.

They might have been scalped and murdered by the Mescaleros!

No, she couldn't think that way. She couldn't live with

such fear. Of course, it wouldn't hurt to tell Michael when she did see him just how scared she had been! It might help him understand.

Then again, maybe Cissy was right. Maybe she had no right to ask him to give up the militia. What would happen to the town without his expert protection?

She didn't care, she thought selfishly.

Yes, she did.

Anne hurried back into the house. "Uncle Jem?" she called. When he didn't answer, she walked through the parlor, with its attractive love seat and Victorian drapes, and passed into the back hallway. Uncle Jem was out back by the corral. He was leaning over the white fence, patting her Appaloosa's nose absently.

"Uncle Jem!" she called again. Still, he didn't look her way. There was a troubled frown on his face.

"Uncle Jem?"

He swung around that time, and there was a guilty look on his face. Then his expression seemed as innocent as a babe's. "Annie! What is it?"

She walked out to the corral, studying him. He gave himself a little shake, like a man trying to ward off some unwanted feeling. Just as she had been trying to rid herself of her lingering unease just moments ago.

"What's wrong?" she asked him. Tamarin, her Appaloosa mare, snorted loudly. Anne patted her nose and the horse came close, then snorted again suddenly, backed away, and started running wildly around the corral. "Seems like everyone around here is kind of spooked," Anne murmured.

Jem stiffened, a lock of white hair falling over one rheumy blue eye. "I'm not spooked, young lady. Now what made you say a thing like that?"

Anne shrugged. "Fine. You're not spooked. But I need you to take a bath and get dressed up a bit. I've decided to go to Mrs. Simmons's party tonight."

"What about Michael?"

"He's not back yet."

"You want me to get gussied up just for some fool dinner party?"

"Please?"

He sighed. "Humph."

"Does that mean you'll do it?"

"Why are you suddenly all fired up to go?"

Anne shrugged again. "That newcomer is going to be there. David Drago. Everyone has been talking about him. I'm curious, that's all."

"Curiosity killed the cat!" Jem warned her.

"Uncle Jem, I just want to meet a new neighbor." She sighed. "All right, if you won't go with me—"

"You'll stay home?"

She shook her head. "No. I'll go alone."

"Dag-nabbit, girl!" He glared at her, then sighed. "No, you're not going alone. It wouldn't be right. Someone has to look out for you."

She smiled. "Thanks, Uncle Jem. And don't forget the bath," she added, turning around. She still had a lot to do before getting ready herself. She had to make out some checks today and straighten out her credit accounts or she wouldn't be able to feed her horses and stock much longer. And there were piles of mending.

But curiously—and pleasantly!—her day moved along quite quickly. She was actually ready early and managed to get Soukie, their half-Cherokee stable boy, to make two trips hauling in water for a bath.

She luxuriated in the bath for a long time, sudsing herself with imported soap from back East. It was a pity that Michael wasn't back, she told herself, inhaling the soap's sweet scent. Then she realized that her thoughts were wandering down decadent paths and she firmly diverted them. Still, after she rose from the tub, she lingered long over her wardrobe. The dinner wasn't a formal occasion, but she found herself choosing from among her best dresses. The yellow silk with the amber bodice was her best gown, and although it went well with her dark hair and golden eyes, she should save it for when Michael would be there to see it.

She started to set it back on its hooks, but some power other than her own seemed to take hold of her. Before she knew what she was doing, she was climbing into the yellow dress.

She stared at herself in the floor-length mirror. The gown was beautiful, the bodice a darker shade in embroidered velvet. The low-cut neckline emphasized her full bosom, while the corset gave her a minuscule waist which flared into curvaceous hips. She'd left her hair loose, flowing down her back.

She frowned as she continued to stare at herself, wondering why she had felt compelled to display her feminine charms. Had Cissy's words made her feel old? That she had to prove her attractiveness to this newcomer?

She didn't know. With a sigh, she turned away from the mirror. Even as she did so, fear and unease rippled along her spine.

If only Michael would come home!

"Annie, you ready?" Uncle Jem called. "The horses are all hitched up."

"I'm coming," she assured him, and hurried out to meet him. He whistled at her in appreciation. She smiled and curtsied to him.

"How do I compliment a beautiful young thing like you?" he asked affectionately.

"The same way I rate a dashing older gent like you!" she teased in return. Then she frowned suddenly. The moon was out. A black shadow seemed to sweep across it, then disappear. She shivered fiercely.

"Annie?" Jem asked with a frown.

What was the matter with her?

"All set, Uncle."

He helped her into their shiny black carriage. Old

Thom, the carriage horse, sprang into action at Jem's urging. In a matter of moments, they were traveling along the road to Mrs. Simmons's huge gingerbready mansion on the hill.

"Looks like the entire town turned out," Jem said, nodding at the array of carriages and buckboards drawn up on the grounds.

"Looks like," Anne agreed.

Jem found a place to leave Thom and their own vehicle, then lifted Anne down from the carriage. He drew her hand through his arm and escorted her up the porch steps to the front door. Lollie Simmons, Civil War widow a decade older than Anne, stood at the doorway, anxious to greet her. "There you are, Anne Pemberton! I'd heard that you wouldn't be coming if Michael Johnston didn't make it back, but I'm so glad you're here. Jem, you old goat, welcome. Anne, I am so aggravated with those boys in the militia! They've just about ruined my seating arrangements, and with so many of the young, handsome, and available gone off, all the girls are just pestering Mr. Drago to death."

Anne kissed Lollie on the cheek. "I'm pretty upset with Michael myself," she assured her. "But the house looks lovely, Lollie. And everything smells divine. I confess, I can't wait for supper."

"Well, you'll have to wait just a few minutes, my dear. You see, Mr. Drago has been dying to meet you."

"Oh?"

"Well, you are such a lovely creature, dear. He's heard about you, of course."

And just what had he heard? Anne wondered. That she was sleeping with a man she refused to marry?

"Ah, there he is now, dear!"

Just as Lollie finished speaking, it seemed as if the crowd parted, breaking away as if by command, just so that she and David Drago could stare at each other.

And she did stare. She felt as if she had become frozen in time and space, suspended there, trapped by his gaze.

He was very tall, perhaps even taller than Michael. He was dark, his hair nearly jet, combed back in a masculine and handsome manner. He was very well-dressed in a dark Eastern suit. His skin was pale, but his face . . .

It was a striking face, one of an indeterminate age. The planes and angles were sharp, nearly gaunt, but very striking nevertheless, classical in their proportions. For all that he was so pale, he appeared to be strongly built, well-muscled and lean. His mouth was broad, full, sensual.

And his eyes . . .

They were gold, and very strange. They were similar to her own amber eyes, but more *gold*. She studied them, fascinated. Perhaps some other color vaguely rimmed them. What color? She couldn't tell. But it was there, framing the gold so strangely. They were incredible eyes. Striking. Commanding. Evocative. She couldn't seem to tear her gaze away from his.

He started walking toward her. In seconds, he was standing before her.

"Mr. Drago," Lollie began. "This is—"

"I know," he said, and his voice was deep and rich, sensual and slightly accented, as peculiarly hot and chilling as his eyes. "This is Anne!" He bowed to her. "I am David Drago." He paused. Somewhere in the room, a fiddle was playing. "Shall we dance?"

"No."

She was certain that she formed the word. She hadn't come to dance. Not with any man. She was in love with . . .

"Come, Anne."

His fingers were on hers. His gold eyes were commanding her.

A searing heat seemed to leap from his fingers to spread throughout her body.

It would not hurt to dance with him.

"I've been waiting for you," he told her.

She fought his hypnotic voice and eyes. "Why?" she demanded.

He arched a deadly dark brow. "They told me you were the most beautiful woman in all of the West. Indeed, in all of the country."

"I do believe they were mistaken."

He shook his head. "I know they were not."

"That is kind, Mr. Drago."

"If I am kind, then perhaps you will dine with me tomorrow night."

"I—I'm afraid I can't."

"Why not?"

"There's another man," she murmured.

"Where is he then?"

"With the militia. He could not be here."

"Then you must let me escort you when he cannot," Drago said politely.

No, never.

"That would be fine," she heard herself say.

He leaned close to her. She thought that she heard him whisper. A very fierce swirl of air, so faint she was not certain she heard it, so intense that the feel of his breath seemed to enter into her very soul.

"There is no other man for you. There can never be. I have waited forever. You are mine. And when you are mine, you will feel my touch and know me—oh, so well, my love!"

She tried to pull away from him; she could not. She must have imagined the words, the passion. But she wasn't imagining the feel of his arms around her, the strength of them. She wanted to break away.

But she couldn't seem to tense her muscles; she couldn't break his hold. His eyes were gleaming down into hers again, and she was meeting them. She wasn't sure that she wanted to break away anymore. There was a staggering warmth in those eyes, a fire, drawing her, compelling her.

He spoke. "Anne . . ." Just her name. So softly.

She gave herself a mental shake. She had to stop this! Then she realized that over Drago's shoulder, she could see her uncle. Jem was watching her.

And there was pure terror in his eyes! Terror that he couldn't seem to hide!

He rushed forward suddenly and tapped Drago on the shoulder. "May an old man cut in on a far younger fellow to dance with his niece?" he inquired.

A look of fury swiftly passed over Drago's features. Anne didn't like it. It was frightening.

But then she thought she must have imagined it because Drago was bowing very politely to her uncle. "By all means, sir! Anne, it is not the end. Only the beginning," he promised.

She scarcely saw him again that night. That was good! He was so strange. So frightening. She didn't want to be near him.

Yet she could think of nothing else but Drago.

And when she returned home that night, she was still thinking about him. Uncle Jem was painfully silent and absorbed, but she barely noticed, her own mind was so fully occupied.

A breeze seemed to be stirring again. But inside the house, and particularly inside her bedroom, it was hot, very hot. She opened her window and lay down in her bed. It was still so uncomfortably hot.

She found herself ripping her nightgown off and lying naked on the bed.

She had never, never done such a thing before . . .

And then she was dreaming. He was there. Telling her to bid him enter. He wanted her. He wanted . . . things . . . from her. He wanted to make love with her.

She was dreaming; surely, she was dreaming. But she wanted him, too. She was twisting on her bed, waiting, wanting him. Twisting, parting her thighs, feeling an ache grow between them.

Drago . . .

He was there, a shadow against the moon.

And all she had to do was bid him enter . . .

2

"**G**OD in heaven!" Billy Trent exclaimed, not able to look at Michael, his eyes still fixed on the scene before them.

Michael Johnston couldn't tear his own eyes away.

And he thought he'd seen everything. Just about everything that one man could do to another. He'd spent five years with the Rebs, butchering the Yanks. He'd seen the Yanks butchering them right back, and he'd seen the landscape in South Carolina—the first state to secede from the Union—once Sherman and his men had marched across it.

Then he'd come west, to this part of Texas. And he'd met the Apaches.

And he'd seen what the Apaches did to the white men, and what the white men did to the Apaches.

This was a Mescalero camp, he tried to tell his numbed mind. They were, to many, the most fiery, proud, and violent of all the Apaches. They were warriors, wild, courageous, and cunning. Few excelled them in the art of warfare.

But this time, none of their skills had saved them.

Not a soul seemed to have survived within the camp. And in all his war years, and in all his years on the Texas plains Michael had never, never seen anything like this.

Far behind him in their militia ranks, someone was sick. He heard the low, soft moan, and then the choking sound . . .

"Colonel, what the hell happened here?" Billy demanded.

"I don't know," he said. There had to be an explanation for this . . . this . . . carnage! Not a single body seemed to have been left in one piece. And the pieces seemed to be scattered so widely that they couldn't be gathered to put one body back together.

And yet, for all the horror that met their eyes, there seemed to be a singular lack of . . . blood.

But that didn't seem to be something that he could just blurt out to Billy. He opened his mouth, trying to say something. Nothing came. "I don't know," he repeated. "I just don't know."

Robert Morison, a freckle-faced redhead who had been with him in the South Carolina artillery and had traveled with him west to Texas when it was all over, rode up beside him.

"Colonel, you don't think that the Yanks from the fort did this, do you?"

Michael shook his head. He knew that everyone in their thirty-man militia unit, most of them Texas boys, was staring at him. "I really don't think that the Yanks are responsible. They were pretty well fired up when they came through South Carolina at the end of the war," he said. "They tore up the countryside pretty bad. It was Sherman's 'scorched earth' policy. So I've seen what Yanks do when they're mad. It doesn't even begin to compare with this!"

"Then what?" Robert asked. "Wild dogs?"

"Maybe," Michael said. No, no maybe. Wild dogs couldn't have been so neat.

There would have been blood.

"I think we ought to get out of here," Billy said suddenly. "What if more Apaches come upon us here and think that we did it?"

Their lives wouldn't be worth a wooden nickel, Michael thought. He lifted a hand and called out to all the men. "We'll have to report this to the Yankee fort. We'll ride north-northwest till we reach them."

But even as he lifted his hand to start the movement, he froze. He had the sense of being watched.

He looked up. They were in an arroyo, cliffs on all sides. And he saw that they were surrounded by Apaches.

There was nothing to do but stand his ground.

Then one of the Apache horsemen stepped forward, and Michael recognized him. It was the war chief, Walks Tall. The man he'd come to meet. He began to pray that the Indian hadn't just arrived, that he had known what was here . . .

"Don't move!" Michael commanded his troops. "For the love of God, hold your ground!"

His men obeyed. The Apaches, excellent horsemen, began to descend the cliffs. Dust and dirt flew in their wake.

Then Walks Tall was riding up before him, his feathered lance lifted in a greeting.

Michael decided not to try his weak Apache with the Indian. Walks Tall had learned English quickly and well because it was the language of the people so determined to encroach upon his land.

"We did not do this," Michael said. "I swear to you, we did not do this."

Walks Tall nodded, and made a gesture to some of his men who dismounted and began to gather the victims' remains. They were a burial detail, Michael thought numbly.

"I've known you since you came to this land, Michael Johnston," Walks Tall told him. "I do not accuse you of this massacre. Women and children, never. Ride back with us. Our camp is not far. We've a fresh buffalo kill. Eat with us before you return home. You must be home before nightfall."

Michael, startled by the Indian's words, glanced at Robert.

Robert shrugged. "You think they really mean to have buffalo for dinner and not us, right?" he inquired beneath his breath.

Michael pondered the question. He had known Walks Tall for a long time, too. They had both tried to negotiate while other white men and Indians had killed one another.

"We're safe," he told Robert.

And they were. Just as the war chief had promised, the white men were welcomed into the camp. Several women saw to their comfort. Walks Tall watched the beginning of the activities, then beckoned Michael to follow him.

There was a certain teepee etiquette, practiced by most of the Plains Indians. Michael knew it well, and entered behind Walks Tall, then sat to the left of his host. He accepted the beautifully carved pipe offered to him. Then he realized that they were not alone in the teepee, that someone was seated in the corner.

An ancient Apache woman, her face lined and leathery, came forward. She nodded to Michael gravely, threw some dust on the fire which caused it to spark, and began to dance around the fire while chanting.

Then she knelt before it and lifted her head, staring at Michael.

"We fight a common enemy, white man."

Perplexed, Michael stared back at the Apache.

"Dancing Woman knows," Walks Tall told him gravely.

Michael shook his head. "Knows what? Does she know who killed those poor people so horribly?"

The Apache woman and the chief exchanged glances. "It is not a *who*," Walks Tall said.

"Animals, then. Coyotes, wildcats—"

"Evil," Dancing Woman told him.

"A white man's evil," Walks Tall added softly.

This was making less and less sense to Michael. If the Indians blamed a white man, they were being extremely kind to him despite it.

"Walks Tall, I swear that no man I know—"

"No man," Walks Tall agreed.

"Evil," Dancing Woman persisted. "An evil whose death lies at the heart."

Walks Tall sighed deeply and tried to explain. "An evil spirit has come. An evil breeze, an evil wind. It is a white man's evil spirit. Dancing Woman felt it when it came. She cried her warning to the Apaches. Here, among my people, we cried to our gods. We made our land holy and brought our children inside at night. But all of our brothers did not heed our warning. You see what has happened to them."

Michael opened his mouth to speak, to protest. But what could he say? Something horrible had happened. Something horrible beyond words.

And even as the chief spoke to him, he remembered the breeze.

He had awakened in the night, afraid. He had known that it was out there.

He didn't believe in ghosts and goblins. But there were times when he wasn't certain that God truly resided in His heaven.

He knew all about hell—he had seen hell, right on earth. He had seen it in the battlefields, in the medical tents.

But now . . .

Now a crazed old Indian woman was talking about spirits, and to his amazement, he believed her.

Because he had felt the breeze . . .

Walks Tall, a man who might have been his enemy, was watching him with pity. He pointed a finger at him. "Dancing Woman says that you must fight the evil."

A cold chill seized him. He didn't want to fight the evil. He didn't want to believe in it.

He lifted his hands. "I don't know what I'm fighting."

The old Indian woman spoke then. "You will see the face of your enemy. He will walk where you walk. He will hunger where you have hungered. He will be more powerful than you could dream."

This was madness.

"If he's so damned powerful," Michael said angrily, "how will I fight him?"

"With the strength of your faith. And your love," the old woman assured him. She was staring at Walks Tall again. The two communicated without words in an eerie silence.

"Dancing Woman says that you must go home. You must ride hard and try to reach your town before nightfall. The fate of your men rests in your hands."

It *was* madness. Truly madness. But Walks Tall was rising and so Michael stood, too.

He was supposed to go. He saw that. So there was no choice.

But just as he was ducking to exit through the flap of the teepee, Walks Tall spoke to him one more time. "Look to your woman, Michael Johnston. Look to your woman."

Fear struck him as it never had before.

Anne!

He had felt the need to protect her that night. Felt it so fiercely. And now he was here . . .

And she was home. Alone.

Look to your woman . . .

It was madness.

He didn't care. He shouted the orders to his men, mounted his horse, and started to ride like the wind, leaving the others to scramble onto their mounts and follow behind him.

He'd never make it. The night wind was coming too quickly.

And it was chill . . .

Ah . . . there she was!

Drago could see her through the window as he hovered in the darkness.

As beautiful as he remembered, as lovely as life and as beguiling as death! She was a picture to set an urgent edge to his hunger—naked, sleek as ivory and writhing against the sheets. Her skin was flawless, her face perfection. Her lips as red as blood, her hair an ebony cloud, her throat . . .

Ah, her throat!

He concentrated, seeking to enter her dreams. If only she knew! He had dreamed of her for so very, very long. Dreamed, waited, and come this perilous way . . .

He had to possess her mind.

He had to force her to bid him enter. Yes, come in, my love! Come in . . .

He was nearly with her. He had sent the wind to seductively stroke her bare skin. Tendrils of swirling air rose and fell, caressing, insinuating, touching her here and then there . . . more and more intimately.

Concentrate, concentrate!

Yes . . . yes . . .

He smiled.

He could nearly feel her. The cool silk of her skin. The velvet brush of that glorious dark hair. Oh, he would take care! He would be so very slow, and very careful, nurturing her all the way. He would not lose her again.

Yes, a stroke here. He closed his eyes, sensing the breeze again. Ah, yes, a long, slow caress with the warmth of the air, along the soft ivory flesh of her inner thigh . . .

Call me, my love, call me . . .

Yes!

She was going to invite him in!

He opened his eyes, gold and all-seeing in the darkness.

And then . . .

3

"ANNE!"

Michael stood at her bedroom door, watching her in amazement. Bathed in an eerie glow of moonlight, she twisted and undulated, her skin sleek and damp.

"Anne!" he cried again, incredulous—and uncaring whether Jem discovered him at that moment or not.

His sense of fear and unease had increased steadily since he had left the Apache camp. He'd never ridden harder in all of his life. His terror had increased when he had galloped into Anne's backyard and seen the horses careening wildly about the corral, snorting, rearing.

The horses were afraid . . .

He had leaped from his own bay, Sandy, and rushed to the back door, the one that was always kept open. He hadn't cared if Jem had heard the door open and close, or if he'd heard the pounding of Michael's footsteps on the wooden floors.

All he'd known was that he had to reach her.

And there she lay . . .

He felt it then. Felt the cool and curious breeze. It made the hair prickle at the nape of his neck, just as if he were a hunting pup. The window! Irrationally, unreasonably, he became certain that the evil was entering through the window. He strode across the room and slammed it shut. Then he hurried back to the bed, falling to his knees beside it, desperate to touch her.

"Anne!" he whispered fervently. She had fallen still now. Her naked flesh was very pale. She opened her eyes slowly, her expression one of confusion and disorientation.

"Michael!" she murmured. Was there disappointment in her voice? he wondered.

Who had she been expecting?

"Yes, it's Michael," he said, somewhat aggravated. He had never expected . . . this kind of greeting.

And now that the breeze was gone . . .

He wondered if he had imagined it. Could it have been real?

"Anne—?" he began, but all at once she seemed to realize how she had been sleeping. She was sitting halfway up, still confused. Her fingers fell on her bare abdomen and she gave a sharp gasp of surprise.

She stared at him hard. "Michael, what—"

He stood, his hands in the air. "I didn't do a damn thing," he said harshly. "This is how you were sleeping."

A blush flooded her cheeks. "The night was very hot."

"The night is quite cool."

"Well, it was very hot in my dreams."

"Just what were you dreaming about?" he demanded.

She wrenched up the covers, staring at him hard. "How dare you just waltz in here like this, accusing

me of things! You take off for days, and I wait for
you—"

"I didn't accuse you of anything!" he flared angrily.
He crossed his arms over his chest, striding away from
her. He jerked the draperies the rest of the way across the
closed window. Damn, she was disturbing him tonight.
He was angry and jealous as he had never been before.
Why? What was the matter with him? He was so afraid,
and his fear was making him touchy. He wanted to walk
right out of the house—and leave her to her dreams.

But he was worried. Worried sick.

He wanted her. There was something so sensual and
evocative about the way she'd been when he had found
her. And still, even though she'd drawn the sheet to her
chin, he knew every exquisite twist and nuance of her
body beneath it. He loved her. He always wanted her.

"I think you'd better go," she said coolly.

Yes, he should go. Just walk out of the damned place
and let her enjoy her dreams!

Suddenly he remembered the Apache camp. The dismembered bodies spread far and wide. The singular lack
of blood.

It was evil. White evil, Dancing Woman had told him.
He couldn't leave Anne. Not in the night. Not when he
felt such strange fear . . .

And the coldness of that breeze.

He sat stubbornly in the rocker across from the bed,
staring at her. "Go to sleep, Anne," he said, suddenly
weary. "I won't come near you. I just want to see that
you sleep safely."

Her eyes widened incredulously. "I just asked you to
leave."

"And I'm not going."

"Well, what if I were to scream loud enough to bring
the entire town crashing in on us?"

He grinned. "They all know that you sleep with me
anyway."

She threw her pillow angrily at him. He caught it. The pillow toss was worth it. Her sheets had fallen. He could see her breasts heaving with the exertion of her breathing. Her skin still held that fascinating sheen. Her breasts were beautiful. Full, firm, with hardened dark-pink crests that now tempted his fingers beyond imagination.

"Michael—"

"I'm not leaving, Anne," he told her. Then he added softly, "I'm afraid."

"Of what?" she demanded, startled.

He shook his head. "I don't know. The night. The breeze. I don't know. But I'm not leaving you. So good night. Scream if you want to, but I'm not leaving this room."

She gritted her teeth, turning her back on him with an angry, huffing sound. Michael's fingers wound around the arms of the chair and he felt his own jaw grow rigid. Then he heard her voice.

"If you're staying, perhaps you'd be more comfortable in bed."

He hesitated, then shed his boots and clothes. He strode to the bed, caught hold of her shoulder, and turned her around. She stared into his eyes. He felt the fierce surge of his desire combine with some strange sense of anger.

"Who were you waiting for, Anne?"

"Oh! Oh, you bastard!" she cried, her amber eyes flashing.

He shook his head sternly, holding her when she would have wrenched away. "I just want to make sure that you're making love with the right man."

She swung back an arm, but he caught it before her palm could connect with his face. Then he kissed that palm quickly. "I'm the one who loves you!" he told her heatedly, and he stretched his muscled length on top of her, his lips finding hers. He kissed her with

searing passion, kissed her long and fiercely. His hand
moved between them, touching her, stroking her. Then
he shifted his weight, penetrating her, determined to
become one with her. The hunger, the passion, riddled
him. He swept his arms around her with a cry and let
the rhythm of desire seize them both.

Later in the night, he thought that she slept. But he
heard her soft, broken whisper in the darkness. "I love
you, Michael. I do love you."

The confusion in the words startled him. There was
something more there. She loved him, but . . .

But what?

He ignored the feeling, wanting only to hold her tight.
He kissed her forehead. "I love you, Anne," he
murmured. "With all my heart. I'll never let you go,
never let anything hurt you," he vowed, his voice still
soft, intense.

She turned in his arms. Her eyes sought his. "Oh,
Michael!" she whispered, and she smiled, laying her head
in the cradle of his shoulder and resting her hand against
his chest. "I just miss you so when you're gone. What
happened?"

He hesitated. Then he decided to give her the bare
facts. "The people of one of the Mescalero camps were cut
down. Everyone was killed—men, women, children."

She gasped, horrified. "My God, how terrible. But
who? Yankees? Other Indians? Oh, Michael! The other
Apaches don't think that you—"

"No, they seem to know that we're not responsible,"
he said. He didn't add, *And they don't think that it was
a who, they think that it was a what.*

Should he tell her everything that the Indians had told
him? Would she think that he had finally and completely
lost his mind?

I'm afraid of an evil breeze, afraid of a spirit, he could
have said. And what then?

"Thank God for that!" Anne murmured. She ran her

fingers along his chest. "Of course, I wouldn't have seen you back here if they had blamed you!"

He had to say something to her.

"Anne, the Mescaleros think that there is some kind of evil spirit at work here."

Her brows shot up. "Evil spirit!" she said.

"I just want you to take care, Anne. Please. Take care of yourself, watch where you go and what you do. Please, be very careful!"

She did look at him then as if he was losing his mind, but it was a very tender look. She kissed him. "I always take care, Michael. Where could I be more safe than here in Green Valley? You're the one I worry about. And," she added, trying to lighten the tone, wagging a finger at him, "you had best take care. There's a new man in town, you know."

He frowned. Yes, he had heard something about it. A rich European. He was building a big house at the edge of town. Funny, though, he couldn't quite remember when the man had arrived. But then, he was gone quite a bit.

His stomach turned. He couldn't leave anymore. Not now. He couldn't leave Anne alone.

"So, is he good-looking?" he asked Anne.

"Very," she told him solemnly.

He slipped his arm behind his neck and leaned his head against it, studying her eyes as she lifted her chin mischievously high. "So, is he the man you were expecting tonight?"

"Michael!" she snapped angrily.

But it seemed . . .

It seemed as if there was an edge of guilt to her voice.

She was suddenly afraid, Anne realized. Because of the strange things she had felt in Drago's arms, the web of seduction that the man seemed to weave?

No, Drago was just a man! She shivered. It was

Michael's talk now, about the Indians and all, that was frightening her.

Drago was just a man. Any other thought would be insane!

She smiled at Michael. "Jealous?" she teased, and the note of fear was gone from her voice.

Michael watched her. Beautiful, sweet Anne. He had best watch out or he'd lose her because of his jealousy. She was smiling, her soft body draped over his, her fingers playing with the dark hair on his chest. "I'm just giving you fair warning. He's offered to act as an escort for me anytime when you're not around."

"Magnanimous of him," Michael murmured. He couldn't wait to meet the bastard.

"It means that you need to stay home more often," she told him primly.

He draped an arm around her, sliding down lower in the bed. For a moment he was still, remembering the Mescalero bodies. Men, women, and children, ripped apart like rag dolls.

"Ummm," he murmured, trying to keep the fear from his voice. "Well, maybe I do intend to stick around for a while," he said. He kissed her forehead. "Think we ought to get some sleep?" He felt that he needed it. He wasn't sure why, except that he was going to need to be awake and refreshed and in full charge of his faculties to . . .

To fight a breeze! he thought.

He closed his eyes. He pulled her more tightly against him. "I do love you, Anne, with all my heart."

She pressed her lips fervently against his chest. "I love you, too."

He was silent then. Sleeping? she wondered.

She eased herself beside him, glad of every place where her flesh could touch his. She felt so secure now. So safe, so cherished, so loved.

And before . . .

She couldn't remember now, but there had been

something or someone out there. Something touching and stroking her. Something incredibly sensuous, beckoning to her.

She'd been dreaming. Awful, decadent dreams that had caused her to . . .

She didn't want to remember. She wanted to lie safe in Michael's arms.

But a feeling of dark unease swept around her heart. If she was safe . . .

Then someone else was in danger. She knew it. She didn't know how, or why, but she did know.

And she was afraid.

Rage filled him. He had been so close, so unbelievably close. She had very nearly whispered the words, thought the thoughts, conceived the ideas that would have given him entry.

It wasn't his only way, of course. But he had to be careful with Anne. He had waited too long for her. He didn't want her perfection marred this time. He didn't want her to die. She mustn't find *that* escape . . .

Furious, he turned from the house.

Michael Johnston. The soldier. The great Indian hunter turned Indian friend.

He was going to die. Slowly. Drago envisioned having him in his power, then slowly draining him of all his strength, so that he could feast even more slowly on his blood . . .

Then tear him to ribbons. Michael had no place in the world of the night. Only Anne! Only Anne would rule with Drago.

A shadow, a wraith, he moved erratically in the darkness.

He heard sounds. Drunkards singing their way from the saloon. He hesitated, melding into the shadows. Then he waited.

Several men, singing, stumbling, paused in front of

the saloon. Two of them managed to throw themselves over their horses. The third tried twice and failed, then swore at the horse.

Drago's lips curled into a scornful smile. It seemed such a pity that he could not be accepted and appreciated for all that he was. He had heard the townspeople do nothing but complain about the Indians since he had come. Especially the Apaches, and most especially the Mescaleros. So he had dealt quite efficiently with a whole campful of the creatures, and instead of being grateful, they were horrified.

And then there was now . . .

And now he wondered what good could one stumbling old broken-down drunk be to the town of Green Valley.

The others had moved off. It wouldn't have mattered. He could have taken them all, just as he had fed his great hunger from the journey with the encampment of savages. But he hadn't come to Green Valley just to feed. He had come for Anne.

Why should they mind the loss of just one drunk . . .

And when he had fed on that drunk, he would be in control again. The night would still be young.

There were other women here. Young ones. Innocent ones. With incredibly sweet, potent blood. Yes, he wanted Anne . . . but he had a tremendous hunger, made stronger by the waiting. Perhaps, once she was his, his need would be truly slaked. But while he waited . . .

It was good to know that there were others.

He smiled again.

So much for the taking!

But first, there was the useless man. Who would notice? And if they did notice, what then?

He almost laughed out loud. And then, as a shadow of darkness and evil, he descended upon the drunk.

Cissy awoke in the night. She'd been having the strangest dreams.

Sweet breezes touched her flesh. The night seemed to be filled with a low, earthly music. The darkness itself seemed to beckon to her.

In her dream she'd been dancing, she thought, with David Drago. He had turned away from Anne and all the other women, and he had been determined to have her. The handsome, sophisticated Mr. Drago, who was so enchanting with his slight foreign accent . . .

Then he wanted more from her. First a kiss . . . then he was touching her. She was powerless to stop it and nothing she had ever been taught had prepared her for such a man. She had never imagined such sensations. . . .

Abruptly, she opened her eyes. She wasn't dreaming anymore. There was a breeze coming in from the open window, and someone was calling to her.

She opened her mouth. She should have screamed. Someone would have come immediately.

But she didn't want to scream. She walked to the window instead. He was there. Smiling at her. Handsome as the devil.

"Cissy . . ."

The sound of her name felt like a caress. Did he really say it? Or did she think it? She didn't know. All she knew was that she wanted him. She could feel the touch of his eyes on her throat, on her breasts. She could feel the heat emanating from him. And oh, that breeze that touched her!

Yes, let me . . . !

Did he whisper it? Yes, he was saying things, thinking things. *You're beautiful, Cissy. Stunning. I want you, I want more, I want . . . please, oh, yes, give to me . . .*

The breeze grew and rippled. She wanted to feel it, had to feel it, all of it. She reached down for the hem of her nightgown and lifted it over her head and tossed it aside. Naked, with a cascade of blonde hair falling all around her, she reached out her arms to the shadowy figure in the darkness.

Yes, take me. Come in . . .

It was all he needed.

He was inside.

In seconds she was in his arms. In seconds, he had touched her.

Kissed her flesh. Swept her into his arms. He was filled now, so he could take his time. Tease and taunt and seduce her. Lull her into complete obedience.

Yes . . .

At last, he reached the sweetest peak of arousal. She inhaled sharply at the pain of his fangs when they first touched her throat.

But that was all. Not a whisper of protest.

He drank. Her blood was achingly sweet, the blood of innocence. Of purity. So damned good.

He would see Cissy again.

And again . . .

He had come for Anne, and he would have her. But now that he had touched Cissy, tasted her sweetness, he might well be magnanimous. He would not maul or destroy her as he had the drunk.

The taste of her was just too good. He would come back and drink again.

And most probably, he would grant her . . . life.

His kind of life.

Just because he had never imagined her blood could be so sweet. He had to taste it again. And again.

Until it was gone.

"Just who is the man and where did he come from?" Michael demanded of Anne.

He'd crawled out the window and come around to the front of the house to knock at the door. He was feeling moody that morning. He hadn't rested during the night at all, and he was irritable.

Anne poured him more coffee. Jem was sitting across the table, looking tired and morose, too. Just what was it with the men in her life lately?

"I'm not sure just when he arrived himself. He has a plump little fellow who works for him and keeps tabs on what the builders are doing up at his house. The servant's name is Servian or something like that. He came in on the stage several weeks ago. I think Drago actually rode in at night."

Michael leaned back in his chair. Anne seemed so amused this morning, so ready to take Drago's side!

"I tell you," he said, eyeing her sternly, "people are amazing. No one even really knows where he came from, and you're all walking around with your tongues hanging out over the man!"

"Why, Michael Johnston!" Anne laughed. "You're jealous!"

"And you're just as pleased as you can be!"

She smiled tenderly at him. "Well, if a bit of jealousy will keep you around . . ."

Jem stood up so abruptly that his chair fell over. Anne looked at her uncle in surprise. He seemed angry. Really angry.

And frightened.

"You're a fool, Anne! You're my niece, and I love you, but you're a fool! Marry this man, and do it quickly, and quit playing your damned fool games!"

Anne stared at him incredulously, her own anger growing, her discomfort great.

"Uncle Jem—"

"Drago is evil!" Jem insisted.

"But you've barely met the man—"

"I'm warning you, young lady! He's evil. You can feel the evil in the air!" He suddenly bent down beside her. "Annie, I know that you've heard the family stories. This man is part of them. This man—"

"Oh, Uncle Jem!" Anne cried in dismay. "You can't be serious! This is America! This is the New World!

It's Texas. We've got Indians, not ancient beasts and superstitions!"

"I'm telling you, Anne—"

Michael stared at them both in disbelief. Jem swung around and stormed out of the house, to the backyard.

Anne looked at Michael. Oh, no. He was going to ask for an explanation and she didn't know where to begin to explain the old stories that had come down through the centuries in her family. They were absurd! She bit her lip lightly, lowering her eyes.

"Anne, what—"

She shook her head, determined to distract him. "I will marry you, Michael," she said softly. "I do love you."

"I love you," he returned, but he was still in an argumentative mood. "When will you marry me?"

She lifted her shoulders in a shrug. "When things are settled. When—"

She wasn't able to finish. There was a pounding on her front door. Foreboding filled her. Michael leaped to his feet and hurried down the hallway, Anne trailing behind him.

Billy was standing at the front door. He looked worn and aged. He stared from Anne to Michael, cleared his throat, and spoke at last. "We need you, Colonel."

"For what?" Anne cried. "You all just rode back—"

"Oh, we're not riding anywhere, ma'am. Sheriff Dougherty just needs to see Michael now." He cleared his throat again.

"Spit it all out, Billy," Michael commanded.

Billy wet his lips nervously. "Old Smokey Timmons is dead."

Michael sighed, feeling sorry for the town drunk. "What did he do, fall off his horse and break his neck?"

Billy shook his head, looking pained.

"Say it!" Anne cried.

Billy exhaled. "No, he didn't fall off his horse. Someone—something!—got ahold of him. Colonel, it's just like it was with the Indians. There's pieces of Billy strewn all over the place!"

"Oh, my God!" Anne breathed.

"I'm coming," Michael said quickly. He turned and gave Anne a shake. "You stay here!" he told her. "Stay here, do you hear me?"

Wide-eyed, she nodded.

Michael started to leave. But some instinct made him pause and turn back to her. He swept her into his arms and kissed her passionately.

Yes, there was evil out there! What was he going to do? How was he going to fight it?

Easy, keep her away from everyone, keep her inside, locked in!

He whispered softly, "Don't let anyone in. Don't invite anyone in, do you understand? Don't go out, don't let anyone in. Not until I'm back!"

She didn't understand. Life had suddenly changed. It had just been breezes and shadows at first. Now it was terrifying.

And Michael was leaving her again.

"Anne!"

"Yes, yes!" she promised. "I understand."

But it was a lie.

She didn't understand anything anymore. Not at all.

4

S MOKEY Timmons was indeed dead.

With Billy behind him, Michael looked on while Mort Jenkins, the town mortician, gingerly collected the pieces of the man, trying to arrange him in the hastily-slapped-together coffin that was to be his final resting place.

They were standing outside Sheriff Dougherty's office, just the sheriff, Michael, Billy, Mort, the sheriff's deputy—and the remnants of poor old Smokey Timmons.

"It's just like the Indians, Colonel," Billy whispered. "Just like!"

Michael felt his throat constrict. Yes, it was just the same. A man, torn to shreds, limb from limb.

And there was that same lack of blood.

Sheriff Dougherty, a good man, a tall man with bushy white hair and a rotund belly, shook his head. "If it don't beat all, if it don't beat all!" he muttered.

This kind of thing just didn't happen in places like Green Valley. Sure, they were tough Westerners. Many of the men had been in the war. And they'd all fought Indians.

But they'd never seen anything like this.

Sheriff Dougherty must have heard Billy's whisper to Michael. He stared at him sharply. "All right there, Colonel Johnston. You think you can shed some light on this subject?"

151

Michael shook his head and the sheriff narrowed his eyes suspiciously.

"Injuns?" he asked.

"I don't think so," Michael replied.

"You just defendin' those heathen Apaches again, Johnston?" the sheriff pressed.

He shook his head again and decided to answer in kind. "Dougherty, the Apaches never mind leaving a calling card. They've never hidden a raid or a battle— or a killing of any kind. What Billy's talking about is something that just happened to the Indians."

"And?" the sheriff said.

"There was a whole tribe of them, a small encampment. Maybe forty or fifty in all."

"Jesus H. Christ, Michael, you gonna make me drag it all out of you?" Dougherty demanded.

Michael faced him. "They were all dead. Just like Smokey here. Every single one of them—"

He paused, amazed at his sudden realization.

"Every single one of them what?" Dougherty exploded.

"Decapitated. The bodies were torn up too, to different degrees. But every single one of them . . ."

"Was missing his head," Billy said. He giggled nervously. "Someone's not happy with scalps, eh? The whole head has gotta go these days!"

"Gentlemen, gentlemen!" Mort complained. He was the perfect undertaker, always dressed in a neat black suit. He was as slim as death itself, with a gaunt face and skeletal cheekbones. He inclined his head toward them, folding his long fingers in a steeplelike fashion. "Gentlemen, I am accustomed to dealing with the dead, but your levity here is—quite frankly!—making me ill."

Michael ignored Mort, frowning, then looked across the dry, parched street that made up Green Valley's main thoroughfare. "The Indians said that it was an evil spirit. A white spirit."

"An evil, white spirit. You want me to find— *and hang!*—an evil spirit for the death of Smokey Timmons?"

Dougherty was going to laugh at him any minute. Michael couldn't quite say that he blamed him.

"Well, I can't help you. I'm damned sorry," Michael told him, "but that's all the Indians would say, and they must have believed it, because they didn't try to blame us."

"Someone killed Smokey," the sheriff said firmly.

"Or some*thing!*" his deputy, Tim McAllistair, said softly. "It looks like something an animal would do."

"Wild dogs," Mort suggested.

"Wolves!" Billy said.

"Right," Tim agreed. Like his daughter, Cissy, Tim was blue-eyed and blonde-haired, a man of forty who looked as young as twenty. There was hope in his eyes. Just like there was a ray of hope in every pair of eyes now meeting Michael's.

"Wolves!" he murmured. "And none of us heard them. And there's not a tuft of fur anywhere—"

"Or a drop of blood, for that matter," Mort commented.

"Well, hell!" Dougherty exploded. "Something went on! A man don't get drunk and tear himself up like this! Now, until we do find out what's going on in this town, you're all deputies!"

"Don't we need some kind of formal ceremony for that?" Billy asked.

"Yeah, real formal! You're a deputy 'cause I said so!" Dougherty said firmly. "All of you, keep a good eye out. Jesu, how the hell did this happen in a fine place like Green Valley? Hell, we ain't even had no horse thieves here in years and years!" He spun on Michael. "Don't you go discounting those Apaches, you Injun lover!" he warned him.

Michael lifted his hands, staring at Dougherty. "I'm

not discounting anything. And may I give you the same advice?"

Dougherty looked affronted, but then he sighed. "Dammit, Michael, I'm just scared. Scared down to my bones."

Mort cleared his throat. "May I—er, take the deceased? Doc Phelan can examine the—er, remains. Maybe he'll be able to give us some clue."

"Yeah, maybe," Dougherty agreed.

Tim, Billy, and Michael helped Mort hoist the coffin up onto Mort's horse-drawn hearse-wagon. Everyone was silent as Mort clambered up to the seat and flicked the reins over his pitch-black horse's haunches. The wagon rattled down the dusty street.

Dougherty pointed a finger at Michael. "If you can spare me an hour or so, I'd like a firsthand report on your latest excursion into Injun territory. I want to hear all about what you found, and what the Injuns had to say. You come too, Tim. I'll buy you both some lunch."

During the meal Michael stared at the bowl of fine stew set before him, but all he could see was Smokey. He had eaten wormy hardtack upon occasion, between battles, with dead men lined up in hearses behind him. But this was different. He pushed the food away and talked as fast as he could, anxious to get back to Anne. He gave Dougherty a thorough report, but he felt sorry for the sheriff because, like them all, the man was left so damned confused.

Tim sat and listened, but with only half his attention. He seemed withdrawn, an unusual way for Tim to be, Michael thought. But then, they had spent most of the morning with Smokey, noon till now with the sheriff, and it seemed that even the afternoon was waning away and they hadn't accomplished much of anything.

"Is that it for now, Sheriff?" Tim finally asked his

boss. He hadn't eaten much of his stew either.

Dougherty immediately looked contrite. "Yeah, sure, Tim. You go on home now. You tell Cissy we're all thinking about her."

Tim nodded, rose, offered Michael a faint smile, and hurried out of the inn's dining room. Michael could see him walking out on the porch and then down the steps to the street. There was a slump to his shoulders.

"What's the matter with Cissy?" Michael asked.

Dougherty shrugged. "She just took sick," he said. "Tim's awful worried. Says she was as pale as death this morning and has hardly opened her eyes all day. There's no fever or the like. It's just as if the life had been drained right out of her."

"I think I'll take a walk over myself," Michael said. "Cissy is a special friend of Anne's. That is—if you're done with me too now."

Dougherty waved a hand in the air. "Sure, I'm done with you, Michael. Evil spirits!" he said. He shook his head. "Jesu, Michael, what's going on here?" Not expecting an answer, he went on his way as Michael went his.

Michael hurried after Tim McAllistair. When he reached the McAllistair house, he found Anne there.

He'd told her not to go anywhere . . .

But what could he say? Cissy was a friend. A good friend. And Anne was obviously fine.

She was sitting by Cissy's bed, spelling Jeannie McAllistair, who looked something like a ghost herself. The strain of her daughter's illness was already showing on Jeannie's face. She had a multitude of children, but she and Tim adored each and every one of their offspring. A cold chill seemed to touch Michael's heart from the moment he walked into the house. He didn't feel any better when Anne's grave gaze touched his. He sat beside her on the bed, trying to think of something to say to make Cissy smile.

But Cissy wasn't going to smile. She was lying there as still as death, as white as a sheet, so very young, so innocent, so lovely. He sat beside Anne, taking her hand, and in silence, they both stood vigil over the girl. In another room, Jeannie was quietly sobbing. Her sons and her husband were trying to comfort her.

"What happened to her?" Michael asked at last.

"No one knows," Anne murmured. "Jeannie says that she was fine last night—but that she didn't get up this morning. She's been more or less like this all day."

"Has Doc Phelan seen her?"

"Yes."

"What did he say?"

Anne's beautiful amber eyes touched his. "He said that we should pray."

Michael nodded. He sat with Anne, taking her hand, and they both watched Cissy.

Time passed. Anne stretched, and Michael looked at her. She probably hadn't had a thing to eat or drink since he had left her that morning. He whispered to her, "I'll stay with her. You go eat something."

Anne seemed startled. "Well, a glass of water," she murmured. She still looked uneasy about leaving Cissy.

"Go!" he commanded her.

She did. Cissy remained still. He looked out the window. What a strange day! The sky was mottled with clouds. Time seemed to slip by so quickly. There were streaks of crimson on the horizon. Far off, in the distance, he could almost see the darkness of night coming. How strange. But then, maybe he had never looked for the night before.

Anne returned. Smiling, she sat beside him again, squeezing his hand. "Any change?" she whispered.

He shook his head. Then he rose and leaned closer to Cissy. "Come back, little one!" he murmured. "Come back." He thought he saw her stir at the sound of his voice. Startled, he sat back down again.

"Michael, look! Her eyes are flickering!" Anne cried.

And suddenly Cissy's eyes were open. Startlingly blue against the pallor of her face, they focused fully on Michael. She smiled slowly. "Michael," she said very softly. Then she gazed at Anne, her smile deepening. "See, he's home!"

Anne leaned over her. "Yes, he's home. And we're both worried sick about you. Your mother is in tears."

Cissy frowned. "Why?"

"You've been sick all day."

"Not sick. Just dreaming."

"I'll get Jeannie," Michael said quickly. He stood and went down the short hallway to the McAllistairs' bedroom. The door was open. He walked in. He gave Jeannie a hug. "She's talking!"

"Oh! Oh!" Jeannie cried. She leaped up and kissed Michael on the cheek. "Oh, thank you, Michael!"

"I didn't do anything," he protested, but Jeannie was gone, and Tim and his young sons, Anthony and Andrew, were grinning at him.

Michael grinned wryly in return.

"How about a drink?" Tim asked him. "I could use a shot of whiskey myself."

"Pa, it's a little early," Anthony, the younger of the boys, reminded him.

"Nonsense, take a look outside. The afternoon is waning. Hell, it's going to be sunset very soon," Tim said. He stood, clapped Michael on the shoulder, and led him into the small parlor. "Damn strangest thing I've ever seen!" he murmured as he poured the whiskeys. They could hear Cissy chatting away with her mother and Anne in the bedroom. "Last night, she was as right as rain. This morning, when Jeannie started screaming, I rushed in and Cissy was as pale and cold as death, barely breathing. We've been praying all day. And now . . ." He lifted a glass to Michael. "You walk in and talk to her and she's just fine!"

"I didn't do anything," Michael protested.

Even as he spoke, they heard a rapping at the front door. Tim excused himself and went from the parlor to the small entryway to open the door.

Michael heard a low murmur of voices. The newcomer was a man with a low, deep, well-modulated voice. An intriguing one, with just the touch of an accent. Definitely European, but with an edge . . .

There was something strange about listening to the murmur of that voice.

The hackles began to rise on Michael's neck, just as if he were an old hunting hound. Something was . . .

No.

Yes.

Evil.

A touch of it, just a trace of it, something that made Michael increasingly uneasy.

He swallowed down the whiskey. After all this time, he was finally losing his mind. An Indian had talked to him about an evil white spirit, and he was hearing and seeing and feeling this *evil* everywhere!

Tim entered the parlor with the newcomer. Michael assessed him quickly, not needing to be told who he was. David Drago.

The man was dark, with ebony hair. More jet than the color of any crow or blackbird Michael had ever seen. His brows were the same shade. But then the concept of *dark* faded, for his skin was a strange shade. It was rather ashen, with a tinge of blue.

No human had blue skin, Michael quickly assured himself.

But Drago did.

His mouth was full and red. His features were handsome, so fine that they were almost too perfect. And his eyes . . .

They were gold. Gold, yes, really gold. Different from hazel, different from brown, different from Anne's beautiful soft amber. They were really, truly gold. With just a hint, just an edge of . . .

Of something else.

He was dressed elegantly in black: handsome black frock coat, trousers, boots, and vest. His white shirt was ruffled. His fingers were long, his nails well-manicured. And also *very* long.

"Ah, I need no introduction to this man," Drago was exclaiming, offering a hand to Michael. Unwillingly, Michael took that hand. "The very, very famous Indian-hunting war hero, Colonel Michael Johnston!"

He had never felt such a jolt of unease. The touch of Drago's fingers was like ice. Michael wanted to wrench his hand away instantly.

Michael was a strong man, but Drago was stronger. His handshake was like a clasp of steel. Michael had the panicked feeling of a man finding himself cast into a pit of rattlers—with no way out.

He gave himself a mental shake, fighting the strange power that seemed to steal away his ability to speak.

"Ah, Mr. Drago, I presume. I'm afraid that I hate killing Indians; I much prefer befriending them, and as for my being a war hero—well, sir, my side lost, and so we are not referred to as heroes but as the vanquished!"

Drago released his hand, his gold eyes gleaming with challenge.

"It is indeed a pleasure to meet you, Colonel Johnston," he said. "I came, of course, because I heard dear Cissy was ailing, but her father tells me she is doing much better."

"And I'm certain that Cissy will want to see you," Tim McAllistair said.

"Well, if I am welcome . . ." Drago said.

"Anytime, sir," Tim said. "You are welcome here anytime."

Drago smiled. Slowly. It gave Michael the shivers.

"Thank you, Mr. McAllistair. I will take the warmth of that welcome to heart, sir! If I may . . ."

Drago bowed to the two of them and started down the hallway to Cissy's room.

A moment later, Anne, smiling with relief over Cissy's improved condition, walked out of the room. Tim excused himself to return to his daughter, leaving Anne and Michael alone. "I see you've met my new beau," Anne teased him, her amber eyes curiously aglow. A ribbon of anger snaked through him. Anne just wasn't the type of woman to pit one man against another.

"I don't like him, Anne," Michael told her honestly. Drago did have some kind of a draw, he told himself, and Anne had obviously felt it.

"Really, Michael," she said coolly. "He's an incredible gentleman. Polite, considerate, concerned—"

"And I'm none of those?" he asked her. He wanted to shake her. She seemed so very tall, elegant, and beautiful with her dark hair and amber eyes—and the rather superior way she was looking at him right now. Since Drago had walked in!

Then her lashes fluttered momentarily, and the Anne he knew was smiling at him. Warm. Sweet. "Mr. Johnston, you are all those things, and much, much more. When— and I do mean *when!*—you're here!"

He sighed. "Anne . . . !"

"Hush!" she murmured. "They're coming from the bedroom. Now, be nice to him, Michael. He's a newcomer in town. You must make him feel welcome. Please."

He wished he could. And yet, as soon as Drago had walked into the room, Michael had felt the presence of evil.

It was his imagination. It was all the awful things that had happened in the past few days.

But the awful things began to happen from the time Drago had come to town.

And, of course, he was jealous as all hell and he really needed to watch himself. Still . . .

He lowered his voice to a whisper. "He's a newcomer in town. I'm not making any accusations. It's just that he did arrive right when things started happening."

"Things?"

"Like Smokey!" he whispered.

"Michael!" Anne gasped, her eyes wide. "What a horrible thing to imply! Why, you've no right, no proof!"

A moment's shame filled him. Was he just jealous? No. Drago was . . . *evil*.

No matter what, that word returned to haunt him.

Tim, Jeannie, and David Drago were back in the living room. Even Jeannie was accepting a whiskey, suggesting that Anne join her. Anne wasn't fond of whiskey, but she cared deeply about Jeannie, just as she cared about Cissy, and the woman seemed to need the drink, so Anne joined her.

Michael noticed that Drago only pretended to sip his own whiskey.

He didn't drink it.

Jeannie politely asked Drago about the progress on his house.

"Oh, it's coming along very well," he said.

"You must be quite busy," Jeannie said. "We never see you during the day."

"Ah, yes, well, I *am* busy."

"And a man all alone! You'll have to come for dinner," Jeannie chided him.

Drago bowed. "A pleasure."

Besides the fact that the man wasn't drinking his whiskey, Michael noticed that he was watching Anne— like a spider about to pounce.

He disliked the fellow more and more.

And Anne! Anne, damn her! She was smiling just as sweetly as could be. "I guess we should all help in that area," she murmured politely. "You'll have to come to dinner at my place too—" she began.

Something in Drago changed. His eyes glittered like gems. He seemed about to burst with pleasure. With . . . triumph.

But then, Anne added, "—sometime. In the future. We'll have to set up a real invitation at a later date."

The glitter left his eyes.

The man was angry, furious, Michael realized.

Drago set down his untouched drink. "Mr. and Mrs. McAllistair, thank you so much for your hospitality. Anne, Colonel Johnston, good night." He bowed deeply, and started to leave.

To his own amazement, Michael suddenly excused himself. Anne stared at him reproachfully. He ignored her, and chased after Drago.

He was down the front porch steps when Michael closed the door behind him. "Drago!" he called.

Drago turned.

In the light of the risen moon, his skin seemed to carry a true tint of blue. And his eyes were surrounded by that other color. He looked as angry as a starved lion.

"Yes, Colonel Johnston. What is it?"

Michael figured he might as well be blunt. He didn't like Drago. Didn't trust him. And he never would.

"You're showing an interest in Mrs. Anne Pemberton. I just wanted to let you know that it's a mistake. She's going to marry me."

Drago was smiling again. He took a step toward Michael.

"Oh, no, little man!" Drago whispered huskily. "I don't think so." Then he went on to amaze Michael with bluntness of his own. "Anne Pemberton is mine!"

Michael curled his fingers around the porch railing, fighting to control his anger. He reminded himself that he slept with Anne, that he loved her. That she loved him.

"Drago, you're mistaken."

Drago shook his head. "No, I'm not. You see, Colonel, I'll best you. Come what may, I will best you, sir. I have the power. It will happen."

A dizziness swept over Michael. Jesu! That was what Dancing Woman had said, that the evil would be more powerful . . .

His fingers bit even more tightly around the rail. What the hell was the matter with him? He was staring at a stranger and believing in his threats!

He needed faith. That's what Dancing Woman had told him.

"No," Michael said firmly. "I will not let you best me."

Drago started to laugh. "I *will* best you! But I will enjoy the fight, I assure you! You have afforded me tremendous entertainment already, Colonel! I bid you good night."

He started away again, into the dark street. Michael ran after him, suddenly determined to have it out then and there.

But it wasn't to be. Suddenly he couldn't see Drago. There was nothing but a dark shadow in the street.

And the shadow seemed to fly. To touch the moon.

Swearing softly, Michael walked back into the Mc-Allistair house. He and Anne stayed a little while longer, then they walked back to her house.

He was silent, and she took his hand. He glanced her way to find her smiling at him. "I'm sorry, Michael, I really am. It's just that sometimes you seem so sure of yourself with me. I couldn't help teasing you, just a little. Please don't be angry."

He shook his head, looking at her, marveling at how much he loved her. She was beautiful to look at, but beyond that, there was something even more beautiful in the warmth of her smile. Anne cared for everyone. She even understood when he tried to explain how they had to find peace with the Indians. He had seen her hold and cradle little Apache babes and never once condemn them for their race.

She was his life. She was everything good in it. And at that moment he realized just how deeply Anne was endangered.

"Anne," he said hastily, "I'm not angry. But I don't know how to make you believe me! I don't like Drago. I'm afraid of him. I'm afraid of what he might do to you."

Her eyes widened in surprise. "Michael! You're not afraid of anything."

"I'm afraid of Drago."

"The man is just different, Michael. He's a newcomer. You're not being fair, and it isn't like you!"

He paused suddenly, chilled. Then he took her arm, hurrying her along. "Let's get inside before we talk more, all right?"

She sighed with exaggerated patience. "All right, Michael, but—"

She never finished. Michael was pulling her along until she had to run to keep up. There was a shadow behind them, he was certain of it. A shadow that was following them, ready to swoop down upon them. It was coming closer and closer . . .

"Michael!" Anne cried out.

He ignored her. They were almost at the house. All that they had to do was reach the porch and get through the door.

The darkness! He could feel it descending . . .

The door to Anne's house suddenly opened. Jem was standing there, beckoning to them urgently. "Come on, come on!"

Michael jerked Anne up the stairs and into the house. He slammed the door behind him.

The shadow, he was certain, lifted.

"What in the hell is the matter with the two of you?" Anne exclaimed furiously.

"Bats!" Jem said.

"What?" Anne demanded incredulously.

"Oh, yes!" Jem said. "I thought I saw some giant fruit bats, hovering right over you."

Anne turned to stare at Michael. "Bats?"

He nodded. "Well, there was *something* out there."

She leveled a finger at them. "You have both lost your minds!"

Jem shrugged. Anne shook her head. "Listen, you two, you just go on ahead and discuss your bats. I'm going to bed."

That was it. Nothing more. She turned and headed for her room.

Michael had a feeling it meant that he wasn't invited. Not tonight.

He didn't give a damn. He'd stay anyway.

Jem was looking at him. "Michael, I've got to talk to you."

He nodded. Jem seemed to . . . to know something. After all, he'd been at the door waiting for them as if he'd known there would be . . . a shadow after them.

He was losing his mind, Michael decided.

"Sure," he told Jem.

Jem walked him back to his own room at the far end of the hallway. He gestured for Michael to sit at the foot of the bed, then dug in one of his desk drawers for an album. There were tintypes and photographs and drawings in it. And letters.

He sat beside Michael, flipping pages. He picked out a letter and handed it to Michael.

"What—" Michael began, staring blankly at the page. It had been written in a foreign language.

"Over, over! It was translated by my English I-don't-know-how-many-greats-grandmother."

Michael flipped the letter over. The words were in English.

"Read," Jem said.

It was an interesting letter, tearstained and very old. It

had originally been written in the late sixteen-hundreds, he realized. Someone had written about a young girl named Helga. She had been beautiful, sweet, innocent. She had died, Michael realized quickly. By her own hand. She had jumped from a castle tower.

Although tears blurred some of the fine print, he was able to read it.

> *He says that he will not give up, that he will search for all eternity, that he will find her again. Oh, how do I explain to the others how strong she was? They refuse her a hallowed grave, for she was a suicide. They do not know her strength in fighting eternal damnation. And now, though my precious daughter is at rest, I am afraid, for he has the power to fight time. Perhaps he can even fight death.*

Michael looked at Jem. "I don't understand."

"You don't want to understand."

"Dammit, I do!" Michael exclaimed. He stood, then began pacing the room. "Jesu, Jem, you weren't there when they found the Indians. You didn't see old Smokey's body. You—"

"You know that there is a connection with Anne, don't you?" Jem demanded.

Michael sighed in exasperation. He didn't know anything except that he'd been plagued with the strangest damned feelings!

"Jem, what the hell are you talking about?"

"Drago is a vampire," Jem said with certainty.

"A what?" Michael almost shouted.

"Shush, shush!" Jem said. He rose and closed the door to his room. "Listen to me, Michael Johnston. If you love my niece, listen to me! These are family papers. I've carried them with me for most of my life. I spent years thinking that it was just a legend, that the letters didn't mean anything. Then the other night, right out of the blue, I felt that breeze, that strange breeze, and I knew. I knew that there really is some kind of strange evil in the world. I knew that Drago is a vampire."

"A vampire," Michael said blankly.

Old Jem shook his head. "I guess you don't know anything about the creatures out here. But they know them real well in the old country of eastern Europe. Some say that the first *nosferatu*, or vampire, was an evil prince named Vlad Dracul, or Vlad the Impaler. He lived years and years ago and—"

"Jem, you're making no damned sense!" Michael cried.

Jem shook his head vehemently. "Michael, you've got to listen to me, you've got to understand. This is the New World, the Wild West. No one else is going to help or understand us, or even believe us! Hell, the damned Indians seem to be the only ones with any sense."

"Jem—"

"I'm getting to it, I'm getting to it. First, let me explain the creature. Vampire. Undead."

"Undead!"

"Listen, Michael—undead, evil spirit, what difference does it make? No one really knows when the first one existed, but a vampire is a creature of evil, of hell, of the night. He must rest by day because sunlight can send him to hell for eternity. He must drink blood to survive. He finds the blood of the young and the innocent the sweetest, but any blood will do for a good meal. This creature had a banquet with the Indians. Then Smokey. Then—"

"My God, my God!" Michael breathed, slumping down, running his fingers through his hair. "I've felt like a lunatic, Jem! But you sound like you want to turn me into a madman!"

"Well, I don't—and you've got to listen and use your senses instead of your mind!" Jem warned him, speaking quickly. "I'll try real hard to make it all clear. My father was Irish, but my mother and her family came from a small place in Romania. Near Transylvania. Right from the area where this Vlad Dracul lived, where he impaled his enemies, where the original legends were all born."

Michael shook his head. "Jem—"

"All right, so you don't understand. You didn't grow up with the legends. But the Transylvanian people knew—"

Michael sank down to the foot of Jem's bed, a headache pounding in his skull. "You're trying to tell me that David Drago is—*a vampire?*"

"The Indians were decapitated, right?" Jem said.

Michael paused. "Yes."

"That keeps them from joining the ranks of the undead. He wanted to feast, not to create other vampires. The same with Smokey. I'm willing to bet he was headless."

Michael threw up his arms. He couldn't tell Jem that he'd been so damned scared himself. Couldn't tell him that all he'd been able to think when he was anywhere near the man was . . . evil.

"I can help you, Michael. Just listen to me. You're not going to believe me, but listen to me. He's come for Anne. I think he started on Cissy because Anne is still strong. Dammit, don't you see, boy? Anne is Helga reborn! Maybe God is giving her a second chance for her faith, for seeking death rather than damnation! But Drago wants her now just as he did then."

"Jem, this is madness! Why would this fellow have come for Anne? You have to be crazy!" Michael insisted.

Jem solemnly shook his head. He reached into his bedside drawer again and produced a locket. Like the letter, it was very old. It was beautiful, crafted in very fine gold.

Jem tripped the lock to let it open. There was a picture inside. A tiny, tiny oil painting of a woman.

It could have been Anne. Anne in the full, stylish

clothing worn by the wealthier classes of the sixteen-hundreds.

"I don't believe this!" Michael whispered.

"Fine. I'm mad as a hatter. Don't believe it. But don't leave her at night, Michael. And don't let her invite him in. Ever. He hasn't been able to touch her yet only because she hasn't invited him in."

Damn, he felt so uneasy! He'd known this morning when he had left her—some instinct had warned him—that she shouldn't let anyone in.

Were they all losing their minds?

Or did old Jem really know the truth, as impossible as it seemed?

There was no mistake, no doubt about it. The portrait in the locket was an exact replica of Anne. His Anne.

"Helga?" he whispered.

Jem nodded.

"Vampire," Michael said, repeating the strange word.

"I know you think I'm crazy. Hell, you must think *you're* crazy! But you've got to think with your heart and your senses now, boy, not with your mind and logic. And most important, you've got to know that he's strong. Very strong. Very powerful. But he can be killed. As strong as he is, he can be killed. Not with bullets, not with a sword. With a stake."

"A stake?"

"A wooden stake. Right through his black heart. Or with sunlight. And, most importantly, with faith."

Dammit! Dammit! That's just what the Indians had said!

Evil spirit . . .

Vampire.

He couldn't believe it.

But how the hell could he deny it?

He rose on shaky feet. "I'm going—"

"Don't leave. Promise me you won't leave."

Michael smiled. "I'm going to be with Anne," he said

softly. "I won't leave her." Then he hesitated. "Jem, doesn't Anne know anything about this family legend?"

Jem sighed deeply. "Stories, yes, she's heard the stories. But none of us ever paid them much mind. Sure, Anne knows that she looks like Helga. She thinks it's an amusing family resemblance. She thinks vampires are really just very seductive men whom innocents fall for a bit too easily. That's the stuff of legend to Anne." He shook his head. "That's why we almost argued this morning. She thinks we're cruel and snobbish, that we're assuming that because he's a foreigner he might be evil."

Jem had a point there. Anne always stood up for the underdog. If she thought that they were being unfair to poor foreign Drago in any way, she'd defend him all the more.

Jem said, "My sister, Anne's mother, never believed in the legend. Neither did Anne's father. Of course, they both died right before the war, so all that's left of the family, that I know of anyway, is me and Anne. She's all I've got, Michael. And as crazy as I've always thought all of this to be, I'm the keeper of the truth at the moment. You've got to help me. Don't leave her. And *believe* me. I think I know enough to help you beat Drago, but I can't take him on alone."

"I won't leave Anne," Michael assured him. He nodded stiffly and he walked down the hall to Anne's room. He paused, then quietly twisted the knob and entered.

He half-expected to feel a terrible chill in the room, to discover that evil had already entered.

But the window was closed. The room was in darkness.

"Michael!" Anne whispered.

He strode across the room to her. She was lying on her bed, clad in white, her raven hair streaming all around her. Her beautiful, warm smile beckoned him. "I love you!" she said.

He took her into his arms. Passionately, tenderly, he made love to her.

No shadows touched them that night. He woke feeling as if the sunlight would allow him to get a grip on the world again.

But he had barely taken his first sip of coffee when word came to him with a message that plunged his heart and soul back into terror.

That morning Billy knocked at Anne's door once more.

Cissy McAllistair had died during the night. Would they both please come?

5

IT was incredibly painful to see Cissy in her coffin, Anne thought. The young were not supposed to perish, and certainly not someone as young and vivacious as Cissy.

She looked beautiful. Perhaps that added to the sadness. She looked as if she was sleeping, as if she might take a breath at any second. As if her beautiful, blue eyes would fly open, and her lips would curl into a smile.

Michael stood beside Anne in the McAllistair house. Instinctively, she groped for his hand. She looked to the window, blinking. Just last night, Cissy had opened her eyes, she had smiled, she had laughed. But this morning . . .

Anne was startled when Michael leaned past her,

smoothing back Cissy's long blonde hair. He was looking for something in particular, she realized.

Nervously, she glanced around them. The McAllistairs weren't in the room at the moment. Doc Phelan had sedated Jeannie, who was lying down. Her husband and her sons were with her.

But they weren't alone in the room. Doc Phelan, gray and grizzled, a veteran of the war like so many of the men, was watching Michael with sharp eyes. Billy was there, too, staring at every move Michael made. Even Mort was there.

Then Anne saw what Michael had been looking for. There were little marks on Cissy's neck. Several of them. Mort had covered them with powder, but they were still visible.

Anne closed her eyes. Dear God, no. They were all going to start believing in the impossible. She'd known that Jem had cornered Michael last night and tried to tell him about the family legends. Now Michael was going to be convinced that there was a vampire in town and that Drago was it. If they weren't careful, they'd cause an awful panic. It might lead to a lynch mob—just because Drago was a foreigner.

Now those damned marks.

Maybe there was nothing to worry about. Surely very few Westerners had ever heard about vampires or the undead, or *nosferatus*, as the old family members had called them. It was all so ridiculous. But with Drago in town and all the awful things happening, maybe people would begin to believe that it could be possible. She was going to have to talk to Jem. It was all so ridiculous.

Then again, there was Drago.

He was an exceptionally charming man. He had the power of seduction. Unbelievably he had even managed to draw her in with his charm. Not when she was away from him, of course. Only when she was near him.

He was just attractive. Handsome. Confident.

Not evil.

Yet she shivered. He did have some . . . power.

Damn those strange marks on Cissy's neck!

Michael stared at Mort, then at Doc Phelan. Mort shrugged. "I thought maybe spiders," he said.

"Would you care to speak with me outside, Michael?" Doc Phelan said. Michael nodded. He glanced at Anne, and she was startled by the intensity of the concern in his eyes. Then he released her hand. "Yes," he told Phelan. "Anne, I'll be right back. Don't leave here without me. Do you understand? Don't leave without me."

She might have gotten angry at the way he was addressing her, but she held her tongue. He was simply worried. She wasn't going to say anything.

Phelan, ancient as the hills but surprisingly spry, clapped Michael on the shoulder and the two men stepped outside. Anne stared at the marks again, then felt a shudder of sorrow sweep through her. Poor Cissy. Poor, sweet, beautiful young girl!

She suddenly became aware of a very strange sensation. A host of tiny shivers was snaking slowly up her spine, and from them both cold and heat seemed to emanate in waves. Before she turned, she knew who she would see.

"She looks stunning, does she not? So sweetly at peace! So very, very lovely."

Drago stared down at Cissy with a tenderness that touched Anne's heart. He was such a strange man. So very good-looking. So very . . . sexy.

She bit into her lower lip with annoyance. The way she reacted to him was absurd. She was in love with Michael. Drago had a certain attraction, but she loved Michael. No man on earth could be more sensual, tender, demanding, sexy . . . all those things. She knew it. And though she found Drago attractive, she didn't find him nearly as attractive as Michael.

He couldn't be an evil spirit, a vampire. Such things did not exist. Certainly not in this world! Only in some ancient little town in eastern Europe.

Still . . . there was that pull.

"How are her parents?" he asked softly.

"Desolate," Anne answered.

"Ah, well, it is to be expected. I came to pay my respects, but perhaps I should not disturb them now."

Anne didn't reply. Just as Michael had done, Drago shifted Cissy's hair. The marks were again visible. He seemed to study them with a curious pleasure. Anne backed away, discovering that she was really nervous around the man.

He stared at her with some surprise, then smiled.

"She is lovely, even in death. But no woman, alive or dead, is more beautiful than you, Anne."

What a strange thing to say!

"Cissy was a very lovely person," she said, her voice cracking.

"You are trying to pretend that you cannot hear all that I have to say to you. You are beautiful. I confess, I am in love with you."

"I'm in love with Michael!" she whispered fervently.

"But you must remember . . ." he said very softly, his voice trailing away sensually, then gaining momentum again. "You must remember my touch. I can still feel the silk of your flesh, the tips of my fingers running along the length of that beauty."

She was suddenly afraid. She couldn't take her eyes from his. Michael was right. She should be frightened.

"You've never touched me!" she challenged.

"I adore you. You will realize it. I will have you and teach you true ecstasy."

"No!"

"Perhaps you have been holding your death vigil too long. I think you should come for a walk with me."

"Oh, no—" she began to murmur. Then she stopped. His eyes were on hers. There was something so alluring in them. Something that brought back very strange memories.

As if she had known him before!

But she hadn't, and Michael was just outside, on the back porch. Even if Drago's gaze seemed to compel her to take his hand, she would not do so.

"Anne . . ."

His voice was soft, sensual. It slipped under her skin. It made her feel as if she wanted to be touched by him, stroked by him. As if she *had* to go with him . . .

"Drago! Get away from here! You're not welcome here!"

Michael's voice was harsh, his eyes flashing with fury.

Anne stepped back, confused. Suddenly Drago was just a tall, handsome foreigner. And Michael was behaving extremely rudely.

But Drago had said things to her, hadn't he? Things that he shouldn't have said?

She couldn't remember. No, it was Jem—Jem and Michael. They were trying to convince her, convince everyone, that Drago was evil. It was wrong. It was just because he was a foreigner. How could they be so prejudiced?

"Michael!" she whispered furiously.

He ignored her. His eyes flashing, his rugged face set, he brought her behind him, still facing Drago.

And David Drago was smiling. Amused with all of it.

"Get out!" Michael insisted.

"Michael, you can't tell the poor man to get out!" she cried, baffled. "This isn't even your house!"

Drago bowed deeply. "I would much rather leave than create a commotion when the McAllistairs are in such deep mourning. Dear Anne, you'll excuse me. Colonel Johnston, I will meet with you one night soon!"

Drago tipped his hat to them and departed.

Michael turned to face Anne. She set her hands on her hips, staring at him furiously. "That was the rudest display I've ever seen!"

"Rude!" He drew her to him, whispering, "The man killed Cissy, and you think that I was rude!"

"Drago killed her?" Anne exclaimed. "Oh, Michael, you are losing your mind. Cissy got sick! She rallied, but she died. How can you blame that on the man? Just because he's a foreigner. Or maybe it's worse. Maybe you discovered that the poor man has been a Yankee, or a Yank sympathizer—"

"Anne—" he began, then broke off. Too many people in the room were beginning to stare at them. He caught her hand and looked around the room, setting his eyes on Billy. "Please tell Mr. McAllistair that we'll be back tomorrow to help with the funeral arrangements."

He turned around, as if to leave. Then he paused. The others were talking softly amongst themselves again. He released Anne's hand, and walked over to help Mort, who had signaled that the time had come to close the coffin for the night.

But Michael didn't seem to be satisfied with the closed lid. He tied something around the center coffin handle to hold it shut. Anne couldn't see what it was.

He had her out the door and on the porch before she came to a dead stop, determined to ask him. "All right, what was that all about?"

He hesitated, staring at her. "Drago is a vampire."

"I've had it!" Anne said, waving her hand in the air. Oh, she knew it! He'd been fighting too long. He was seeing demons in the man just because he was different.

A vampire! Michael probably hadn't even known about vampires. Jem must have convinced him. Oh, they'd be seeing ghosts and all sorts of things soon!

"Michael, I love you, but this is ridiculous. What—"

"Three times, Anne," he said, swallowing quickly. "He bit her three times. That's what the marks were.

Three is the number. She'll come back to join him now."

"Where did you hear that?" she demanded.

"From Jem. And it's your family legend—you should know, you should see the truth!" he told her.

"You've lost your mind! Jem has heard this legend all his life, and he never believed in this ridiculousness before!"

"Drago was never around before."

"Oh, come on, Michael!" Anne exclaimed.

"You come on, Anne! Look at what's happened."

"Michael," Anne told him coldly, walking around him, "you were unbelievably rude, and now you've lost your mind." She started down the steps, and toward home.

He followed on her footsteps. If she weren't so very worried about his mental state, it would be touching. He'd been in half the major battles of the war. He'd ridden out into Indian country for years now. It was only natural that he would crack eventually. He needed peace!

"Anne, he wants you!"

"Michael, I've told you, I intend to marry you. There is no need for this—"

"Anne!" He caught hold of her, swinging her around to face him. "Anne, I'm worried sick! You must know that you look exactly like Helga—"

"She's an ancestor! I *should* look like her! There's nothing so unusual there."

"Anne, dammit, I'm worried about you—"

"And I'm worried about *you!*"

"Anne, listen to me. When I discovered the Indians' bodies, they were all but bloodless. And they were all decapitated. A vampire can't rise from the dead if it's been decapitated. Then there was Smokey. Bloodless, decapitated. And now—"

"Cissy, whose head is in place!" Anne reminded him painfully.

Michael let out a cry of aggravation. "Because he wants Cissy to join him!"

"I thought he wanted me?" she reminded him.

He threw up his arms and sighed. "Anne, he does. He thinks that you're the woman he loved centuries ago, and that you've come back to life. I can't read his mind. Maybe it was just taking him a little bit too long to get to you. Maybe he wants company in the meantime, and maybe he just really liked Cissy, too, and wanted her to have eternal life. I don't know!"

"Oh, Michael! This is just getting better and better! My uncle has been filling you with the family tales, and you're turning a handsome foreigner into a vampire! Michael, please, get out of my way! I love you, but I want you to go home, and get some sleep! This has all been too much for you."

"No." He shook his head stubbornly. His jaw was set.

She gritted her teeth, feeling a little tremor of desire. She was frustrated, but she loved him like this, when he was so determined.

"I'm going to be with you."

"Suit yourself," she said, walking again. "But I don't want to hear any more about it!"

She walked for a few steps and was surprised to realize that he wasn't following. She turned back. His hands on his hips, he was looking up at the sky.

His gaze touched hers. Suddenly he ran forward, sweeping her off her feet and into his arms. And then he was running like a jaguar with her held to his chest.

She couldn't breathe!

"Michael!" she cried out. It didn't do a thing. He kept on running, all the way to her porch steps.

Once again, Uncle Jem was waiting for them. Michael ran through the door. It slammed shut behind them.

"I've had it!" Anne cried out. "I've had it! Uncle Jem, you quit with the stories. Michael—you quit behaving like a lunatic or I'll not only refuse to marry you, I'll refuse to—" She broke off, remembering Uncle Jem.

"Watch it," Uncle Jem said dolefully to Michael. "She's threatening to not sleep with you anymore."

"Oh!" Anne cried in total exasperation. She walked down the hall to her room and slammed the door shut behind her.

Jem looked at Michael. "Well?"

"There were six marks on her neck."

"Three bite marks," Jem said.

"Maybe," Michael murmured.

"And I'll bet Doc Phelan told you her blood was half gone, too."

Michael nodded.

"Don't leave Anne in there alone," Jem warned him.

But Anne wasn't in her room. She was bursting back into the hallway. "Uncle Jem! Why is my room decorated from floor to ceiling in *garlic bulbs?*" she demanded.

He shrugged. " 'Cause there's a God-darned vampire out there!"

"I don't believe in vampires!"

"Then humor an old man."

She tossed a garlic bulb at him and stormed back into her room. Michael winced and followed her. She was sitting at the foot of her bed, looking morosely around her. "I do not believe this!" she exclaimed. "This behavior from two grown men."

Michael smiled and reached into his pocket, producing a jewel case. He handed it to her.

She looked at him suspiciously, then flicked up the lid.

It was a delicate, beautiful gold cross. "Oh, Michael!" she moaned.

He sat down beside her. "Humor a young man as well as an old one?" he said softly.

She smiled, handed him the cross, and turned so that he could clip it around her neck. "It's a lovely gift," she said softly. "But Michael . . ."

"Ummm?"

"I don't think I can sleep with all this garlic."

"How about giving me a chance to make you forget it's here?" he asked her huskily.

She was so angry with him. He was driving her crazy. Both he and Uncle Jem were already halfway there!

But she loved him.

She kissed him gently, meaning it to be just a brief touch, but he pulled her into his arms. His lips molded sensually over hers. His tongue penetrated between her teeth and stroked her mouth deeply.

She did forget the garlic.

Later that night, she awoke. Or perhaps she didn't awake. Perhaps she dreamed.

Drago stood outside her window. Far outside, shivering. He was telling her that it was cold, but that he couldn't come in.

"Come to me!" he whispered to her.

No.

"Come to me, come to me. Please . . ."

No. She was in love with Michael. But Michael had been so rude. She had to apologize. She just had to apologize.

It was only a dream, but she was suddenly walking. Walking to the window. The garlic was pungent. She needed to crawl over it.

"Anne!"

She awoke with a start. To her amazement, she was standing at the window. Ready to open it and climb out.

But Michael was there, wrapping the sheet around her, wrapping his own warmth around her. "Anne, Anne, Anne!" He cradled her, held her, swept her up and against him.

"It's all right!" she cried. "I was just sleepwalking." She lifted his dear head, cradled his cheeks with her hands. "I was just sleepwalking. Oh, Michael! There are no such things as vampires."

Truly, there weren't such things as vampires, she assured herself with a mental shake. Drago was powerful, handsome, sexy—and far too bold. But there were no such things as vampires!

Michael held her, too weary to fight with her.

He slept finally, his limbs entwined with hers, his arms locked around her, his thigh cast over her hip.

Jem pointed a finger at him over a cup of morning coffee. Anne was out back, feeding the chickens.

"You've got to kill the creature!" Jem said.

Michael slumped back, staring at Jem. "And just how do I do that? If he is a vampire, he won't die with a bullet."

"But he will die if you decapitate him, or force him into daylight—or drive a stake through his heart. But Jesu, boy, you've got to be careful! Vampires are tremendously strong . . . Holy water helps," Jem reflected. "But I'm not so sure you can actually kill a vampire with it. Not unless you have a tubfull."

"What a help you are, Jem, what a help!"

"You can't just accost him. I mean, you can't go out and beat up a vampire!" Jem warned him.

"I wasn't planning on trying," Michael assured him. He sighed. Maybe Anne was right. Maybe they *were* crazy. Nonetheless, he was growing more and more frightened. "I've got to find him by day. In his coffin, I imagine. Oh, God! What am I saying?" he demanded with disgust. Then he shrugged. "I'll speak with Father Martin after Cissy's funeral today."

Jem nodded. "Good idea. And you'd better hush up for now. Annie's on her way back in and she doesn't seem to have a lot of patience for either of us at the moment."

Anne came in. Michael went on back to his own house to change into his black suit for the funeral. He returned with his carriage for Anne and Jem, and the three of them attended the service together.

It was the saddest service Michael had ever been to. Jeannie cried as if her heart would break.

Then Cissy was lowered into the ground. Father Martin tried to say all the right words, but a sudden dust storm came up. It started slowly, just as Father Martin began. Then suddenly, it became ferocious. Father Martin, holding on to his hat, looked to Jeannie. "Mrs. McAllistair, we'll start all over tomorrow, don't you worry, we'll see it done right by tomorrow afternoon." By then, people were shrieking, and heedless of the need for a decent funeral for Cissy, they were beginning to run. Father Martin got no further. They would all come back for the service tomorrow.

Everyone there was running for his or her carriage.

As Michael covered Anne and they headed for shelter, he couldn't help but wonder if the cross he had wedged into the coffin the night before had kept its occupant sleeping through the night.

And he couldn't help but wonder if it was still there.

At the McAllistair house, the women made coffee and served food that everyone pushed around on their plates.

While Anne supervised in the McAllistair kitchen since Jeannie was still unable to, Michael took the opportunity to slip outside with Father Martin.

The priest was a young man. For some reason Michael was glad that Green Valley's one man of God happened to be a Catholic.

Father Martin had soft brown hair and brown eyes. He was of medium height and build, but as he crossed his arms over his chest, Michael decided that he was probably stronger than he looked.

Michael tried to talk. He tried again. "Jesu, Father! I can't believe I'm saying this to you, but I think we have a vampire in Green Valley."

Father Martin's brows flew up. "A vampire?"

"I know you can't possibly believe me—"

Father Martin interrupted him quickly. "I'm not sure I know what that is."

Michael patiently explained everything Jem had told him.

"I know it sounds crazy, and it's a long story. It started with the Indians, and they were absolutely convinced that there was an evil spirit afoot, a white evil spirit. Oh, Lord! I—"

"Michael," Father Martin said passionately, "we know that there is the power of good in the world. We believe in God, in the Holy Spirit. So perhaps there are evil spirits as well."

Stunned, Michael stared at him. "Then you believe me?"

"I don't believe or disbelieve you." The young priest suddenly shivered fiercely. "But something is going on here. Jesus in His heaven, my friend, something is going on here. And I'll do anything in my power to help you! I'd be pleased to bless you and your efforts in any fight against evil."

Michael smiled. "I don't exactly know what I'm doing myself, Father Martin, but I've been given some advice, and you might supply me with a few of the things I've been told I'm going to need." He hesitated. "You don't think I'm insane?"

Father Martin paused for a minute. Then he spoke in a rush. "I felt it—something, a while back. One night. I don't know how to explain it. Something came with the breeze, something that had a strange feel of . . ."

"Evil?" Michael suggested softly.

Father Martin nodded somberly. "And then there was the Indian massacre. Then old Smokey. And now poor Cissy. I don't know the truth. And, of course, the Church isn't taking any official stand, you realize."

Michael nodded. He didn't give a damn if anything was official or not.

"There is something out there," Father Martin said. "Ask what you will. I'll help you."

Michael went to the church with Father Martin, who blessed him and gave him a wooden walking stick with a pointed end—a stake.

He left the church with a small cross around his own neck, a vial of holy water in his shirt pocket, and the stick at his side.

He walked slowly along the empty street until he looked up and realized that it was almost dark. Then he began to run.

Anne looked worriedly out the window. Almost all the others had gone home now. Jeannie was lying down. The boys were sitting in their sister's empty room. Tim was getting drunk.

Jem and Billy were still there, quietly sipping from glasses of beer.

Anne, growing more anxious, was just about to jump up and run out to look for Michael when he entered the front door. She frowned, worried that he might have hurt himself, because he seemed to be leaning on a walking stick. He gave her a faint smile. She frowned, lifting a brow to him. But before she could say anything, they heard a loud shriek from Jeannie McAllistair's bedroom.

In a panic, Anne flew up. She raced into the room, followed by the others.

Jeannie was sitting up in bed, shaking, pointing to the window. "She's out there. My baby is out there. I swear it! I saw her. She was calling to me. She said that she was cold, that she was lonely, that she needed me!"

"Oh, Jeannie!" Anne cried, taking the woman into her arms. "It's all right, Jeannie, it's going to be all right! I'm here with you. Cissy isn't cold! She's with God now. She's going to be fine. But she loves you so much! She'd want you to be well!"

"There's nothing in the window, Ma, nothing at all!" Anthony told her.

Jeannie collapsed in Anne's arms. Anne soothed her until she ceased sobbing.

Michael swung around and walked through the house, past Tim McAllistair who sat in a stupor in his armchair.

He walked outside. There was nothing to be seen in the front of the house. He leaned against his walking-stick stake, then rounded the corner.

And then he stopped still.

It was true, all of it.

Because she was there. Cissy McAllistair, dressed in the beautiful white spring gown her mother had chosen for her funeral, was there. She looked as young and sweet as ever, but she smiled at him in a way that was no longer innocent.

"Michael . . ."

The sound of her voice was hypnotic. He wanted to go to her.

"Michael, I'm so cold. Come, put your arms around me. Warm me. I beg you, Michael . . ."

He was moving before he knew it. Somehow Cissy's blue eyes now resembled Drago's gold ones. There was a rim around them. A rim of a different color.

"Cissy?" he said softly. They must have been mistaken. She hadn't really been dead. They had buried her prematurely; he had heard of it happening before. He went closer and closer to her.

That batty old Jem had been right. Drago really must be a vampire. He had given Cissy his deadly kiss . . .

No, it couldn't be.

Her blonde hair tumbled all around her. Her pretty smile was in place.

"Oh, Michael! I always envied Anne so much. Come to *me* now, Michael! Come to me. You think you've found ecstasy with Anne. It's nothing—nothing, Michael, like the things I can show you. Like the way I can make you feel. Let me touch you. Let me show you. Let me kiss you."

Something glittered in the moonlight. He realized it was coming from her . . . mouth. Her lips had drawn back. He saw with mesmerized horror the incredible length and sharpness of her teeth. They dripped clear liquid . . .

"Michael!"

She called his name in dismay, as if having sensed that she had lost something.

And then he noticed much more. The pieces of grave-yard dirt in her hair. The subtle, putrid smell of . . . death.

"Michael!" she whispered. "I'm so cold. You're sup-posed to be my friend, Michael. Please come, make me warmer . . ."

He wanted to. She had caught his eyes, and her power was so strong, he wanted to do just as she asked.

No! Oh, no!

He wrenched his anguished gaze from hers. This wasn't Cissy. Cissy was dead. This was some hellish creation with Cissy's sweet face and youth, yet with the devil's own eyes.

"You come to me, Cissy," he said softly.

She started to move toward him. Smiling. Moving slowly. She was in front of him, ready to sweep her arms around him.

Ready to taste his flesh.

He drew his stake between them. It seemed his silent scream echoed inside him. He took the stake and drove it into her chest with all his strength, seeing in her eyes the shriek of absolute horror she never voiced.

Then she was falling to the ground. He leaned over her. Her eyes were still open. She smiled, and for an instant she was once again the sweet innocent Cissy who had been Anne's best friend. "Thank you, Michael!" she whispered, and her eyes closed.

"Oh, God!" he breathed. He sat back on his heels, covering his face with his hands.

"Michael!"

It was Billy, coming around the corner of the house. Michael looked at his friend and waited for him to express his shock, but apparently Billy had been seeing and understanding a lot more than Michael had realized.

Billy crossed himself. "She come up from the dead like a devil, right?"

"Something like that," Michael told him.

"You've got to help us all, Michael."

Michael swallowed hard. He nodded. "I'm going to try Billy. But now, you've got to help me, before her parents see her. Let's bring her back to the cemetery."

Together they carried Cissy back to the graveyard and laid her in her coffin. And once again he felt the cold breeze of fear suddenly crash down upon him.

Anne!

She was in the house. It was nighttime. Drago's time.

Somewhere, a wolf howled. Michael stood in the cemetery and looked back toward town. The breeze picked up. It was cold.

He started to run.

6

JEANNIE was sleeping at last.

Anne returned to the living room. Tim had fallen into a drunken sleep in his chair. The boys were gone. Uncle Jem was on the sofa in the parlor, trying to keep his eyes open.

Anne went into the kitchen and started washing the dishes as best she could. She was worried. Michael had been gone for a long time now, and he had been acting very strangely.

She looked out the kitchen window and thought she saw him hurrying toward the house. She wiped her hands on a dish towel and went out the back door, onto the porch. There was a shadow against the darkness.

"Michael?" she said softly.

But it wasn't Michael. David Drago quite suddenly stepped into view, smiling. "Anne!" he said softly.

All at once she felt uneasy, and was sorry she had come outside. She backed away, watching him. "The funeral was this afternoon, Mr. Drago," she said. "The McAllistairs are all sleeping, if you have come to pay your respects."

To her dismay, he kept walking toward her. She backed away from him. He stopped, reaching a hand out to her.

"I didn't come to see the McAllistairs, Anne. I came for you."

She shook her head, fighting the confusion that threat-

ened to engulf her very soul. There was something about
the man that mesmerized her. She had to think carefully
to speak. "Mr. Drago, I don't know what impression
I gave you, but I'm very much in love with Michael
Johnston. I'm going to marry him. I—"

"I intend to change that."

"But I don't want it changed," she said firmly.

Abruptly he was furious. "Well, it *will* be changed this
time, Anne! I have waited hundreds of years for you! I
have searched nations, continents! And I finally found
you here!"

"I don't know what you're talking about!" she cried,
starting to back away again. Centuries . . .

How strange. She'd once had the feeling that she'd
known him before. She had dreamed about him, again
and again.

She was attracted to him.

She feared him . . .

They were all losing their minds. Or else it was true,
and David Drago was a vampire.

No, that couldn't be! It was legend, superstition. It just
couldn't be true!

She should have paid more heed to Uncle Jem, to
Michael . . .

"No!" She mouthed the word. "I have to go in. Michael
is coming. Michael will be here at any minute."

He started to laugh. "And you think Michael can keep
us apart? My love, you are mistaken!" His golden eyes
were latched upon hers, and to her horror, she discovered that she could not move. "I can break your
precious Michael's neck with the snap of my fingers,"
he whispered. "I can send him flying across the state
with the whisper of my breath. Anne, you are now
mine!"

Deny him! Fight him! she charged herself. But she
didn't know how. Why had she been such a fool? She'd
sensed his power before. Now she was trapped in it. Its

strength was incredible! She couldn't move. His gaze touched her, and she couldn't move.

Fight, fight, she had to fight . . .

Over and over she whispered, "Michael will come. He will come."

Drago reached for her, finding her wrist, wrenching her toward him. He held her shoulders, staring down into her eyes, murmuring, "I meant it to be so slow! A sure, sweet seduction of the senses. You would have come with me so willingly then. But fast or slow, it doesn't matter. You must still discover all that I can give you."

"I'll never want you! Never."

"But you will. Once I touch you, you will know my power and you will want what I want. Just once, when your blood has trickled from your body into mine, warming it, giving it sustenance, then you will be my creation. Three times, Anne, and you will be mine for eternity!"

He brushed aside her hair. Then he paused, swearing violently, and Anne dimly realized that Michael's small gold cross lay around her neck.

Dear Lord, please . . .

He swore again, dragging her with him. "I wanted you! I esteemed you above all women! I searched for you forever! Don't fight me!"

She *was* fighting him, though, struggling with every ounce of strength she possessed, and still, unable to dislodge his secure hold on her. He was taking her with him. Running with him. But then it seemed they were not running anymore; they were not touching the ground at all.

He had lifted her. He had become a shadow in the night. He was holding her, and they were soaring over the town.

She looked down. There was Michael, running back to town from the graveyard.

From the graveyard?

Oh, dear God! Michael was running *away* from the direction in which they were rushing. She began to shiver with dread. Drago was a creature of death and shadows, and he was taking her to the cemetery.

He was taking her toward death.

"Michael!" she cried out.

Drago was laughing. His whisper, hot, throaty, encompassed her. "You'll come to my home, my pet. I'm sure your fool uncle has been wondering where it is. A patch of earth in unhallowed ground has warmed and welcomed me nightly. A small tunnel beneath it leads up to my newly built house on the hill. Richard Servian lives there. You'll come to like the fat little bug, my dear, for he serves me well. Watches over my coffin by day, cares for my comfort at night."

Impossible . . .

Oh, why hadn't she believed?

She was dreaming. No, they were standing on the unhallowed ground, where the suicides were buried. The atheists who had scorned God. The poor, the unknown, the unloved.

Drago just looked at her, smiling. She heard a noise behind her. She turned to see Richard Servian, the fat little man who had arrived one day on the daily stage coach. Short, plump, he should have been the picture of health, but instead his skin, too, was as pale as death.

"The cross!" Drago roared.

Caught between the two of them, Anne spun around. Servian started toward her. She backed away, striking out. She caught his face, his throat. The man was human! She should have hurt him. But he didn't cry out. And he kept coming for her.

She backed into Drago and his fingers, cold as steel bars, curled around her arms, holding her in place before Servian. The servant reached out and wrenched the cross from her throat.

The fight was finished from that moment, for Drago held her immobile with absolute power.

First she felt the warmth of his breath against her throat. Then she felt the razor-sharp jab of his teeth. She cried out. His teeth sank deep into her neck. And suddenly, it wasn't painful anymore. A coldness entered her body. And with it, a curious feeling of sweet ecstasy. Yes, she wanted more.

More and more . . .

Michael reached the McAllistair house to find it dead quiet. Frantically, he searched for Anne, and stumbled upon Jem Turner, fast asleep.

"Jem!" He shook the man. "Anne . . . where's Anne? Jem, you have to help me. Where is she?"

"Anne, Anne!" Jem cried, waking. He shook his head. Michael's heart sank. Jem gripped his arm tightly. "My God, she's gone. He's taken her! You'll have to go for him, you can't wait until morning, you have to find him. Three times! All he needs to do is drink three times!" He leaped up. "I'm coming with you. Get Billy to come with us, too. We've got to fight—now!"

Michael knew there wasn't time to dissuade Jem from coming. Billy, as white as a sheet, was still willing to stay at his side.

"Where?" Michael cried. "Where would he have taken her?"

"Where else would the dead find a home?" Jem replied. "The cemetery. He must have taken her to the cemetery, probably to the unhallowed ground. He'll make her sleep with him!"

Michael rushed out of the house with Jem and Billy behind him. Then he realized that although Billy was right behind him, Jem was falling back.

He turned for just a minute. He had forgotten Jem's age. The old man was panting, gasping, his face lobster-red. They should have taken the carriage. They should have—

No, there was no time.

"Go on, go on!" Jem urged him, catching up. He gripped Michael's shirtfront. "Don't forget how powerful he is! Have faith, Michael." Jem was shaking him. "You've got to win! You've got to win."

Michael nodded and spun around. He and Billy ran the rest of the way to the cemetery.

At first he didn't see Drago or Anne. All he could see was a squat little man standing amidst the makeshift crosses on the unhallowed ground.

The fat man raised his arm. Michael realized he was holding a pistol. "Down!" he shouted to Billy, who fell to the grass and rolled. The pistol exploded. Michael butted the fat man in the gut with his shoulder, and the man went down easily, sending the pistol flying.

When Michael stumbled back to his feet, Drago was standing there. Billy was staring at him in awe and horror. Drago walked straight toward him, but he never moved. Drago swung his arm, and it was as if he were swatting a fly. He slapped Billy against the side of the head, lifting him into the air. Billy crashed down upon a tombstone, unconscious . . . or dead.

Drago turned his attention to Michael. "All right, little man. It has come down to you and me. It is over. She is mine. And I will tear you limb from limb!"

Michael heard something soft—a word, perhaps—and realized Anne was standing behind Drago.

"Anne!" he cried. Drago stepped aside. She didn't move. She didn't even seem to see him.

There were two tiny puncture marks on her throat.

Michael was overcome with anguish. "No!" he cried in despair.

Drago need touch her only twice more—touch her throat, drink her blood—and she would be lost to Michael forever.

His stake was gone, imbedded in Cissy's heart, buried in the ground beyond. The holy water remained in his shirt pocket. Drago beckoned to him, circling him.

"Come, Michael Johnston, proud Indian hunter, great soldier, warrior, all! Come, fight me!"

Drago was laughing. Anne stood perfectly still, touched by the vampire.

"Anne!" Michael whispered again.

"Don't you see, you fool creature," Drago said to him. "She cannot help you. She is mine, and mine alone. Only I have the power to keep her!"

He moved toward Michael. Impatient, he was now ready for the kill.

Michael reached into his pocket and found the vial of holy water. He splashed it onto Drago's face.

The man let out a chilling scream of pain. He backed away, then fell to his knees.

Good God! Michael thought. Was that it? Had he won?

But Drago was stumbling to his feet. His face was burned where the water had hit him. "You will die slowly!" he promised.

He walked straight to Michael and struck the side of his head.

Michael flew into the air and landed hard, all the breath knocked out of him. He felt broken, bruised, stunned.

Drago was standing over him. A furious Drago.

"First I shall feast upon you, drain the blood from your body. I will leave you barely alive so that you may watch while I take your beloved Anne, here in the moonlight. We will make love upon the earth, beside your rotting, dying flesh, and in the end, I will make her one with me. Then I will grab your near-lifeless form and twist your head from your pathetic body."

Drago smiled and started down upon him.

Michael lashed out, catching Drago in the jaw. Drago just grunted. Michael stumbled to his feet, swinging again.

The vampire struck once more.

Michael sailed, then crashed down upon the earth. Drago dragged him to his feet and struck him again. Michael fought back the best he could, but Drago was gaining strength where he was losing his own.

No matter how many times Michael struck Drago, the vampire seemed to show no sign of discomfort.

"I have the power!" he whispered triumphantly.

And he hit Michael again. Michael felt the sensation of flying once again. Of hitting the ground.

He hurt from head to toe. He couldn't move. He struggled to regain his breath.

What a fool he had been to have left his best weapon embedded in Cissy's heart. But he hadn't wanted to jeopardize her soul, and so he had left it there.

All at once he realized a cross lay mere inches from his grasp. It had been crudely fashioned from branches sharpened at the bottom and thrust hard into the ground, a grave marker to stand guard over some poor soul, made by someone who must have believed in the power of God.

But at some time it had fallen free and intact from the dust.

It could be used as a stake . . .

The thought had barely entered Michael's head when Drago pounced upon him.

Michael furiously pitted his waning strength against the vampire's puissant force. The dusty old cross lay inches away, just where the fence signified the beginning of the hallowed ground. He could see it so clearly now! Someone had whittled the wood into a very sharp point. And with the rawhide binding around the horizontal, crooked piece of branch, it was both a weapon and a symbol of holiness. If Michael could just get his hands upon it, curl his fingers around it, and plunge it into the creature's heart.

That would be the end, Jem had promised him. Even old Dancing Woman had said death lay in the heart.

Just as life sprang from it.

But he needed more, Michael reminded himself. Father Martin had warned him that he needed faith.

Faith . . .

God help me, he prayed silently. God help me.

But Drago was over him now. And Drago knew that Michael's strength was failing him.

Anne stood just feet away, watching with her sightless stare, caught in the vampire's hypnotic spell.

She could not help Michael now.

And God, it seemed, had deserted him.

He stared at Drago, determined never to give up to his evil. Not until death, not beyond. Faith was the key. Faith in the strength of goodness.

As the vampire smiled down at him, Michael finally realized the true color of his eyes. They were red. Redder when he had drunk his fill of human blood. Gold when he was hungry . . .

Right now, they gleamed with both colors, hard gold orbs surrounded by red. An awful red.

Blood-red.

Blood-red with the stolen life of his many, many victims.

The vampire opened his mouth. The fangs were fascinating, just like those of a rattler but far more deadly. They were dripping. Coming closer and closer to his throat. Michael remembered all of Drago's words. He did not intend to make Michael a creature of the night. He meant to rip him limb from limb, and leave him a dismembered carcass as he had done with the Apaches . . .

"Anne!" Michael shouted suddenly. "Anne, I love you!"

His cry was powerless, but maybe she would hear him before he died. Maybe it would touch her heart. Maybe somewhere, in heaven or hell, she would know how very much he had loved her.

"Anne!"

He heard her sharp gasp as she sharply inhaled. "Michael!" His name, coming softly from her lips, was a cry of anguish. She could see him. She could feel him. She wanted to help him. But she could not fight the vampire's power.

"She's mine now, you fool!" Drago shouted, his fingers biting harder into Michael's shoulders. And then he started to laugh. "By the devil, dear fellow! You've yet to understand the full extent of my powers! But you will, soon. Oh, I promise you. You'll know very, very soon." And he opened his mouth again. The fangs seemed to extend, his whole face to contort. He meant to drink, and drink deeply.

Michael renewed his struggle, pitting the bulk of his strength against the arms and chest of the vampire, keeping those fangs just inches from his neck. Drago swore, and Michael thought he could count it a minor triumph to have held him off for so long, during a vicious fight . . .

Michael blinked suddenly. Perhaps he was losing his mind, hallucinating. Men in the desert often talked of seeing things that weren't there . . .

But it was happening. Anne was moving.

He could hear her soft voice. Or maybe it was a voice from her heart, because Drago didn't seem to hear it. It was Michael's name she was saying again and again. "Michael, oh, Michael. God help us, God help us . . . oh, Michael!"

Miraculously, she *was* moving. He could see her eyes. She was fighting the creature's supernatural power. Ah, that amber fire within her eyes. In it, he could see the fantastic strength of will with which she was fighting.

And he could see her tears, evidence of her love.

She had sunk down to her knees. She was thrusting the stake forward.

Closer. Closer.

He stretched out his fingers. He could almost touch it. Almost! He groped and strained . . .

Try! He willed her. Oh, Anne! Please try!

And Anne pushed the cross forward once again. His fingers closed around it.

And he found new strength.

For a moment, he faltered. What would happen to Anne? The vampire had touched her, put his mark upon her. If he did manage to slay the vampire, then . . .

"Do it! For the love of God, do it!" Anne pleaded. "Save us both!"

He had to. Whether she perished or remained on the earth to love him, he had to do it. To free her, one way or the other.

"I love you, Anne!" he cried out.

Drago was laughing, laughing, deep within his throat.

The teeth were almost ready to sink into Michael's flesh, to draw his blood. To steal away his life.

Michael gritted his teeth. With a burst of raw energy, he drew up the crosslike stake and managed to wedge it between them even as he struggled with Drago.

And just as the cold teeth touched his flesh, he thrust the pointed stake straight into Drago's heart.

He pushed it hard, again and again.

The vampire glared at him, his red-gold eyes widening. Michael looked on amazed. The vampire was surprised. Stunned.

Drago fell back, his long pale fingers curling around the stake that protruded from his heart. He looked at Michael again. His hands fell away from the stake.

Miraculous things began to happen. Years and years of decay began to take place before Michael's very eyes. Drago became a wrinkled old man. Then his skin turned to leather, which began to turn to dust and ash, crumbling around him.

In horror, Michael backed away. Then he heard Anne cry out.

Anne! They had won, they had bested the creature. They had fought it and bested it with love and faith and someone's pathetic cross from a dusty grave . . . Anne!

She was still on her knees, just inches away, as beautiful as ever, tears staining her cheeks, her eyes wide and luminous.

"Oh, Michael!" She threw herself into his arms. He held her tightly. He felt her warmth, her trembling. She was alive and well, and fire in his arms. He touched her frantically. Even the tiny pinpricks on her throat had healed.

She reached for him, and he was there. Ready to hold her, finding new strength, sweeping her into his encompassing grasp. She was trying not to look at Drago.

She stroked his cheek. "Oh, Michael. We made it! You saved me from him."

He smiled crookedly. "No, my love. *You* saved *me* from him." He was trembling again in remembrance. "God saved us both from him, Annie. He gave us . . . life."

Just inches away, a new, cleansing night breeze, warm and balmy, was lifting away the ashes of the vampire's corpse.

Neither of them looked at the remnants.

There was too much to be discovered in each other's eyes. Anne's smile deepened. "I'll marry you," she whispered.

"I haven't asked lately!"

"You will."

"And you'll understand about the militia?"

She nodded. "I'll understand that I'm blessed. You have a rare strength, Michael Johnston. A very rare strength. I pray that our children will have it too."

"Our children?"

"Yes. We'll be starting with just one, of course. Very soon."

"Anne . . ." he murmured.

Her arms tightened around him. "You mustn't worry! I knew long before Drago came. I just couldn't tell you because I wanted to convince you to quit the militia. And now . . ."

"Now?"

"Now I know that would be wrong. The town needs you. Cissy said so. We all need you."

He lowered his head for a moment. Cissy. They would all mourn her for a long time. She would keep them all from ever forgetting.

And maybe that was good. They would cherish life so much more because of her!

Anne cupped his face. She kissed him long and deeply before releasing him and stepping away.

"Billy," he murmured. He left her for a moment, going to his friend, fear lodging again in his throat. But even as he knelt beside him, Billy stirred.

He stared at Michael. "Did we lick him, Colonel?"

"We licked him, Billy. Come on, let me help you up."

Billy wavered for a minute, then stared at Anne, wide-eyed. "You all right, Annie?" he asked.

She smiled and nodded. Billy let out a Rebel cry that pierced the night. He hugged her. Then he turned to Michael. "I'll hurry on ahead. I'll let Jem know you're all right and that—"

"Right. Tell Jem that we had enough faith. Get the sheriff to send someone out here to pick him up," he said pointing to Richard Servian, who was still lying unconscious on the ground. "And take care, Billy! We don't want the McAllistairs to ever worry about Cissy. She is at peace now."

"I know," Billy said softly. He shook his head. "I don't think that I believe it, Colonel. I was here, but I still don't think I believe it."

He headed back to town. When he was gone, Michael realized that he was trembling. He spun around. "A baby?"

Anne nodded, smiling.

"And you're going to marry me?"

She kept nodding.

"Well, you're going to do so right now. I'm going for Father Martin the minute we get back, and I don't care how long he's been sleeping. Jem and Billy can be our witnesses. We'll have to be quiet out of respect for the McAllistairs, but I'm not giving you any chance to change your mind!"

"Michael!" Anne protested.

"And I don't want you to step away from me. Ever."

Her arms curled around his neck. They might be standing on unhallowed ground, but Michael was certain that God was smiling down upon them.

Maybe the legend was true. Maybe Anne *had* lost to Drago once before. Maybe this was their turn for happiness.

All he knew for sure was that she was kissing him, and that it was good. Sweet, tender, loving.

Oh, she could stir his senses so easily!

They needed to get home. Her home, he decided. That would be where they would live. She'd already imbued the place with her special warmth.

And tonight . . .

Tonight he wanted to return quickly. To hold her in a darkness that no longer harbored evil shadows. To make love to her with a breeze caressing them that was soft and warm and good.

"Let's go home," he said softly.

"And just leave . . . him?" she murmured.

Michael pressed her head against his shoulder and stepped around what was left of the vampire. There was the stake that now protruded from a swatch of black cloth. There were pieces of bone and ash on the ground.

Michael held Anne very tightly. "Perhaps I never truly understood the extent of your powers," he told the remnants of the creature. "You told me about them over and over again. But there was one power you underestimated. One you never understood."

He paused, then smiled.

"The power of love, old boy. The power of love. It's the strongest in all the universe!"

Then, holding Anne to him, he walked away from the shadows.

And into the light of life and love.

Shannon Drake

Spooky things and things that go bump in the night!

"I love the entire concept of a lover who's just a little bit different. Truly from the moment I first laid eyes on Patrick Swayze's "Ghost," I knew there could be love after death. But I'm a believer in happy endings and so in my story I leave the question open—When emotions are involved and they are strong enough, can there be a second chance at love and life?"

SHANNON DRAKE is the author of nine historical romances, including *Bride of the Wind*, which Avon Books published in September 1992. She has received numerous awards from Waldenbooks, *Romantic Times*, and *Affaire de Couer*. She also writes under the names "Heather Graham" and "Heather Graham Pozzessere." The mother of five children, she lives in Coral Gables, Florida.

My Aunt Grizelda

Kasey Michaels

Prologue

Wherein the stage is set for what is to come

MY home stands in solitary majesty on a pleasant stretch of headland above the chalky cliffs of an area known as Beachy Head, near the southeasternmost end of the South Downs and close by the charming village of Eastdean.

The estate I speak of is aptly named the Rookery, and is a much-loved holding of Douglas, Fourteenth Earl of Wilmington, and his countess, the fair Antonia. The site is best reached by following the considerable length of a wide, winding gravel drive that leads off the Duke's Road. I tell you this only so that you might understand the relative isolation of the spot.

In the spring and summer, spindle berries, split open by the sun so that bright orange seeds peek through their vermilion cases, hang like lighted lanterns along the drive, while in the far distance can be seen the many-armed tops of working windmills, grinding out the grain produced on nearby farms. Wild strawberries tempt the passerby, while the sight of fat cattle contentedly grazing on the turf of a sloping meadow lend an air of bucolic simplicity to the landscape. Everywhere is the song of birds, with the thrush's clear-throated music soothing the ear in the midst of the gull's angry screeches, so that the unwary visitor might not realize that the thrush is considerately warning of an approaching storm.

Autumn arrives each year rainy and mild, carpeting the drive with brightly colored leaves, with winter slipping in over the downs unannounced, covering everything with a pristine frost, and fierce storms buffet the area, only the shelter of the primeval beech weald the first earl prudently left intact shielding the Rookery from nature's more ambitious assaults.

But the stark scenery of Beachy Head remains perhaps the greatest attraction of this beautiful countryside no matter the season, overpowering the estate with its sheer chalk-white cliffs that thrust upwards more than five hundred feet from the Channel sea. The awe and majesty of those cliffs make this, my adopted home, very dear to my heart.

The estate is also haven to a multitude of gulls and rooks that roost in the mellow brick gables beneath the vaulted roofs, although they are quiet this late autumn night, their heads prudently tucked beneath their wings as a storm rages all around them, flashes of blinding white lightning streaking across the sky, followed swiftly by the rumble and crack of thunder as the wind bows the treetops to its will and a driving rain sheets against the brick walls.

I have closed the heavy oak front door on the sight of the storm raging outside and the disappointment of the still-empty gravel drive, my bottom lip firmly clamped between my teeth—a childhood habit long abandoned except in times of worry, times like now, when the splendid privacy of the Rookery seems more of a handicap than a virtue. It is no more than another storm, I try to convince myself, and not an early onset of winter, with its inherent icy conditions and danger.

It can't be. Not when he is on the road.

Inside the main saloon of the sprawling, centuries-old, four-storied building that same persistent wind has set the hems of the heavy velvet window draperies to waltzing, and occasionally whooshes down the chimney, teasing the bright flames so that sparks shower onto the wide marble hearth.

Gathered on the soft Aubusson carpet that fronts the fireplace, three rosy-cheeked, blond-haired children— Augusta, aged four; Harry, nearly six; and Edward, almost ten—sit wrapped snug in their nightclothes, with their sturdy legs tucked up tight, watching me as I enter, a bright smile now painfully pinned to my face. Lifting my skirts a fraction, comforted by the reassuring whisper of silk, I join them on the floor, my back turned to the hearth, my ears attuned to the sounds of the storm, still listening for the crunch of carriage wheels against the gravel.

"Well now, my darlings," I say, looking to each of the children in turn as the mantel clock chimes out the hour of nine, "as you have coerced me into allowing you to stay up past your bedtime, what shall we do while we await your papa's return from Lewes?"

With one voice the children cry, just as I expect them to do, "A story! Tell us a story!"

"One with scary ghosts, or monsters, or mean old witches!" Edward adds, almost-ten being an extraordinarily bloodthirsty age.

"No, Neddy, no," Augusta protests, moving closer to the hem of my gown. "It should be a tale of princesses and fairies."

"Oh, bother," Harry grumbles, for Harry, bless him, is the middle child and therefore constitutionally compelled to expend his energies arguing against any suggestion made by either of his siblings. "Let us hear about our papa, and how he won the war against Boney."

Edward leans over to cuff the side of his brother's head. "Papa didn't beat Boney on his own, you numskull. Wellington helped."

"Princes, and fairies, and a beautiful princess locked in a tower!" Augusta trills, the voice that will one day be beautifully feminine still sometimes unfortunately high-pitched.

"Children, please!" I interrupt, clapping my hands to silence them. They are good children, for the most part extremely cooperative, and quite well loved by everyone at the Rookery. But the storm has put them on edge. It has put us all on edge. "If you will be so kind as to resist the temptation to become a mob, I shall tell you a story that contains bits and pieces of nearly everything you wish—a witch, a war of sorts, a beautiful maiden in dire need of rescue, a brace of mean-spirited monsters, and even a handsome prince who rides to the rescue. And it all took place here, at the Rookery."

"Yes, yes!" the children answer, scooting closer to me, their wide blue eyes alight with eagerness as they anticipate my tale.

"Is this to be a true story?" Edward questions, for he is the oldest and gives fairy tales short shrift.

"Is it true? How you wound me, Edward. Now please, don't interrupt, or I may remember that you children are here on sufferance."

"Yes, shut up, do, Ned," Harry orders, leaning his chin on his hands. "Gussie and I want to hear the story."

"I remember it well," I begin when they are quiet once more (Augusta having taken momentary umbrage at being referred to so informally by her brother), leaning forward slightly, again looking to each of them in turn. "My tale begins many years ago, although I hesitate to reveal the exact year of our princess's travail, for no female is best pleased to have herself dated, you understand. I will tell you that dampened muslins were much the rage, and dear Lord Byron's verse was still openly quoted in all the best London salons."

"No later than eighteen-sixteen," Edward offers in an aside to his brother, nodding sagely. "Byron booted himself off the island then and sailed away to die in Greece."

I ignore this outburst, for the child is correct, and continue, "My story concerns a young lady we will call Arabella. A dear creature. A lovely creature, actually. And sweet. Definitely sweet of nature. Alas, she is also pockets to let—orphaned, you understand—and totally without prospects."

"How old is she?" Harry inquires, the child showing all the signs of being a stickler for facts. I'll have to be on my toes as he matures.

"Three and twenty," I admit. "But age is not important. This wonderful creature—due to circumstances entirely beyond her control—is forced to seek employment in order to feed her belly and, as she lives in the very back of beyond—near Polegate, Harry, before you are tempted to interrupt again—she is forced to relocate herself to a village near Eastbourne and hire herself out as governess to the regrettably nasty twin sons of the even nastier Lady—*um*—the Lady Mary Knox, widowed sister of the current earl. The earl, not liking his sister overmuch, spends precious little time on his estate, preferring the relative quietude of London."

I watch Edward as he nudges his brother. "Sounds like what Papa used to do, don't it, Harry? And Aunt Isobel—and even the twins, although, of course, they're all grown up now." I wait patiently until he turns to me again, smiles, and says, "Sorry, ma'am. You may continue now."

"Thank you, Edward. How very kind of you. Now, where was I?"

"You were talking about Arabella. She's the princess, isn't she?" Augusta, hugging her doll close, has picked up the hem of my gown and is now rubbing the silk against her cheek. I doubt she will be able to remain awake until my story is concluded.

"Ah, yes. Arabella. Well, children, Arabella is not a happy young woman, considering the fact that Freddie, one of the twins, delights in putting frogs in her bed and, Bertie, the second twin, considers it the height of levity to mix salt in with the usual contents of Arabella's sugar bowl.

"Penniless or nay, Arabella decides she must leave her employment, for she cannot abide life under this roof for another moment." I lean closer, my voice dropping to a whisper, and add, "But then, as she walks near the cliffs one night just at dusk, building up her courage to leave, Arabella comes face-to-face with—"

"The witch!" all three children shout in unison, and my story is begun . . .

1

In which the characters mount the stage and our play begins

ARABELLA Brawley was not the sort to frighten easily. She couldn't be, else she would have packed her portmanteau long since and fled the terrible Knox twins and their nasty little tricks with all the apparent haste of one escaping the jaws of hell.

However, when she was out and about on her own, as was her custom while the harassed nursery maid oversaw the twins' dinner hour, and deeply lost in thought, Arabella did not expect to encounter anyone as she walked along the cliffs behind the estate. After all, she had been walking these same solitary cliffs every evening, fair weather or foul, for the past four months without meeting another living soul.

Perhaps that was why Arabella was heard to issue a short squeak of surprise before marshaling her wits and addressing the woman who seemed to have appeared out of thin air, to land solidly no more than three feet in front of her. "Good evening, ma'am," Arabella said after a moment, and not unkindly, for it mattered little to her if the woman were trespassing upon private property. It wasn't *her* property, was it? "May I be of some assistance? Have you lost your way?"

"What? Lost my way? Me? Goodness no. At least not lately, and not in a way you'd suspect," the small, round female of indeterminate years, a woman dressed neck to toes in a voluminous cloak of midnight-black wool, returned in a sprightly manner, her voice as high-pitched and winsome as a young child's. "I never lose my way around here, my dear girl. Impossible, you know. I've been here for ages." Her bright smile, which turned her round red cheeks to small hard apples, faltered, draining the shine from her innocent blue eyes. "Ages and ages and *ages*."

"Really?" Arabella responded, frowning as she leaned slightly forward, the better to see the woman in the gathering dusk. "I feel that way myself sometimes, although I have not been in residence here at the Rookery above four months. It's strange, our not having met before today. I'm Arabella, by the way. Arabella Brawley, governess to Lady Mary Knox's twin boys."

The woman's smile was once more firmly planted in the middle of her apple-dumpling face, although her truly ludicrous bright-yellow chip straw hat was not likewise placed centered on her head, the thing having somehow slipped forward to cover her eyes. She pushed it back atop her tight gray curls with an impatient swipe of one pudgy hand. "I know, Arabella. They need a good thrashing, don't they? All three of them, if you take my point. Oh, yes, I imagine it would be allowed to tell you my name as well, as long as we're being friendly. I knew you'd be friendly. It's Grizelda. My name, that is. *Grizelda*. I had a surname once, I believe, although it is long forgotten. Gone—*poof!*—straight out of my head. You may call me Aunt Grizelda. Yes, I believe I'd like that, Arabella."

What a droll little creature! Imagine, to meet a person one moment, and to extend a request for such wonderful familiarity the next! Such things simply weren't done in polite society. But, now that Arabella thought of it, the Rookery was an eternity away from polite society. Who would know? Who would care? And she did so long for a friend.

Arabella felt a smile tugging at the corners of her mouth. *Aunt Grizelda*. She'd never had an aunt. She'd never had an uncle either, for that matter, or any cousins, being the sole offspring of two only children. She was, in a word, alone in the world, and had been for more than three years. "Yes, I think I'd like that—Aunt Grizelda. Do you live nearby?"

The little old lady—for even the most generous of souls, operating in the most flattering of lights, could not bring themselves to call Aunt Grizelda young—bobbed her head, nearly dislodging the bonnet once more. "I do. I do. I live very much nearby, as a matter of fact, although I am here only for the space of one cycle of the moon every twenty-five years, although you needn't worry your head about that, for this time I think I have just the right plan to put a stop to this appearing-and-disappearing business. I have a pot brewing just beside the fireplace even as we two speak, and would like nothing better, truly I wouldn't, than for you to come to my cottage and share a dish of tea with me. And some scones?"

Arabella looked toward the Rookery, where her duty lay, and then to the woman called Aunt Grizelda. The twins were in the Rookery. The twins, and Lady Mary, and another long evening of drudgery. She then looked toward the clearly daft ("I am here only for the space of one cycle of the moon every twenty-five years . . ." How droll!) yet gentle old woman, who stood smiling up at her, wordlessly repeating her invitation with a quick, friendly wink of one eye.

"I suppose it couldn't take *that* long to have a cup— I mean, a *dish* of tea," Arabella put forth at last. "That is, if your cottage is not too far from the Rookery. I shouldn't like to leave the nursery maid, Peggy, alone with the twins for too long. She is prone to tears, you understand, and wringing her hands, poor child."

Aunt Grizelda took hold of Arabella's hand and began to walk toward the acre-wide stand of trees that protected the Rookery from the Channel winds. "Far? Never think it, my dear. My cottage is just over there, a step or two into the weald—or what is left of it. Used to be trees from here to there—everywhere. Trees, trees, and more trees. Couldn't see the cliffs for the trees, as a matter of fact. Young Will nearly toppled to his death one night, walking through the trees one minute, just to have one of his boots dangling over the edge of the cliff the next. And a fine dance that young'un did, getting himself back on solid ground—and not without help." She sighed as if the memory pained her. "Gone now, child, all gone. Young Will, the heart and soul of the weald. All my friends are gone, everyone except for me."

Arabella felt her heart go out to the woman. "I'm so sorry, Aunt Grizelda. You must miss your friends terribly."

Aunt Grizelda squeezed Arabella's hand. "Miss them, my dear? No, I don't miss them." She lifted her free hand and pointed at the stars that were just beginning to appear above the horizon. "See—there they are. To your left, child—do you see that rather yellowish star? That's young Will. Nice boy, although he was ever prosing on about thundercloud kings and blighted lovers and the like, and finally stopped visiting altogether. Stayed

up north somewhere after that, as I remember. But no
matter. He's back with us now. Just below him is Maisie,
and Heloise is to her left. Galls Maisie no end, for she
never could abide Heloise. Flirts, you know—Heloise,
that is. But she has a good heart for all of it. And then,
to your right, to the other side of the North Star, that
one is Hester. I'm to be just beside her, on Number
417. Lovely number, isn't it, 417? There were the four
of us, you see—Maisie, Heloise, Hester, and me. Only
I forgot the words, and never did see much point in
running about moaning over Birnam Wood moving
and doubled trouble. Anyway, in the end I was left out
altogether. But I'm used to it. Indeed I am. Ah, here we
are, my dear."

Arabella, who had been shifting her gaze from Aunt
Grizelda to the stars and back again as they walked
along, her eyes widening more and more as the woman
spoke, shook her head and blinked twice as she saw the
small cottage nestled just inside the stand of trees.

How could this be? She had come this way a dozen
times, a hundred times, and never seen this cottage. Yet
here it was, nestled snugly between two ancient trees,
a lovely little half-timbered, thatched-roof building no
larger than the buttery, with overflowing flower boxes
at each of the two front windows and a thin stream of
smoke rising lazily from the chimney.

It looked as old as the world, and as bright and shiny
as a new penny.

"How could I not have noticed?" Arabella mused aloud
as Aunt Grizelda opened the front door and ushered her
inside—although Arabella had to dip her head so as not
to strike it on the low lintel.

The cottage seemed even smaller once Arabella was
inside, and crowded from one end to the other with
rush brooms and black iron pots and precious little in
the way of real furniture. The ceiling was hung all over
with drying flowers and herbs, and a strong aroma of

garlic filled the air. There were two comfortable-looking rocking chairs pulled up near the fireplace. But, although she could see no doors leading to other rooms, there was no bed anywhere, so that, although Arabella could see no ladder, she supposed that Aunt Grizelda must have a bed tucked away in the loft, under the roof.

Aunt Grizelda untied her cape—tossing it into a corner so that it landed, quite conveniently, atop the handle of one of the brooms, keeping it from falling onto the floor—to reveal a plain gray gown of no recognizable style. "Here we go, my dear," she said, bustling across the room to open a cabinet that hung on the back wall. "You just sit yourself down and I'll have our tea and scones in a moment. Please excuse any mess. I just got here late last evening, you understand. Do you like butter? I do, although my churn has refused to perform the office ever since the last full moon—it must have been something I said, I suppose—so we shall have to make do with green-apple jelly."

"That—that will be just fine, Miss—*um*, Aunt Grizelda," Arabella answered abstractedly, gingerly settling herself into one of the rocking chairs. "Really." She sat very still, trying to make herself small as she looked at the large stone fireplace, wondering why she felt absolutely no heat from the roaring fire that burned within it.

"Here you are, my dear," Aunt Grizelda said a moment later, setting a round wooden tray down upon the table that stood between the two rocking chairs. "Scones and jelly and nice hot tea."

Arabella looked to the kettle that stood on a flat stone just to one side of the fireplace, then to the pot that so obviously held a quantity of steaming hot tea. When had Aunt Grizelda availed herself of the kettle? Arabella certainly had not seen her do so. Not only that, but the scone she now held in her hand was also warm, and Arabella was quite sure that Aunt Grizelda had not paid a visit to the small oven chamber built into the stones beside the fireplace. "How?" She barely realized she had spoken aloud.

"Yes, dear? How what?" Grizelda spoke with her mouth full of scone.

Arabella spread her hands, as if to indicate the tray, the fireplace, the entirety of the small cottage, then let her hands flutter back into her lap. What did the "how" of it, of any of it, matter? Her smile was apologetic as she lifted the dish of tea with both hands. "Nothing, Aunt Grizelda," she said before taking a sip of tea. "Oh! This is delicious!"

Aunt Grizelda patted her gray curls, frowning slightly as her fingertips touched the brim of her straw hat. "Thank you, my dear. I have quite mastered some things, you see. Drat this bonnet! It's not supposed to be here now that I'm indoors." She sighed, untying the bright-yellow ribbons that were tied to one side of her double chin. "Mastered some things, and been mastered by others. No wonder Hester is still alone up there."

As this statement was completely indecipherable, Arabella ignored it, leaning back in her chair and sipping the tea as she stared into the fireplace. "What a lovely refuge from the outside world," she said almost to herself as she smiled toward the big white cat napping on a rug on the hearth. "An hour spent in this lovely cottage could almost make one forget that Freddie and Bertie exist."

Aunt Grizelda leaned forward expectantly. "Would you like that, my dear? It would be difficult, but if you'd really like that—well, I suppose I could make them disappear."

Arabella nearly choked on her tea. "Disappear? You're talking about making Freddie and Bertie *disappear?*"

"Yes, of course, my dear girl. What else could I mean?" Putting down her tea, Aunt Grizelda rose and began looking about the cottage, the fingers of her right hand tapping against her chin—her first chin. The second chin was not subjected to a similar attack. "Let me think. Eye of newt? No, that never works. Besides, do you have any idea how difficult it is to find a newt these days? I do have some adder's tongue left over from that spell I cast the last time I was here—or was that the second last time? No, it was last night. Yes, I'm quite sure it was yesterday, and not a moment longer. Silly me. Doesn't matter, for it didn't work anyway. If it did, the earl should have been here by now, to rescue you from your drudgery, my dear. Oh, let me think, let me think."

Arabella carefully put down her dish of tea and rose as well. Clearly the dear old woman was slightly to let in the attic. Perhaps even fully vacant in her upper stories. Poor thing. And such a nice old woman. "That's quite all right, Aunt Grizelda," she said soothingly as she watched the woman open a small round-topped wooden chest and begin digging through its contents. "I really don't want the twins to disappear. Truly, I don't. If only they would behave. That's all I really want."

"Here it is—my most important possession. Strange how I am always misplacing it." Aunt Grizelda popped her head and shoulders back out of the chest, holding a rather old, strangely lopsided, melon-sized ball that appeared to have been fashioned out of lead crystal. Rubbing at it with the skirt of her gown—for the ball was quite dusty—she turned to her guest, a rather sheepish smile on her face. "You don't want them to disappear? Really? Oh, that is most amenable of you, my dear. I, however, believe the best way to prod them into minding their manners is to give them a small dose of their own vile medicine. And this will do nicely, I'm sure," she said, returning to stand beside the table and depositing the ball into a wooden holder that seemed fashioned for just such a use. "I never did much like working with newts. Heloise was quite good with them, however. Now, tell me, what is it these boys do that most offends your sensibilities?"

A prudent person might be running for the door just about now, Arabella concluded, staring at what she at last realized must be a witch's crystal ball. As a matter of fact, a prudent person *would* be running for the door—and screaming all the way!

But Aunt Grizelda couldn't really be a witch. There was no such thing as a witch. Never had been, no matter how much the general populace had been bent on dunking or burning females a few centuries ago. Witches were nothing but creatures from rather dark, uninspiring fairy tales—or characters in William Shakespeare's *Macbeth*. Nobody really *believed* in witches.

William Shakespeare's play? Oh, dear. Arabella swallowed down hard on a sudden, unsettling suspicion. Aunt Grizelda had spoken of someone she called "young Will." She had also spoken of three women—Heloise, Maisie, and Hester. Did the witches in *Macbeth* have names assigned to them? Arabella didn't think so. And what was that business about "doubled trouble" and "thundercloud kings"? No! That was ridiculous! William Shakespeare never set foot in Sussex, at least not as far as Arabella knew, and besides, he had been dead and buried for over two hundred years!

All these thoughts, and more, passed through Arabella's head in a matter of seconds, and were just as quickly dismissed. Aunt Grizelda was a sweet old woman. A sweet old woman who lived, most happily it appeared, in a world all her own. And if she wished to play at being a witch, play at casting spells—well, what of it? Surely it could do no harm?

"Do?" Arabella responded at last, subsiding once more into the rocking chair, one eye still on the lopsided "crystal ball." The tea was still piping hot, and the scones were delicious. She might as well finish them—then go. "Well, Aunt Grizelda, Bertie put salt in the sugar bowl yesterday and then sat by, his hands neatly folded in his lap, while I availed myself of two teaspoonfuls for my morning tea. And Freddie—oh, what can I say about Freddie? Where could I start? Yesterday, to tell you only of his latest prank, he slipped a rather large frog into my bed. It's not that I'm afraid of frogs, you understand, but I wasn't expecting one as a sleeping partner."

"You would if I could make him into a prince," Aunt Grizelda said, winking at her. "But only Hester can do that. She's most prodigiously talented."

"I'm sure she is, Aunt Grizelda," Arabella said soothingly, more than slightly aware that it was time she took her leave. She stood yet again and walked to the door. "Don't worry about the twins, please. I'm sure I can discover some way of making them behave. Truly. And thank you so much for the tea and scones."

"Will I see you tomorrow?" Aunt Grizelda asked, following her to the door. "It has been so pleasant having you. I'll talk to the churn about some butter—and I will want to hear how the twins are behaving once I've concentrated my powers on teaching them a lesson about good manners."

"Of course I'll come see you tomorrow, Aunt Grizelda," Arabella said, smiling as she ducked her head and stepped outside the cottage. It would do no harm to humor the old woman. "Only you must promise me you won't be too hard on the boys."

"Such a sweet child," Aunt Grizelda answered, reaching up to pat Arabella's cheek. "I knew you were the right one. So sorry I couldn't get the earl to come home. London's a long way for spells, you know."

Arabella bit her bottom lip to restrain a giggle. Not only did Aunt Grizelda fancy herself a witch, but she fancied herself a matchmaking witch. As if the earl would ever become enamored of a penniless governess of three and twenty, a woman who, if not at her last prayers, was definitely past her prime. "I shall attempt to overcome my disappointment, Aunt Grizelda," she said with as much solemnity as she could muster, leaning down to kiss the woman's apple-red cheek. "Good night."

Arabella walked away without turning back, intent on finding her way out of the stand of trees without stumbling in the near-dark. It was only when she was completely clear of the trees and the Rookery was once more in sight that she turned about, to take one last look at the cottage and, perhaps, understand how it was that she had never seen it before today.

But there was no cottage. No half-timber. No quaint thatched roof. No colorful flower boxes beneath the windows. No trail of smoke rising lazily toward the now nearly dark skies.

There was absolutely nothing—except for the lingering sweetness of Aunt Grizelda's green-apple jelly on her tongue.

The man traveling along the Duke's Road at dusk was clad in the height of fashion. His Hessians shown like black mirrors as he braced his legs against the floorboards of the sleek curricle. His pantaloons, form-fitting in the extreme as they flattered his long, muscular legs, were of the lightest fawn shade, a fine contrast to his midnight-blue jacket. His many-caped driving coat had been left open and was flung back over his broad shoulders, easing his touch on the reins.

Beneath the fawn-colored curly-brimmed beaver hat, his dark brown hair was a mass of artfully disarranged curls, two of which hung down over his brow. A fine aristocratic nose was nicely balanced between two clear blue eyes and above a wide, well-formed mouth. All in all, he looked to be just what he was, one of the foremost peers of the realm.

Yet this man, Duncan, Earl of Willoughby, had not the faintest idea why he was traveling the Duke's Road at this time of night. As a matter of fact, he did not understand why he was on the road at all.

He liked London. He enjoyed the people, the parties, and the general air of good feeling that had been prominent in the metropolis this past year, following Bonaparte's final rout at Waterloo and his dispatch to that tiny island. He felt he deserved to enjoy himself, seeing as how he had been gone from England off and on—mostly on—for nearly six years, either fighting the French, or chasing after them, or settling the articles of peace once the war was over.

He deserved his fine London mansion, his good friends, his splendid luck at cards, his not-too-demanding mistress, and his fine Viennese chef. Truly, he did. The sobering fact that none of these people or things were tucked up in his luggage as he tooled his curricle along the Duke's Road was partially responsible for the fierce frown that marred the Earl's otherwise handsome face. The remainder of that responsibility lay with the fact that ahead of him, not a mile off the Duke's Road, residing in *his* house, was his sister, the Lady Mary Knox, and her two pernicious offspring, Frederick and Bertrand.

"Damn and blast!" Duncan shivered in the comfortably warm spring evening, remembering his last visit home. His sister, the elder by three years and not quite one year a widow (dying was the only intelligent, wholly unselfish move his late brother-in-law had ever made, or so thought the earl), had been a thorn in his side since he was in leading strings and she had locked him in the cabinet under the servants' stairs, thus ensuring that she would get all the Christmas pudding delivered to the third-floor nursery.

Age had not improved their relationship or allowed the earl to see the past through rose-colored lenses. He couldn't abide his sister, simply could not abide her!

It didn't seem fair. He had provided his sister with a most lavish Season in London upon her come-out, and advertised a generous dowry to all who would listen, his way of assisting Lady Mary in finding herself a husband who would take her away—far, far away—from her loving brother. Forever. But Lord Knox had died, breaking his neck in a fall from a hunter, although not before he had frittered away every cent in the Knox coffers and at least ten thousand pounds more than he would have ever hoped to have seen if he had lived until a ripe old age.

That had left Lady Mary—and the twins; heaven knew Duncan couldn't forget the twins—adrift and penniless. Not that Lady Mary had worried overlong about her precarious financial condition. Within a fortnight of her sad bereavement she had descended upon the Rookery like a man-of-war in full sail, twins in tow, rigged out in funereal but extremely stylish black from her head to her toes and issuing orders with the cutting precision of the most fearsome officer of the line.

The servants had scattered to their quarters to regroup, and Duncan had abandoned the Rookery entirely, taking himself off to London, leaving his valet to follow along behind as best he could—vowing never to return.

And yet here he was, driving along the Duke's Road at a neck-or-nothing speed, trying his best to beat the darkness, heading for the Rookery.

Why? Duncan cast his mind back to the previous evening, trying to remember exactly how it had happened.

He had been preparing for an evening at the theater, followed by a private dinner with friends and some amiable gaming. A normal enough schedule of entertainment, in the midst of a normal enough Season. He had dressed in his new evening clothes, allowed one of the footmen to drape his coat across his broad shoulders, and had been about to place his hat upon his head when, suddenly, without warning, a vision of the Rookery had come flashing before his eyes, followed by a wave of nostalgia that rocked him to his toes.

The Rookery. His beloved home. The place of his youth. How lovely it would look in this season. Not smoky or sooty, like London. Not noisy or crowded. The air fresh and clean off the Channel. The birds soaring on the breeze, calling to their mates. Long walks along the cliffs. Long rides through the fields. Bucolic splendor. Scene after scene, memory after memory, called to him like a Siren song.

It had been so long since he'd been home. Too long. He missed the estate, his beloved home, so much that it had suddenly, unexpectedly, been difficult to breathe.

The theater had been forgotten, as had the private supper and a night's gambling. All he could think of was the Rookery, and how long it might take him to reach it.

He had been on the road within the hour, once more leaving his valet to follow along as best he could, filled with an anxiety to reach the Rookery as quickly as possible. Nothing else mattered, nothing.

It was only now, now that he was within a mile of that beloved home, that he had remembered his sister. And the twins.

"Damn, damn, damn!" he repeated, pulling expertly on the reins so that the matched pair of bays was neatly turned onto the gravel drive that led away from the Duke's Road. "But perhaps she has improved, mellowed with age. It has been nearly a year that her husband is underground. Perhaps she has put off that infernal black. Perhaps she is ready for a trip to Paris—or America. Anywhere she wants, and never mind the cost, as long as she goes and takes those infernal brats of hers with her!"

A minute later the Earl neatly brought the curricle to a halt in front of the Rookery, although he was still frowning. The sight of his boyhood home was usually enough to put a smile on his face and a spring in his step, but not tonight. Tonight his sister was in residence.

Tossing the reins to one of the grooms that had followed after him on foot as he passed by the stables, Duncan alighted from the curricle and bounded up the wide steps to the front door, seeking a measure of solace in the notion that he kept a fine wine cellar at the Rookery, laid down by his great-grandfather and grandfather. A bottle or two of wine with a late dinner of country ham and whatever else was in the kitchens should lend him the courage he needed to face Lady Mary.

He had taken three steps into the foyer, intent on heading for the main drawing room, before he noticed the young woman entering the foyer from the opposite direction. Had his sister hired a companion? *Hardly*. Duncan dismissed the thought barely before it had formed in his brain. Lady Mary (even in his thoughts he found it difficult to think of her simply as "Mary") had no need of a companion. She was a creature entirely sufficient unto herself.

A second conclusion, one he felt more certain of, entered his mind even as it escaped his lips. "Governess, aren't you?" he asked, removing his hat and bowing in the young woman's direction. "My condolences. Have they set fire to your hair, or are they saving that for some sort of grand finale, subsisting for the moment on lesser pranks such as tying all your clothes in knots, or slathering glue on your chair?"

"I—I beg your pardon," the young woman returned, her steps slowing as she came toward him, a look partway between interest and unreasoning fear marring her clear features. Now that he thought of it, the look of fear had already been on her face when he had first espied her, before she had caught a glimpse of him. And she was pale. Extremely pale, so that her hair, nearly black in color, seemed almost too dark, and her emerald eyes too green.

Pretty thing; not in her first youth, but appealing enough in her own way. "What's your name, girl?" he asked, as it appeared as if she had lost the ability to speak.

She didn't answer. She merely stood in front of him, her emerald eyes growing wider and wider until he thought they might pop straight out of her head. "You— you're the earl, aren't you?" she questioned at last, pointing a finger in his direction as if she were accusing him of some terrible wrongdoing. "*Our* earl—that is to say, the Earl of Willoughby?"

Yes, there was no question about it. The woman had to be the governess. And tending to the twins had sent her straight round the bend. Poor creature. Smiling kindly, Duncan said, "Right you are, my dear young woman. I am the earl. I know I am unexpected, but as I only last night thought to travel down here on the spur of the moment—I'm still pondering the why of the thing, to tell you the truth—there was no way to announce my intention to visit. Here, here—what did I say?"

The young woman had gone even paler, if such a thing was possible, and began to sway on her feet, so that Duncan feared she might swoon dead away into his arms.

Her finger continued to point in his direction, although it wavered slightly, as if her strength was rapidly deserting her. "You're him. I mean, Aunt Grizelda did *say* she had tried to summon—but who would believe such nonsense? *I* certainly wouldn't believe—I mean, it's *impossible*. Isn't it? Yet it couldn't be coincidence. Everyone knows you swore never to return as long as—but then, I do still taste the green-apple jelly, don't I? And there was no smoke. But eye of newt? I mean, *eye of newt?* Young Will? *Heloise?* No one believes in such things anymore. Oh, Lord . . . I don't think I feel very well . . ."

Duncan had been right to be concerned. A moment later his arms were full of fainting female flesh. It was an odd development, not to be looked for, but at least she had stopped babbling. And, surprise of surprises, something else unexpected had happened. He was smiling!

2

In which our players become aware of a Situation

"**B**UT my lady, if you would but come into the foyer—"

"And I told you, Rutgers, I don't care if it's the Prince Regent himself who has come to call. I have the headache, remember? I feel absolutely *beastly*, and have ever since I was so foolish this morning as to open the mail pouch and see all those plaguey tradesmen's bills stuffed inside. It was all I could do to push two slices of roast ham past my lips tonight. I cannot and *will* not see anyone, Rutgers—*anyone!*"

"Not even me, dear sister? I call that rather poor sporting of you, considering that it is I who will be paying all those plaguey bills."

Lady Mary, who had been reclining on a lovely blue-and-white-striped satin settee, a lace handkerchief draped lightly over her eyes, leaped to her feet with an alacrity that belied both her claim of the headache and her seven and thirty years. The sight that met her eyes was one of a well-dressed—excellently dressed, *superbly* dressed—sophisticated London gentleman. He was young, tall, darkly handsome, and appeared to be so much at ease that her teeth immediately began to ache. "Duncan!" she exclaimed in accents of disbelief. "Can that possibly be you?"

"Why, yes, dear sister, as a matter of fact, I believe it could," the earl said affably, for he had espied a nearly

228

full decanter of brandy on the drinks table and made for it even as he looked in his sister's direction, suppressing a shudder as he did so.

She hadn't changed a hair (or, as he had feared, her funereal mode of dress), and was quite obviously the same Lady Mary he had known and avoided all these years—although she had put on about a stone, most of it concentrated on her always ample hips. Her brownish hair, the little he could see of it, was tucked up beneath a starched white cap that tied beneath her chin—causing her to resemble an overgrown baby—and her completely unpainted face held the same ashen lips and startlingly black eyes. Once, she had held the power to intimidate him—reminding him so very much, so very depressingly, of their dear, departed father. Tonight, however, he seemed to see her as she really was—an unlovely mass of feminine anxieties and bluster, a beast without fangs.

Duncan winced and quickly poured himself a generous three fingers of brandy. "Is this the same headache that plagued you when I saw you last, or have you grown tired of that one and traded it in for another?" he asked, turning from the drinks table, cradling the snifter in his palm to warm it. "That headache, I recollect, came as a result of your unfortunate circumstances in having been relegated to the Rookery."

"Oh, shut up, Duncan," Lady Mary said, sniffling into her handkerchief. "You are so smugly healthy. You can have no idea what it is to be a woman, what it is to suffer the way we females are made to suffer. No idea at all."

He took a sip of the brandy and paused, eyes closed, to savor the taste on his tongue. How strange. He didn't feel in the least intimidated by his sister anymore—even with her rigged out to look like a scavenging crow. Life, he realized suddenly, was wonderful—time and distance having somehow combined to prove that, at last, he had become the man he wanted to be. He had been that man everywhere else for years and years—just not in his own home, when confronted with his headstrong older sibling. She had dominated his life before her marriage. Why had he thought she could still dominate it all these years later? Silly notion. They were neither of them the same people they had been when last they had shared this roof. Whole years had passed. A lifetime of years.

Duncan raised the snifter once more, deciding that his emancipation called for another drink. "Well, you've got me there, I must admit, dear sister. I am totally ignorant of a woman's sufferings. I only pay their bills when they attempt to alleviate those terrible sufferings with an orgy of shopping. Tell me, how much have these peculiar, particularly female travails set me back this time?"

Lady Mary tilted her head to one side, assessing her brother with anxious eyes, for something in his tone had alerted her to the notion that he, and not she, had assumed command of this conversation. He seemed to have gained some consequence not obvious to her before—probably in large part due to the fact that he, thanks to her late husband's lamentable lack of foresight, now held the purse strings. "Have you eaten, Duncan?" she asked, convinced that a diversion was in order. "I believe we might have something left in the kitchens to tempt your palate."

"Changing the subject, Mary? Oh, dear, that is ominous. Will I have to mortgage the Rookery? Or would it be sufficient for me to sack the governess and economize by having you ride herd on the twins yourself?"

Now Lady Mary was indeed confused. "Miss Brawley? You have seen to keep yourself distant from the Rookery for nearly a year, and all you can find to talk about when we meet again is the *governess?* Duncan—I don't understand."

He stood in front of his favorite chair, motioned for his sister to be seated, and then sat down himself, carefully spreading his coattails in his most elegant, gentlemanly fashion. "Neither do I, dear sister, but as I had your Miss Brawley fainting into my arms not ten minutes ago in the foyer, I thought we might bring her into the conversation for a moment. Does my allowance to you stretch to feeding her? I hate to think she might have been delirious with hunger."

"Don't be ridiculous, Duncan," Lady Mary snapped, raising a hand to her head only to realize that her headache had become a thing of the past. There was never any time for her own pain when her darling boys could be in danger. That's what being a mother was all about—fighting past her own pain for the sake of her offspring. "But she may be sickening for something, I suppose. I'll have to isolate her from the twins at once. Bertie sniffles so easily, you understand."

Duncan crossed his legs and leaned back negligently in his chair. He was really beginning to enjoy himself. "Bertie sniffles *incessantly*, dear sister. If I recollect correctly, that is how I tell the little demons apart. And don't worry about my stomach. Rutgers is bringing a tray to my room in fifteen—no, ten minutes. But first, could we possibly get back to this Miss Brawley person of yours? Does she by chance suffer from flights of fancy?"

The matter of the trademen's bills seemingly forgotten and her brother's dining plans already in place, Lady Mary was more than pleased to divert the conversation in Miss Brawley's direction. "Why, yes, brother, as a matter of fact, she is. Only imagine. The other day she suggested that Freddie might be hiding her tinderbox in his room. She wanted to launch a search—as if I could allow such an invasion of the boy's privacy. I think she means that he might burn the Rookery down around our heads, for heaven's sake! As if the child would do such a thing. I soon disabused her of that notion, I tell you. My Freddie is an angel. Both my boys are angels." Having made that pronouncement, she added, frowning slightly, "And I'm sure that little blaze in the library yesterday was purely accidental. Just a few books, and a bit of one drapery. Nothing serious."

Duncan resisted the impulse to roll his eyes in disbelief. If nothing else, this small chat with his sister was going a long way toward easing his mind over the "why" of his sudden impulse to travel down to the country. Obviously his love of the place had knocked on the door of the deepest recesses of his mind, reminding him that he had, in a moment of incredible stupidity undoubtedly brought about by his concern for her widowed state, allowed his sister and her pernicious offspring to run tame on his best-loved estate. It was only a wonder that his unconscious mind hadn't jabbed him long since into realizing that he was needed at the Rookery. Moreover, it was beyond all that was wonderful that this same estate was still standing. He had been fortunate not to come tooling up the drive to see blackened chimneys, crumbled walls, and little else of his boyhood home.

"Duncan? You haven't said anything. Surely you don't believe Miss Brawley's assertion? You do! Don't bother to deny it! You do! You never did like Freddie—not since that day he mistook your pistol for a toy and shot down the chandelier in the dining room in Portman Square. He told you he was sorry. I never imagined you'd be so small as to hold a grudge, Duncan."

He rose, consulting his pocket watch. "And that small I am not, dear sister. However, having a grown woman babble about newts and swooning into my arms within seconds of my arrival is not conducive to convincing me that everything is wonderful here at the Rookery, missing tinderboxes and library blazes notwithstanding. Therefore, I shall be expecting Miss Brawley in my study at ten o'clock tomorrow morning."

"But interviewing Miss Brawley is my domain, brother," Lady Mary protested, feeling the rein of command slipping further through her fingers. "There is no need for you to trouble yourself with such mundane matters."

"Ah, dear sister, but I cannot allow someone in your enfeebled condition to so strain yourself. Not and remain a gentleman." He bowed and headed for the door, not bothering to hide either his smile or the new spring in his step. "I will be going to my rooms now, Mary."

He turned, putting his fists on his hips, to survey the drawing room. "Damn and blast, but I'm happy to be home. I should have done this months ago! I can't imagine why I ever left in the first place. You may reconvene that headache now, if you so desire, dear sister. Good night."

Arabella woke a few minutes after dawn, an action that surprised her, for she was sure she would have perished of shame sometime during the night, then laid quietly as the rest of the household staff rose and left the servants' wing, to go about the business of beginning another day.

She didn't know how long she could lie here before Lady Mary summoned her, chastised her, and turned her off without a recommendation, but she wasn't about to move until she had to do so. Perhaps they would forget her, and she could just stay in this bed, hiding her head beneath the covers, until she curled up and died.

Hour after hour passed as Arabella berated herself for her behavior of the past evening. How could she have carried on like such an hysterical nodcock? Nodcock! No, that was too tame a word for it. She had behaved like an idiot! A fool! A totally brainless twit!

Yes, she had been unnerved by her encounter with Aunt Grizelda—or, rather, her encounter with the workings of her overactive imagination, for surely she had dreamed that entire interlude on the cliffs. But being unnerved was a far cry from rushing into inane, incomprehensible, and mindless speech when presented with the Earl of Willoughby.

What *was* the man doing at the Rookery? Stupid question. He *owned* the estate. Why shouldn't he visit the place?

Unless her imagination had conjured up the earl as well? No, that would be too wonderful. He had been in the foyer last night all right, and she had fainted straight into his arms—but not before she had spouted a mouthful of gibberish that would have sent any sane person running for a straight waistcoat and calling to the servants to have a carriage set-to for a fast gallop to Bedlam.

Yes, the man had definitely been the Earl of Willoughby. Arabella had tiptoed into his private study on more than one occasion, to look up at his portrait that hung above the fireplace. She had been intrigued by the twinkle in his blue eyes that the artist had captured on the canvas, as well as the slightly devilish smile that seemed to mock her as she stood below the painting, admiring the view. She had even, as of late, begun to talk to him, warning him that he had better soon show his face at the Rookery, before Freddie and Bertie demolished the place.

That was how she had recognized him last night, by the twinkle in his eyes. If he really had been there. If anything that had happened last night had been real. If Aunt Grizelda had been real. *Especially* if Aunt Grizelda had been real, and if Aunt Grizelda really was a—

There was a knock on the door and a moment later Sara, one of the housemaids, poked her head inside the door. "Mornin', miss," she said as Arabella hopped from the bed, drawing on her dressing gown. "His lordship wants ta see ye 'bout ten, iffen ye be up ta it. Ye feelin' more the thing now, miss? Thought ye'd died last night, truly we all did. Rutgers said ye were ever so heavy when he carried ye up the stairs. Ain't had such a rare treat round here since Cook dropped a pot on her toe and tumbled inta the fireplace."

"Thank you, Sara," Arabella replied, knowing she was blushing. "You and Rutgers and everyone else are all very kind. I am fine now, truly. Um, where is his lordship?"

"In his study, miss. He said ta let ye sleep in this mornin', which I did, fer it isn't often us workin' folk gets ta rest our noodles past six, but ye'd best be up now." Sara turned to leave, then added in a kind tone, "Excuse me, miss, but who's Aunt Grizelda? Rutgers said ye were goin' on about her somethin' terrible last night. Someone from yer family, I suppose? Did she die or somethin'?"

"No," Arabella answered quietly. "She didn't die. As a matter of fact, I just met her. Sara—do you know of any cottages in the woods, I mean, in the weald near the cliffs?"

"On the estate, miss? Here, at the Rookery?"

"Yes, Sara. Here, at the Rookery."

Sara shook her head, eyeing Arabella as if she had suddenly shown signs of becoming dangerous. "Nary a one, miss. The earl wouldn't allow it, would he? This bein' his land and all. Um, miss—are ye sure ye be up ta seein' his lordship?"

Arabella merely smiled. It seemed safer than opening her mouth again, thus taking the chance of landing herself in more trouble.

Within moments of seeing Miss Arabella Brawley again his lordship concluded that things at the Rookery were looking better with each passing moment. She was wearing a simple morning gown of green-and-white sprigged muslin, for one thing, which was a welcome change from the depressing black of his sister's wardrobe, and her young, fresh face seemed to bring sunlight and new life into his study.

And he could not help but remember how she had felt in his arms, her young body so sweetly curved, yet light as a feather as he had scooped her up, high against his chest, before reluctantly delivering her over into Rutgers's care. She had smelled sweetly of apple blossoms, as he recalled. Apple blossoms and innocence.

"Good morning, your lordship," she said now, rousing him from his reverie, her voice soft and well-modulated— a sharp contrast to its rather hysterical tone of the previous evening. "You asked to see me?"

"Indeed I did, Miss Brawley." The earl motioned her to be seated in one of the large burgundy leather chairs that stood like accenting commas on either side of the fireplace, then took up his position behind its mate, leaning his long frame against its back as he visually inspected her. "You are looking much recovered this morning. I imagine that means that you have not as yet encountered my nephews."

Arabella nodded, unable to keep her gaze from darting to the portrait over the fireplace and then back to the earl, realizing that the artist had not been as brilliant as she had supposed, for he had failed utterly in capturing the full force of the earl's charms. The man was more handsome than she had expected, even more so than he had looked last night, standing big as life in the foyer, draped neck to boot-tops in his driving coat. Memories of her daydreams that had a lot to do with a magical prince— a prince looking very much like the man now smiling at her with what seemed to be genuine compassion—coming down to the Rookery to rescue her from the twins brought a rush of hot color into her cheeks.

The sobering thought that Aunt Grizelda, this figment of her clearly overstimulated imagination, had told her that she had attempted to summon him to the Rookery expressly in order to "rescue" her, effectively erased that same color.

"No, your lordship, I have not yet mustered sufficient courage to climb to the nursery," she admitted honestly. "No doubt they will soon be forced to amuse themselves by trussing up the nursery maid and dangling her out the window by her shoestrings, so bored they will be that I have not yet appeared to give them their history lesson. We are studying English history at the moment and, to my horror, Bertie is showing an inordinate interest in beheadings."

"So, they diversify, I see." Duncan came around the chair and sat down. "I thought Freddie was into burning the place down this week. Or have you been able to confiscate the tinderbox?"

"I suppose Lady Mary told you about that," Arabella said, smiling yet again. It was easy, almost too easy, to talk to this man. "I am sorry about the damage to the library, your lordship, but yes, I have the tinderbox back—and under lock and key." Her smile wilted marginally as she added, "I am truly sorry for my behavior last evening, your lordship. It was unforgivable. I can only say that I have been under a tremendous strain these last months, attempting to deal with Freddie and Bertie, and must have suffered an overset of nerves. I actually believed, only for a moment, you understand, that I met a wi—an elderly woman, a woman with the most odd way of speaking, last night while I walked along the cliffs. Silly, isn't it, for we are quite isolated here at the Rookery and no one on the estate is a stranger. Because of this incident of imagination I have determined to seek other employment before I slip my wits entirely and begin to imagine that I can talk to the angels."

"Please, don't apologize. We shall speak no more of the incident, Miss Brawley, for I quite understand," Duncan said, dismissing her explanation with a wave of his hand. "But I do understand your intention to leave the Rookery. Riding herd on Freddie and Bertie would, I imagine, be enough to have you seeing pink elephants and dancing bears."

She leaned forward, his understanding of the pressures under which she was asked to perform prodding her to put forth the question that had been bothering her ever since she came to work there. "Why, sir? It is the height of impertinence for me to ask, I know, but why do you allow them to stay here, terrorizing everyone? The Rookery has got to be the most beautiful estate in all England. Rutgers has told me that it is also the best-loved estate of all your holdings—your childhood home—yet you have steadfastly refused to visit while your sister and her children are in residence. Is there no other place to put them?"

Duncan laughed out loud. "Impertinent, Miss Brawley? Perish the thought. It is a question I have asked myself often, most especially since viewing the damage to my library this morning. Do you, perhaps, have any suggestions that might help me dislodge my sister from what is, alas, also *her* childhood home?"

Arabella, who knew herself to be leaving this place just as soon as she could arrange another position, ventured boldly, "Marriage, sir? Lady Mary's year of mourning is almost over, and there is a gentleman living nearby, a Sir Harold Yates, who has been seen visiting here several times these past weeks. If he were to get wind of a substantial dowry—"

"Oh, Miss Brawley, I knew I'd like you!" Duncan leaned forward conspiratorially. "But don't you dare go running off, my dear girl. Not while I am still in residence at least, for we have to stand together if we are to defeat my sister's intention to take over the Rookery for life. Tell me more of this Sir Harold and, if this glimmer of an idea just now flickering to life inside my skull works out, *you*, dear Miss Brawley, may never have to work again!"

They smiled at each other then, two near-strangers now very much in charity with each other, so that Duncan found himself struggling not to lean even further forward, to sniff at the elusive fragrance of apple blossom, or even to dare to steal a kiss.

Arabella seemed to sense his mood, her beautiful green eyes softening as she remained very still, as if awaiting his next move. Possibly even anticipating his next move.

Time very obligingly stopped as Duncan debated his better self, sure that he should not be taking advantage of this young woman, yet not really able to convince that same better self that he was sufficiently in control of his baser instincts to draw away.

"Duncan!"

Both Arabella and Duncan leaped to their feet at this shotgun burst of shrill feminine exclamation, nearly colliding as they turned toward the doorway.

"Duncan! Come at once!" Lady Mary exclaimed, racing toward him, her black dressing gown, hanging open over her equally dark nightdress, flapping behind her. "My boys! Oh, my dearest, dearest boys! They are afflicted! Do you hear me, Duncan—they are *afflicted!"*

"Lady Mary," Arabella implored, ushering the over-wrought woman to a nearby chair, "please. You must calm yourself. How are Freddie and Bertie afflicted? Are they ill? Do they have fevers?"

"Fevers? Ill?" Lady Mary searched in her pocket for a handkerchief, forestalled only when Duncan considerately offered his own before taking up a pose in front of the fireplace, safely out of the line of fire. And he had worried that the country might seem boring after the hustle and bustle of London? Silly man.

"If only it were that simple," Lady Mary continued. "No, it is worse. Much worse! They have been cursed. Peggy—" She reached up to take hold of

Arabella's wrists. "—you know—that thimble-headed nursery maid—says there has been a curse put on them. And indeed, I can think of no other explanation. Oh, what to do, what to do!"

Duncan pushed himself away from the mantel, barely containing a chuckle as he watched his sister and Arabella. His sister's histrionics he dismissed, for she had ever been the dramatic sort, but Arabella's almost comical look of dismay was really quite humorous.

"Could—could they possibly be funning with you, madam?" Arabella asked, her tone more than passably hopeful. "You know how inventive the twins can be when they put their heads together."

"A curse, dear sister?" Duncan commented when his sister did not answer, cautiously approaching the ladies. "How very intriguing. Tell me, how is this curse manifesting itself? Have they been turned to stone, or are they spouting Greek and rolling their eyes?"

"You—you are familiar then with curses, brother?" Lady Mary immediately released Arabella's now-nerveless hands to turn to Duncan, a faint glimmer of hope flaring in her otherwise dark eyes. "Oh, thank heaven you are here! Come with me now, brother, and see for yourself. Perhaps you have been sent here purposely by a kind Providence, to save my poor darlings."

"A fair Providence? Mary, please, contain yourself," Duncan protested as his sister made as if to take his hand, probably to pull him pell-mell up the stairs to the nursery at the top of the house. "Just tell me what has happened to the boys. What are they doing that makes you think they have been cursed?"

The handkerchief came into play once more as Lady Mary, belatedly remembering that she was a delicate, high-strung lady who really should be calling for her hartshorn and burnt feathers, collapsed into the chair once more, furiously fanning herself. "Freddie has lost the power of speech, brother. Completely and totally lost it! He opens his mouth, his eyes all but bulging from his head as he tries desperately to communicate with me—his beloved mother—but the only sound he can make is to croak. Like this—*ribb-itt, ribb-itt, ribb-itt*. Oh, Duncan, it is terrible. He sounds just like a frog! And if Peggy, the ungrateful chit, doesn't stop giggling each time my Freddie tries to speak I will have her sacked!"

Arabella's eyes widened, a reaction Duncan did not miss. "Go on, sister dear. And Bertie? Does he also croak, or has he taken to bleating, like a sheep?"

The handkerchief fluttered once more as Lady Mary continued to labor under the nearly unbearable strain of reciting her children's afflictions. She sighed soulfully, then went on. "Bertie's condition is, if anything, worse. He woke this morning to learn that his lips had settled themselves into what seems to be a permanent pucker— as if he had spooned salt into his mouth or some such thing. Oh, Duncan, my poor baby looks just like a fish stranded on the beach! What will we do? What will we ever do?"

"Frogs—salt," Arabella murmured under her breath, so quietly that no one save herself heard. "*Aunt Grizelda.*"

"What was that, Miss Brawley?" Duncan asked, wondering if the strain of widowhood had finally gotten to his sister and she had slipped into some mother-love–induced insanity—a nasty turn of events that would do little to forward any romance he might have hoped for between Lady Mary and Sir Harold. "Do you have anything to add to this business about curses?"

Arabella pressed her hands to her chest. "Me? Do I have any notion of what caused the twins' distress? But how could I? I mean, who could think that *I* have anything to add to this unfortunate development? I am only a governess. I suggest we send someone into the village for the doctor."

"And this matter of curses?" Duncan persisted, certain he had heard her mutter something about an "Aunt Grizelda" last night, just before she had fainted. Yes, and something about newts, if his memory served him correctly. He could not help but wonder how Arabella felt this unknown woman might figure into things. "Do you, like the nursery maid and, it seems, my dear sister, believe the boys have been cursed?"

"Cursed, your lordship? Hardly. Why, if I were to believe in curses, it would stand to reason I also believed in witches, those cackling, humpbacked, warty-nosed creatures who stir cauldrons, keep cats as familiars, and wish misfortune on others. And we all know there are no such things as witches. Don't we, your lordship?" Her smile, beautiful as it was, did not quite convince him that she believed what she said. As a matter of fact, if he didn't know better, he'd think she was pleading with him to agree with her.

"*Witches!*" Lady Mary exclaimed, looking from her brother to Arabella, and then back again before continuing in an awed whisper, "Oh, my stars— why hadn't I thought of it? Brother—the worst has happened. The absolute worst! Aunt Grizelda has come back!"

Duncan's head came up with a jerk and he looked straight into Arabella's wide green eyes, figuratively pinning her to the spot on the carpet upon which she now stood, while showing every indication that she really did not wish to be standing there at all. "Aunt Grizelda, dear sister?" he questioned, still staring at Arabella. "The name sounds vaguely familiar, yet I don't believe I can place it. Pray tell, exactly who is this Aunt Grizelda?"

"Don't you know anything, brother?" Lady Mary fairly spat, standing up so abruptly that she nearly clipped his chin with the top of her head. "She's a witch, of course. She shows up every generation or so, expressly to bedevil the people who live at the Rookery. It's all in the family history—look it up for yourself. For now, I must go to my babies."

"I'll go with you, madam," Arabella offered quickly, avoiding his lordship's eyes.

And with that, Lady Mary quit the room, calling loudly, "Mama's coming, my darlings. Never fear, Mama's coming!" Arabella was hard on her heels— leaving Duncan to wonder if the whole world had run mad.

3

Wherein the plot proverbially thickens

DUNCAN had risen before dawn, intending to watch the sun rise over the estate. Dressed in comfortable trousers, a comfortable white shirt, and with a hacking jacket tossed over one shoulder, he set off on foot for his favorite walk, the path that led along the cliffs, reaching the area just as daylight broke through the mist.

Stifling a yawn, he looked out over the sea, trying to marshal his thoughts. In truth, he hadn't slept very well, spending half the night reading through several volumes of the family history, marveling over repeated references to a woman named Aunt Grizelda, and wondering why his papa had never deigned to warn him of the woman's intermittent presence. Although, now that Duncan thought of it, his papa hadn't been the most talkative of parents, preferring the company of his peers to that of his only male child.

According to the histories, this Aunt Grizelda person appeared four times a century, and only for a space of one cycle of the moon, wreaking havoc all over the Rookery, although some of his ancestors seemed to believe she had not really meant to be destructive, but was only inept.

But inept at what? The histories were maddeningly vague, as well as impossible to believe. No one woman could exist in three separate centuries, at least no mortal woman. Which, of course, was how the legend grew, passed mostly from mother to daughter for, incredible as it seemed, Aunt Grizelda supposedly could be seen and heard only by females (as men, the earl decided, were made of sterner stuff and immune to such nonsense). And the legend was simple—or perhaps simpleminded. The conclusion drawn by his female ancestors, and obviously shared by his sister, was that Aunt Grizelda was a witch.

Duncan had visited the nursery yesterday afternoon at the insistence of his sister, to see that she had been correct. Freddie croaked like a frog whenever he opened his mouth. Bertie resembled a beached fish. After shaking his head and commiserating with Lady Mary over the sad plight of her beloved sons—the same little angels who had packed snow into his best riding boots last Christmas Eve—he had prudently escaped into the hallway as quickly as good manners dictated, to laugh soundlessly until his sides ached.

But he had sobered at last, remembering that Miss Arabella Brawley hadn't found any humor in the twins' dilemma. Not by a long chalk. And why should she? Although she had done her best to deny it, it was Miss Brawley who had actually seen Aunt Grizelda.

No. She hadn't seen Aunt Grizelda. There was no Aunt Grizelda. Sad as it was to contemplate, Miss Brawley was no more than another hysterical female. And he had harbored such hopes in that direction, admiring her beauty, appreciating her high opinion of the Rookery as well as her low opinion of Lady Mary and the twins. Why, she had even offered him a possible way out of his current problem, that of boosting his sister off the estate by way of the marriage bell.

Duncan found himself almost wishing there really were an Aunt Grizelda, for then he could continue to develop his friendship with Miss Brawley without fear that he would be wooing a woman with goose feathers for brains.

He abandoned his gloomy thoughts to watch a trio of noisy gulls circle over the narrow spit of sand at the base of the cliff, intent on finding themselves some breakfast among the sea life that hadn't had time to safely burrow out of reach beneath the surface of the beach. How long he sat there he could not know, for he seemed to have misplaced his pocket watch somewhere in his dressing room, but he couldn't have been there more than a quarter hour before the enticing aroma of brewing coffee came to him on the morning breeze.

Lifting his head, he sniffed again. Coffee? Not very likely. He was too far from the house to smell coffee brewing and, as he well knew, there wasn't another residence within miles of the place. Yet Miss Brawley—Arabella—had said something about seeing a cottage just inside that stand of trees over there. But no. It was impossible, no matter what his ancestors had written in the histories. The whole idea was farcical.

Abandoning his comfortable seat on the rock and his view of the sea, the Earl of Willoughby determined to follow his nose, still disbelieving that there was any such thing as an Aunt Grizelda, but not quite as sure as he had been only a few moments earlier.

"Thank you, Aunt Grizelda," Arabella said, gingerly accepting the mug of steaming coffee. Saying no to the woman seemed to be an exercise in futility, so that

Arabella had agreed to have coffee, and more scones with green-apple jelly, hoping that once they had eaten the old lady would answer a few questions for her.

Arabella had sneaked away from the Rookery just before dawn this morning, not really sure she knew what she wished to find when she stepped into the stand of trees near the cliff walk. Finding the cottage again had gone a long way toward convincing her that she had not in truth slipped her wits, but to learn once and for all that she had indeed seen and spoken with a witch last night wasn't the sort of knowledge that lent itself to maintaining a sound mental state. It smacked of the supernatural, after all. And herself, the daughter of a minister!

But seeing the twins in such a quandary, while an amusing enough spectacle for a space considering the horrors they had put her through these past four months, had touched Arabella's kind heart. Besides, Lady Mary's hand wringing and hysterical lamentations were upsetting the entire household. If there really was an Aunt Grizelda, and the woman really was a witch, it wasn't a far leap of imagination to decide how Freddie and Bertie had come to be afflicted with such unusual maladies. Freddie had put a frog in Arabella's bed. Bertie had laced her sugar with salt.

And Aunt Grizelda had said they should be made to suffer a taste of their own medicine!

Aunt Grizelda who, Arabella recalled, couldn't "make" her churn produce butter for her because "of something I said." As a matter of fact, to listen to her tell it, if Aunt Grizelda was a witch, she was a sadly incompetent purveyor of the dark arts. Therefore, a frog in one's bed could easily become a frog in one's throat, and a tart taste might readily become a sour face.

"How are the twins this morning, Arabella?" Aunt Grizelda asked now, her eyes twinkling as she took up her seat in the other rocking chair. "I removed the spell at dawn, but I do hope they have learned their lesson. I know I should have if I discovered a dozen frogs in my bed or tasted sour for sweet."

"Oh, dear." It was no longer possible to deny the obvious. Arabella had been right. Lady Mary had been right. The histories had been right. All the way to the cliff path Arabella had been hoping, praying, that this was all a dream, a bad dream—a nightmare!—but it was all true. Aunt Grizelda was, Lord help them all, a witch. And, according to what Lady Mary said she had read in the family histories, Aunt Grizelda was to be in residence at the Rookery until the next full moon.

"Um, Aunt Grizelda," Arabella ventured, deciding if she was already in for a penny she might as well be in for a pound, "you're a witch, aren't you? I mean, that's the only explanation that makes any sense." She added, somewhat under her breath, "If anything makes sense anymore."

Aunt Grizelda's smile was beatific. "How very clever of you, Arabella, to have found me out so quickly. I knew as soon as I saw you in my crystal ball that you were a knowing one. Yes, I'm a witch, although I doubt Hester, Heloise, and Maisie would say so. They're so much more talented than I, which explains why they have their stars and I am still earthbound. It's just that I have not quite gotten the knack of spells, you see. Sometimes they don't work out all that well. I am given another chance every quarter century to prove myself, but if I do not learn how to get my spells right in the space of one cycle of the moon, I am sent whirling back into the skies, to wander until the next quarter century. Arabella, I tell you, I am so very weary of spinning around in the middle of nothing. It makes me dizzy, for one thing. That's why this time I simply must get it right. At least three of my spells must come about exactly as I have planned them, or it's off into space I shall go in another three weeks."

"I see," Arabella said, not really seeing at all. First of all, she had thought all witches were mean, and Aunt Grizelda certainly was not mean. And second of all, while she was thinking about it, she had never imagined that a witch could be termed incompetent. After all, what made a competent witch? Was there really some sort of test? Apparently so. If only she could say something to make Aunt Grizelda happy. "Would it help you to know then that the earl is currently in residence, having driven down from London without knowing why he felt bound to do so?"

Aunt Grizelda's round face lit in a grin as she clasped her hands together in glee. "I did it! I did it! That's one spell that worked! Oh, Arabella, I shall surely earn my star this time. I came within Ames ace of my star in 1666, but missed out when my spell meant to create lighted streets for people traveling about after dark led to that little blaze in London—"

"*You* are responsible for the Great Fire?" Arabella asked, completely appalled. "But that's terrible!"

Aunt Grizelda had the grace to blush. "I imagine so, although the residents did erect a lovely monument at the very top of Fish Street Hill when it was over, as if the fire had been a good thing. And Sir Christopher Wren did a wonderful job rebuilding the city, or so I'm told. Of course Hester did not agree with my declaration that, all things considered, I had done a good thing. That's when I was permanently confined to the Rookery during my excursions on Earth."

"I—I'm sorry," Arabella said, unable to think of any more intelligent rejoinder.

"I'm not. I like it here well enough. But enough of past glories. Tell me—did Freddie wake yesterday to frogs in his bed? And Bertie—did he taste sour for sweet each time he ate? My, my. That would be three then, the earl and the twins. Unless they count the twins as one, which is just the sort of thing Heloise would do. But I must be prepared. I should be packing, shouldn't I, if I am going to be called to my star."

Arabella winced, reluctant to burst the old woman's bubble of happiness. "Well, actually, Aunt Grizelda, it wasn't quite that way. Although you came close—truly."

"Oh, pshaw!" Aunt Grizelda exclaimed with some heat and reached down to pick up a large, dusty book that lay beside her on the floor. "What did I forget this time?" Opening the book on her lap, she began paging through it, her forehead creased in concentration. "Ah, this is the correct page," she said, running a fingertip down a page filled with—to Arabella at least, who was leaning sideways, surreptitiously trying to get a peek—completely indecipherable gibberish having something to do with hagstones and eel's tongues. "Here it is, Arabella," she announced, jabbing the page with her fingertip. "A tricky step, you understand. I must have gone wrong right about here. I should have found another word for the second verse of the incantation. But 'said' was the only word I could think of that rhymes with 'bed' Don't tell me—I already know, my dear, for I am not entirely stupid. The frog landed in his throat, didn't it?"

She closed the book with a snap, sending a cloud of dust into the air. "A slip of the tongue, my dear. That's what did me in this time. I won't even bother to ask what went wrong with the spell I placed on the other young scamp. It's enough that I removed the spells this morning. Isn't it? Not that Heloise will count that. Oh, no, she never counts that sort of thing."

Arabella found herself nodding her head in an indefinite, apologetic sort of way. "I suppose. But you did get one spell correctly, Aunt Grizelda," she reminded the woman in hopes of brightening her mood. "You still have time to get two more—and then you can earn your star." Arabella was aghast, listening to what she was saying. What was she talking about? She was sitting here, calmly nibbling on a scone, discussing the finer points of witchcraft, just as if it were the most commonplace of occurrences!

"I have to get back to the Rookery now, Aunt Grizelda," she said, rising. "Lady Mary, happy as she must be to see that her children are back to normal, will still doubtless be extremely upset, worrying what you will do next. You *are* going to do something else, aren't you, Aunt Grizelda?" she ended in tones of amused resignation. "To earn your star?"

Aunt Grizelda bustled ahead of Arabella, to open the door. "Yes, yes, of course I am. I have already begun, as a matter of fact, although I doubt it will work out. After all, what can you think of that rhymes with 'watch'? Only I don't know exactly what else I should do." She tapped one pudgy finger against her cheek, then brightened. "Although I do make a tolerable love potion, if I must say so myself. That might be the ticket, rather than what I've planned. Arabella, child! Would you like me to mix one up for the earl, so that he will fall desperately in love with you? You could slip it into his wine. It would be ever so helpful to me, I vow it would."

Arabella took a moment to remember how handsome the earl was, how affable, how intriguing. She could think of worse fates than to have such a man fall in love with her. She had fallen half in love with his portrait before she had ever met him and learned that he was a very nice man. If Aunt Grizelda truly did have a way with love potions—but no! It wouldn't be honest. Besides, no matter how noble the witch's intentions, if she had indeed been struggling in vain to successfully perform three witchy acts in the space of one cycle of the moon for more than three centuries, heaven only knew what damage she could cause. Poor Lord Willoughby could end up falling in love with a potted plant!

"No, thank you, Aunt Grizelda," she said at last, dismissing the idea, not without a pang for what might have been. "But," she added brightly as another thought struck her, "if you truly would like to practice your mastery of love potions, I could suggest you brew one up for Lady Mary and one of our neighbors, a man named Sir Harold Yates. I know the earl would be extremely appreciative."

"Do you really think so? I shall set to immediately!" Aunt Grizelda abandoned her post at the doorway to snatch up a thin stick of charcoal, writing the name *Sir Harold Yates* straight onto one of the whitewashed walls of the cottage before opening a large leather strapped chest and digging through the contents, speaking as if Arabella had already departed. "Let's see. I shall need a large pot, and this bag of herbs, and . . . oh, yes—Archibald! Gather me up some nice cobwebs, please, and don't harm either Lucille or Gertrude while you're about it, else I shall have to find myself new spiders, and you know what a bother that can be." The top half of Aunt Grizelda's body nearly disappeared into the chest. "And I shall have to find some nightshade—just a touch—and three eggs from a white hen, laid just as the cock crows, and . . ."

Arabella didn't hear any more, nor did she wish to hear the remainder of Aunt Grizelda's list of ingredients. It was enough that one of the rush brooms that were stacked in the corner seemed to fly into life right before her eyes, skittering around the rafters, sweeping up cobwebs. She didn't even say good-bye. She just backed carefully out the door, turned on her heels, and began to run just as fast as she could.

She didn't get more than a few yards before crashing into something solid, nearly all the wind knocked from her lungs as two strong hands came out to steady her, keeping her from tumbling to the ground.

"I say, Miss Brawley, you really should be more careful when you run," she heard the earl say in his well-modulated voice. "You might hurt yourself. Is something amiss?"

"Amiss? *Yes!* No! I mean—*no*, of course not." Swallowing down hard on her sudden acknowledgment that, no matter what apprehension she had felt watching Aunt Grizelda gathering ingredients for her potion, she was now five times as apprehensive concerning her reaction to the touch of the earl's hands against her bare flesh. It took every ounce of fortitude she had not to throw herself into his arms and smother his handsome face with kisses. Appalled, she avoided his eyes. "And yes, my lord, you're correct. I could have ended by toppling over the edge of the cliff, like young Will nearly did, which would have been a most disastrous turn of events, as what would the esteemed Mr. Kean have done for a living without the chance to perform in *Macbeth?*"

"I beg your pardon?"

Now she had done it—opened her mouth only to spout gibberish worse than anything she might have been able to see printed in Aunt Grizelda's strange book. But he was *so* handsome. Could he hear her heart beating at twice its normal rhythm? She could. "Please, never mind me. I have not slept well, nor have I eaten very much this morning," she said quickly, daring to smile at him, her knees turning to water as she saw the little laugh lines beside his eyes. She should have had another scone. She was becoming absolutely giddy, her head spinning.

"Nor have I," the earl said, taking hold of her elbow in a most intimate way and guiding her a few steps away from the trees. "As a matter of fact, I have been spending the past ten minutes chasing an elusive aroma of brewing coffee in these woods. This business of a witch on the premises has us all edgy, I suppose."

"Coffee, my lord? Searching? But that's above all things silly. You should have located the cottage within moments, as it sits just behind us—*oh, Lord, not again!*" Sure enough, as Arabella had turned to point out the obvious, Aunt Grizelda's cottage, she saw nothing but trees.

She turned back to the earl with what she knew to be a rather sickly smile on her face, slipped her arm through his—oh, how that innocent touch made her fingers burn—and burst into rapid-fire speech. "Um, yes, well—never mind. Shall we go back to the house? Yes, yes, we should. What a splendid idea! We'll go back to the house. I'm sure you'll find a lovely buffet awaiting you in the morning room. My lord—shall we go?"

But the earl wasn't budging. Not that he pushed her away, for he didn't. He merely turned to face her, taking hold of both her hands and squeezing them, hard. "You saw it again, didn't you? The cottage, I mean. And Aunt Grizelda as well, I suppose. You did seem to appear in front of me from out of nowhere, now that I think back on it. Did you enjoy your coffee, Miss Brawley?"

Arabella hung her head, speaking into the bodice of her simple morning gown. "Yes. I saw her. We did have coffee—and . . . and some lovely scones. I'm sorry," she ended, raising her eyes to him. "Truly I am."

"I see," Duncan responded succinctly. "Then that much of the legend is true. Aunt Grizelda only appears to females. Strange as it seems, I find that I feel abused, not to be allowed to see this witch who has taken up residence on my estate. That seems rather unfair of the creature, don't you think?"

"Unfair to the *females*, yes," Arabella said, regaining some of her confidence and deliberately tamping down the urge to reach up and run her fingers through his dark curls. "It makes it that much easier for the males to laugh at all of it as nothing more than a recurring figment of feminine imaginations. No woman seems able to gain credibility easily—even a witch. It's not fair. And it isn't any great wonder that witches began making up love potions. It seems a fitting revenge on the male of the species, although in this case it might be of considerable help to us."

Duncan pulled on Arabella's hands, bringing them close against his chest, so that she found herself feeling hot and cold both at once. "Love potions? Could it be? Miss Brawley—Arabella—have you got Aunt Grizelda to consent to help us pop off m' sister?"

Arabella looked up into Duncan's extremely appealing face, breathing in the fresh, intoxicating scent of him and wishing yet again she'd had enough confidence in Aunt Grizelda to ask for a potion to slip into the earl's brandy. "Then you do believe in her, my lord? You don't think I'm insane for having seen her?"

"Insane? Is that why you avoided me all day yesterday, Arabella?" Duncan smiled, and Arabella's heart all but leaped from her breast at his casual and repeated use of her Christian name. Was he feeling what she was feeling? Even half of what she was feeling? No. That was impossible. Otherwise, how could he not be kissing her? "Why, my dearest young woman," she heard him say, "it is quite the opposite, I assure you. You seem to have great affection for the Rookery, and have volunteered to help me reclaim it by helping me bracket my sister to this Sir Harold person. That is not insane. That is wonderful. As a matter of fact—and I know I should not be saying this—I have not been so in charity with another person in my life. From the moment you appeared in the foyer, and most definitely from the moment you swooned so gracefully into my arms, I have been inordinately in charity with everything about you. Arabella—I know this is rather precipitate of me, but—"

"Yes?" she prompted when he suddenly fell silent. He *did* want to kiss her! She had never been kissed before, as being the daughter of a minister had served to convince the young men in her home village to steer clear of her, but she was sure the earl wanted to kiss her. Almost as much as she wanted him to kiss her. "But what, my lord?"

The earl stared at her for a long time, then released her hands, to slip one arm companionably about her shoulders. "But Miss Brawley—my dear Arabella," he continued, guiding her back along the pathway, "would you consider breakfasting with me this morning? We could speak more of this proposed match between my sister and Sir Harold, a man, you'll remember, that I have not as yet met."

Arabella's heart dropped to her toes, then rebounded slightly. Duncan wasn't attracted to her, he was only being gentlemanly. What was the matter with her, that she should even dare to think differently? "I should like that above all things, my lord."

"Please, Arabella. We are in the country now, where manners are more relaxed. I should like it if you were to call me Duncan."

"Yes, my lord—*Duncan*."

Duncan and Arabella disappeared around a curve in the pathway, heading in the direction of the Rookery.

A moment later two carroty-red heads popped out from behind a large tree not ten yards from where Duncan and Arabella had been standing.

"A witch?" Freddie questioned, looking toward the small cottage that sat nestled in the trees.

"Mama and Sir Harold? A love potion?" Bertie queried, his gaze following his brother's. "Mama was right. There *is* an Aunt Grizelda. Freddie, what are you thinking? You *are* thinking of something, aren't you?"

Freddie stood up very straight, briskly rubbing his hands together, and grinned as wickedly as only a twelve-year-old on a quest for revenge can. "Aren't I always, dear brother? Let's go! It's time we presented ourselves to our visitor and thanked her for showing us the error of our ways with that 'marvelous trick' she played on us yesterday."

4

"Double, double toil and trouble: Fire burn and cauldron bubble . . ."

THREE days passed in relative calm, with Lady Mary at last announcing herself recovered from her fright that had confined her to her rooms until she could be assured that her dear babies were once again right as trivets, these aforementioned "babies" curiously well-behaved, Duncan and Arabella rapidly developing an extremely amiable relationship (complete with undertones of friendship and overtones of mounting passion, thank you), and Aunt Grizelda being most conspicuous by her absence.

But then it takes a fair amount of time and bother to gather three eggs laid by a white hen just as the cock crows.

"Have I told you lately how very much I appreciate that you continue to believe in Aunt Grizelda? It is not every man who would be so amenable, especially as even I have not seen her lately."

Arabella put forth this observation as she and Duncan took their ease beneath an ages-old tree just beside the cliffs, the former delicately leaning her back against its sturdy trunk as the latter (a rakishly tilted chain of daisies adorning his dark curls) rested his head in her lap.

What a strange three days it had been for the two of

them. Neither could remember eating much of anything, or sleeping more than a few hours a night. They were happiest when in each other's company, and therefore spent most of each day together, Duncan's gentlemanly upbringing the only thing standing between himself and the nearly overriding urge to kiss Arabella until she was gasping for breath, and only Arabella's maidenly insecurities holding her back from declaring her love for him.

And it all seemed so blessedly normal to them both, not in the least out of the ordinary.

"I have always been known as the most generous of fellows, Arabella," he answered, grinning up at her. She was so lovely. Lovelier than Venus, Aphrodite— all the goddesses. If he died at this moment he would die happily, in her lap. "Especially when it comes to beautiful young ladies."

"Wretch!" Arabella responded, laughing while lightly tapping the tip of his nose with her fingertip. She felt so entirely fortunate, so carefree, as if the world had narrowed to include only the two of them, as if they were two kindred souls that had been searching for each other over the years, only to have found each other at last. Talking with him, walking with him, seeing his smile, had become her very life and breath. Bless Aunt Grizelda for having brought Duncan to the Rookery!

"I have invited Sir Harold to dinner this evening, Arabella," the earl said, boosting himself to a sitting position and removing the daisy chain, to place it atop Arabella's ebony curls. "I've already informed Mary of the invitation, and she is at the moment running about her chambers at sixes and sevens, deciding which of her dreary, funereal gowns would best serve to capture his interest. If only she would put off those horrid caps! You will join us, I hope? Although I am not a coward, I believe I should enjoy the support of your charming presence."

"But it isn't done, Duncan," Arabella responded reasonably, longing to help him. She would walk over hot coals for him, swim the deepest sea, climb the highest mountain. But she could not eat at his table. "I am governess to the twins, a servant. Lady Mary would be incensed, her sensibilities insulted."

"Hang Mary's sensibilities! If I want you to be at table with us, then you will be at table with us. I am the earl, and the Rookery is my estate. Or do you think I have been trifling with your emotions these last days?" Leaning toward her, he took her hands in his, his dark eyes eloquent with emotion. "I haven't been, you know. Arabella, I am painfully aware that I am rushing my fences, but we are neither of us children—not that you are old, precisely, so don't pull a face at me. We cannot either of us deny that there is an attraction, a very strong attraction, between us. An almost magical attraction. And it is time I set up my nursery. Just think of it. If I were to die tomorrow, Freddie—oldest of the twins by some five minutes, I believe—would inherit. It's a disaster not to be thought of. But that is not my only reason for asking this question. Arabella, I feel a great affection for you—a *great* affection—and I believe you return those feelings. And so, if you are feeling awkward about appearing at table as a governess, perhaps you will feel less so if you were to sit in a place of honor, as my affianced bride. You have to marry me, Arabella. It's the only answer to this longing I have for you—this love I have for you."

"Oh, Duncan," Arabella fairly gushed, ready tears springing to her eyes. It wasn't the proposal of her dreams, but she felt confident that Duncan had meant every word in the most flattering way, and she loved him for it. As he loved her. "I never thought, I never dared to dream, but—*magical?* You did say *magical*, didn't you? Why didn't I see it? Why didn't I understand? Oh, dear Lord—*no!*"

"*Pssst!* I say—*pssst!*"

Arabella's head jerked upward and she looked about, trying to locate the source of the sudden, extremely intrusive sound.

"*Pssst!* Over here, my dear. Over here."

"Arabella? Darling?" Duncan asked as Arabella frowned, casting her gaze into the shadow of the stand of trees. "What is it? No, don't tell me. It's the witch, isn't it? It's Aunt Grizelda. My God, I never thought of it before now. Can she see and hear everything we're doing? Damned uncomfortable thought, that, especially when a man's in the midst of baring his soul to the woman he loves. I don't appreciate that, Arabella. Really I don't."

Arabella nodded in embarrassed agreement, her heart breaking as she bit her bottom lip and continued to search the distance for some sight of the little old woman. If Duncan was embarrassed now, what would he feel when she told him that they had been the victims of one of Aunt Grizelda's spells? "I hear her, but I can't see her. I can't see her cottage either, now that I think on it. I always see it when I see her, and I've seen neither for three days. I had thought she was too busy mixing up the love potion for your sister and Sir Harold to take time out to entertain visitors. But we really need to talk to her, Duncan. *Really.* Aunt Grizelda? Where are you? What's wrong?"

"It's my crystal ball!" the disembodied voice of Aunt Grizelda returned, the sound so close that Arabella nearly leaped out of her skin. "It has gone missing."

"Your crystal ball is missing?"

"Her crystal ball is missing?" Duncan echoed, slightly intrigued, but more than a little put out that his proposal had been forgotten the moment Aunt Grizelda had come upon the scene. He'd much rather be nibbling on Arabella's shell-like ear—in *private!* "You *are* kidding, aren't you? The woman actually has a crystal ball? I see now that I haven't given all of this enough thought. Does she have a flying broom as well? You've seen her. Does she also wear a pointed black hat and have a wart on the end of her crooked nose?"

"Hush, Duncan, please," Arabella said, laying a hand on his arm, doing her best to ignore what, she realized now, must be her "unnatural" attraction to him. "Something is very, very wrong. Aunt Grizelda told me that first night that her crystal ball is her most important possession." She raised her eyes to the treetops, for it seemed that the witch was floating somewhere above her. "Aunt Grizelda? Why can't I see you or your cottage?"

"You can't see her either? Well, that's some small solace, I suppose," the earl said cuttingly, "considering that I can neither see nor *hear* her. You told me she isn't a very good witch. What did she do, accidentally cast a spell on herself?"

"Duncan," Arabella ordered, exasperated, and at last totally forgetting that she was speaking to the love of her life, "shut up. This is serious. Or are you forgetting that Aunt Grizelda has promised us a love potion for your sister? Besides, if Aunt Grizelda can't perform *two* more spells before the moon cycle is complete, she will be cast into space for another quarter century—*because one of her spells has to be undone!*"

"Really? Which one is that? I thought bringing me here from London was her only success so far. But you have a point about having Grizelda back in another quarter century, my dear," Duncan conceded, admiring the way her complexion deepened to a lovely pink in her agitation. He leaned over to kiss her cheek. "I don't think our children would much appreciate the visit. We must help her. Only you must promise to repeat to me everything our resident witch says, my darling, if you please."

"I will, Duncan," Arabella promised, looking deeply into his eyes, openly adoring him, yet knowing that her adoration, her nearly unbearable desire for the man, was, at least in part, undoubtedly the result of Aunt Grizelda's meddling. And if Duncan was also under a lover's spell, a lover's spell soon to be broken, this might be the last time they would be together. He had proposed to her? Confessed his love? Not truly. Why, left to his own inclination, he might not even *like* her. "You are wonderful," she told him fervently, tears stinging her eyes. "You do know that, don't you?"

"Ah, Arabella, on the contrary, it is you who are wonderful. And beautiful. And loving."

Arabella's head dipped close to his, longing for his kiss—one sweet remembrance. "Oh, Duncan—"

"Oh, Arabella—"

"Oh, *bother!* If you two are quite done billing and cooing, I should like to get on with this *important* issue," Aunt Grizelda said peevishly from somewhere above Arabella's head, effectively shattering the mood. Arabella dutifully repeated the witch's sentiments to her bewitched beloved, whose muttered response was, fortunately, for the most part unintelligible.

"Thank you, my dears. And now, down to cases," Aunt Grizelda pronounced, sighing. "My crystal ball is gone. Vanished! Disappeared just this morning into the air like thistles on the wind. And my book of spells with it! Luckily, I had already finished the love potion and placed some in your room, my dear. Look under your bed—or did I have it transported to your jewelry box? Oh, well, it's there somewhere—I'm sure you'll locate it. Just pour some in Sir Harold's drink and a similar measure in Lady Mary's glass. I have every expectation that they will then fall on each other's necks within the hour, declaring undying love. Such a pity. I had nearly got it right this time, Arabella, fulfilling my assigned quota of spells correctly, but without my crystal ball I shall never be allowed to gain my star. You see, how else do you think I am to light my star, my dear Number 417, if not for my crystal ball? Why, I cannot even materialize without it, nor make it possible for you to see my cottage. You know what I should have done? I should have pierced the thing, put a stout leather cord through it, and hung it about my neck! Oh, woe is me!"

"Your crystal ball does all that?" Arabella was truly concerned. Perhaps it would even be impossible for her to break the love spell she had cast on Duncan and herself. Arabella felt tempted, oh, so tempted, to leave well enough alone, but she knew she could not. Duncan must be told that they were not really in love, but only bewitched. But not yet. Not until Aunt Grizelda had been convinced that she must remove the spell. "Perhaps you have only misplaced it again, Aunt Grizelda," she suggested hopefully. "Are you *quite* sure you have searched the cottage thoroughly?"

At Arabella's well-meant but obviously not as well received question a bolt of white lightning sliced through the air, to split a nearby tree from top to root. "Sorry, my dear," Aunt Grizelda said a moment later, as Duncan clasped his beloved tight against his chest in a protective embrace, cursing under his breath. "Sometimes my temper gets the better of me, try as I might to be a good witch. And yes, of course I looked. I have looked, and looked, and *looked*. Besides, I know who took it. It's those dratted boys!"

"The boys? Do you mean to say that Freddie and Bertie took your crystal ball?" Arabella questioned, confused. Calling upon all her fortitude, she pushed herself out of Duncan's arms.

"It figures," the earl supplied drolly, brushing a few stray fallen leaves from the sleeves of his hacking jacket before looking at Arabella sharply. "Now, just a moment. I thought only females could see or hear Grizelda. How could the boys steal her crystal ball if they couldn't see the cottage?"

"Women and children, Arabella," Aunt Grizelda explained, and Arabella quickly repeated to Duncan. "I had the boys to tea the other day, to lecture them on good behavior. They seemed most receptive, so I invited them again this morning. I should have known better. Bertie stepped on my cat's tail when they had been in the cottage only for a moment. It must have been while I was tending to the poor dear thing that they filched my crystal ball and book of spells. One moment I was petting my dear cat, and the next I was all alone in my cottage as it floated above the treetops, the boys visible below me, running lickety-split toward the Rookery. I have been powerless ever since."

Arabella pointed to the lightning-blighted tree. "Powerless, Aunt Grizelda? I think not."

"Pshaw," the witch countered. "That was nothing, a truly piddling display. You know, like making things go thump in the night, and moving furniture, and all that silly business. I can still do that sort of simple parlor trick. Always could. I am, after all, a witch. But I cannot do spells, and I cannot get my star. Not without my crystal ball! The book is unimportant, but the crystal ball—ah, that is irreplaceable! Arabella, you and the earl must help me. *You must!*"

"Of course we will help you, Aunt Grizelda," Arabella declared feelingly, her heart going out to the old woman's plight—and her own. She turned to face her beloved, yet soon to be *former* beloved companion, whose frown was more contemplative than commiserating. "Won't we, Duncan?"

"Yes, yes, of course," he answered, absentmindedly committing himself to the project. Arabella was so beautiful, so generous, so willing to help others. The perfect female. The most wonderful creature the good Lord ever fashioned. Perhaps he could whisk her away from Grizelda's prying eyes for a moment and demonstrate how much he loved her. Kiss her rose-red lips. Touch her creamy skin. Lay her back against the grass and—

"Duncan? Are you going to help us or not?"

He sighed, the mood broken. "Only have Grizelda answer one question for me," he said peevishly. "Can Freddie and Bertie *do* anything with this crystal ball and book of hers?"

Aunt Grizelda's answer came swiftly, in the affirmative, and even went so far as to explain that there was nothing—or next to nothing—Arabella and Duncan could do to stop them as long as the crystal ball was in their possession.

"Damn and blast!" the earl exclaimed, pulling Arabella to her feet. Arabella had asked for his help, and he would slay this dragon for her or know the reason why not. But it wouldn't be easy. "We're in for it now! Arabella—tell Grizelda to come back to the Rookery with us, 'parlor tricks' at the ready! This, ladies, is *war!*"

Arabella was all but breathless by the time they entered the main drawing room through the French doors that led off the terrace on the east lawn, so that it took her several moments to recover herself, moments during which the earl blistered the air with curses that made her ears burn, calling the twins names usually reserved for the lowest soldier of the line.

The drawing room was upside down! Literally. Every carpet, each stick of furniture, from the matching satin settees to the drinks table, was stuck to the ceiling. The tops of all the decanters had become unstuck, so that the contents of those same decanters—some of the earl's beloved stock—made puddles on the bare floor.

"Oh, dear," Arabella said, suppressing a somewhat hysterical giggle. "This will make tonight's dinner party somewhat awkward, won't it, Duncan?"

"I'll kill them!" her beloved vowed with considerable heat, grabbing Arabella's hand as she stood, open-mouthed, surveying the scene. Together they raced to the foyer.

The furniture in the foyer was, fortunately, untouched. The same, however, could not be said for the three footmen who stood just inside the door, frozen into immobility, like statues in a waxworks. Arabella tiptoed cautiously to stand in front of one of them, waving her hand in front of his unblinking eyes. Nothing. She reached up to slap the fellow lightly on the cheek. The footman failed to react.

"Duncan?" She turned to look at the earl. "They—they seem to be breathing," she said encouragingly. "That is something, isn't it?"

"I don't understand it," said Aunt Grizelda. "I've tried that spell a dozen times—two dozen times—and it has never worked. Yet those dratted boys have mastered it, and the upside-down-room spell, in less than two hours. But don't worry, it will all wear off in a day or so."

The earl spun in a circle, his gaze darting a thousand ways at once. "I heard that. Arabella! I *heard* that! I can hear Grizelda!"

"You can?" Arabella questioned, relieved, for repeating everything the old witch said had begun to wear on her nerves.

"He can?" Aunt Grizelda repeated, clearly confused. "He shouldn't. I mean, you shouldn't, your lordship. Unless—"

"Yes, yes. Unless—go on, woman. I'm listening."

"Unless it has something to do with my being inside the Rookery. I've never been here before, you know. It's too large by half. I much prefer my cottage. Goodness, isn't this nice? Now we can all have a comfortable coze. I haven't spoken to any man save young Will in centuries. I can remember our last discussion as if it was yesterday. He was working on something having to do with Cromwell and ambition. He said—"

"Some other time, Grizelda," Duncan replied shortly, taking Arabella's hand once more, grinning at her. "And if either of you think I believe she meant William

Shakespeare, I suggest you think again. There are some things that pass beyond belief. Besides, right now we have to run Freddie and Bertie to ground before they can conjure up any more spells."

"Yes, dear," Arabella said meekly, knowing when to keep her thoughts to herself, although she agreed that the notion of Aunt Grizelda with the Bard was a rather difficult scene to contemplate with any degree of credulity. "Do you think we should check on your sister? They wouldn't have cast a spell on their own mother, would they?"

Duncan stopped midway up the first flight of the divided staircase to glare at her owlishly. "Arabella, think a moment. Given half the chance, they'd cast spells on *each other!*"

Upon entering his sister's room, however, it became abundantly clear that Freddie and Bertie had not yet been forced to descend to turning each other into toads. They hadn't had time. They had been too busy wreaking havoc—was it really havoc? Really?—upon their mother.

"Hello, dearest brother," Lady Mary said pleasantly, turning from her full-length mirror, where she had been avidly drinking in the glory of her reflection.

"Mary? Is that really you?" His jaw had dropped to half-mast at the sight of his sister. "You—you look *wonderful!*"

And indeed Lady Mary did look wonderful—if just a tad overdressed. Rigged out in a rose silk ball gown worthy of a Court presentation, she was also clad in ivory kid gloves that ended just past her elbows, a long, lovely double strand of pearls, and—unbelievably—her no-longer-graying curls were piled high atop her head and crowned by a diamond tiara.

"Look, dearest brother—only look," she said, extending one stout yet shapely foot for his inspection. "*Glass*, Duncan! My slippers are fashioned of sheerest glass!

Isn't it the queerest thing? I had been sitting at my desk, making an extensive list of new duties for Miss Brawley here—lovely child, isn't she?—when all at once I felt so odd, almost light-headed with a strange new happiness. I tore up the list, deciding that the boys shouldn't have any studies again until at least the fall. A few moments later I looked across the room, measuring the distance between myself and the bellpull, intending to summon the servants to give them all a three-pound raise in their yearly wage, when I caught a glimpse of myself in this mirror. Well, how can I tell you what I thought? I must have a million questions as to how this happened, but I vow I cannot think of a one. Not when I am so nearly overcome with love of my fellow man. I feel positively giddy with good nature."

A slight frown marred her unusually smooth features, and then she giggled. Lady Mary Knox, who, in Duncan's memory at least, had not ever found humor in anything, *giggled.* "Sir Harold is still coming to dine with us this evening, isn't he? He shall be so pleased to see that I have put off my black, for the good Lord only knows how often he has hinted that I should. The dear man fair dotes on me, you know."

"Duncan?" Arabella slipped a hand through his arm, leaning against him as if for protection. "Is she all right?"

"Oh, laws, of course she is," Aunt Grizelda answered, her voice seeming to come out of the heavens. "It's just the Cinderella spell. Mere child's play, although I have had some difficulty with the mice. None of them really like coaching, you understand. And pumpkins are out of season, although the boys may not have invoked the entire spell. It will all wear off when the clock has struck twelve—midnight, that is."

Lady Mary roused herself from her joyous reflections long enough to inquire sweetly, "And who is that speaking, dear Miss Brawley? Is there someone behind you perhaps?"

"Yes, Mary," the Earl supplied hastily, holding tight to Arabella's hand and already backing from the room, "there is someone behind us, in the hall. One of the servants. We—er, I am needed belowstairs. Please excuse us, won't you?"

Lady Mary returned to looking in the mirror, holding out her lovely rose silk skirts and tilting her head so that the sunlight coaxed small bursts of brilliance from her tiara. "Yes, yes, my dear. You go on now. I shall remain here until I am summoned for dinner."

The door to his sister's bedchamber had barely closed when Duncan let go of Arabella's hand and demanded, "All right, Grizelda! What's going on?"

"She mentioned the Cinderella spell," Arabella said quickly. "You remember the story, don't you? My mother told it to me as a child. It concerns a poor but beautiful young girl, sweet of disposition, who is cruelly treated by her stepsisters. A fairy godmother comes to her one night and—"

"I am familiar with the story, Arabella," Duncan interrupted testily, pulling her along the hallway.

"Ah, but do you know all of it?" Aunt Grizelda's voice seemed to travel along with them, hovering just above their heads. "It began in China, about the ninth century, I believe, then traveled slowly to the rest of the world— Germany, even France. Charles Perrault—such a good soul—finally wrote it all down for us only a little over a century ago, but in French. He couldn't say 'witch,' of course, or it would make the children cry, so he used 'fairy godmother.' We didn't mind for, although most of us are good, we know that the bad witches do cause more than their fair share of trouble. Anyway, when our story was translated into English the word *vair* was mistaken for *verre*, and poor Cinderella's fur slipper has been glass ever since. I can't imagine how the twins got it right the first time. Even Hester had a spot of trouble making that one work. Fur is much easier, you must understand, Duncan, what with the wealth of pelts to choose from here in—"

"I don't have to understand *anything*, Grizelda," Duncan cut in, assisting Arabella in climbing the staircase that led to the third floor—and the nursery. "All I have to do is feed your love potions to m' sister and Sir Harold while she is still being so amenable."

"No, no, no!" Aunt Grizelda protested in some agitation. "Now I know why we don't deign to appear for males—they're simply too thick to understand! The spells will all be undone at the very moment I have my crystal ball back in my possession. We cannot wait to rescue it. We just can't! Besides, if Lady Mary meets Sir Harold while she is being so conformable, we will never know if he falls in love with her because of my potion or the Cinderella spell, and then I'll *never* get my star. I am so close, dearest Arabella. So close. We must retrieve my crystal ball!"

Duncan was caught on the horns of a dilemma. If he understood correctly, rescuing the crystal ball (and the book of incantations—he mustn't forget the book, for heaven alone knew what the twins could do with it), would lift the spells the boys had woven from one end of the Rookery to the other.

The drawing room would turn right side up. That was good.

The footmen would break free of their statue-like state. That was good.

And his sister, so mellow, so in charity with the world, so unusually gentle on the eyes, would revert to her normal, depressing, harping self.

That was not good at all.

Oh, yes, there was this business about a love potion, the supposed answer to all his problems. But how could he put his faith in such a scheme when the woman who had mixed it up had been bungling her witching duties for several centuries? And if the potion didn't work, if

Sir Harold Yates did *not* fall in love with, marry, and take Mary away, what would happen to the earl's hopes to live a life of unfettered joy here at the Rookery, with his newly discovered yet deeply beloved Arabella by his side?

Yes, he could throw his sister out. He had that power. He could insist she transfer herself and her brood to one of his other estates, or even to London. It wasn't as if he was some knock-kneed looby who was afraid of a mere female. But he loved his sister—at least he knew he should. He wanted her happiness.

He wanted her *gone*, but he also wanted her happiness.

"Duncan?" Arabella prompted, tugging at his sleeve. "You seem a million miles away. Aunt Grizelda asked you a question. Are you going to get the crystal ball for her now?"

"Hmmm? Oh—oh, yes, of course." Duncan shook himself back to attention, remembering not only his promise but the condition of his drawing room. The crystal ball could not remain in the twins' possession for a single moment longer than he could help! "Grizelda!" he called, pushing past Arabella and heading for the door to the nursery wing. "Stay by my side at all times, if you please, and follow my lead."

"I will," Aunt Grizelda promised, her voice so close by his ear that the earl flinched. "But, as I will be going back to my cottage the moment the crystal ball is mine once more, I am afraid that we will have no further opportunities for speech between us. I wish to thank you for all your help while you can still hear me. I mean, if it weren't for you, my lord, I would still have only two spells to my credit."

"Aunt Grizelda—" Arabella began hesitantly. "About those three spells—do you think you could meet with me tomorrow morning to discuss them?"

"Certainly, my dear," Aunt Grizelda answered cheerfully, as it evidently had still not occurred to her that

Arabella didn't seem to be overjoyed to be the recipient of spell number two. "You can even help me pack for my trip. But now, my lord, do you suppose you might humor an old woman? As I already told you, I will not be able to talk to you once I leave the house. Could we perhaps say good-bye?"

Arabella squeezed Duncan's hand, wishing she could hold it forever. "Isn't that sweet? I think Aunt Grizelda has taken a liking to you."

The earl felt himself beginning to blush, a childish response he had given up at the same time he had forsworn short coats. "You are welcome, madam," he said gently, raising his eyes to a point near the ceiling. "And I thank you, for without your appearance I might never have had the pleasure of having my nephews' governess swoon into my arms, thus infinitely changing my life for the better. Good-bye, Griz—*Aunt* Grizelda. I'll look for your star."

Arabella and Duncan then proceeded through the doorway hand in hand, the sound of soft, witchy sniffling following behind them.

5

In which mayhem doubles, potions trouble, and love, at last, triumphs

THE nursery was still furnished as it had been the last time Arabella had seen it, but the room smelled strange—rather like wet puppies—and appeared to be dark and brooding, even though the sun still shone behind the oddly darkened windows. The walls seemed damp and dripping, and the air was cold and dank.

"When I get my hands on those miserable scamps . . ." Duncan ground out, allowing his sentence to drift off into nothingness.

Arabella swallowed down hard on her apprehension and tiptoed past Duncan, her head stretched forward on her neck, tentatively calling to the nursery maid: "Peggy? Peggy? Where are you, dear?"

There was no answer, unless one were to count the sudden fluttering of what seemed to be a rather large bat high against one corner of the tall ceiling. Quickly putting her hands over her hair, for everyone knows that female hair is a bat's most favored nesting place, Arabella retreated to cower behind the earl. Then, feeling somewhat silly, for she had long ago decided that a woman forced to make her own way in this world must necessarily be made of stronger stuff, she peeped around Duncan's waist to look more closely at the bat.

"Why, the thing has red pigtails—just like Peggy!" she exclaimed. "Duncan! They've turned poor Peggy into a bat!" Striding purposefully forward, so incensed she completely forgot that she could very easily become Peggy's companion on the ceiling if she took a misstep, she declared hotly, "This is the outside of enough! The drawing room was more than sufficient outrage, and to freeze the footmen into statues was definitely not nice— but this I will not stand for! Freddie! Bertie! Show yourselves at once!"

She had gone no more than three paces before Duncan grabbed her around the waist and pulled her back behind him. "Much as I admire your spunk, I'll handle this, if you don't mind, my dearest," he said firmly, before adding in a whisper, "Aunt Grizelda? Are you still with us?"

"Bats," Aunt Grizelda said, sniffing in disapproval.

"Mere child's play. And the air of wet dog. How infantile. Why anyone would wish to transform a room into a cavern is totally beyond me, I tell you, although I suppose it is the sort of spell that would appeal to young boys. Mere child's play, I say. I can't see why everyone is making such a fuss, as if they did something so out of the ordinary."

"Aunt Grizelda!" Duncan ground out from between clenched teeth. "Pay attention, if you please. This is no time to indulge in professional jealousy. Where are the twins? Can you see them?"

"Of course I can see them," the witch answered peevishly. "They are in the next room, standing just behind the door. And Freddie's holding my crystal ball," she added, sniffling once again. "Oh, that horrid, horrid child. I wish—I wish—"

"What do you wish, Aunt Grizelda?" Duncan asked, holding Arabella's hand as, together, they slowly progressed toward the doorway to the schoolroom.

"I wish I knew what I should wish!" Aunt Grizelda's voice was somewhere to the left of Duncan, so that he turned and smiled. A rather evil smile, Arabella noticed, wincing.

"I know what I wish, Aunt Grizelda. Now pay attention, because here we go," the earl said easily, then raised his voice as he continued: "I, Duncan Estherbrook, Earl of Willoughby and lord of this manor, call upon all the powers of the ancient kings that once roamed this great land. With a heritage of strength born of adversity and a power ten times ten more than that of any mere witch or her incantations, I command that this power come to me so that I might vanquish my enemies and restore order to my manor. Door!" he intoned heavily, pointing at the door to the schoolroom. "You offend me. *Begone!*"

"Duncan?" Arabella whispered, wondering if the strain of the past days, combined with the love spell, had at last proved to be too much for the man. She certainly knew that she was feeling none too good at the moment. But then, Duncan didn't know about the love spell, did he? "Are you sure you're quite all right?"

"Hush, darling," he returned quietly out of the corner of his mouth, his quick, loving wink making her want to sit right down in the middle of the room and wail. "Aunt Grizelda? You're on. Make it look good—blast that door to bits!"

"Bats with braids? Ridiculous. I could do that. I'm sure I could. At least, I think I could."

"Aunt Grizelda!" Arabella prompted, sniffling. "Duncan said to do it now, please."

"What? Oh! Oh, yes, of course! Sorry. One door—gone!"

And it was. One moment the door to the schoolroom was there, standing slightly ajar (all the better for the twins to hear what was taking place in the nursery), and the next moment it had disappeared in a large puff of pink smoke, so that the twins, standing close together and seemingly leaning toward the nursery in the age-old position of eavesdroppers, were exposed to view.

"I say, Uncle," Freddie commented, gathering his dignity about him as he threw back his shoulders and entered the room, the misshapen crystal ball held firmly in both hands, "that was very good. But you don't suppose we have been convinced that *you* did it, do you? You cannot possibly believe that Bertie and I are frightened of your powers. You can't even come near us, or else we'll do something terrible to you. Something even more terrible than we did to the others. Besides, we heard you speaking to Aunt Grizelda."

"Heard her answer you, too," Bertie added, joining his brother in the nursery, the dusty book of incantations tucked beneath one arm. "Spirits of dead kings, indeed. Uncle, you should be ashamed of yourself, trying to frighten us children. Mama will be extremely put out when we tell her. If she's not too busy looking in her mirror," he ended, poking his brother in the ribs.

"I live only to amuse you, boys," the earl replied, his grip tightening on Arabella's hand. "However, now that you know what I am about, perhaps you will consider returning Aunt Grizelda's possessions, before she gets really angry. After all, bright, intelligent boys that you are, you do realize that you have not completely defanged our resident witch with your robbery. This time it was the door that disappeared—gone heaven knows where, dear nephews. Next time? Well, I wouldn't care to dwell on such things. I wouldn't, as you so neatly pointed out a moment ago, wish to be accused of frightening my sister's dear children."

Freddie and Bertie seemed to pale beneath their freckles, so that Arabella thought they looked much like they had suddenly come down with a nasty case of measles. Being a lover of children (didn't she wish to have at least three or four of her own someday?), her heart went out to the boys who, after all, were probably only indulging themselves in what they considered to be a lark, an adventure.

But, although the sight of their suddenly woebegone faces touched her heart, Arabella was also aware of the red-braided bat that was visible just out of the corner of her eye, the bat whose squeaks sounded very much like sobs. "Oh, poor Peggy," she said, wringing her hands.

"Perhaps Aunt Grizelda could turn Freddie and Bertie into bats as well," Duncan suggested while glaring at the twins.

"Yes, perhaps she could," Arabella agreed, inwardly cringing. "What a splendid idea, Duncan."

"No. Couldn't do that," Aunt Grizelda supplied quickly, so that Arabella longed to choke her—if only she could see her. "Not without my crystal ball. That's the whole point of this thing, remember? I can't do spells without it. Honestly, Arabella, are you sure you wish to marry this man? It's a good thing that you're coming by tomorrow to help me pack. Perhaps I could do something to help, as I'm really getting the hang of spells this time around. Men are so extremely dense at times, don't you agree?"

"Thank you, Aunt Grizelda," the earl articulated dampeningly as Freddie and Bertie grinned at each other. "The twins, I am convinced, greatly appreciate your having so candidly pointed out that you cannot cast a spell on them."

"You're welcome, boys," Aunt Grizelda said, dismissing Duncan's sarcasm (if, indeed, it had registered with her), her voice suddenly cheerful, as if she had suddenly remembered that, if she could not cast spells, there still were things she could do. "Freddie, place my crystal ball on the floor, won't you? I shouldn't wish for it to come to grief when I call down a lightning bolt to split you in two. Bertie—I would step away from Freddie if I were you. Lightning bolts are not my best trick, and I might miss."

"You'd better listen, boys," the earl commented, for he was nothing if not astute and had immediately understood what Aunt Grizelda was about. He made quite a business of pulling Arabella in the direction of the hallway. "She cut a tree in half just an hour ago. Straight down to the roots, wasn't it, Arabella? Very impressive."

"Oh, indeed," Arabella agreed, not really needing his warning pressure on her arm to understand what part she had been elected to play in this hastily improvised farce. "And if she could do it to a tree—why, imagine what could happen if she did it to Freddie? Pity," she said, shaking her head. "For all the trouble he has caused me, I had been rather fond of the little scamp. I believe I might even miss him."

Bertie, who had always been more of a follower than a leader, yelped and scooted to the corner of the room as Freddie, obviously made of sterner stuff, thrust out his chin and declared, "You wouldn't. You're a good witch. You told us so when we came to your cottage and you served us tea and scones and green-apple jelly. You would never hurt a little boy. Bertie, stop being such a goose and come back here. Nobody is going to hurt us."

There was complete silence in the room for several moments—save for the squeaking of a certain oddly coiffured bat—before Arabella looked toward the ceiling and inquired, "Aunt Grizelda? Are you still here?"

"Yes, my dear, I am," the witch answered, her tone so defeated that Arabella longed to weep. "He's right, of course. I can't split his head with a lightning bolt. I'm allowed, you understand—it's not against the rules—but I simply don't have it in me, I suppose. Oh, Arabella, I'm a failure. I can't be a good witch, and I can't be a bad witch. Come to think of it, without my crystal ball I can't be any sort of witch at all. I'll *never* get my star now. No, I'm doomed to appear here at the Rookery every quarter century, from now into eternity."

"Into eternity? *That tears it!*" Duncan was more incensed that he could remember ever being. Have Aunt Grizelda appear again in twenty-five years, when he most likely would still be in possession of the place? Have her rushing about the estate in his children's time, in his children's children's times—mucking up their lives with her misfiring spells and inane tricks? No. Oh, no, no, *no!* Not while he still had something to say about it! "Freddie!" he commanded, walking toward the boy, "Give me that crystal ball—now!"

"Stand back, Uncle," Freddie warned, holding up the crystal ball in a threatening way. "Stand back, or I'll—I'll turn you into a great ugly bug and step on you!"

"Duncan, dearest, come back!" Arabella exclaimed, truly frightened.

"Don't do it, my lord," Aunt Grizelda warned. "He

can do it. The spell takes no more than a single incantation."

"I don't care," Duncan informed them, taking another step forward, glaring malevolently into his nephew's eyes. "My drawing room is a shambles, my footmen are no more than resting places for pigeons, the nursery maid is fluttering about the room seeking to swoop down on some unsuspecting rodent, and my sister—" He hesitated a moment, as if considering his sister's recent transformation, then ended, "Well, it isn't normal, no matter that it is a marked improvement. But to continue—I have a resident witch flying about, spying on me while I try to woo my soon to be affianced bride, I have a most important guest coming to dinner, and I have no more time to waste with these two miserable, disrespectful, *larcenous* little monsters! I want my house back!" he ended on a roar. "I want my *life* back!"

"Sir?" Freddie, rather than beginning the two-verse incantation that would render his uncle into an ugly black insect, began to sidle toward the doorway to the schoolroom. "You're angry, aren't you? You don't think any of this is at all funny? I mean—you're *really* angry?"

"Livid," Duncan agreed levelly, stopping just in front of Freddie and holding out his hands. "It may have taken you some time to realize this, but now that you understand just how angry I am, perhaps you will listen closely while I describe what it is I intend to do to you as your punishment. Once you have given me the crystal ball and that dangerous book, I shall most probably confine both of you to the nursery floor for a week, with extra lessons scheduled in all of your studies. There will be no puddings, no toys, and you will read sermons when you are not writing very long, very sincere apologies to everyone whom you have hurt with this nonsense you have been indulging in all day."

"Will you cane us as well, sir?" Bertie asked, rejoining his brother. "We've never been caned, either of us, but I understand that it is extremely painful."

"No, I will not cane you," the earl said, adding facetiously, "as I'd much rather prefer having the two of you lined up against the garden wall at dawn and shot. Alas, this will not happen, as I am the adult here and you are but children. Children, I see now, who have never learned the meaning of the word *discipline*. I believe it is time you learned."

Freddie and Bertie exchanged quizzical glances before Bertie nodded and Freddie said, smiling, "You really do love us, don't you, Uncle? I mean, Mama loves us. We know that because she calls us her darlings and gives us sugarplums. But you love us too, or you wouldn't want us to behave, or to learn."

"Yes," Bertie piped in, also smiling in a way that brought tears to Arabella's eyes. "Papa didn't care if we learned or if we behaved, as long as we stayed out of his way. That's why we started to misbehave in the first place—so Papa would pay attention to us. But he never did."

"Oh, Duncan," Arabella said, rushing to embrace Bertie. "I've been so caught up in their pranks that it never occurred to me to ask why they were being so naughty. Freddie and Bertie aren't monsters—they're simply little boys who have been crying out to be noticed."

The earl rolled his eyes, not so easily taken in by this sudden change of heart, then found himself struck by a sudden inspiration. "Freddie? Bertie? How old are you boys? Eight? Ten?"

"Twelve," Freddie responded in aggrieved tones. "Old enough to be in school, if Mama didn't think we would get the sniffles and die once we're away from her. Why?"

Now inspiration was practically beating the earl over the head. "Twelve? Why, you boys should be in school with other boys your age, not boarded up here in the country with a governess, like some girl-child. Why didn't I realize this before now?"

"School?" the twins repeated in unison. "Truly?"

Freddie's delighted smile was the first to crumple. "Mama will never allow it."

"She would if she were married, and had something other than you two boys to occupy her time," Duncan reasoned, holding out his hands to receive the crystal ball. "Of course, I can't foresee her ever marrying if you two persist in behaving like wild Indians, frightening off people like the very eligible Sir Harold, who just by chance is to be my guest at dinner this evening."

"In your upside-down drawing room," Bertie added, jabbing his brother in the ribs. "That's why we did it, isn't it, Freddie? To scare Sir Harold away. But we were wrong, Freddie—give over, do. I want Mama to marry. I want to go to school. Besides, it smells in here."

Freddie hesitated for only a moment before holding out the crystal ball to his uncle, who took it with some alacrity before gingerly placing it and the book of incantations on a nearby table.

"Oh, isn't this just lovely?" Aunt Grizelda exclaimed from somewhere near the window. "If the potion works tonight—and it will, I just know it—I shall have done my three spells and Hester will come for me. This time I shall surely get my star! Everyone—close your eyes and slowly count to three. Farewell, my darlings!"

"One . . . two . . . three!" they all counted together, then opened their eyes to see that the nursery was once more as it should be—except for Peggy, who was sitting rump-down in the corner, totally back to normal but looking faintly dazed and quite unaware that anything out of the ordinary had occurred. When questioned, she could only apologize for, it seemed to her, napping while in charge of the twins.

"Three spells, Duncan," Arabella began nervously a few minutes later as Peggy, acting on the earl's instructions, ushered the boys into the schoolroom to begin writing their apologies. "Aunt Grizelda's first successful spell brought you to the Rookery, and her third, if it works, will be the love potion for your sister and Sir Harold. She has already told us that lightning bolts and disappearing doors do not count. Have you thought about what her second spell could be?"

Duncan slipped an arm around Arabella's waist and guided her down the staircase to the foyer, to see that the footmen were once again going on about their business. He had no doubt that the drawing room was once more neat and orderly, and feared that his sister was once again gray-haired, dowdy, and ordering the servants about in her usual harping way.

"I have no idea, my dear heart," he admitted honestly, dropping a kiss on her cheek—their first kiss, and not exactly the one he'd planned, but it would do until he could get her alone, which he was now in the process of doing. "And I don't think I care."

"Oh, Duncan, I wish I could be as uncaring," Arabella said as he led her into his study at the back of the house.

He kissed her again, this time on the lips. It was much more satisfying, but not as much as he had hoped, for Arabella pulled away from him. What a dear child; so modest, so ladylike—so utterly bewitching. "Enough of Aunt Grizelda and her infernal spells, my darling. That good woman interrupted us earlier at a most inopportune time—in the middle of my proposal, as I recall." He sat in one of the leather chairs, pulling Arabella down on his lap. Feeling her body so intimately placed against his urged him to hurry his words, eager as he was to get on to other things. "I believe we had gotten past my initial question and you were about to answer in the affirmative. Now, if you'll allow me to help you, I believe you should be saying, 'Yes, my dearest Duncan, I would very much like to marry you.' Go ahead, sweetings. Say it."

"I wish I could, Duncan. I wish I could be dishonest, and let my heart rule my head. But I can't. I can't even know what my heart truly feels, what you truly feel in *your* heart. Duncan—you have to listen to me. Aunt Grizelda's second spell was a love spell—directed toward us. I'm convinced of it."

Duncan, who had been concentrating on the delightful way nature had fashioned Arabella's lips, blinked hard and looked at her as if she had just announced that the moon was made of cheese. "A love spell? You? Me? Us?" He put her from him and stood, to begin pacing the carpet, then wheeled about on his heels to look at her in utter amazement. "*Us?*"

Arabella nodded, unable to speak. She pressed a hand to her mouth, her eyes swimming with tears as her heart went out to him. Her heart, which was rapidly crumbling into little pieces.

"Are you sure?" Duncan asked, already knowing that his attraction to Arabella had been immediate, and definitely intense. How had he thought of her just a moment ago? As bewitching? Yes, that was it. Bewitching. Was it possible? Even now he was having a difficult time concentrating on the idea that they might not be in love, but the unfortunate victims of Aunt Grizelda's zeal to get her own star. Arabella was too near, and he longed to kiss her. He didn't want to think of unfortunate things. *Unfortunate?* Was it unfortunate to feel this way about Arabella? Was it unfortunate that she was so clearly in love with him? "Arabella, are you sure?"

"Quite sure. I realized it just before Aunt Grizelda appeared to tell us about her crystal ball, and I've been thinking about it ever since. Your watch is missing, isn't it, Duncan—I mean, my lord? The other day Aunt Grizelda mentioned something to me about finding a word to rhyme with *watch*. I've now realized that one of my hair combs has gone missing. I believe she used them to help her cast her spell. My lord—we have not fallen in love. We have been *bewitched*. I'm sorry. I'm so sorry."

"*No!*" Duncan picked up a figurine that stood on a nearby table and hurled it into the fireplace. "I don't believe it! I won't! That daft woman couldn't even keep track of her own crystal ball—she could not possibly have cast a spell on me. I know how I feel, Arabella, and I love you!"

Arabella began to cry in earnest, and Duncan went to her, taking her in his arms. He felt the quick swell of passion that had become his familiar companion whenever he touched Arabella, whenever he looked into her eyes. "Oh, God, Arabella, maybe you're right. I've never felt this way in my life. All I want to do is to hold you, to love you. And you feel the same way?"

She nodded, then looked away from him, biting her bottom lip. "What—what are we going to do? Aunt Grizelda will leave tomorrow morning if her love potion works tonight with Lady Mary and Sir Harold. As I'm the only one of the two of us who can see her, talk to her, I'll have to explain that she must remove the love spell. Poor Aunt Grizelda. Now she'll never get her star."

Duncan drew Arabella's unresisting form tighter against his chest. "Poor Aunt Grizelda? Arabella, I couldn't care less about that dotty, interfering woman. She has complicated our lives. Who are we to say that we would not have eventually tumbled into love without her ridiculous spell? I cannot resign myself to the idea that a witch's spell can control my emotions. I was born to love you, Arabella. I'm convinced of that."

"Oh, Duncan." She gently disengaged herself from his embrace, remembering how she had believed herself to be half in love with his portrait before she'd ever met him. "And if Aunt Grizelda removes the spell and we find that we don't feel at all inclined to love each other? What then, Duncan?"

Marshaling all his reserves of willpower (for he still longed to kiss her, hold her, claim her for his own), the earl smiled and said teasingly, "Please, my darling, one crisis at a time. If we get safely through this evening, we shall think about that tomorrow."

Sir Harold Yates was nearsighted. Shortsighted. Unable, with even partial clarity, to register things beyond the space of less than three feet, even with the assistance of the spectacles that seemed more at home perched atop his round, balding head than they did on the bridge of his bulbous nose.

Sir Harold had nearly come to grief three separate times while they all were gathered in the drawing room for drinks before dinner, tripping over footstools and small tables, and Duncan had been so amused that he had leaned close to Arabella to whisper that, strange as it might seem, the man would have been safer if the drawing room had remained in its earlier, upside-down condition.

But it was just this helpless ineptness that seemed to most appeal to Lady Mary. From the moment of his arrival she had been no more than a few feet from his side, ordering him about, helping him to find his wineglass, assisting him into the dining room, treating him like the helpless child the twins no longer were. And Sir Harold, bless him and his nearsightedness that kept him from noticing that Lady Mary was past her first blush of youth—about twenty years past it, as a matter of fact—seemed to be lapping up her attentions like a cat laps up cream.

Arabella's presence at the dinner table had been neatly arranged by the earl, who had avoided needless argument by pointing out to his sister that Arabella's presence served to even the numbers. With the earl at the head of the table and Lady Mary at its foot, Arabella was placed on Duncan's left side, close enough to warn him with a stern look when he showed signs of breaking into laughter as Lady Mary recounted her strange afternoon, which seemed to have gone missing in her memory, leaving her to ponder why the servants were thanking her for her generosity concerning their yearly stipend—she who had learned to squeeze a penny until it squealed. But, as the additional funds would be coming out of her brother's deep pockets and not hers, and because she felt so very rested, so very much in charity with the world, she had decided to let the matter pass.

Arabella picked at her food, delicious as it was, waiting in mingled dread and anticipation for the moment between the third and fourth courses, when Rutgers had been ordered to bring "a new wine just arrived from London" to table for Lady Mary and their guest to sample. It had taken Arabella considerable time that afternoon to locate the small brown vial in her bedchamber but, after at last running it to ground in the bottom of her wardrobe, tucked into the toe of one of her jean half-boots, she and the earl had very carefully instructed the butler as to its disposition in the two wineglasses.

And now the moment had come. The footmen had cleared away the third course, and she and Duncan waited breathlessly for the butler's appearance.

And waited.

And waited.

Duncan lifted the small silver bell at his side and rang it.

And rang it.

And rang it again.

"Excuse me, please. There must be something amiss belowstairs. I'll be right back," the earl said at last, rising, as the moments had stretched into minutes, long, anxious minutes; and Lady Mary prosed on and on about the sad state of servants today and her precarious health;

and Sir Harold's chin slowly lowered toward his chest, a slight glaze—undoubtedly of boredom—clouding his nearsighted blue eyes.

"I would be happy to accompany you," Arabella put in quickly, laying down her serviette and hastening to follow him.

"Well, *really!*" Lady Mary exclaimed, clearly taken aback by this unorthodox defection. "And am I to remain here—unchaperoned—while the two of you go off on some mad start?"

Fortunately, neither Duncan nor Arabella was forced to point out that Lady Mary had long since given up any claim to being an innocent debutante by the arrival of Rutgers, with the young housemaid, Sara, at his side.

In his right hand Rutgers was carrying a small round silver tray with two goblets on it—the love potion, carefully divided and mixed with wine. However, his left hand—Duncan blinked twice as he stared, openmouthed at the sight—was firmly holding on to Sara's right hand, and the maid was smiling up at him with such moonstruck devotion that it was painful to see.

"Had the devil's own time getting her to leave go this much, my lord," the butler said, his face purple with shame. "Says she loves me, sir," Rutgers whispered, his voice so deep that no one in the room could mistake what he had said for anything but what they'd heard.

It didn't take much in the way of deep thought to understand what had happened. The maid had been sipping some of the "new" wine. Aunt Grizelda had been correct. She may have made a sad botch of her attempt to light London's city streets a few centuries ago, but she was quite proficient in the making of love potions.

"Ah, Rutgers," Duncan said, taking the man's elbow and leading him and the seemingly attached-to-his-hip Sara to a corner of the large room, carefully turning all their backs on the rest of the assembled company, "I'm not the sort to pry, and you don't have to answer if you so wish, but—are you by any chance at all fond of this young woman?"

"Well, sir," Rutgers began, clearing his throat, "I do like her. Even been thinking of asking her to walk out with me, as I do have my butler's keys and can support a wife. Why do you ask, if I may inquire, my lord?"

Duncan smiled, patting the butler on the shoulder before relieving him of the silver tray. "No reason, Rutgers. You may go now. Oh, by the way," he added as the butler turned to leave, "is there any more of that wine additive I gave you? In the kitchens, you understand."

The butler nodded, trying in vain to keep Sara from picking up his hand and placing small kisses on each of his fingertips in turn while Lady Mary shuddered and was heard to mutter, "Why, I *never*" from her chair halfway across the large dining room (a totally superfluous comment, for Duncan was already quite sure his prudish sister had never in all her years "ever-ed" much of anything).

"Yes, my lord," Rutgers answered quietly, obviously operating under quite a strain. "There is still some left. I used it sparingly, as you suggested. Do you wish for me to bring it to you, my lord?"

Duncan smiled, winking at Arabella, who was seated once more and holding her serviette to her lips to cover her sudden smile of enlightenment. "No, indeed, my good man. I would much rather you drank it yourself— every drop, mind you. It is much too dear too share. Oh, and Rutgers—after you have drunk the wine, you and Sara may have the remainder of the evening free to 'walk out' if you wish."

"Thank you, my lord," Rutgers answered, his brow furrowed in confusion. "Thank you very much."

Once the servants had gone, Duncan played at butler, placing one of the goblets before both Lady Mary and Sir Harold and inviting them to taste his newest acquisition.

"What? Wine, you say? From London?" Sir Harold heaved himself forward, groping for the glass. "Don't mind if I do. Where is it?"

Duncan swiftly placed the goblet in the man's hand before it could come to grief and then returned to stand at his own chair and just as swiftly proposed a toast to His Majesty's health—the one toast even his sister would not dare refuse to drink to, no matter that she didn't much care for wine.

"Drink up, my dear lady! To his Royal Majesty!" Sir Harold cried, stumbling to his feet and raising his glass, tipping it in salute in Lady Mary's general direction before draining its contents to the dregs.

A moment later Lady Mary took a drink from her own glass.

Two moments later Duncan and a blushing Arabella prudently took their leave from the dining room, warning the serving staff that Lady Mary and her fiancé were not to be disturbed.

Early the next morning Arabella sat inside the small cottage with her legs tucked tight against the rungs of the rocking chair, careful to keep her feet out of harm's way as Aunt Grizelda went on in her own peculiar way of packing her suitcases.

All around her, bits and pieces of things were either walking or flying into one of the three large leather strapped chests placed in front of the unlit fireplace. Brooms and pots and glass jars holding things Arabella would much prefer to remain ignorant of were hopping off shelves and arranging themselves in the chests. Aunt Grizelda, sitting in the matching rocking chair, then pointed to a succession of objects on the far wall, and wiggled her index finger in a circular motion, causing another exodus from the shelves and adding another layer to the chests. All this time the clearly ecstatic old witch excitedly urged Arabella to divulge even more details about the success of her love potion.

"And after they finally reappeared, hand in hand, in the drawing room—Lady Mary smiling from ear to ear like the village idiot and Sir Harold with his waistcoat misbuttoned—then what happened?" she asked, taking a sip of tea.

"And then Sir Harold applied most formally for Lady Mary's hand," Arabella told her, "which would have been a very touching scene if he had but asked it directly of Duncan. As it happened, however, Sir Harold bowed in front of a portrait of the late earl to make his declaration of undying love."

Aunt Grizelda giggled like a young girl, then frowned as her large white cat refused to jump into one of the chests. "Stubborn thing. Been moping around here since last night, saying she doesn't want to leave. Told me she's afraid there won't be any mice on Star 417. Arabella— I've just had a lovely thought! Would you like me to make her a present to you and his lordship? A wedding present?"

Unknowingly, Aunt Grizelda had given Arabella the opening she had been looking for, the opportunity to utter the speech she had spent the entire sleepless night preparing. She opened her mouth, ready to tell the witch that she must remove the love spell she had cast on the earl and herself, ready to break the old woman's heart by informing her that she now must cast about for another spell before gaining her star—and then she closed her mouth once more.

She couldn't do it. She couldn't hurt Aunt Grizelda, not when the woman had meant well. Not even to save herself a lifetime of longing for the man she now knew she must leave. Today. This very afternoon. Before they could allow their spell-induced passion to lead them into even more trouble than it already had done. For they could not live a lie, even this very lovely, mutually pleasing lie. Perhaps, in time, the spell would weaken, and they could both get on with their lives.

Perhaps.

But for now, Arabella knew she had to continue the lie, for Aunt Grizelda's sake.

Arabella looked at the cat consideringly, then shook her head. "Thank you, Aunt Grizelda, but no. It is very generous of you, but—um, it might be difficult explaining to the servants that we have taken in a talking cat."

The witch shrugged, giving up the idea. "Very well." She stood, reaching into her pocket to extract a large gold watch. "Here—I nearly forgot. You'll return this to his lordship, won't you?" She dug into another pocket and pulled out one of Arabella's hair combs. "And this is yours. I don't need them anymore, do I, now that the spell has worked."

Holding out her hands to accept the articles, Arabella asked, in what she hoped was a confused tone, "The spell, Aunt Grizelda? And just what spell would that be?"

Aunt Grizelda shook her head, as if disbelieving that her guest did not understand. "What spell? Why, my second spell, of course. The earl's arrival was my first success, the love potion for Lady Mary my third. *You*, my dear, were my second, you and his lordship. I couldn't use the same love potion twice, you see. That wouldn't count. Not with Hester. She's such a stickler for the rules, our Hester is."

Arabella stood very straight, frowning as if trying to understand. "Aunt Grizelda," she began, ducking quickly as the witch gestured with one hand and a small black iron pot went whizzing past her head, to land in the third trunk, "this spell—your second spell—does it last very long?"

Disentangling herself from a voluminous cloak, which had somehow wrapped itself around her head as it made its way from the hook on the wall to the chests, Aunt

Grizelda said, "Why, forever, of course. It's very simple, although I had failed at precisely that spell at least six times, beginning with Henry and that poor Boleyn person. That one wore off with a vengeance. Bloody boy, Hal—but he did compose a fair tune or two in his day. Why, I remember—"

"Aunt Grizelda!"

"Yes, my dear? I'm right here. There's no reason to shout."

"Forgive me," Arabella apologized, although her heart wasn't in it. Her heart, her poor, aching heart, was too busy breaking to be interested in apologies. "Aunt Grizelda, are you saying that Duncan and I are destined to love each other until the day we both die?"

The old woman grinned. "Exactly! Precisely! And I did a wonderful job of it, too, if I must say so myself. Never saw such a case of April and May between two people."

Arabella longed to weep, to throw things, to crawl into some dark corner and stay there forever. But she couldn't tell Aunt Grizelda that—not while the old woman was so happy. Not while the old woman was at last about to get her star. Summoning up every bit of composure left to her, she smiled and said, "Thank you, Aunt Grizelda. It was indeed most generous of you to think of us. And yes, it was a very good spell. Um, is there any way to get it to wear off on its own?"

"Wear off?" Aunt Grizelda seemed confused. "Why would you ask that, my dear? Aren't you happy with my spell? Oh, dear, oh, dear, oh, dear. This won't do. This won't do at all. You have to be happy with my spell or Hester will disallow it!"

Arabella quickly assured the old woman that she had only been speaking idly, and had no more reason for asking that particular question than simple curiosity. She didn't think she was overly convincing with her lies, but Aunt Grizelda was immediately mollified, for people and, it would seem, witches, are always eager to believe that which they want to believe.

And then it was time to go. Hester would be here soon, and Aunt Grizelda thought that Arabella should not be about when the grand high witch made her entrance, a sentiment the young woman fervently seconded.

"Remember me, my dear," Aunt Grizelda said, walking Arabella to the door. "I know I shall always remember you. And if you should ever need me, just gaze up into the sky and look for the guiding light of my crystal ball. That way you will know you will never be quite alone."

"Oh, Aunt Grizelda!" Arabella felt tears pricking at her eyes and threw herself into the old woman's arms, truly sad to see her go. Aunt Grizelda, for good or nay, had changed her life forever. "I will miss you so much!"

"Yes, yes, of course you will," Aunt Grizelda said, gently pushing her away and stepping back inside the cottage. "But you must be off. I hear Hester now and I am not yet done with my packing. Remember to watch for the light of my crystal ball, Arabella. It will always be there for you and yours!"

Arabella's bottom lip began to quiver as she watched the cottage door close behind the old woman. Slowly, as she continued to watch, the cottage began to swim in front of her eyes, becoming more and more transparent as it waved back and forth, like long grass in a breeze, then disappeared entirely.

Aunt Grizelda was gone.

And Arabella had to go back to the Rookery and tell Duncan the heartbreaking news that it was true—they were no more in love than Lady Mary and Sir Harold, or Rutgers and Sara, although at least those four had been on their way to falling in love before Aunt Grizelda had hastened the matter. She would have to tell him that they were nothing more than the living proof of the success of Aunt Grizelda's second spell. And, worst of all, she would have to tell him that she had not been able to summon the courage to ask Aunt Grizelda to remove the spell.

What would she say? How would she find the words? And where would she go now that she must leave the Rookery, leave Duncan?

Her head down, Arabella began walking back along the cliff path, her vision clouded with tears, so that she didn't see the woman standing beside one of the large trees until that woman said, "Here, here, now. We can't have this, my dear."

Arabella's head jerked up, so that she had a clear vision of the woman. Dressed much as Aunt Grizelda had been on the occasion of their first meeting, this woman was no more like the smiling, comfortably pudgy Aunt Grizelda as chalk was to cheese. Impressively tall, and quite angular in shape, this woman had the presence and bearing of a queen. And quite the largest nose Arabella had ever seen!

"I—I beg your pardon?" Arabella inquired politely, knowing in her heart of hearts that she was looking at none other than Hester, chief of the witches.

"Nonsense, girl," the old woman chastised her, waving one long-fingered hand. "If anyone should be begging anyone's pardon it is I, for having foisted that bird-witted Grizelda upon you in the first place. It was a stupid punishment, banishing her to the Rookery, but needs must when the devil drives, you know. And the *devil* of it is, Grizelda could *drive* anyone half out of her head. It's time she moved on. But that's not why I'm here."

"It isn't? But I thought you had come to take Aunt Grizelda to her star—Star 417, right next to you. She is all packed and ready to go. She'll be so disappointed if you tell her she has failed again."

The witch shook her head. "You mistake my meaning, child. Grizelda is already firmly entrenched on her star, setting up housekeeping with that dratted cat of hers. That is all settled. But I could not leave until I had eased your mind. You and the earl, my dear girl, are not the recipients of Grizelda's sad attempts at love spells."

Arabella felt her pulses leap with renewed hope. "We're not?" Then her spirits fell a notch. "But—but we were her second successful spell. I don't understand. How can Aunt Grizelda have her star if she has not completed three spells?"

The witch smiled, revealing a stunning set of what appeared to be golden teeth. "Grizelda brought the earl to the Rookery. That was a good spell. Elementary, but well executed. The love potion for Lady Mary—a horrid woman, actually, but then Sir Harold will be happy with her—was totaled up as Grizelda's third success. We cannot in good conscience count that business with the butler, you understand. But her second spell, the love spell she believes she has worked on you and the earl? Hardly successful. No, no, no. You and the earl were already more than halfway to falling in love when she cast it."

"We were?" Arabella asked, then smiled, her heart full. "Yes, we were, weren't we? We were already falling in love. We *are* in love. Truly in love. Isn't that above everything *marvelous?*"

"Please, child, don't interrupt. As I said, you and the earl were already on the road to love when Grizelda cast her spell. Therefore, according to the rules, it could not work and does not count. We could not allow you to believe otherwise, for we could see it had caused you pain—although you certainly should have seen the difference between what you and the earl feel for each other and the ridiculous carrying-on that is a result of a true love spell. Lady Mary and that nearsighted ninnyhammer?" Hester rolled her eyes. "Dreadful to watch. Truly dreadful. No, you and the earl are not like that, are you? And so, you see, our poor deluded Grizelda has only cast two workable spells—one more than she has ever been able to cast before this, I grant you, but nonetheless only two."

Arabella didn't know whether to be happy for Duncan and herself or sad for Aunt Grizelda's failure. Remembering that the old witch had been granted her dearest wish anyway, she settled for remaining at least slightly confused. "Then how has it come about that you have granted Aunt Grizelda a star?"

"Simple, my dear. Grizelda had a chance to wrest her crystal ball from that little scamp, that Freddie, but she refused to do harm in order to help herself, no matter that she might be condemning herself to another visit to the Rookery in twenty-five years and yet another trial. Heloise, Maisie, and I were extremely impressed by this act of humanity. Heloise most especially. And so, we voted to allow Grizelda to join us. We agree that she can be a ninnyhammer at times, but we have missed her. Besides, with the havoc she helped create by misplacing her crystal ball, we were reluctant to allow her loose much longer. You do see our dilemma, don't you?"

Arabella's smile was wide. "Oh, yes, ma'am, I most certainly do. You won't ever tell Aunt Grizelda that her spell didn't work, will you? She seemed so proud of her accomplishment."

"We won't," the witch promised. "But don't you think you should be getting back to the house?" she added, winking. "I have consulted my own crystal ball, my dear, and I can tell you that there is a very anxious, very loving gentleman waiting for you in the drawing room. Good-bye, my dear, and thank you for befriending our Grizelda. It won't be forgotten."

The tears Arabella had been fighting now flowed freely down her cheeks, but they were tears of happiness. She watched through the mist of those tears as Hester—

a clearly most exalted, yet definitely prone-to-drama witch—lifted her cape in a flourish, covering her head, and disappeared in a puff of pink smoke.

A moment later Arabella was running. Running toward the man now standing just outside the opened doors that led directly into the drawing room, as if searching for someone—and toward the lovely future that awaited them both.

Epilogue

In which illusion becomes substance

"

... AND, after a short courtship during which their love grew, and deepened, and laid a solid base for the future, they lived happily ever after," I say finally, as I can see that Harry and Edward have begun to lose interest now that Aunt Grizelda is gone and my story has turned to love and all that "sloppy stuff."

"Tell us again how the nursery looked," Harry pleads, lying on the rug, his chin cupped in his hands. "It was our nursery, wasn't it? Did it really look like a cave?"

"Dolt! None of it's true, you know, even if it was a nice enough story," Edward puts in, brushing at his knees as he rises from his position near the hearth. "Freddie and Bertie would have been turned into great ugly toads if it were true. This whole story was made up only to show us that the reason we get punished when we do wrong is because we're 'loved.' Bother! In two years, when *I* get to go off to school, I wouldn't dare tell such a silly story. Come on, Harry, let's go to bed. Papa won't be home for hours and hours."

"You two run along upstairs to Sally," I tell them. "I think I will keep Gussie here with me for a while longer."

After dutifully kissing my cheek, the boys depart, Edward teasing that he and his brother will find their way to the nursery by following "Aunt Grizelda's star." I should have known better than to tell them a love story. Next time I will have to spin a tale of dragons, and bold knights, and a beautiful damsel in distress. No, not a damsel in distress, or else I will bore them yet again. Perhaps it is time their papa took over the chore of storytelling.

Augusta has been sleeping for nearly an hour, ever since just before Freddie turned the drawing room upside down, her curly blonde head tucked into my lap. I reach down to stroke her sleep-flushed cheek. Augusta, being female, would have appreciated my happy ending. She would have sighed a soulful sigh and clapped her hands to hear of Arabella's and Duncan's fairy-tale happiness. That is one of the wonderful things about daughters.

There is a flash of lightning that, for just a moment, illuminates the room as if it were day, followed by a long rumble of thunder, both the sight and the sound reminding me that he is now two hours overdue. I sigh, thinking how lovely the world would be if there truly were an Aunt Grizelda. Then I should be able to ask her to light the path that leads to the Rookery.

"Ma'am?"

I look up to see the butler standing just inside the doorway, my heart leaping in anticipation. "Yes, Rogers? Is he coming?"

"His lordship? Not that I can see, my lady. Nasty night, isn't it? But he'll be fine. Just you wait and see. Sally was just wondering if you'd like me to fetch Miss Augusta upstairs for you?"

I am reluctant to give my daughter over, fearful that once she is gone I may give in to my fears, and my tears. But Rogers and his wife Sally will worry if I appear troubled, and so I allow the butler to lift the sleeping child high against his chest and carry her off to her cot.

Now, my silly, hastily invented fairy tale told and my children in bed, I am free to do what I have tried so desperately not to do—stand at the window and look out over the drive, waiting.

Waiting, and trying to be brave.

I stand at the window for long, anxious minutes, staring into the darkness and seeing nothing, and then I hear the great oaken door in the foyer open and a sleepy footman greets the Earl of Wilmington—Douglas—my husband.

"Thank you, Tweed. Wicked weather out there! My wife?" I hear him ask as I run toward the foyer, relief flooding me.

Still shaking himself out of his rain-drenched greatcoat, his dark curls pressed to his head with the force of the storm, he turns to smile at me. "Darling!" he exclaims as, not caring that my actions show my concern, I launch myself into his arms.

Holding onto my husband's dripping hat, Tweed and the rest of the footmen scatter as we kiss, more than twelve years of marriage not yet having reduced our passion and deep love, before Douglas guides me back into the drawing room and toward the warmth of the fire.

"It's the very devil of a night out there, dearest," he says, holding me close as we stand before the fire, my head resting on his shoulder. "More than once I thought I should have to either turn back or face the night on the road, sheltering as best I could under the hedgerows. But then the strangest thing happened."

I look up at him, drinking in the sight of his beloved

face. "Strange, Douglas?" He is so handsome. Even more handsome than Duncan, my mythical earl. "What do you mean?"

Taking my hand, he leads me toward the window I have tried so hard to shun. "I was nearing the turn off the Duke's Road, and having the very devil of a time finding it, when all of a sudden the clouds broke and a single star appeared. Not the North Star, but one very close by it, I believe. Anyway, this star seemed to shine down expressly for me, lighting the turn that leads into the Rookery. That light guided me every inch of the way from that point on, until I reached our door. Here— I want you to see it."

I stand very still, unable to believe what I am hearing, unwilling to see what I might see.

Douglas pulls back the drapes and peers out the window and up—up into the heavens. "Never mind, Antonia. The clouds are back, covering the star." He turns back to me, then frowns as he sees the tears on my cheeks. "Antonia? Is something wrong?"

I have told my children a story, a fairy tale, a fanciful piece of nonsense scattered with little fact and ample fiction, meant only to pass the time, meant only to ease my worried heart. And now my husband has told me of a star that has appeared where no star should shine, to guide him through a storm and home to me.

Stepping past him, I push back the drape to look out the window and up, up into the heavens. The clouds have parted again, and I see a single star twinkling above me—for only a moment—and then it is gone, and the storm rages on. I remember Aunt Grizelda's words as I have invented them and told them to my children, *"Remember to watch for the light of my crystal ball, Arabella. It will always be there for you and yours!"*

Had the thought become the wish, the wish given life to the dream, and the dream become the reality?

I will never know.

"Wrong, darling? No. Nothing's wrong," I say at last, letting the drape fall into place and turning back to my husband. I am not a woman prone to fancy. I have borne three children and know that I carry another just under my heart, a secret I have yet to share with my beloved.

It is the only secret I will tell him this night . . .

Kasey Michaels

Kasey Michaels has written thirty-five books in twelve years, including Regency, contemporary, and historical romances, as well as one non-fiction book about her oldest son's first kidney transplant. She has garnered several writing awards, such as the *Romantic Times* Outstanding Regency Writer of the Year, and the Romance Writer's of America Golden Medallion Award. Kasey resides in Coplay, Pennsylvania, with her husband, three of her children (who refuse to leave), two spoiled felines, and half the children in the neighborhood (who think she is their mother), while her oldest daughter, her son-in-law, and her grandson live only a block away—all of which explains why Kasey wears stereo headphones and locks her office door while she writes.

What Dreams May Come

Christina Skye

With warmest thanks to Karen Plunkett-Powell for aspects, trines, and transits.

To sleep: perchance to dream: ay, there's the rub;
For in that sleep of death what dreams may come . . .

—William Shakespeare, Hamlet

Prologue

Sussex, England
June 1991

RAGGED clouds flew before a three-quarter moon. Saturn was trine Uranus. Mars was in Scorpio.

Damn and blast, the black-clad figure thought, staring down into the darkness. No auspicious alignment here.

Idly he swept a fall of lace from the braided cuffs of his frock coat, watching racing clouds shadow the stark, weathered parapets beneath his feet. Before him Draycott Abbey's one-story gate house lay silent, dappled with silver in the moonlight.

A man and yet not quite a man, the tall figure stood in brooding silence, while moonbeams played over his black damask waistcoat and elegant lace cravat.

In this world he was, yet somehow not quite *of* it.

Around him drifted the scent of roses, rich and fine now in the full flush of summer. 'Petite Lisette,' 'Gloire des Mousseux,' and 'Fantin Latour'—their names were as rich as the heritage that had bred them. Ornate and densely clustered, their velvet petals opened to the night, scenting the warm, still air with beauty.

Far away in the distance, past the rolling downs, past the silver river, past the sleeping village of Highgate, a bell chimed the dead of night.

Twelve times it rang, and then once more.

High atop the granite parapets, Adrian Draycott turned and stared out at the lush park, the glossy waters of the spring-fed moat.

At the shimmering mullioned windows of this ancient house that he had always loved, not wisely but too well.

His lips twisted in a ghost of a smile.

He sensed more than heard the low rustle of fur against granite. He turned, looked down, his smile growing to a boyish grin. "Ah, Gideon, have you come to keep me company this night? If so, I'll thank you for it, old friend, for there is something about this night . . . something troubling." He looked up, his eyes ranging over the dark, wooded fields. "Something that summons up long-forgotten hopes and dreams that are better left buried." Slowly his smile faded and his expression hardened.

A cat glided over the parapet, long and starkly gray, paws tipped in black. Great amber eyes glowed against the darkness, keen and intelligent.

Too intelligent for a cat.

Frowning, the figure in starkest black stared out toward the Channel, watching a finger of lightning arc over the wooded hills. "Yes, there is something else out there tonight. You feel it too, don't you, my friend? A gathering. A heaviness of spirit. And every second I sense that danger moving closer."

Sleek muscles flashing, the cat jumped to the top of the parapet and padded along the weathered stone face.

His companion's lips quirked. "Brazen as always, I see. You really must curb this impulse to recklessness, old friend. It will beget you much trouble otherwise, I fear."

The cat's eyes shone as he settled back on gray haunches. His ears twitched and then he looked down, initiating a delicate toilette in brazen disregard for the granite edge only inches away.

Beside him Adrian Draycott sighed. "So you think it's over, do you?" He leaned out across the wall and into the wind, the white ruffles at his neck tossing sharply as he studied the dark patchwork of fields and forest below. His long fingers smoothed his damask waistcoat thoughtfully. "Because my brother is wed and the men who chased him are dead?"

For a moment Adrian Draycott stiffened, tasting the bitter dregs of sadness. He had saved his brother from a pair of cold-blooded adventurers in search of a treasure buried far away in the mud of Thailand, where Nicholas Draycott had spent nearly a year in captivity.

Adrian had saved Nicholas from them, and in the process he had saved one other, a woman with golden hair and sparkling eyes. A woman to whom he'd lost his heart.

Two hundred years before.

Ever since, there had been a great emptiness in his life, which he'd tried hard to fill with his duties as guardian of this beloved abbey. Two centuries had passed since he'd slipped away from his dying body, and over the years Adrian had found himself missing that physical form less and less.

1790. Yes, it had been a fine year—for wine, for women, and for dying. But he still remembered what it felt like to walk in soft spring grass, to breathe the summer air and feel all the things that a physical body entitled one to feel.

And, of course, there had been those seven short years of boyhood, when he had been Nicholas's twin. But an accident had ended that life tragically.

Yes, those years counted hardly at all, Adrian thought.

But Nicholas and Kacey deserved their happiness, and Adrian was determined that they have it. His job now was simply to watch, to guard, to intervene in what small ways he could to protect this ancient place and all who resided within it.

Which meant that he was left alone once more, with no company but Gideon and the cold stone walls. With nothing but dark memories and the sad cry of the wind sweeping up from the sea.

But this duty was by Adrian Draycott's choice. He'd have it no other way.

So he'd always thought, at least.

Until tonight.

Until he began to remember things he shouldn't have remembered.

Things like the haunting scent of lavender on a summer breeze, the velvet texture of a woman's cheek. The slow, slanting smile that spoke of pleasures soon to come . . .

At the foot of the moat a small night creature rocketed from the darkness, screeching in pain as it crashed away through the underbrush.

With a sigh, the man on the parapet shook his head, his raven eyes hardening. "Aye, there is danger abroad tonight, Gideon. *Great* danger. I can almost feel it growing, somewhere out there in the darkness." He closed his eyes. "Dear God, not another test . . ."

At the edge of the parapet the great cat meowed.

"Indeed, I hope not, my friend. Long have I guarded these beloved walls, these fertile fields, and it has always been my joy as well as my duty. But now—now I'm tired. Dear God, Gideon, I'm so . . . tired . . ."

In a dark rush the sadness returned, crushing him with thoughts of all the things he'd never have again.

His fingers, washed with moonlight, tightened abruptly.

Slowly Adrian Draycott turned, lace fluttering at his braided cuffs. He began to pace the abbey's lonely battlements.

Just as he had done every night for the last two hundred years.

And for six hundred before that.

Atop the sheer granite wall the great gray feline sat motionless, his body a slash of shadow against the rising moon. His amber eyes glowed keen and phosphorescent as the moon rose higher, wreathing him in a nimbus of silver. Purring softly, the cat watched his friend and liege keep a lonely vigil with dark memories and lost dreams.

Meanwhile the night slept on below them.

And with every passing second the malevolence that had no name crept closer.

1

London

THE roses were glorious.

Heavy-petaled, crimson, peach, and palest blush-pink, they glowed through the florist's window. Even through the glass Gray Mackenzie could almost smell their lush perfume.

Around her the honking horns and squealing brakes of Oxford Street faded away to nothing. As if in a dream, she watched herself turn and push open the door to the neat little florist shop.

She would buy a dozen of them.

For herself. Just because she wanted to.

It was a gesture totally unlike her, of course. Lingering jet lag, perhaps?

Gray worried her lower lip. She'd arrived only last night after a hellish flight from Philadelphia, and this morning her pale cheeks showed the strain.

"Yes, miss. 'Ow can I 'elp you?" The proprietor was short, red-cheeked, and impatient to get on with his work, though he was trying hard not to show it.

Gray pointed. "Those roses in the window. They're—magnificent. No, not the modern hybrids. There to the right—the old ones. The centifolia roses with the densely packed petals. 'Lisette,' aren't they?" She delighted in the cluster of rich fuchsia blooms tucked in an elegant crystal vase.

There was something sad about her, the bald-headed proprietor thought. Not like the usual Yanks who came in here, flashing their plastic, talking fast and loud. Only hybrids would do for their sort.

But this one was different. Careful and slow in her speech, she was. And she was a rare and proper beauty, what with that auburn hair spilling over her shoulders and skin that seemed almost too translucent to be real.

And those eyes! Purest sea-blue, they were. They put him in mind of a tropical beach at dawn.

The florist frowned, wondering why such a beauty went about dressed in a dark skirt and a nondescript gray jacket. Then he sniffed. None of his business, after all.

But the flowers were.

He nodded, approving her choice. "Quite right, miss. 'Petite Lisette.' 'Normandica' over 'ere. I've a few 'Fantin Latour' as well. You know something of roses?"

"Not a great deal. It's just . . . a hobby." Gray knew the blooms must be terribly expensive. "I think—yes, I'll take them. All of them."

The florist's estimation of her soared several notches. She had good taste, this red-maned Yank. But perhaps she didn't understand exactly what she was looking at. "That will be ten pounds each," he murmured discreetly, just in case she wanted to back out.

Gray's eyes flickered. The figure was extortionate!

She did a quick calculation, counting nearly two dozen cut stems. In one sweep she saw most of her cash going.

But those roses would be worth every penny. Every shilling, she corrected herself, savoring the rich-veined damask of the petals, drinking in their heady scent. "I'll take them all," she said decisively.

Yes, it was time she put the past where it belonged and treated herself to something special.

The florist gave her an approving smile. "Very good, miss. I'll just fetch some paper to tie them up." A moment later he disappeared into a curtained alcove.

Behind Gray the front door opened with the tinkle of a bell. Chill air swirled through the little shop. Crimson petals dipped in the swift currents and Gray brushed a curl from her cheek.

Behind her came the creak of a floorboard, and then the rasp of a dry voice.

A familiar voice, even after five years.

A voice straight out of her nightmares.

"Lovely, aren't they?"

She spun about, her heart pounding. *Dear God, don't let it be him. Anyone but him!*

But the man in the shadows by the door was broad-shouldered, his skin bronzed from long hours in the sun. Bleached nearly white, his long hair feathered low over his eyes.

Brown eyes, not green.

Not like her ex-husband's at all.

Gray squinted into the shadows. Appearances could be changed, after all. *She* of all people knew that.

The low, dry voice continued. "Such a pity that they die so soon after they're cut." The man's brow rose when Gray did not answer. A smile drifted over his lips. "Sadly, that is often the way with things of beauty. They never last, you know."

Suddenly all the old panic arose. Gray felt her hands begin to quiver. The cold eyes narrowed, studying her, frankly curious now.

"Ex—excuse me. I—I must go." She spun about and stumbled to the door, fear tightening her throat.

Behind her the curtain swished open.

" 'Ere, miss, come back! You've forgotten your roses!"

But Gray was too busy stumbling through the impersonal crowds of Oxford Street to hear.

"Just over the hill, it is. Take the first roundabout and then watch for the second turning. That road will take you direct to Draycott Abbey, miss."

Gray smiled her thanks to the healthy, red-faced village boy and put her rented Mini into gear, trying to forget the curiosity that had gleamed in the boy's eyes as she had asked directions to the abbey.

When are you going to stop being so jumpy? she asked herself angrily. *It's been five years, after all. Why can't you just let it go?*

But Gray knew why.

Because her ex-husband was free again. Because all the high-tech equipment in the world hadn't kept him behind bars.

Away from her.

And now it was just a matter of time until he tracked her down, just as he'd sworn to do.

Her fingers clenched against the steering wheel as she fought down dark memories. Memories of what he'd threatened to do if she revealed any part of the dirty little arrangements he excelled at.

But Gray *had* revealed what she'd heard. Every detail, every damning fact she had spilled to a packed courtroom and an army of eager reporters.

And the last thing Matt had screamed before he was jostled out of the courtroom was that he'd find her somehow. And when he did, he'd make her pay.

Biting down a jerky breath, Gray sailed through the roundabout and eased the gearshift to low. She tried to tell herself she was making too much of the situation. Matt had escaped, yes, but the security officers in Washington had assured Gray it would be just a matter of days until he was back behind bars.

Meanwhile, they had told her, a visit to England—especially to this quiet little backwater of Sussex—would be an excellent idea.

As Gray drove she went over the conversation, looking for details she might have missed then. But no, the officer—Harrington, wasn't it?—had been calm, professional, and totally unalarming.

There was absolutely nothing to worry about, he'd promised her. Not with all the levels of protection and security that had surrounded her case.

Yes, she was to go off to Sussex and work. Leave the heavy stuff to them, he'd ordered briskly.

The man was a professional. Of course he was right, Gray told herself as forested estates rushed past in a blur of green. She had to forget all this brouhaha about her ex-husband and concentrate on her work.

Especially now, when she had the assignment of a lifetime before her.

At that moment a second lane came into view. Above the trees Gray caught a quick glimpse of weathered towers and stark stone walls.

Her heart began to pound.

How well she remembered her friend Kacey's letters describing the great moat-encircled structure with its picturesque stone gate house and climbing roses. Blonde-haired Kacey, the new bride of the Twelfth Viscount Draycott, had been an unshakable friend to Gray at a time when she had desperately needed one.

And Gray was determined to do her best work for Kacey now.

She shoved the gearshift into second and sent gravel flying up, savoring the feel of the Mini as it hummed down the narrow drive.

As she passed beneath a line of overhanging oaks, the years seemed to slip away. Suddenly she was young again, with all things possible.

Without warning a speckled brown deer darted across

the road. She slammed her foot onto the brake and wrenched the wheel violently, barely managing to avoid the animal.

Gray's breath hissed free. Her fingers gripped the wheel. Abruptly she remembered another time she'd driven down a quiet country lane, remembered how much she'd been enjoying the feel of speed and control when a dog had shot out onto the road.

Matt had cursed and wrenched the wheel away from her.

That night they'd had their first disagreement. Their first full-blown quarrel. Their first—

White-faced, Gray clutched the wheel, struggling with fear and raw despair. Down, down, she pushed them, back into the dark cubicle she reserved for her past. For anything to do with the other woman she'd been before her name had been changed, and her features altered.

Before she'd become Gray Mackenzie.

Put everything to do with Matt out of your mind, the counselors had ordered. You're Gray Mackenzie now. Forget that Moira Jamieson ever existed.

With a ragged breath, Gray sat back.

She ought to be happy, after all. She was making a name for herself at last. Her work was found in architecture quarterlies and trade publications on three continents. She was almost established enough to pick and choose her assignments.

She was a success, by anyone's standards.

But inside, Gray knew differently. Inside she was still shy, gawky Moira Jamieson, an uncertain little nobody from a backwater town in central Maine.

Matt had known that too. In fact, he'd never let her forget it.

Out of the corner of her eye Gray saw a dark shape separate from the thick woods.

Her heart lurched as a tall figure emerged from the dark tree line. Gray stiffened, half-expecting to see her ex-husband's sullen face swim into view before her.

But it didn't, of course. Matt would never find her here, not on this quiet estate tucked away in the middle of the English countryside. With any luck he might even be back behind bars already.

Keeping that thought firmly in mind, Gray turned to study the man walking toward the car. The moment she did, she regretted it.

Heat poured into her cheeks; her breath caught in her throat.

He was nothing at all like her former husband. Hard, keen eyes the color of wintry seas stared back at her from a rough, weather-hardened face. His nose was high and his lips were full. Dark and thick, his hair brushed the top of his broad shoulders.

It was a face capable of much pride, Gray thought. A face capable of much stubbornness. It was also a face dark with secrets, secrets that would not be easily revealed to anyone.

And it was indeed the face of a stranger, just as she'd known it must be.

Yet somehow not quite a stranger?

Something nagged at the back of Gray's mind. Something Kacey had told her in one of her short letters before she'd left on her honeymoon with Nicholas Draycott?

Gray frowned as she saw the man scowl, then move directly in front of the car. Of all the colossal arrogance! The insolent fellow was blocking the road!

Reluctantly Gray coasted to a halt, making no attempt to conceal her irritation. Muttering under his breath, the man stalked straight toward her.

A moment later his black-clad legs banged full against the front fender, almost as if he were unaware that the car existed. Cursing roundly, he stared down at his knee, then looked back up at Gray.

Drinking, no doubt. Just her luck to run into an English

lush! But sweet heaven, the man was tall—well over six feet.

Unconsciously Gray studied the hard muscles rippling beneath his soft dark shirt and the long thighs that braced and tensed as he moved around to stare at her through the open window.

And Gray stared back, pointedly and quite rudely.

Her interest was strictly professional, of course. Merely the impersonal concern of an artist assessing a possible subject.

But that explanation didn't stop strange tendrils of heat from licking at her cheeks and uncoiling through her stomach. And that knowledge only made Gray angrier.

She gulped down a deep breath, fighting for calm. *Get a hold on yourself, Mackenzie. The man's a stranger, remember? Just a stranger.*

"Where are *you* going, woman?"

His voice was low and richly accented. For some reason the sound of it made Gray flush, made the fine little hairs at the back of her neck prickle and rise.

"Straight up this drive—if you'd just move out of the way, that is." *Maybe even if you don't*, Gray thought irritably.

"What business have you here?"

Her hands tensed against the steering wheel. "I might ask the same of you!"

Gray glared, but even then the man did not move back from the window. Clearing her throat, she tried a more direct attack. "Do you mind? I've just had a long ride from London and I was hoping to—" She halted abruptly. "This *is* Draycott Abbey, isn't it? Don't tell me I missed the second turn."

With every word the man's black mood seemed to deepen. "Yes, of course this is the abbey, woman! And these are Draycott lands. But how in the name of all that's holy did I—" He stopped, then plunged long fingers through his thick black hair.

Gray barely noticed his tension, too relieved by the assurance that she was finally near her destination. Soon she would be ensconced in one of the lovely old chintz-and flower-filled rooms Kacey had described. There she would be safe from Matt, safe from any and all distractions while she completed the work she'd come here for.

But the man outside the window continued to frown, showing no sign of being finished with his interrogation. "What sort of game are you playing at, woman?"

Gray felt her cheeks redden. *Game?* Was the fellow mad or just terminally rude?

"I've come on an assignment—for Lord Draycott, not that it's any of *your* business." Suddenly she stiffened. "You can't be—good heavens, you aren't Lord Draycott, are you? That is, I expected someone—"

Shorter? Younger? Less imposing?

She didn't finish, held captive by the intensity of his slate-dark gaze.

"*I?* Nicholas Draycott?" The man's dark brows rose as he laughed bitterly. "By God, that's rich! The woman thinks—"

Suddenly a rustling at his feet called his attention to the ground, where a sleek gray cat pressed against his black-booted ankles.

He seemed to catch back his words, his eyes narrowing.

Gray didn't mean to give him time for any more questions. "Well, if you're not Lord Draycott, then I'm wasting my time here. So if you don't mind . . ." She gestured at the gravel drive. "I really would like to reach the abbey before the light goes."

The man's frown grew to a decided scowl. "Mind? Who am *I* to mind? When am *I* ever consulted about anything?" Suddenly he bent closer, his eyes scouring her face. "Ah! You must be the artist. American, I believe."

Gray merely glared. "Are you going to move or not?"

The slate eyes glittered. "I believe not—Miss Mackenzie."

Suddenly Gray felt cold—very cold. So what if he knew her name? Why did any of this matter?

But it did. For some reason it mattered intensely. Perhaps it was something about the man's face, something sad and bitter in the way he laughed . . .

Enough, Mackenzie. Get out while you still can.

One last question leaped to her lips. "Who are you? What gives *you* the right to cross-examine me?"

Did she merely imagine that he stiffened? "I? I am . . . Adrian. The caretaker, as you would call it."

Gray frowned. Caretaker? He was like no caretaker *she'd* ever met before. A tiny network of lines radiated from the corner of his eyes, and she had a sudden urge to touch them, smooth them.

"Have I ever—I mean, have we ever—"

Ridiculous! Of course they hadn't met before.

But how else was she to explain the familiarity of that lean face, her instinctive knowledge of the pain that haunted those wintry eyes? The heat hidden in that stern mouth?

With a gasp, Gray recovered herself. "N-never mind. Of course we haven't."

Outside the car the man smiled slightly. Draping his arm along the metal roof, he bent closer, his eyes darkening. "If you mean by that obscure bit of gibberish have we met before, the answer is no. But I do have the advantage over you, Miss Mackenzie. Kacey told me you were coming."

It was a lie, of course. The viscount's bride had said nothing to Adrian Draycott about Gray Mackenzie. But a ghost had ways of hearing nearly everything that happened within his domain, particularly when he was a resident ghost of the guardian variety.

In that sense Adrian supposed his answer about his identity had not been a lie. In his role of guardian he had chanced to overhear Kacey and Nicholas speak about Gray Mackenzie several times before their departure.

But no amount of discussion could have prepared Adrian for the pure beauty of the woman who sat before him now.

Nothing could have captured the glow of her alabaster skin, the fiery sheen of her wild auburn hair.

The wariness that darkened her azure eyes.

And those things made Adrian want to sweep her against him and drive the fear from her eyes. To kiss her and tease her and coax a laugh from her soft lips.

And then carry her down to the ferns beside the moat and slide deep inside her, filling her with his hard heat until she shuddered and arched in breathless abandon beneath him.

Adrian stiffened. What in the name of heaven was wrong with him? He was a *ghost*. He hadn't had such raw impulses for years!

Two hundred years, to be exact.

He scowled, trying to fight down the heat that rose insidiously toward the seat of his manhood. Abstracted, he ran his finger down the rim of the roof, leaving a long trail in the dust atop the car.

But how was it possible? This woman *saw* him. She *heard* him. And somehow he was beside her in physical form, with fingers that moved and felt and left a visible mark against dusty metal.

He had managed to materialize once or twice before, of course, in times of dire need. He had even appeared to Kacey once, desperate to warn her of the danger that she and Nicholas faced unless they found a way to trust each other.

But never had those appearances been more than temporary, and never had they involved a tangible flesh-and-blood body such as he now possessed. Certainly Adrian had never before felt the intensely physical things he was feeling now.

Yet here he stood, the wind ruffling his long black hair, the sun warming his neck, the metal of this clamorous four-wheeled conveyance cool and smooth against his all-too-real fingers.

In physical flesh-and-blood form, by God! Accomplished without conscious thought or effort of any sort. Damn, but it was unnerving.

Was this another test? Or was it simply a new twist to his ancient duties at the abbey?

He smothered a curse, trying to understand, knowing already that he would not succeed.

Meanwhile the look in the eyes of the woman beside him told Adrian that to her he was only *too* real, and that the sight made her vastly uncomfortable.

Somehow *that* hurt Adrian Draycott most of all.

For at that moment he felt a stunning need to sweep the fear from those wary azure eyes forever. To see those petal-soft lips curve up in joy and wonder.

Shocked by the force of these unfamiliar emotions, he could only stare down at her pale face, fighting to understand this sudden and intense need to protect her.

Beside him, Gray swallowed. What was happening to her?

The man was handsome, there was no mistaking that. But the sun would soon be setting and if she dawdled any longer she would miss the best time for viewing the abbey. "I—I'd really better go."

She tried to look away, but the storm-dark eyes continued to hold her. Motionless, the black-clad stranger merely stared back at her.

And the look was pure heat, a beam of summer sun poured through leaden clouds straight into her heart.

Frowning, Gray swept unsteady fingers over her forehead, then clutched the wheel. "I—I'm going to go now. If you don't want to lose a toe or two, I'd suggest you move back."

She tried to make her voice cool, but all she felt was

utterly foolish as she looked down and fumbled with her keys. What in heaven's name was *wrong* with her?

In that second a hard hand reached out to catch her fingers, pulling them from their trembling hold on the steering wheel. His eyes were tense, unreadable. "Don't go."

Gray's heart beat wildly. "I b-beg your pardon?"

"To the abbey. *Don't go.*" His voice was harsh. "Go back to London instead. And then go back home, Gray Mackenzie. Back to wherever you come from in America."

Gray nearly flinched. "*Don't go?* Just like that? After I've come ten hours by plane and another five by car?" She felt her cheeks burning. "Not on your life, mister!"

A vein pounded at Adrian's forehead. "Wretched female! There is danger here, don't you see? And somehow *you* are involved, though I cannot yet say how. But I bloody well won't permit my abbey—"

"*Your* abbey?" Gray laughed in disbelief. "Funny, I could have sworn that Nicholas Draycott was the abbey's owner!"

The caretaker's fingers tightened on hers. His calloused thumb inched across her cold palm, leaving an odd trail of warmth against her skin. His eyes flashed dangerously. "Of course he is. But Nicholas left me here to . . . to keep an eye on things, shall we say? In his absence, of course."

Muttering angrily, Gray tried to tug her fingers free but failed. "You take your duties very seriously, don't you? But then, I'm clearly a dangerous sort, just bristling with evil designs upon the abbey's treasures."

"You might be more dangerous than you know, Miss Mackenzie." For long seconds the frowning caretaker stared down at their entwined fingers. Abruptly he released her. "Mark me well. If you go farther, know that you do so on *my* land." His slate eyes narrowed. "And it will be *me* to whom you'll answer then."

Gray glared back at him. "No, I have a much better idea! You stay out of *my* way! My work will keep me quite busy enough as it is. Believe me, the very last thing I need is an ill-mannered, supercilious junior gardener with delusions of grandeur and an advanced case of paranoia poking around while I'm trying to concentrate!"

Without waiting for an answer, Gray wrenched at the gearshift and sent the car plunging forward. Gravel hissed and spun beneath the flying wheels and a moment later the forest bled away in a blur of green.

But with every second Gray felt her neck prickle, felt her cheeks flush. Somehow she knew the unblinking slate-gray eyes were following her still.

And she couldn't help but wonder at her nagging certainty that she'd seen those strange, implacable eyes somewhere before.

He watched motionless as her car sped down the drive and disappeared over the hill.

Damn and blast, he hadn't meant to frighten her! In fact he hadn't meant to say most of the things he had. He'd only meant to warn her of the danger he felt and then try to find out if she could explain its source.

He *certainly* hadn't meant to touch the woman.

But he hadn't been thinking straight at the time.

After all, he hadn't expected to be knocked speechless by the vision of a wary beauty with a mane of auburn hair and azure eyes. He hadn't expected to see full crimson lips that trembled slightly at some private fear.

He certainly hadn't expected to feel this fierce compulsion to protect her. From everything and everyone.

Even from yourself?

Cursing roundly, Adrian turned away from the road. He raised one hand before him, then the other.

Slowly, almost hesitantly, he ran his fingers over his tense forearms, feeling soft wool and hard, bunching muscle beneath.

Frowning, he dragged his booted toe through the rich dark earth, then stared fixedly at the small furrow raised in its wake. "So I really am here. And I haven't the slightest memory, the slightest clue as to how it came about."

Grim-faced, he raised his head and stared at the spot where the noisy green car had just disappeared. "One minute I'm caught up in dreams and the next I'm thrust down without a hint of warning into dirt and noise and a body I can barely remember how to maneuver. The whole thing is bloody impossible!"

But there were the powerful forearms, the booted legs to prove him wrong. He scowled down at his outstretched palms. "Muscle. Blood. How strange it all feels. How . . . heavy. And how vast a responsibility . . ."

A butterfly with azure wings skimmed past, looped around his fingers, then settled onto his calloused palm.

For a moment Adrian Draycott's face darkened. He stood unmoving, mesmerized by the sight of those frail wings fluttering upon his long, calloused fingers.

Just like her eyes, he thought.

Azure with flecks of gold. Like sunrise on a warm summer sea.

He shook his head abruptly, forcing away that particular memory, feeling a half-forgotten heat rush through his legs and move inexorably upward in a way that was distinctly disconcerting.

And all too human.

But Adrian Draycott was not about to be deterred from his ancient obligations. Not by anyone or anything.

And before the night was over, he was bloody well going to know just what in the blazes was going on here at his abbey!

2

B Y the time Gray left the woods and circled up the drive to the gate house, her heart had stopped pounding. But her cheeks were still flushed.

Damn the man! Who did he think he was?

Then even he was swept from Gray's mind as Draycott Abbey's massive granite walls burst into view before her.

Her first thought as she looked upon the ancient structure was that she was glad she wasn't psychic. Within such a place there must be many ghosts. Even she who'd never felt a hint of special intuition sensed an odd prickle at her spine as she stared up at the crenellated roof and mullioned windows.

The granite walls gleamed back at her, bathed with light in the slanting rays of the afternoon sun. Beneath the sheer stone faces, white swans skimmed across a lily-studded moat.

Gray's breath caught. There was a sense of timelessness to the place, a sense of utter peace that invaded one's very soul. It was almost as if past and present merged here, then formed a boundless, eternal present.

Oh, right, Mackenzie! Next you'll be seeing mounted knights jousting for their ladies' honor!

Somewhere over the hills came the sound of bells and the faint bleating of sheep. The engine died with a cough. Suddenly Gray was enveloped in a vast, luminous silence.

It was then that the house began to sing to her.

So long . . . so long since she had known such peace.

Her azure eyes rose to the granite parapets. For a moment she thought she saw a hint of movement in a corner tower. But that was unlikely, of course, since Lord Draycott and his new bride were almost certainly in Paris by now, enjoying their honeymoon.

And Gray knew just how much Kacey and Nicholas deserved that happiness after escaping death at the hands of a pair of cold-blooded murderers searching for secrets Nicholas didn't possess.

Kacey had said little about the ordeal and Gray had known enough not to press her. In the meantime Gray was delighted when Kacey had phoned with a commission to do a detailed rendering of the abbey. She was determined to give her friend the very best work she had ever done.

Already her practiced eye was at work, scanning the abbey for balance points, shadow values, and angles of perspective. For these things were Gray's life now, the source of her few pleasures.

And in the last year she had finally begun to make her mark. Offers poured in and she had actually had to turn down commissions. But a house had to sing to her, to give of itself freely before she agreed to take on an assignment, no matter how impressive the fee.

And Gray invariably left her clients delighted. As any one of them would have agreed, to own one of Gray Mackenzie's sketches was to own the heart of a house, its very soul.

But oh, *this* house—this proud, magnificent abbey sang to Gray already and in many voices. Of heroic days, of bards and warriors girded in leather and mail. Of dark seasons when brother turned against brother and father against son.

As she sat silent, listening to a lark trill out a gay tune, Gray lost her heart. Somewhere behind her a fat trout jumped from the sparkling moat.

Already she knew that the sketches she did here would be her very finest work.

She was still sitting wide-eyed, fingers taut on the wheel, when the crunch of gravel roused her. She turned her head to see a man in a black jacket and incongruous red running shoes striding toward her, a careful smile on his ruddy face.

"Miss Mackenzie? Welcome to Draycott Abbey. I am Marston."

As Gray stepped from the car, she remembered Kacey's last, hasty note, which had reached her barely a week before.

> *Marston, Nicholas's butler, is a dear, but I'm sure the man will be overjoyed to see the last of us. He claims he can't concentrate on his work with the two of us forever mooning about. He swears it's making him dangerously matrimonial.*

Gray smiled to herself at the thought of this sober, correct gentleman's gentleman feeling "dangerously matrimonial."

The man looked about as emotional as a mackerel.

"Shall I take your bags up, Miss Mackenzie?"

Gray nodded, still enthralled by the massive walls hung with climbing roses. Quickly she dug into her satchel and tugged out a spiral sketchbook. Without another word, she settled herself against the hood of her rental car and began to work. Already her mind was humming with ways to capture the elegant angles of the ancient stone edifice.

Yes, the lovely centifolia roses would curl and climb just *so*, and the swans would glide just a little left of center . . .

Footsteps crunched softly over gravel. Gray heard

them only dimly, already lost in balance points and texture sources.

In the only thing that had saved her life five years before.

The sun hung golden atop the trees when Gray finally looked up. Beside her lay her first three renderings of the abbey.

Slowly she sat back and massaged her aching neck.

And then she saw the letter, cream vellum stock with an embossed coronet surrounded with double dragons. Vaguely Gray recalled Marston saying something about a letter—a letter from the viscountess, was it?

A smile flitted about the corners of her mouth. Gray wondered if she would ever get used to the idea of sweet, forthright Kacey Mallory being a viscountess.

Her smile grew as she tore open the envelope and read her friend's scrawled note, dated only two days earlier.

> *Sorry, Gray, not to be there to meet you, but our flight has been changed yet again. Marston will take care of anything you need though. The man is truly a wonder!*
>
> *Thanks again for coming on such short notice. I wanted the very best person for these renderings, and you were it. By the way, I'd like to keep these a secret from Nicholas until his birthday. Only Marston is to know about them for now.*
>
> *But I absolutely forbid you to bury yourself in your work the way you usually do. As your employer I hereby order you to borrow the car. Take a walk around the downs. The Sussex countryside is lovely in high summer. And you, my girl, were looking far too pale the last time I saw you.*

Gray's eyes crinkled as she recalled the last time they'd met. Their lunch had consisted of soft pretzels loaded with mustard, which they'd gulped down on a crowded Philadelphia street corner between jobs. Had it been only two months ago?

Gray's eyes returned to her friend's letter.

By the way, if you should happen to hear thirteen bells, don't be upset. The locals say it has to do with an old abbey legend. You see, along with a moat and a priceless art collection, the abbey also has a resident ghost. And when the bells ring thirteen times—

Here the letter ended in a jagged scrawl, then picked up a line lower, with the scrawl even more pronounced.

Sorry, but Nicholas is growing impatient (as usual) and I really must go. I believe I have a way to put a smile back on his face, however. The limousine taking us to Heathrow has curtained windows and a smoked glass divider. The mind positively boggles at the possibilities . . .

Love you.
K.C.

Gray found herself chuckling. No doubt Kacey would find a way to coax a smile from her husband. A certifiable beauty, she was also something even rarer: a kind and generous person. Only she seemed unaware of her beauty, and perhaps that was part of her charm.

Now *she* was a different matter entirely, Gray thought ruefully. Tall, auburn-haired, she had always been a little too tall, a little too shy, a little too bony. Most men felt uncomfortable just looking at her.

Or looking up at her, since she neared six feet without shoes.

For years she had never seemed to fit into any mold and that had bothered her keenly. Then she had begun making her own mold.

That had worked well for a time. And then she'd met Matt . . .

Gray's fingers stiffened. Frowning, she brushed back a wild strand of wine-dark hair.

No, she refused to think about *him*. Her ex-husband belonged to that other life, to that dark time she was not supposed to think about anymore. The only way her change would be complete was if she made it *inside*, or so the counselors had warned her.

But it had been hard, far harder than she'd thought. She hadn't dreamed there would be so many cues, so many tiny details that bound a person to a specific place, a specific time, a specific identity.

But your identity became a threat, she reminded herself grimly. *Because of that it had to be changed, and the truth buried forever.*

Beyond the moat a curlew exploded from the woods and hurtled through the air, gray wings outlined as it cut through a cloudless turquoise sky.

Do you really think that will stop him? a cold voice whispered. *Do you think anything can stop a man like that?*

And now he's free. The first thing he'll do is come looking for you. And when he finds you, he's going to—

Gray bit her lip, feeling the old, familiar fear gnaw at her stomach. *But I'm safe here!* she told herself, watching the sun melt like warm honey over the forested hills above the moat.

He can never trace me here.

Yes, here at Draycott Abbey she would be safe.

Wouldn't she?

Marston was every bit as efficient as Kacey had promised. After an elegant dinner of marinated white asparagus, feather-light salmon mousse, and an unforgettable crème brûlée, he'd led Gray out to the flower-hung gate house flanking the moat.

The taciturn butler had first offered her a room in the main house, but the gate house's floor-to-ceiling French doors overlooking the moat had instantly captured Gray's imagination.

And there she had stayed.

Now, after sketching for several hours, Gray still found herself no closer to sleep.

She glanced down at her watch. Three A.M. Jet lag for sure.

Not that she could have slept anyway. There was something too rich about the air in this ancient, history-haunted place.

Yes, she could well believe that phantoms walked the parapets of Draycott Abbey. Hadn't Kacey mentioned something about a legendary family ghost?

A shiver played down her spine. She realized the night was growing cool. Pulling a wool throw over her shoulders, Gray curled up on an armchair before the opened doors, watching moonlight play over the shifting silver water.

Somewhere in the distance came the first faint peal of bells.

What was it Kacey had said about bells?

Gray frowned, unable to remember. She stifled a yawn as the scent of roses enveloped her, warm and inviting. Nice, she thought. More than nice . . .

Not that she'd be able to sleep, of course. She was far too keyed up. But at least she could rest and run through several possible compositions to try out in the morning.

Moments later, clutching an architecture manual in one hand and a Royal Geological Survey guide in the other, she sank onto the bed. Her eyes fluttered, then closed. Her head slid forward, auburn hair spilling over an embossed leather cover.

She never even heard the thirteenth chime.

*   *   *

The roses swayed. A cloud ran before the three-quarter moon.

Mars in Scorpio. Saturn trine Uranus.

The house seemed to catch its breath—to shudder. Quiet and yet not entirely quiet, the great walls slept on, caught in a restless silence.

Moonlight touched the edge of the opened French doors and a shadow that was not quite a shadow fell across the threshold.

Dear God, she was beautiful, he thought.

Her skin was like finest bisque, her lashes a dark curve against her cheeks.

And that glorious auburn hair . . .

The figure in the doorway moved closer, making no sound in these, the dead hours of night. Just as before he sensed the danger, enveloping her like a sullen black cloud.

Had she no idea at all?

At the window the curtains fluttered. A large cat crept through their swaying folds, gray tail all atwitch. Leaping to the white coverlet, he stretched out comfortably, his body curved like a dark comma against the apricot damask pillows.

Moonlight bounced off the moat, poured through the window, and gleamed back from a small gilt mirror opposite the French doors. The room seemed to shimmer, ablaze with light, while the air filled with the dense summer scent of honeysuckle and roses.

On the bed Gideon stirred. Flicking his tail, he gave a soft meow.

The man at the threshold frowned. She was nothing like Kacey, Adrian Draycott realized. She was nothing like any woman he'd ever known.

Or maybe she was . . .

A hint of memory pricked at his consciousness. A dim image of sad eyes in a pale and very noble face.

A flowing gown cut from silk that flashed like hammered gold.

The black-clad figure stiffened. Where in the blazes had *that* image come from?

A dream?

Or was it something more?

Faint, so faint, the phantom images danced before him, teasing and elusive, finally fading away into nothingness. Smothering a curse, Adrian Draycott slipped past the drifting curtains, then laughed bitterly at his unnecessary care.

For no one could hear his curses or his footfalls. Just as no one could see him when he walked his ancient parapets and gazed upon his beloved roses.

Not until *she* had come, that is.

The sense of uneasiness that had dogged Adrian grew sharper. Once more he was being pulled in, and he liked the prospect not at all. Aye, whether the obdurate female was a rare beauty or not!

After all, he'd succeeded once. After that precarious chase upon the cliffs, during which he'd saved Kacey and his brother from death, Adrian had bloody well earned the right to be left alone for a century or two!

The newly married couple was probably ensconced in a lovely old *auberge* outside Paris right now, resting and enjoying the fruits of Adrian's work at reconciling them.

The ghost of Draycott Abbey frowned, one brow rising.

Well, perhaps *resting* was not precisely the word for what the two would be doing in that great silk-hung bed . . .

Adrian tensed, feeling the old bitterness, the gnawing memories of regret and betrayal. Once, long ago, Kacey had been his, but in his arrogance he had lost her.

Now it was Nicholas's chance to know the joy of her love.

Frowning, Adrian gazed down at the woman asleep

on the bed, sensing the black wall around her grow ever more solid.

At her feet Gideon stirred and raised his head.

"Yes, my friend, there is danger here—great danger. Perhaps even more than my brother faced from his old enemies."

Adrian sighed. He had a choice, of course. There was always a choice. But he had never before shirked a duty to his abbey, and he didn't intend to do so now.

Yet something told him this time there would be other complications. Complications that included all the heated demands of this uncertain physical form he'd been given.

Lord, what was the use of it?

Gideon meowed softly from the bed.

"Yes, I know there are *some* things a body is useful for, old friend." As Adrian's eyes returned to the figure on the bed, he felt a sharp current of heat sweep down his spine.

His frown grew. Damn and blast! He hadn't felt such things for years. Even with Kacey it had been merely a remembered response. But with this woman . . .

The heat twisted, shimmered, coiled about him like a bright mist. Dim memories gathered, teased, took tangible form in the ashes of a desire he'd thought dead and long buried.

Buried, yes, but far from dead, as Adrian soon discovered.

It seemed desire had merely slept, century after century, awaiting this moment.

Time ground to a halt. Adrian stood rigid, staring at the auburn hair spread upon the pillow. His heart seemed to lurch, his hands to tremble. Who *was* she to affect him so?

Suddenly he was tasked with all the old dreams, all the thoughts of things that could never be his.

Because it was too late for him, far too late.

Outside in the moonlight a fish leaped from the moat and fell back in an explosion of light. Water scattered in a fury of silver, flashing ever outward beneath the moon.

Gideon blinked as the curtains danced, then drifted back to stillness. A moment later the abbey's resident ghost disappeared into the night, trailing sadness behind him like a shimmering stream of silver.

Sussex, England
February 1191

Out beyond the moat, out beyond the old Roman track and the quiet rowan wood, blood-red fingers of light gathered across the darkening Western sky. Even now the first beacon fires were being lit.

Dressed in a rough cloak and wimple, a woman moved past the unfinished stone tower and leaned over the crenellated wall. Tall and fair, she stared out into the gathering night while somewhere in the darkness a lone wolf howled. In the far hills above her others took up the wild, sad chant.

Desolation. It sat upon her like a shroud, inexorable as the coming of night.

Not even in her native Brittany, where the iron-gray seas heaved against the barren cliffs, had she known such dolor, such utter loneliness.

She shivered, clutching her homespun cloak closer about her shoulders. Gone the furs, gone the velvets in her liege's absence. And as so oft of late, she was gripped with ominous premonitions.

When would he return, the man she loved so well? Seven long months had passed, and yet she'd had no word, no news at all from the Holy Land where he marched at Richard's side.

She gripped the granite parapet with trembling fingers, in desperate need of the stone's reassuring strength.

His strength. *Gleaned from* his *beloved stone walls.*

*Now they were among the few things she had left
to remember her husband by. Even the brooch he had
given her was gone, stolen in the night while she slept.
Carefully worked in gold and jewel-like enamels, it was a
clever piece, with two dragons intertwined about a golden
coronet.*

His device. And the Lady Anne of Draycotte knew
she would never see the treasured brooch again.

She sighed. There was still so much to be done here.
The south tower of the great house was only half-finished,
its inner and outer faces truncated in a jagged shell. Only
half the merlons rose above the high parapets. Even now
mounds of carefully made mortar lay discarded in heaps
near the gaping wall.

But masons, quarrymen, and smiths were gone, dismissed just as the rest of Draycotte's loyal servants had
been. And now the walls stood jagged and unfinished,
a silent mockery of all that Draycotte's lord had sought
to create here.

At least his beloved roses, gathered from far-flung
Aquitaine and Castile, were now settled in fresh beds,
the Lady Anne thought. This she had done with her own
hands, trusting the job to no one else. Soon they would
begin to put forth their first green shoots.

How sad her lord would be to miss their first budding
against his granite walls.

Another beacon took flame, blazing in the black hills.
The cottagers and villeins moved about it, keeping their
silent vigil.

Just as Draycotte's lady did.

Where are you, my love? her heart cried out, as if it
could cross the thousand lonely miles to his side. *Are
you fallen before an infidel blade? Is your broad brow
even now dry and baking beneath a cruel desert sun?*

The Lady Anne flinched and nearly cried aloud at the
thought of it, her fingers pressed to fists.

No, he must be alive! He had sworn he would return

to her. Had he been felled with mortal wound, she must know it, feel it in her very limbs!

No, he would return, her liege and lord. He would come back to Draycotte and this land he loved so well. She had to believe that. Even on this blackest of nights when her hope was nigh gone, she had to remember and be strong.

Crying shrilly, a kestrel winged home through the night. The manor's lady hoped that the bird found a safer roost than she had done, surrounded by sullen enemies who never let her from their sight.

But such was the lawlessness on the land. And now by royal writ her home was no longer her own.

She pushed back her wimple, feeling the coarse linen flow loose at her cheeks. Her fingers flexed, easing around her ripening stomach. At her gentle touch the babe within stirred and kicked.

Once she would have smiled at such a movement, but now it only made her catch her fingers tighter to protect the fragile life growing inside her. Feeling a moment of dizziness, she reached out to the granite parapet, pressing her fingers into the smooth, honed stone.

In two more months the babe would come. She prayed that his father would be home in time to see his son's birth. And a son she knew the child would be. Yet somehow in her restless dreams she could never see more than a glimpse of the tiny face and keen, bright eyes.

And then naught but darkness . . .

To cheer herself, she tried to think of brighter things, recalling the image of their last meeting, out by the witch's pool.

There in the ferns he had loosed her kirtle and cloth-of-gold gown. Swiftly he had caught her to him, his fingers desperate, searching, his manhood hot and pulsing. All through the long hours of night he had held her and claimed her, ever more fierce, ever more urgent, almost as if he could drive away the morrow with the raw force of his desire.

Her eyes blurred with tears as she gazed out at the distant glitter of the pool. There they had loved and laughed seven months before.

It might have been a lifetime, in truth.

If only he would come to her again.

If only there were some way to drive these sullen wolves from her hearth.

But she knew it was impossible. Not even with a score of able men could such a thing be done.

And the Lady Anne had no more protectors. One by one they had sickened and died, or simply gone beyond the walls and never returned.

Now she was left alone, without waiting-maid or kin, a prisoner attended by those who wished her only ill.

Out in the darkness another beacon flamed white-hot to life. Watching the sparks shoot up, the Lady of Draycotte straightened her shoulders and shoved down her fear, knowing her lord would expect that of her. Aye, his pride was fierce; he would have demanded no less from her.

For those were his *people out there in the darkness. Serf, villein, and cottager, they waited, with no other way than this to show their loyalty.*

Now more than a score of fires glowed golden through the valley, turning night to day. The sight heartened her as nothing else could have. The Lord of Draycotte would have been proud, so proud of them.

Her hands curved protectively over her stomach. In the meantime she must be strong, just as he would wish her to be. She must wait and pray for her own true love's return, even if it took ten years more, and a hundred after that!

Still she would remember and still she would be here waiting when he returned from his holy quest.

By the witch's pool at midnight. 'Tis there I'll seek you. Forget it not.

Even as the wrenching loneliness gripped her, the Lady Anne vowed to remember. And she would be there waiting for her lord and love when he came riding back to her over the lush green Draycotte hills.

With a choked moan, Gray shot upright in the soft bed, in the peaceful night, in the ancient gate house by the silver moat.

Her heart was hammering wildly. Her eyes were wide and haunted.

She peered into the shadows, frightened and disoriented. Her fingers dug into the damask coverlet as she tried to remember what had woken her.

A dream? If so,'twas more real than her gray, cheerless reality.

She tried to catch back the shifting images, but her dreams poured through her fingers like white sand, leaving her with nothing but emptiness and an aching sense of loss.

And with fear, her old, familiar companion.

The room was wrapped in silence; moonlight glittered like frost before the half-open French doors.

Then Gray saw the perfect, densely petaled rose. It lay beside her on the bed, centered on an ivory pillow.

"Dear God . . ." she whispered.

But she was not the same person she had once been. No longer would she shove down her fear, shivering and waiting in silence and dread. This new person that she was exploded from the bed in an angry white storm of linen and damask.

Without a thought to the brevity of her satin nightshirt she flung back the curtains, determined to find the person who dared invade the privacy of her room.

But there was no one.

Beyond the narrow flagstone terrace only a pair of swans moved, necks arched and proud as they glided beneath the moon's opaque silver eye.

Nothing else stirred in this silent nightscape of black and glittering silver. Of soft mist and hard shadows.

Only the swans moved.

Only her dim, restless memories lingered.

Gray's fingers tensed against the chill metal of the terrace railing. She fought to hold back a wracking sob.

Dear God, when would she learn how to forget? When would she ever be truly whole again?

A rustle of the curtains drew her eyes behind her, where a gray blur slipped through a beam of moonlight. A great cat, it drifted through the curtains out onto the little flagstone terrace.

It was the same cat she had seen this morning, curling about that insufferable caretaker's booted feet.

Amber eyes rose to study Gray, moon-bright, oddly keen.

They glittered at her, then narrowed as if in secret query.

Gray caught back a shiver. What new fancies were upon her now?

With the barest bunching of sleek muscles the cat jumped to the delicate wrought iron rail at the edge of the terrace and moved closer, stopping just short of Gray's right hand.

The hand that still clutched the rose.

A moist, black nose shoved at her closed fingers, tongue lapping, warm and faintly rough. A low, rich purr poured from the cat's throat.

Gray felt wild laughter build in her chest. Slowly she slid her fingers over the soft pelt, delighting in the cat's silken warmth.

A hint of perfume drifted on the warm, still air. She turned, sniffing to trace its source. Abruptly she saw the dark outline of a climbing rose. Crimson petals spilled across the wall to her right, where the moat lapped against the side of the gate house.

Centifolia roses. Just like the ones she had left behind in London.

Just like the rose clasped within her fingers.

A wild joy swept through Gray. It came unbidden, as if from some other place, some other time.

Without taking time to think, she swept over the railing and inched along the narrow strip of damp soil that ran between gate house and moat.

Twice her bare feet slipped, mud-slick, and twice she caught herself.

And then she seized the vine itself. Struggling upright, she feasted on the wide-petaled beauty of the ancient roses covering the wall before her.

As if in a dream her fingers circled the satin petals. Perfume spilled around her, drowning the night in beauty, making her throat constrict with pain and a flood of exquisite, nearly forgotten memories.

In just such a place two lovers might have met to share whispered vows beneath the wind-tossed petals. Here too they might have shared lingering kisses, warm and gentle.

Then kisses not gentle at all . . .

"What in bloody hell are you doing to my roses?"

The words came at her without warning.

Gray started, let go of the vine, and instantly lost her balance. Swaying wildly, she slipped down the muddy bank and realized that any second she was going to fall.

But strangely she did not.

Hard hands seized her shoulders, dragged her upright, spun her around.

And she gazed into eyes of slate, into eyes of pride and cunning.

She stared at an angular, weather-beaten face. *The caretaker?* But surely the man did not take his duties so seriously as this!

Her heart still thundering, Gray fought to recover her control. She frowned, shoving at his hands. "Just what do you think *you're* doing, Tarzan?"

"I believe I asked first, Miss Mackenzie. Your work

here does not entitle you to decimate my gardens, after all."

Fury speared through Gray. And then she realized they were trapped on the narrow band of soil between rock and water, thigh to thigh, chest to chest.

Heart to pounding heart.

And it felt sinfully, *painfully* good.

Most of all, it felt oddly familiar somehow . . .

Red-faced with fury and embarrassment, she wrenched at his hands. "Let me go, you arrogant—" Her hand lashed out, driving against his chest.

His grip only tightened. "Who are you, woman, that you try me so sorely?"

What was the madman talking about? Painfully aware that she wore nothing but a satin nightshirt that barely skimmed her thighs, Gray tried to twist free.

And got nowhere. Her hands were captured securely between hard, calloused fingers.

In her struggling, Gray's hips brushed his taut thigh. Heat flared through her as she felt the powerful muscles bunch and flex at her touch.

Her captor flinched. His breath seemed to catch. "Who *are* you?" he repeated, his voice as raw as Gray's had been. "Is this some new sort of test?"

But when her eyes rose, Adrian Draycott read nothing but bewilderment in their azure depths. Sweet heaven, what was happening here? In truth he was at least as confused as she!

A vein hammered at Adrian's temple as heat swept between their tense bodies. Around him the night swayed, and time slid to a halt. Had he been even halfway sane at that moment, he would have pulled away, stopped before it was too late . . .

But maybe it had been too late the first moment he'd seen this stubborn, exasperating creature. And sane was the very last thing Adrian Draycott was feeling right then. How could he be sane with her soft breasts caressing his chest, her slim thighs brushing his belly?

"By all the heavens above, woman, you task me beyond measure! But arrogant I always was. Damned, too, perhaps. If so, then it makes no difference if—"

It was reckless, of course. Worse yet, it was utterly dangerous. And yet . . .

And yet he cared not.

The next moment Gray was swept close, molded to his urgent body.

"S-stop this! What do you think you're doing—"

She got no further, her protests drowned beneath the hot silk of his probing lips, the velvet fury of his kiss.

Kiss? she thought dimly. Kiss was far too tame a word for this total possession, this storm of heat and hunger he unleashed.

And even as she struggled, cursing, Gray felt his need kindle an answering heat within her.

Impossible! Unthinkable!

And yet . . .

With a gasp, she wrenched at his iron grip, kicked at his legs, but all her efforts won her only a peal of dark laughter.

Mouth to mouth they strained, caught on the very edge of the moat, where the slightest misstep would send them both flying into the water.

Neither cared in the least. In furious silence they struggled, she to wrench free, he to drive closer. To claim and possess.

Infinitely. With a hunger that Adrian Draycott realized he had never known before, nor even dreamed of in a life spent pursuing every imaginable form of pleasure.

Somehow there was a fatedness to the moment, as if his roses had been left here over the long centuries, waiting for just such a meeting.

And in spite of all her fire and struggling, Adrian knew the woman in his arms felt it too. Her breath was too ragged, her pulse too wild for it to be otherwise.

He knew he ought to let her go. He knew he should turn and melt back into the night where he belonged. But somehow he could not. Not tonight, not when he found such searing pleasure in her touch.

Just once, he told himself.

His mouth opened. He captured her velvet underlip in his teeth and savored the mystery of her mouth.

At that single exquisite movement, desire raged full-blown through Adrian's frame. His fingers sank into her hair as he slanted her face up to his, desperately afraid that if he released her she would be torn from him forever.

Just a little longer, he promised himself . . .

Caught against his chest, Gray bit back a moan. What was *wrong* with her? "L-let me go, you—you snake, you—"

Too late she found out her mistake. Her black-clad captor seized the moment and slid his tongue deep, caressing the inner textures of her mouth and searching out all its hot, forbidden secrets.

Suddenly the night was ashimmer, electric with danger. With a wild, reckless hunger that made Gray moan and strain against him.

She who had never moaned, had never wanted, had never even *imagined* that such desire existed.

And now, in the span of an instant, she had discovered a thousand exquisite textures that she could no longer deny herself. Ablaze with wonder, she combed her fingers through the long hair that swept his shoulders, feeling it part like silk at her touch. She shivered as his breath surged ragged at her neck, raw and hot against her cheek.

His pulse hammered, echoing her own.

Blindly, Gray dug her fingers into his hard shoulders, glorying in his instant stiffening, in the groan that tore from his lips.

There beneath the moonlight, hunger flared between them like summer lightning and Gray felt herself tossed like a leaf in the wind.

She moaned restlessly, sliding closer against his hard thighs, which clenched like forged steel in response.

Shivering, she felt the unmistakable thrust of his rock-hard arousal. Even then she could not pull away, could not forsake the heat she had discovered in his granite body.

For that, too, was somehow familiar.

"Damn and bloody blast!" Strangely enough, it was he who pulled free and stared down at her, scowling. "By the name of all the saints, woman—"

He never finished. His eyes glittered down into the flushed beauty of her cheeks, the dazed depths of her eyes, bright with passion still.

And as Adrian Draycott watched, a single tear squeezed free and inched slowly down Gray's cheek.

He cursed, his jaw clenching. Slowly his calloused finger rose to the salty bead.

As if in a dream, Gray felt his hard hands anchor her cheeks, saw his face slant down.

"I never meant . . . by God, I swear I never planned—"

And then, slow and infinitely gentle, his lips covered that single tear and eased it onto his tongue. Dazed, Gray felt his lips close, felt him draw the bead into his mouth.

In truth, she had no idea what had caused the tear. Not pain, of that there was no doubt. Nor did it stem from anger. Perhaps it was the sheer violence of the sensual discovery she'd just made.

And then Gray had no time left for thinking.

His lips tightened.

Slowly, exquisitely, he drew her delicate skin tight, molding every captive inch with his teeth. Heart pounding, Gray swayed, feeling the dark force of his possession. A low moan tore from her throat.

Heat.

Need.

Dear God, the unimaginable power of touching and being touched in such a way, as if the whole world began and ended in texture and sensation.

Sweet heaven, she'd never imagined the reckless wonder of it, the wild, sweet splendor of it.

She shivered, her nails digging into his neck.

An eternity passed. Around them the abbey slept and the night hung still, caught in timeless dreams while an ancient, primal drama raged on beneath its weathered walls.

Then, with one sleek tugging movement, Gray was free. Her intruder stood back, his eyes hooded, glittering.

"I'll not apologize, so don't expect it. For you puzzle me sorely, woman. You raise too many questions for which I have no answers. But I'll have my answers, every one. And until then, Gray Mackenzie, I leave you with something to remember me by. It has always been the punishment for stealing a Draycott rose." His fingers swept her flushed cheek. "Here. Here you will wear my mark."

Overhead, ragged clouds ran before the moon. Gray shivered, realizing she was standing half-naked in the reckless, heated embrace of an utter stranger.

"You arrogant, p-pigheaded—"

His smile was the merest curve of brightness in his dark face. "Completely, I'm afraid. And yet at this moment I could almost wish that—"

Somewhere in the night a clock began to chime. Gray felt him stiffen.

And then, with a faint rustle of the ferns along the bank, he was gone, loping across the little terrace and skirting the bridge to disappear into the shadows beyond.

Even then Gray did not move, shaken profoundly, feeling that a new person now occupied her body, a stranger complete.

Blood leaped to her cheeks. She shivered, feeling as if the man stood before her still, his breath ragged, his body tense with need.

Just as your own is, a mocking voice whispered.

Dazed, she raised trembling fingers to her cheek and traced the flushed skin where his mouth had lingered only seconds before.

Already she could feel his mark rising.

3

S UNLIGHT spilled through the opened French doors. Gray yawned and burrowed back beneath the satin pillows, smiling drowsily.

Roses. There had been roses.

Her lips curved as she remembered her rich, heady dreams of the night before.

Beacon fires burning in the darkness. A golden brooch with intertwined dragons.

A cat with eyes of unblinking amber.

And roses—roses everywhere, in every shape and color, their scent spilling out into the night.

But they were only dreams, she told herself, stifling another yawn. In one fluid motion she stretched, then tossed back the covers and came to her feet.

And there she went absolutely still, reeling as the full truth of the night returned. The hard truth of a man, brooding and reckless, driven by implacable need.

The raw truth of her own wanton response.

She, who had seemed fated to feel nothing. She who

was always distant, cool, detached.

Grieving. For what, Gray was never quite sure.

Her hands cupped her flaming cheeks. What in the name of heaven was happening to her? How could she possibly have—

A faint movement shifted the coverlet. Looking down, Gray saw a sleek figure curled at the foot of her bed.

It was the cat she'd seen last night, gray-furred with paws of black. The same cat who had trod so delicately across the terrace railing.

His cat.

Anger shot through her. Who was this infuriating man to invade her privacy, to thrust his pet upon her even while she slept, defenseless?

Angrily she jerked the pillow from the bed, sending her two architecture books crashing to the floor.

The cat did not move.

"Go! Shoo!"

But the creature only inched down onto his paws and curled his tail around his haunches, his keen eyes never leaving Gray's face.

"*Go*, I said!" Gray waved her hands wildly.

Still the cat remained, content, unmoving, silkily alert.

So he meant to be stubborn, did he?

Grimly Gray began to tug at the coverlet, wishing that it were the cat's master she was dumping onto the floor instead!

At that moment she caught a glance of herself in the gilt-edged Regency mirror across the room. Her cheeks were flushed, her hair a wild cascade of auburn at her shoulders. During her restless sleep, the top buttons of her nightshirt had come free, revealing the shadowed softness of her breasts.

She looked, in short, like a woman who'd just come from her lover's bed, flushed with memories of sensual excess.

Like a woman who'd enjoyed every wanton second of it.

With a low cry Gray stumbled backwards, unable to tear her eyes from the image in the mirror.

What in the name of heaven was happening to her? She was never so reckless, never so emotional.

And what about the rest? a dark voice asked. *What of the other thing he promised you?*

She inched forward, her pulse like thunder in her ears.

The mark was just where she had known it would be, a faint pattern of raised skin where her captor had pressed a love-mark onto her creamy cheek.

His mark, given in wild, reckless passion.

And oddly it looked like a perfect, dense-leaved rose.

Gray stood frozen, her gaze fixed upon the mirror. Behind her on the bed the great cat began to purr.

"More eggs, miss? Or kippers perhaps?"

Marston was as cool as ever, dressed in a crisp navy blazer that fairly screamed Burberry. This morning, however, his formality was muted by neon-green running shoes that peeked out beneath sober gray flannels.

Gray shook her head absently, not really listening. She had barely slept the night before and all through breakfast she'd toyed with her food. All she could do was stare out blindly at the roses climbing in riotous color across the abbey's granite walls.

The night had shaken her profoundly.

Even now a thousand questions pressed at her, each one screaming for answers.

But she had work to do, sketches to finish. She had absolutely no time for or interest in an arrogant, insufferable Englishman with more libido than sense!

Gray set down her Limoges cup too forcefully, trying to shake off her distraction. She realized belatedly that Marston had asked her a question. "I beg your pardon?"

"You slept well, I trust?"

Gray frowned, twisting the fragile cup between her fingers. "Passably, but this deafening silence of yours is going to take some getting used to. In Philadelphia it's never really quiet—not *this* quiet, anyway. There's something . . . unsettling about so much silence."

Marston bent to refill her teacup, his sharp eyes flickering over her face.

Had he noticed her distraction, the dark circles beneath her eyes? Gray wondered. And what of the other marks left from the night?

Her fingers rose, tracing the bandage she had shoved over the telltale mark at her cheek. At the thought of that wild, savage kiss, fire swept across her face.

Damn the man anyway!

Suddenly her eyes narrowed on Marston's back. "Are you—the only one here? That is—" Blast it, how was she to phrase this? "I mean, the abbey must require a large staff, but I've seen no others about."

The butler straightened, staring out over the moat. "Oh, at one time there must have been well over a hundred working here. In more recent years, Edward, the last viscount, employed a staff of thirty or so. But now, what with government regulations and the crippling inheritance taxes . . ." Marston sighed. "Ah, well, now there's only myself, miss, though Lord Draycott has others in when the need arises."

Gray swirled the tea idly in her cup. "But the grounds are so extensive. There are the formal gardens, the maze, the moat, and all those lovely roses. Surely you can't manage all that."

Marston unbent so far as to smile slightly. "Indeed not. Not that his lordship wouldn't set me at it if I showed the slightest aptitude. You see, a rose sees me coming and immediately withers—which suits me just fine, for I've no patience with greenery, no patience at all. No, his lordship has a professional in to care for the grounds. A nice enough chap, although he seems a bit on the quiet side. Brewer, his name is."

Gray's fingers tightened on the fine porcelain saucer. "He—he lives nearby?"

"Brewer? Down by the main road, as a matter of fact. There's an old cottage there, and I understand he's done wonders with repairing the thatched roof and flower beds." A crease appeared between Marston's brows. "I heard he's taken his daughter and gone abroad for a holiday. He has relatives in the south of France, I think."

Gray stared out at the rose-covered wall, trying to make sense of this new information. "Well, he's back now." She flushed faintly. "I passed him yesterday on the way in."

For a moment Gray considered telling Marston the rest of the night's happenings, but in the end she decided not to. Some things were better left unmentioned. No, she would just push the whole wretched business from her mind. Besides, she could handle the insufferable caretaker on her own if she had to.

"Ah, well." Marston shrugged. "He must have returned, in that case. Jolly well time, too, what with the roses in high bloom and the weirs to be tended."

Gray swallowed. "His daughter—and his wife—live there too?"

"Oh, he's no wife, not now. Widower, he is. No, there's just the two of them."

"What about the cat?"

Marston stiffened. "Cat?"

"The great gray thing that follows him about."

"You—you *saw* it?" Marston looked shocked.

Whatever was wrong with the man? "I more than saw him—I touched him, too. He was prowling about the terrace last night. The impudent creature even snuck into my room and spent the night curled up on my bed."

Marston made a strangled sound that might have been a cough or a gasp. "Did it—were the cat's paws black?"

"That's the one," Gray said, starting to grow impatient. "But why—"

"The ghost." Marston's voice was low and very soft. "The ghost and that infernal cat of his."

"Ghost?" Gray felt tendrils of fear brush her neck. Abruptly she remembered Kacey's letter. *Along with a moat and a priceless art collection, the abbey also has a resident ghost.*

But that was impossible, of course. There had to be a simple explanation. "The cat was every bit as real as I am, Marston. And as for this ghost Kacey mentioned, don't you find that a little bit hard to swallow in this day and age? I mean, we've put men on the moon, after all. We've split the atom. We've . . . we've invented panty hose. Non-smudge mascara!" she concluded triumphantly, setting down her cup with a decisive click. "No, the cat was simply a stray looking for a warm meal and a soft berth for the night."

Marston nodded slowly, folding and unfolding a napkin. "Yes . . . of course, you're right. These cats do come nosing about occasionally. The moat's full of fish, after all." He dropped the napkin, nodding resolutely. "Yes, a stray, that's what it was." A moment later he looked up at Gray, his lips pursed. "Just the same, if the cat bothers you, keep the French doors closed. Which might be a good idea anyway, considering . . ." His gaze wandered off to the moat.

"Considering what?" Gray prompted impatiently.

"What? Oh, yes, well, old places such as this seem . . . seem unpredictable somehow. They have hidden corners, extra shadows that appear when you least expect them. They . . . play tricks on you." The butler looked grave for a moment, then shrugged.

Gray found herself wondering just what sort of tricks Marston was talking about. But the butler was already busying himself with the tea things, and his somber expression did not invite further questioning. "Will you be requiring anything else, Ms. Mackenzie?"

"Gray."

"I beg your pardon?"

"Gray. Call me Gray, please. Whenever you say 'Ms. Mackenzie,' I look around expecting to see my mother."

Marston's eyes crinkled. "Very well, miss—er, Gray. It was just the same with the viscountess, as I recall." The butler's veneer of formality slipped away for a moment. When he bent back to his work his lips were curved in a secret smile.

Ghosts! Gray thought angrily. No doubt it suited that insufferable gardener to see such a story circulated. All to protect his precious roses, no doubt! Lazy, that's what the man was. Probably hadn't done a decent day's work in his life! And that cat of his was most likely purchased to enhance the effect.

Well, I'm not about to be cowed so easily, Gray swore. *And this is one handyman who will soon have a few lessons coming!*

Twenty minutes later, sketch pad in hand, Gray edged along the far side of the moat, searching for the best angle to capture the abbey's massive walls.

The problem, she soon decided, was not which wall or which angle but how she was going to choose from the wealth of magnificent possibilities.

She tried angle after angle, composition after composition, until the ground at her feet was littered with crumpled paper. Again and again she attacked the rough, textured sheets she favored, only to cast down another effort in disgust.

Wrong and wrong again! Something was still eluding her.

Squinting, Gray looked across the moat at the south tower. Yes, that area was particularly bothersome. No matter how she varied contour lines and tone values, she couldn't seem to capture the effect of those sheer, curving walls.

Muttering beneath her breath, she flung down another aborted effort and held up her charcoal pencil, sighting the crenellated roof of the tower. Yes, the proportions at the top *were* inconsistent, as if the tower had been built in stages, to different plans.

But Gray meant to stay right where she was until she got the elusive tower down on paper at last.

Sunshine shimmered off the moat, bouncing from the high, mullioned gallery windows. Seconds trickled into minutes and then hours.

Hunching her shoulders, Gray studied the weathered battlements, trying to concentrate. Passing bees droned noisily in the climbing roses and the moat murmured from some hidden, spring-fed corner. With every passing second she found it harder and harder to focus on her work.

Even now the scene fought her, always slightly out of kilter, the perspective wrong.

She squinted up at the corner tower, half-expecting to see an ominous, ghostly figure loom out from behind a merlon.

But nothing moved in the hazy midday heat. The tower was empty.

Of course it's empty, Mackenzie! Were you expecting to see the abbey's so-called ghost?

Muttering angrily, Gray snapped her pad open to a fresh sheet and sent charcoal slashing against fiber.

But with every stroke the abbey's surfaces seemed to shift infinitesimally, as if to deny Gray the solidity she sought.

And somehow, between the droning of the bees and the whisper of the wind, Gray found herself nodding, slipping back to an earlier age.

An age of dreams.

An age when armor flashed and destriers pawed the ground into raw furrows.

"Heat stroke," she muttered, jerking upright and ripping off another half-finished sheet. A second later a misshapen ball of paper struck the wall. "Jet lag! Maybe even incipient senility!"

Frowning, Gray sat back against the sun-warmed wall. Her charcoal pencil hissed as it sped back and forth over the vellum sketch sheet. Against the paper weathered stone walls took shape, followed by a bank of mullioned windows, and finally the haze of the moat and the dark home wood beyond.

This one was good. Gray could feel the surging emotion, the intensity of vision that went far beyond mortar, stone, and plaster.

All great buildings had an inner intensity, of course. And it was Gray's singular skill to be able to unveil that central essence and render it on paper in grays and black.

At that moment peace descended upon Gray, a peace such as she hadn't known for years. For five years to be exact. The day she'd discovered about Matt.

Matt.

Fear pricked at her neck, but she shoved it away, refusing to allow anything to disturb the peace that Draycott Abbey seemed to impart so well.

In the sunlight the far bank of the moat seemed to shimmer and blur. Gray rubbed her eyes, which had begun to ache from hours of steady work in the sun.

And as she watched, the haze twisted, then resolved into glittering images. Sunlight flashed off steel breastplates as a row of ghostly war-horses pounded along the far side of the moat. Banners twitched in a phantom wind, red silk swirling with intertwined dragons.

Far away Gray seemed to hear the stamp of great hooves, the harsh call of a leader to his men. Over the green land the spectral army stamped, armor ablaze, pennants snapping.

Moving a foot and more above the ground.

And as they thundered past in blazing splendor, the rose shrubs beside the moat seemed to straighten, to raise their branches and climb up into walls of blue-gray and green, their foliage twisted like some wild, living thing.

The leader raised a sword of steel and crystal, then cried a single word of command—low and rich, the remnant of some old, forgotten tongue.

Gray shivered and drew her hands across her watering eyes, even then unable to tear her gaze away.

As she watched, speechless, the foliage formed a living arch above the riders' heads. Every stem burst into wild bloom—crimson, fuchsia, and white scattered against a vivid sea of green.

She caught back a moan. Dropping her sketch pad, she stumbled to her feet and spun around, putting her back to the moat.

A dream. A mirage. Merely a trick of light and shadow, just as Marston had warned her . . .

Behind her came a wild, excited shout as the phantom company thundered onward, ever closer to the steps of the gate house, where the great oak door creaked open in welcome.

And then there was a new sound, a high female cry.

Shivering, Gray opened her eyes.

A woman ran from the opened gate, her long gown gleaming golden in the sunlight. The man at the front of the line let out a shout and shot forward, bending low and swinging her up before him on the saddle.

Suddenly Gray felt a savage pain tear at her heart, a raw anguish such as she had never known before.

Tears began to flood down her face. Her breath came sharp and ragged as she swayed beneath a flood of churning emotions beyond logic or comprehension.

"N-no! It—it's a dream, all of it!"

Fingers trembling, Gray rubbed her eyes, willing the madness to pass.

Overhead she heard the shrill cry of a kestrel. An errant gust of wind played through her long hair.

Slowly she opened her eyes.

The parade was gone, the bank empty. Only the roses moved now, their dense petals nodding sleepily on the far shore.

Gray fought back a sob, wrenched by a raw, ineffable longing. For what, she could not say.

Clenching her fingers, she stared at the sunny ground. "Way too much sun and fresh air for you, Gray Mackenzie, to say nothing of Marston's excellent cooking! But now the hocus-pocus is over. It's time to get back to work."

With a sigh, she looked down at the sketchbook dangling from her fingers. At least this one was passable. But the sketch still lacked something.

She yawned, brushing a glistening strand of hair from her eyes.

Pondering the problem, she sank down against a sun-washed boulder and braced her back.

She stifled another yawn and smoothed the half-finished sheet. Yes, there was something decidedly troubling about that south tower jutting out over the moat. The proportions were all wrong . . .

And that was Gray's last clear thought.

A moment later her eyes blinked, then fluttered shut.

Her head eased back against the sun-warmed stone. Unnoticed, the charcoal pencil slipped from her fingers.

He slid out of the shimmering noonday heat, his face angular, brooding.

In taut silence he stood, an imposing figure in dark clothes that seemed ill-suited to his powerful frame. His face was bronzed, carved with deep lines. Smaller lines of laughter, care, and concentration radiated out from the corners of his glittering eyes.

It was his eyes that moved now, hooded yet keen, blazing from slate-gray depths. They flowed over the woman before him, anger and resentment warring with even more primitive emotions.

Why are you here? It was a silent shout of frustration. Of confusion. Of something that bordered on pain.

And Adrian Draycott was not used to being confused about anything.

Another test? he asked himself, as the wind tossed silky auburn strands about her shoulders.

Damn and blast, he had not known it could be so troubling, so personal, so intensely *physical* to return this way!

Frowning, Adrian stared down at his arms and legs, slanting a look of particular disgust at his dusty shoes.

By heaven, there was no dignity in such clothes! No beauty. No grace whatsoever.

But your velvets and lace were put down centuries ago. Right now they lie hidden in dusty, forgotten chests, fallen to threads and fragments.

Slowly Adrian dragged a hand through his long black hair. Yes, this new age, this garish, clamorous age, called for different clothes and he must adopt them or withdraw.

Suddenly a sleek shadow loomed at his feet, long tail atwitch.

"What of the danger, old friend?" he asked of the animal beside him.

The cat meowed softly, his amber eyes never leaving Adrian's face.

"So bad as that?" For a moment rage coursed through the abbey's dark-clad guardian. If only he could see more clearly! In the past he had always been able to summon up at least some intuition of the dangers that threatened his beloved home.

But not now. Not with *her* on Draycott lands.

With her before him, Adrian found he couldn't think normally at all. All he could do was *feel*. All he could do was drown in the sweet scent of her, in the silver heat that spiraled through him as he watched the soft rise and fall of her breasts.

Her hair was really quite extraordinary, he thought, fighting an urge to run his hand along its silken length. In the sunlight the auburn strands flashed in a thousand shades of red and bronze.

The wind caught a thick curl and tossed it playfully about her cheek. Adrian felt a sharp prick of jealousy that he could not do the same, burying his fingers in those gleaming depths.

His hands curled into fists as he was rocked by a knifelike desire. Bone by bone, it slammed down his spine, from his head to his feet.

He stumbled backwards, breathless, fighting for control.

Who *was* this woman? Why did she affect him so? And what in the name of heaven was he doing here beside her, with a physical ache that threatened to burst his tenuous control any second?

Only inches away, the subject of these ruminations shifted. Sighing, she turned her head. Her fingers brushed the sun-warmed stone.

As he stared down at her, Adrian felt a need too long suppressed explode to life.

Dear God, he had never expected, never imagined—

He caught his hand just as it rose to comb through her hair. To skim the perfect curve of her cheek.

Stay clear! he warned himself grimly, even while his fingers trembled at the effort. *Look, advise—assist, even. But she is not for you to touch. For like the rose, she bears fierce thorns.*

Even for a between-worlds creature like yourself.

But still he stared—and still he dreamed, pondering the sleeping face before him, luminous in all its innocence and peace.

For a moment regret clung to him, raw as a winter wind. His eyes narrowed, dark with regret and a thousand shattered dreams. He shivered, feeling images that were too faint to be called memories press at his head.

But when he tried to seize them, they vanished like thistledown on the wind.

At that moment Adrian's eyes fell to the sketch pad balanced precariously on Gray's knees. An odd, sad smile twisted his hard lips.

"So you love my abbey, don't you, Gray Mackenzie?" His voice was carried in the whisper of the wind, in the drone of the passing bees and the murmur of the moat.

Already he was fading. He could feel the telltale lightening, the not quite painful tingle at wrist and ankle.

Surely not so soon?

He lifted his head to the sun, closed his eyes, and centered his thoughts.

Slowly the tingling faded. With a faint sigh he knelt to study Gray's sketch more intently.

You've come close, woman. Perhaps too close.

Something about the sketch left him distinctly uncomfortable—naked and vulnerable. Perhaps it was because no one had ever before come so close to capturing the abbey's heart as she had just done.

And in a very real sense, Adrian Draycott knew that the abbey's heart was *his* heart.

Yes, you're good, Gray Mackenzie. You're more than good.

Nearly as skillful as you are innocent and beautiful, in fact. But that stunning innocence of yours is deadly. Already it captures me, entraps me, until I can think of nothing else but you.

Is that what you've come here for? To threaten every bloody thing I've ever loved and valued and fought to protect?

Adrian expected no answer, of course. But as he studied the hot blaze of the sun in her hair, he had the raw certainty that the next hours would bring danger—and a testing such as he had never known before.

Yet even with that knowledge he could not seem to pull his eyes away.

Catching himself with a muffled curse, Adrian forced himself to look away. As he did so, he saw her rendering of the south tower. It was slightly off, he realized. The tower's curve should have been broader and the crenels deeper. The moat, too, was off, twisting to the right where it should have veered slightly toward the left . . .

A wrenching pain exploded up his spine. The day flashed like lightning before his eyes. He felt reality heave and twist, then slowly begin to fade.

Or perhaps to return.

It was all a question of perspective, after all.

Slowly he bent down, his face lined with pain as he struggled to finish one last task before his vision faded and the darkness reclaimed him.

Grimacing, he shoved the charcoal pencil into Gray's fingers, circled her hand, and began to draw.

The sun poured like warm honey onto Gray's closed eyelids. She swept a hair from her eyes and stretched dreamily.

Her eyes finally opened. She frowned, looking down and searching for her pencil. Everything was blurred, her head throbbing.

Too much sun, she thought, rubbing her stiff neck, feeling as if she'd been asleep for a hundred years.

Eight hundred years, more like.

Now where had *that* thought come from? she wondered. And then she froze, recalling the strange images she had seen across the moat. Wide-eyed, she studied the far bank, recalling her dream of the night before.

Chill darkness lit by a score of beacon fires.

Danger on every side.

She gasped. Could the two things be somehow related?

Her fingers tensed and a moment later the charcoal pencil in her hand snapped cleanly in two.

Dear Lord, what was happening to her here? What was it about this beautiful, crazy place that affected her so?

A gust of wind eddied up from the moat and tugged at the corner of her sketch pad. Slowly the paper rose. Whispering softly, it fell open to her last sketch.

At least it *had* been her sketch. But no longer. Now it showed the mark of a stranger's powerful hand.

A shiver worked through Gray as she stared down into a landscape of dreams, captured in exquisite, inspired strokes such as she had never seen before in all her years of work and study.

At that moment Gray realized she was looking down into a distant age and a world long gone. Into a valiant time, when the world rang to the cries of heroes and magic was commonplace. Each stroke captured the power of that distant era, suggesting but never quite revealing whence the magic sprung.

More dreams?

She shivered, studying the proud walls sketched upon the paper. Wrought with strength, they were yet insubstantial, their edges softened and blurred. Like poured emotion, like feeling made tangible, they stood with all their textures dreamlike and hazy.

And at the same time stunningly real.

The sketch was utterly different from her own work, which was almost superrealistic. In fact, the sketch was totally unlike any work Gray had ever seen before.

And it was absolutely beautiful, almost alive somehow, a dream spun of charcoal, patience, and love. A love so strong that Gray could almost touch it.

Dazed, she studied the sketch, understanding none of it. And something told her the longer she stayed in this ancient place, the less she would understand it.

Then Gray saw the other sheet. A mere scrap, it had been torn from her sketch pad and tucked into the pocket of her flowered skirt. The charcoal lettering was as bold and restless as the sketch of the abbey.

She shivered as she read the two scrawled lines.

Tonight at midnight. By the witch's pool.

If you dare.

4

G RAY'S breath caught. Raw indignation swept over her.

But in its wake came a fierce, forbidden curiosity.

She wouldn't dream of going, of course. There could be no question of that. She had far too many other things on her mind to worry about an insolent caretaker with an attitude problem and a dislike for women who didn't know their place.

Which for him probably meant the kitchen or the bedroom.

At that thought her cheeks flared with furious color.

Muttering angrily, she slapped open a new page, determined to complete her quota of sketches before the best of the sunlight was gone.

Yet her fingers, as she smoothed down that last, odd sketch, were surprisingly gentle.

*   *   *

"Where is the witch's pool?"

To Gray's utter horror, the words burst from her lips the instant Marston finished pouring tea after dinner. Cursing silently, she glared down at her rose-strewn porcelain cup.

Horrified.

Infuriated.

But most of all gripped by curiosity as she waited for Marston's answer.

Abruptly she shook her head, her cheeks aflame. "Never mind. I can't imagine why—" Her fingers tensed on the base of her teacup. "It—it doesn't matter."

Of course it didn't matter! She wasn't about to go anywhere tonight!

"The witch's pool." Marston straightened slowly, his brow creased. "Ah, now there's a term I've not heard in years. Let me think." His expression grew distant. "Down on the far side of the moat, it is, Miss Gray. Spring-fed and surrounded by thick reeds. A strange place, sure enough. Water bubbles up crystal-clear there, warm all year round. The problem is that sometimes a swan gets caught beyond the reeds and can't get back out. I hear them crying there sometimes, in the silence of the night. Several times I've gone down to carry them back to the moat, but they never seem to want to go. The crazy things just struggle back as if they're searching for something."

The butler folded and refolded a damask napkin, his eyes fixed on the twilight shadows beyond the dining-room window. "Aye, it's a strange place, sure enough. Some say it's a haunted place. Legend has it that long ago a thane's wife, distraught and despondent after her husband's long absence, was found drowned there."

Gray swallowed. Suddenly she was finding it difficult to breathe.

Somewhere in the house a clock chimed seven o'clock. Marston studied her curiously. "But why were you asking, miss? You're not going to work down there, are you? I can't say as I'd advise that, for it's an odd sort of place. And what with the mist always drifting about, you could find yourself lost before you knew it."

Lost? Gray felt as if she were hopelessly lost already!

Somehow she managed a lopsided smile. "No, I won't be working down there, Marston. I was just . . . curious. Kacey must have mentioned the pool in one of her letters."

"I see. Will you have more tea?"

Gray shook her head. Speech was entirely beyond her. Dear God, what was happening to her in this strange place?

She started, realizing Marston was speaking to her again.

" . . . mousse. Or maybe some chocolate soufflé, if you'd prefer."

She shook her head, feeling panic wash over her. Dear God, she could feel all the old vulnerability, all the raw, choking helplessness creep over her again. Only now it was worse, because now she wondered if her very sanity was in question.

" . . . quite all right? Shall I call a doctor?"

Around her the air seemed to hum and shiver, light and sound swirling together in odd, churning waves. And with it came the fear, like cold fingers inching down her spine.

"No!" In a sharp burst of movement, Gray tossed down her napkin and jerked to her feet, her hands clenched to keep them from trembling. "No, everything was lovely, Marston. Thank you s-so much. I'm—I'm afraid I had a bit too much sun this afternoon, though. I'd better make an early night of it."

Once again the keen sideways glance, the slightly pursed lips. "Of course . . ." The kind voice drifted in and out of her hearing. " . . . hotter than you think, no doubt . . . better in the morning . . . good night's sleep."

But as Gray walked through the quiet courtyard and over the narrow stone bridge to the gate house, she had a sharp sense of purple shadows pressing close, menacing somehow.

And with them came an inexplicable sense of loneliness, of bitter regret and utter fatedness.

Almost as if the ancient abbey had been merely sleeping, merely waiting, guarding its dark secrets until the day she returned.

She wouldn't go, of course.

Gray squared her shoulders.

She wasn't about to be goaded and manipulated. Not again. She had learned that lesson too well with Matt.

And the first thing she would do to prove it would be to rip up the note. Then, after a long hot bath, she'd go straight to sleep.

Ten minutes later steam twisted around Gray's head. Lulled by the warm water, she shifted idly, stirring the crystal waters and watching mist rise in frothy white plumes.

For some reason the drifting shapes made her think of the moat, shimmering with heat beneath the noonday sun.

Glowing silver beneath the rising moon.

At midnight.

Jerking up with a start, Gray seized a bar of hand-milled lavender soap and scrubbed her arms with a ferocity that bordered on pain.

And still the words lingered, haunting her.

At midnight. By the witch's pool . . .

"I won't go, do you hear?" Scowling, she rinsed off the white suds, wishing she could brush away the nagging voice with equal ease.

If you dare.

Muttering, Gray slid low in the heated water. Yes, let the bloody man wait in vain! She would just sit here and soak in sweet contented peace.

She stifled a yawn. Plumes of steam drifted up, twisted, enveloped her.

Once more the beacon fires were lit.

The Lady of Draycotte watched numbly, clutching her shawl closer about her shoulders while the wind keened across the half-finished south tower.

Far below, dim laughter echoed up from the great hall, where her jailers sat to their ale, busy with belching and toasting.

If only Draycotte's lord would return! If only she could be wrapped in his strong arms once more, safe and secure.

But he did not come. And here she remained, a prisoner surrounded by vengeful, cold-eyed spies.

Without warning the first pain came. Sudden and wracking, it bent her over double, made her clutch blindly at her swollen belly.

No, it could not be! Not so soon.

But nature had different plans, it seemed. Another spasm ripped through her and she slid down along the granite wall, her lips locked against the pain.

Something was wrong, very wrong. The child was not due for almost a month yet!

Too late she remembered the broth they'd forced on her at dinner. It had tasted odd, heavy with herbs and something else that left a faint, metallic taste.

Poison?

Slowly she slid to her knees. A terrible roaring filled her head. Wildly she clutched at her middle, where already the first terrible convulsions had begun.

She had promised him she would wait! She must be waiting for him when he returned.

There by the silver-black glade when he came riding across the lush green Draycotte fields.

Tears wet her cheeks as she struggled to rise. Blindly

she felt for the wall's reassuring bulk, even as her head throbbed with the malignant fury of a thousand war drums.

And then, as if from a vast distance, she saw a blurring shadow detach from the ragged edge of the south tower.

"Dear God, is that you, my love? Are you c-come back to me at last?"

But the torchlight danced lower, playing over flat, sullen eyes. Over thin, cruel lips.

Not the man she wished to see at all.

"No!" she cried, inching back along the cold stone.

The sullen eyes tightened; hard lips curved to an ugly smile. And the man in the darkness was still smiling as the Lady Anne fell senseless to the parapet's cold granite floor.

Except that Anne was not her real name, not to those who knew her best.

Back in her native Brittany, where she'd spent twenty summers before being summoned to Draycotte, she was called Griza. Griza for the iron tones of the wintry seas she loved. Griza for her velvet eyes the color of a cooing dove.

Griza.

Gray.

A bell was chiming over the hills when Gray awoke.

She shook her head, fighting her way up through angry dreams, feeling the clutch of terror and something else she ought to remember but could not.

Wind rushed into the room, playing through her unbound hair, sending steam up in ragged eddies. Goose bumps broke out on her chest, across her shoulders, along her neck, where it rose above the warm water.

If you dare, Gray Mackenzie. The words echoed through her head.

"Forget it! Just *forget* it!"

Scowling, she sloshed from the tub and wrenched a

towel embroidered with intertwined dragons around her trembling body.

The room beyond was silent, just as it should have been. Yet when Gray looked at the great gilt mirror on the wall, she saw it wore a light haze of steam.

And there in the mist hung a faint mark.

The lush, perfect outline of a densely petaled rose.

And beneath it hung three words, traced by the same phantom hand.

If you dare.

5

FURY crackled through her.

In its raw showering force Gray felt the long years of denial and regret burn away. Never again would she hide or give way to her fear. She would go or not go, but it would be by *her* choice and no one else's!

"Oh, yes, I dare! I *dare*, do you hear?"

Damp towel clutched to her chest, she turned, searching for her robe, only to find it was no longer on the chair where she'd left it.

Muttering furiously, she stalked to the mahogany dresser across from the bed and flung open the top drawer.

Her eyes widened in disbelief.

She opened drawer after drawer, all with the same result.

Empty, absolutely empty. She hadn't a stitch of clothing left! "You loathsome, despicable—"

Only then did Gray notice that the French doors were

open, their silken curtains fluttering in the breeze.

And the door of the heavy oaken armoire was also ajar. Grabbing a chair and holding it before her, Gray stalked closer.

"Come out, you miserable—"

The door creaked open.

But it was only a cat, slipping like a gray shadow across the polished floor.

White with rage, Gray pounded to the armoire and flung open its doors.

Inside hung a film of white lace.

Film was the only word to describe the gown's white froth, as thin and fine as thistledown.

Low-necked and long-sleeved it hung, cut of alençon lace so sheer it might have been worked of faery webs. And at the bodice, caught between lacings of silk ribbon, hung a perfect centifolia rose.

Without quite knowing why she did it, Gray ran her hands across the cloud-soft fabric, delighting in its exquisite textures. As she did, she had a sudden impression of a similar dress from an age long gone. A dress such as a great lady might have worn in the privacy of her chamber.

To entrance and delight the man she loved.

With a sigh, Gray closed her eyes, enveloped in a fantasy which quickly progressed to something more. Suddenly she was flooded with images so real that they verged on being memories.

Memories of hard hands that loosed a filigree girdle and slipped a line of lacing free. Memories of calloused fingers that eased a froth of white lace over restless, heated skin.

And then a woman's breath hissing out in a sigh while she ran her fingers over taut male flesh.

Gray froze.

Dear God, it was *her* breath she heard. *Her* fingers she felt!

White-faced, she stood before the armoire, her heart pounding at the savage force of the images exploding through her. And as Gray stared at the exquisite gown, she had a shattering vision of lovers from a distant age who met at midnight beneath a climbing rose.

Lace parted over flushed skin. There in the quiet of midnight two dreamers strained close, twining urgent limbs and restless fingers as they pledged a love that could not die or ever be forgotten.

A love to light the coldest night.

A love that would last beyond the bounds of time or space or hope itself.

With a choked cry Gray stumbled back from the armoire, staring at the white gown in shock and bewilderment. Her breath came wild and ragged as a thousand questions churned up inside her.

But there was only one way she would have any answers. That was at the witch's pool.

At midnight.

As the moon rose over the dark, wooded hills a car glided from the highway and slipped along the narrow graveled drive that led to Draycott Abbey.

It was a nondescript car, of no striking color or make. A car that moved slowly, careful not to invite attention or comment.

Just like its driver.

At the first turning the headlights dimmed. Carefully the car inched onto the grass and came to rest behind a copse of beech and oak.

Abruptly the twin beams disappeared. Darkness closed over the landscape once more.

Only now it was a restless, fitful thing.

A boat was waiting for Gray at the edge of the moat.

The bloody man thought of everything, didn't he?

Frowning, she tugged her shawl about her shoulders, trying to cover the elegant wisp of lace that had been her only choice of clothing. But with every movement the sheer fabric clung and teased her skin, as light as a lover's fingers, making it impossible to forget the sensual images that had flooded over her earlier that night.

Images? Or were they memories?

Memories of herself and a man with slate-gray eyes? A man she barely knew and certainly did not like?

With fingers oddly unsteady, Gray untied the frayed rope and cast off in silence, feeling the night press wary and watchful around her.

Almost as if it were waiting.

Through the steam the boat glided, parting the strange shifting shapes that eddied upward as she passed.

It was like entering another world, Gray thought, a world resembling the normal world but not quite the same.

A world where magic lived and dreams were real.

In silence she glided on, the only sound the faint *splosh* of her pole. And then the far bank was before her, and with it the narrow reeded channel that led to the pool.

The witch's pool.

At midnight. If you dare.

Gray's lips tensed. Oh, yes, she dared! She only wished it hadn't taken her this long in her life to realize it.

As her foot touched the fern-soft shore, a bell began to chime, far away across the forested hills.

Twelve times it rang, and then once more.

Beyond a thick screen of reeds, Gray glimpsed the little glade that Marston had spoken of. And at its center, circled by yew, rowan, and beech, heated water shone silver in the moonlight.

But glade and pool were empty.

Gray wasn't sure whether to be relieved or irritated by that fact. What was she *doing* here, anyway? Especially dressed in this wretched, ridiculous, *beautiful* dress!

She heard the step only an instant before he loomed up beside her, dressed all in black with a soft shirt that clung to his broad shoulders.

For long, tense moments he did not move, his eyes probing her flushed face. "You came." And then, simply, "I'm . . . glad."

"Of c-course I came!" Gray snapped. "How could I ignore such diabolical messages?"

The next moment she bit back a cry. Looking down, she saw blood pool up on her fingers, where she clutched her forgotten rose.

His rose.

At her cry the wind seemed to swirl around her, shaking the rowan boughs and roiling the silver surface of the pool.

She heard him smother an oath. "You've hurt yourself." His voice was low, rough.

Pure heat. Just like the hands that circled her wrist a second later.

Before she could draw a ragged breath in protest, his lips covered her finger, tugging gently.

Gray shivered, fighting his sensory onslaught. But even as she struggled she had a vision of his lips sliding higher, foraging hungrily over a thousand aching pleasure points.

"D-don't!" she cried, jerking free and stumbling away from him.

He did not seem to hear. His eyes glittered, lit with inner fires. Slowly his hand rose.

Gray flinched as she watched the rock-hard arm ascend.

Memories flooded over her, memories of Matt and all his twisted games, memories of the fear that she could never quite escape, even now.

With a shriek, wind gusted through the glade, sending dead leaves and fallen twigs skittering up in a dark circle.

With the whirling wind came a chill so fierce that it caught at Gray's breath.

And in its wake came a raw, inchoate anger. A black regret.

A savage, wordless longing.

Suddenly Gray saw that Adrian's hand was stayed, his fingers rigid. Her eyes widened as she realized they were trembling slightly.

"Don't move, Gray Mackenzie." His eyes narrowed, smoky with desire. Dark with unnameable secrets.

Very gently he reached past her and plucked a great white moth from her hair. The pale wings fluttered against his long fingers, open and closed, open and closed. Then the insect sailed back into the darkness.

Adrian's face hardened. "Next time you might not be so lucky. Did my warning mean nothing to you?"

"I can take care of myself!"

"Can you?" One black brow rose to a commanding point. "Are you so sure of that, Gray Mackenzie?"

"Of course I am!" Gray's glared up at his shadowed features.

"I only wish I could say the same." His voice was low, raw. "But when I'm near you as I am now, thinking is the very last thing on my mind."

Gray could only stare, her breath coming fast and jerky. A vein began to pulse at his forehead, and somehow she could not drag her eyes away from it.

She wondered what it would feel like to touch that tiny throbbing inch of skin, to ease her lips close and touch his ragged pulse. To tease a moan from his hard, chiseled lips.

Gasping, she forced down her unruly imagination and summoned up her anger instead. She pulled her shawl tighter across her lace-clad chest. "You broke into my room! You drew in my sketchbook!"

"How do you know it was I?"

For a moment Gray faltered before his unblinking gaze.

She had no proof, of course. But outside of Marston who else was at the abbey?

"Did you view me at these infamies perhaps?"

"Of course I didn't. You're far too clever for that."

"Ah, if you thought that, you'd be right, Gray Mackenzie. But come, name me my other sins. On your lips . . ." Adrian's dark gaze fell to her trembling mouth. "On your lips, my sweet, they sound almost like virtues."

"I'm not your sweet!" Shoving her hands onto her hips, Gray called up her fury as armor against his caressing look. "And you—you took my clothes, you arrogant snake!"

Adrian's lips curved faintly. "They are merely hidden, I assure you. And that gown looks utterly ravishing, if I may say so."

"No, you may *not* say so! Who are you to leave me notes, to interrogate me? To meddle in my affairs?"

The dark eyes glittered. "Affairs? Now there's an interesting word."

Gray ignored his innuendo, ignored his mocking smile. Angrily she seized a gossamer bit of lace at her hem. "And then you left me nothing to wear but this—this *thing!*"

"Beautiful, isn't it?" His voice was dark and smooth as the night. "Especially with you filling it, my love."

As he spoke, a breeze tugged softly at Gray's hair and brushed the fine lace until it clung to the aching swell of her breast and thigh.

So sweet. So soft. Like a lover's touch.

Would his hands feel just as good?

She shivered, fury forgotten as a new heat began to build inside her. A rich, insidious heat such as she hadn't known for years.

For centuries?

"I'm not your love! I'm not *your* anything!"

"Then why did you come?"

Gray's heart pounded wildly. "Because I had no choice. Not after all those sneaking messages you left me! And because I had something to tell you." With trembling fingers, she clutched at her shawl, trying to quell the creeping heat that grew stronger every second. "S-stay out of my room, do you hear? Stay out of my sketch book! Most of all, stay out of my life!"

"What about your heart, Gray Mackenzie?"

Gray's breath caught at his dark, rough words. "What has my *heart* got to do with anything?"

The black-clad figure before her did not move. His eyes were all smoke and heat. Dark with an infinity of need, they roamed her face, missing nothing of her trembling response. "Everything, I should imagine. Because I want you, Gray Mackenzie. I want you very badly."

His voice dropped to a husky, intimate whisper. "And tonight, stubborn one, tonight I'm going to have you."

6

GRAY blinked, suddenly dizzy. Suddenly hungry. For things she could not even name.

She stumbled backwards, her hands tensed atop her heaving chest. "You're—you're crazy, do you know that?"

"I've little doubt of it." Adrian took a step closer.

"Stay away from me."

His eyes glittered. He moved again.

"Stop it! You don't—you can't possibly be serious about this!"

"No? Why not, Gray Mackenzie?" His voice was dark, compelling. Utterly ruthless.

Gray tugged desperately at her shawl. "Because you—you just can't!"

"Why not?" he repeated, softly this time.

"Because—because you don't know me. Not the slightest thing about me."

He was close enough to touch her now, but he did not. He only stared down at her, his eyes dark with the hunger of hundreds of wasted years.

Thousands of lonely nights.

"I know you've a temper to match that glorious auburn hair of yours. I know you snore quite impudently when you sleep." He gave her the ghost of a smile. "Marriages have been built on less familiarity than that."

Mine certainly was, Gray thought bitterly.

"So enlighten me, if you will. Why can't I want you? Tell me all the reasons. Tell me that my pulse isn't racing painfully right now. And that yours isn't racing just the same," he added huskily.

Gray swallowed, fighting for control. "Because you—you just can't!"

His eyes never left her face, harsh with need and something else Gray couldn't quite make out. "Why? The truth, remember?"

Her face turned a shade paler, and the sight made Adrian curse silently. Had he any other choice, he would have left off then and there. But now, in this place and this time, he could not.

For time was the one thing Adrian Draycott did not have.

"Well?" His eyes were mocking. "Not turning faint-hearted on me, are you?"

Instantly her chin rose.

Ah, that had done it. Somehow he'd thought it would.

He arched a jet-black brow and waited.

His patience was soon rewarded.

"All right, damn you, I'll tell you why! I'll tell you *all* the ugly little reasons." With trembling fingers Gray flung the shawl from her shoulders, baring her slim, lace-clad form to his hungry gaze. "B-because I'm t-too tall. Because I'm all bones and sharp angles. Not soft. Not de-desirable at all. B-because touching me is the next best thing to t-taking an ice bath!"

With a wild cry she spun about, her arms locked rigid about her chest.

Adrian could only stare at her back, wordless, uncomprehending. Even then heat licked at his loins, made his gut tense and churn.

Bony? Ugly? Undesirable? What in the name of heaven was the crazed female talking about?

Abruptly his eyes narrowed. Sweet saints above, could she really believe—

His fingers clenched to fists. "Who told you such things? Who made you believe such lies?"

He heard her smother a soft sob.

"Does it matter?" Gray countered bitterly. "All that matters is it's true, every last word of it."

Adrian went perfectly still. He ached to seize her, ached to press her trembling body against his. Damn and blast, a minute or two would do it. One hot slide of lips and tongue, one slow foray over her unbound, pouting breasts and she'd be his!

But even as the realization hit him, Adrian fought it down.

He didn't want it that way, didn't want *her* that way.

For some unnameable reason he'd been called here, called back through space and time to find her. And he bloody well wasn't about to settle for anything less than knowing why—all the reasons why. And for every sweet inch of her, given to him willingly.

"Oh, it matters. Far more than you can imagine. And whoever told you such things was either an utter fool or a patent liar. Probably both."

Gray's fingers shook. "It's no business of yours! Why do you care about any of this?"

"Because you affect me, Gray Mackenzie. In ways I've never been affected before. And I intend to find out why."

"Oh, why don't you just go! It's—it's better this way, don't you see? *Safer*." Gray brushed a furtive hand across her cheeks. Only then did Adrian see the glint of tears in her eyes.

The sight made him stiffen, made his innards twist to furious knots.

But he hid his anger well, knowing she would mistake its cause. He took another step closer. "Better off *this* way? With you dead inside? Oh, well said, woman, except you've no notion of what you're talking about." His voice hardened. "You've no notion of—death, and you can thank God for it. For you, Gray Mackenzie, were meant to hum with life. To burn with passion."

"I *can't*, don't you see? Maybe I never could. Matt told me often enough that it was all my fault he—"

Adrian cut her off with a hoarse curse. "Enough! I'll hear no more of the bastard's name, nor of his lies. For lies are all they were, Gray!"

Gray's face was a mask of alabaster in the filtered moonlight. "I—I've tried to believe that. Dear God, don't you think I've tried?"

Adrian reached out slowly. "Then give me your hand, Gray Mackenzie. Give me your hand, and I'll give you answers in return."

She studied him warily, her chest rising and falling jerkily.

In the moonlight he could see the shadowed aureoles strain against the fine lace at her chest.

Instantly he was on fire. Sweet Lord, he couldn't bear another aching second!

Somehow he managed to keep his face impassive. "If you truly want answers, that is. If you truly want to leave the past behind. The choice is yours."

Gray took a ragged breath. Her shoulders straightened. Without a word she raised her hand and put it in his.

White fingers fitted to hard bronze.

Perfect, Adrian thought, feeling that one light touch rock him all the way to his suddenly shaky knees.

Unimaginably perfect. Just as if they'd been made for each other.

He wondered if the rest of them would fit together so well.

But at that thought, a storm of erotic images rushed over him, shaking his resolve. He drowned in dreams of rose-tipped breasts, of restless, naked limbs, of dew-slick skin that eased apart to sheath him.

Endlessly.

He cleared his throat loudly. "Good. There, we've made a beginning." His thumb trailed slowly over her pounding pulse. He would have liked to think that pulse leaped with the same passion he felt. But Adrian knew her too well now, knew it was a darker emotion than desire that made her tremble. That thought helped him combat the angry need that roared and screamed and threatened to overrun its banks.

Impulsively he raised her hands to his lips, permitting himself the luxury of a slow, hot slide across her palm, along her fragile wrist.

He carried her fingers to the open collar of his shirt, then lower until her hand rested over the warm skin where his heart hammered madly.

"There's a first answer for you." He stared at her, letting her see the heat in his eyes, the hard need that gripped him. "Does that feel like a man who's repulsed? A man who's had a—what did you call it?—a bloody ice bath?"

Her fingers flinched slightly, but did not draw back.

And what she did next stole Adrian's breath away.

Her fingers curved and slid gently through the crisp black hair at his chest.

At the simple gesture his eyes turned to smoke. His breath slid hoarse between his taut lips.

He didn't even try to hide the force of it. He wanted her to see, to know every single blessed thing she was doing to him.

He watched her eyes widen, watched a hundred different emotions war in her face.

"There it is, woman. Plain enough for even your doubting eyes, I should think."

Her surprise was all too obvious. Surprise, and then disbelief. But she was brave, this woman. Watching her lips clench, her eyes darken with determination, Adrian began to think she was the bravest person he knew.

And she didn't even know it.

He framed a silent prayer, knowing he was going to need every shred of patience and strength tonight. And Adrian Draycott had never been noted for his patience.

A second later she inched closer, ran her hands gently over his rigid shoulders and cupped his face.

And then she drew him down to her.

He exploded like a Roman candle, halfway between heaven and hell by the time her lips settled light as cobwebs against his own.

Sweet. Dear God, so unbelievably sweet. He was going to die grandly from that sweetness any second!

But when his hands rose to caress her neck, they were gentle, as tentative as her kiss.

Even at that, she shivered, pulled away. Her wide eyes locked upon his face. "Did you—did that—"

"I did and it was," he said hoarsely.

Her face flushed crimson.

"Ah, God, don't blush, woman. Every time you do it sets me off, and I'm near to dead already. Sweet Lord, have mercy on a poor, defenseless male!"

Instantly Gray's face flamed brighter, but Adrian hadn't missed the faint smile that tugged at her lips.

He groaned softly, burying his fingers in her hair.

"Did you really? Like it, that is? Just—a little?" Her voice was as soft as the night breeze. But Adrian wanted to shout with triumph when he heard it, to crush her close.

Instead he merely crooked one sable brow. "No." And then as her beautiful forehead furrowed, "Not just a little, stubborn one. Endlessly, unimaginably more than *just a little*. In fact, the way I want you right now is causing me mortal, wracking pain!"

Gray's eyes narrowed thoughtfully. She caught her lip between straight white teeth.

Dear God, what torture had the woman in mind for him next?

It had been two hundred years, after all, since he'd last felt such things! But of course, she couldn't know that, Adrian reminded himself wryly.

Absently she slid the tip of her tongue across her lip. Adrian smothered a raw curse at the sight.

"Did—did you say something?"

"Who, me?"

Reassured, she turned back to her contemplation of his mouth.

At her slow scrutiny Adrian felt his manhood throb painfully. Closing his eyes he began a rather desperate cataloguing of some of the finer paintings in the abbey's collection.

Two Turners.

The Whistler, of course.

A few middling sketches by da Vinci.

An indifferent Constable.

A rather masterful portrait of the Tenth Viscount by Sargent.

And of course, he mustn't overlook that one thoroughly forgettable canvas by—

Adrian was jerked back to agonizing reality as her lips slid wetly down his neck and caressed his suddenly bared chest. "What in the name of all the saints—"

He got no further. His breath exploded and his pulse went wild as her lips circled, then closed softly over his nipple.

A groan tore from his lips. His hands went utterly still against her neck. The pleasure was unbearable, unspeakable.

And all that he'd ever expected heaven to be.

In a fraction of a second he was gone, six feet under, toes cocked, drowning in sensation. He shuddered, feeling her soft fingers at his shoulders, her sweet breath playing over his chest.

Most of all, he felt the wild, erotic slide of her lips, gentle and tentative with discovery.

He started to speak, and found to his fury that he had to clear his throat. "I think—yes, I really think that that's enough, my dear."

His fingers tensed in her silky hair. He was perilously close to the edge, Adrian realized.

But she did not cease. Her tongue slid back and forth across his taut skin.

"Gray—stop." He grimaced as her teeth brushed the aching nub of his sensation. *"Now."*

Something in his voice penetrated her haze. She pulled back, eyes dazed, breath ragged. "Did I—is something wrong?"

Adrian managed a raw laugh. *"Wrong?* On the contrary, my heart. Something's far too right—and that's what is wrong."

"Well then—why can't I—"

"Because, my sweet, dim-witted, splendid little fool, there are *two* of us here, in case you've forgotten. And if you keep doing such wildly abandoned things to me, *one* of that pair is going to lose his head and bury himself inside you until we both go over the edge."

Adrian tensed as soon as he'd said the words, certain she would flinch and retreat from him.

But wondrously, miraculously, she did not. Instead her eyes narrowed thoughtfully. "It's . . . really true then." Her glorious lips curved gently.

The sight was like pure sunlight poured into all the dark corners of Adrian's ancient, embittered heart. If he had nothing else, it would still be worth all the pain, all the frustration just to know the sight of that one soft, sweet smile.

"But now, I really think it's time you had a taste of your own medicine, temptress." His eyes glittered with a hint of wickedness.

Gray pursed her lips. "Oh, no, I don't think—I never planned—"

Adrian groaned inwardly. He had his work cut out for him, that was certain.

He took a measured step forward—and watched her take one back. "Fair is fair, woman. You must realize that." He took another step.

She retreated in turn.

"Afraid, my stormy one? I can hardly believe it." He moved again.

She countered with another step of retreat.

"There's nothing to fear, I assure you."

She retreated once more, but the movement was slower this time, indecisive.

Adrian's smile grew to a wolfish grin as he watched her back right into the gnarled trunk of a rowan tree.

He didn't give her time to think, time to run. He lodged his hands beside her head and eased his hard body close, his lips pressed against her trembling mouth.

Heaven fell. The sky sang. Light, time, and matter dissolved into dreams.

But no dream could taste as good as she did.

And then her lips opened and Adrian groaned, catapulted into a whole new universe of sensation.

"Gray," he murmured. "Can you feel it now? Can you feel how much I want you?"

He felt her lips curve beneath him in answer.

Emboldened by that gesture, he drove his tongue deeper, seeking out the secrets of her mouth.

When he felt her fingers clutch at his shoulders, felt her tongue slide softly against his, Adrian thought he would howl from utter pain and perfect pleasure.

And then—only joy. Only wanton, breathless discovery.

Only Gray.

He knew it would be enough to last him forever.

But it wasn't, Adrian soon discovered, enough for her.

Her fingers curved, insistent at his shoulders. Her hips moved gently against his rigid thighs.

And her tongue, dear God, her tongue was doing *carnal* things, forbidden things, indescribable things.

Things that Adrian Draycott, profligate though he'd always been, hedonist and confirmed cynic, had never even dreamed existed.

And had certainly never expected to feel. Not two hundred years dead as he was.

A moment later his lips closed around her restless tongue. Somehow his fingers were unlacing her bodice, exploring the exquisite curve of her breasts, his nails grazing the pebbled nipples that strained upward beneath the flimsy lace.

"Gray . . . sweeting . . . you're heaven itself . . ." Heat raced through him, white-hot, blinding.

Unimaginable.

It left Adrian stunned, breathless, shaking.

Maybe that was why he didn't hear her moan, didn't feel her tense against him until it was too late.

But her soft, breathless cries were unmistakable in the ragged silence, as was the tension that suddenly gripped her slender frame.

Her eyes widened. She cried out against him, passion cresting through her.

Adrian caught her close, smiling as he felt the first velvet tremor rip through her. Her suddenly locked fingers and shuddering body told him everything he needed to know.

And he gloried in every tremor, in every soft gasp. Sweet Lord, the woman was nothing short of magnificent!

Shifting slightly, he captured her between his braced thighs. With a delicate movement he triggered her sensory storm anew, sending her arching wildly against him.

And he caught each moan, each breathless, shuddering sigh against his lips, cherishing every one.

Without warning, her fingers tensed. With a wild cry Gray stumbled sideways, a trembling hand locked to her mouth, her eyes hazy with unshed tears. "N-no! I don't want—I never wanted—"

And then she was gone, her gown a spiral of moonlight against the soft, dark grass.

7

SHE turned and ran, her heart hammering painfully. What had she done? How had this man broken down all her defenses? It was inconceivable. Sheer madness!

Branches ripped at her hem, vines caught at her feet, but still Gray stumbled forward, blind to everything but her pain and shame.

How? How could she have let such a thing happen?

She stumbled, her foot catching on an unseen vine. With a wild cry she pitched forward. Her head struck stone with a dull, sickening thud.

But Gray barely noticed the pain. Not the pain in her head, at least. For at that moment Gray Mackenzie, *née* Moira Jamieson, was beyond feeling little things like contusions or fractures. It was the pain in her heart that tore her apart and sent hot tears spilling down her cheeks.

Dear God, how *could* she have?

She shuddered, still reeling from the sensual explosion she'd just experienced, from the unforgivable bliss she'd just discovered in the arms of a stranger.

When his strong hands circled her shoulders, she flinched and wildly shoved them away. "G-go away!"

Adrian ducked to avoid her flailing ,arms. "Contain yourself, woman. It's hardly worth such a fuss."

"It is! I h-hate you!"

"Very well, but must you—ah—struggle so while you do it?" Sharp nails whipped past Adrian's cheek, and he growled a graphic oath.

Gray was beyond hearing, nearly beyond reason. "You see—how soon it begins? But I don't want it, do you hear? Not this cursed thing you call love. This raw, bleeding wound that never heals. I don't want to *feel* again, not ever. There's just too damned much pain in it!"

Adrian ducked again. "Sometimes, just sometimes, it's the pain that lets you know you're alive."

Gray wiggled furiously. "Never! You'll never set a hand—not the slightest finger—on me again, do you hear?"

He caught her grimly, hauled her up struggling into his arms. "Stop fighting me! Your head needs tending, you intractable harridan. And—by God, you're bleeding!"

"What are you—where in the—"

"Enough arguing, woman!" He strode over the dark, soft grass until he came to the far side of the pool. There Adrian settled her gently in the ferns, then dipped his fingers into the water and caught up a palmful of moonlight, which he trickled carefully over her bleeding forehead.

It was not a deep gash, but it would pain her when the shock wore off. Grimly, he tugged at a handful of fragrant grass, then brushed away the last traces of blood.

"Better?"

Gray shivered, catching the fragrance of verbena and mint leaves crushed in his fingers.

"W-why?" she stammered. "Why do you care? Just let me go. I—I don't know how much more I can take." It was an admission given shudderingly, at great cost.

Adrian heard how much the admission pained her, and the knowledge filled him with fury for the man who had left her so vulnerable. But he gave no sign of his inner rage. His hands simply continued to move, gentle at their task. "I don't know why, sweeting. But I do know this. I could no more let you go than I could cease to breathe. For you're in my blood now, Gray Mackenzie, part of my very soul. And you're not leaving here until you accept that."

She shoved unsteadily at his fingers. "I don't want this, do you hear? I never wanted it!"

"It's too late for that. Too late for running. Too late for wishing things were different. What's done is done. And the sight of your sweet, shocked passion was the most beautiful thing I ever hope to see." His voice hardened, as fierce and angry as Gray had ever heard it. "So don't bloody try to twist it into something dirty and contemptible—for that it never could be."

Gray wanted to scream, wanted to shout that he was wrong. But the barely leashed hunger in his eyes held her silent, made her dream it might be so, just for a second or two.

And damn him, he noticed—noticed the exact instant she hesitated. At that very second his patient nursing turned to raw, premeditated seduction.

His fingers slid into her hair. His thigh wedged against her hip.

"No, damn you! I won't . . ." But her voice was husky.

"You want it, Gray. Let me give it to you. Dear God, this one thing at least I can give you."

She fought it. Oh, God, how hard she fought it. But he was part of the night, part of her dreams, part of the soft scent of mint and verbena.

Part of *her*.

And it had all begun with that damned, beautiful dress he'd left entwined with a perfect blood-red rose.

It was unfair, totally unfair! Everything conspired against her, even her own traitorous body.

"Don't touch me."

His hands curved gently, anchoring her neck.

"Don't bloody touch me."

He eased closer, his need an unbearable seduction.

"I'm going back now. Don't try to stop me."

He didn't believe her bluff for a second. "Why can't you admit it, sweeting? Admit you're already half in love with this place. I saw it in that sketch you did today. And if you love my abbey, then you're halfway to loving me."

"Do you have answers for *everything?*" A reckless instinct drove Gray to attack. Anything to avoid facing the truth of what he said.

And the pain of decision.

"And you, sweet harridan, do *you* have nothing but questions?"

A distant peal drifted over the hills, faint and crystalline. The sound was ethereal, otherworldly.

Achingly sad.

Adrian sighed. "I've one answer, at least." Before she could pull away, his head slanted down. His lips skimmed over hers. Slowly his hands moved lower, molding her rigid shoulders. "Gray. Gray . . ." His mouth played over her, hot and light. "Sweet Gray. Soft Gray. Beautiful, stubborn Gray."

The first touch sent sparks shooting through her. Suddenly she was finding it hard to breathe.

Adrian raised his head, his expression unreadable. "You wear my rose. It dims before your beauty." His hands tightened. Gray could have sworn they were trembling.

And that slight sign of vulnerability shook her as nothing else had. She felt the hard walls around her heart heave, shudder, and finally crack.

Heat. She had never felt, never imagined such heat.

Such yearning, blind and sweet . . .

Without knowing quite how or why, she was lifting her face to his, flowing into the wine-dark beauty of his kiss.

"Dear God, Gray—" He caught her close, his breath ragged at her cheek. "Let me touch you. It's . . . you can't understand, but this is the only bloody thing I have left to give you."

At his words, at the slow glide of his hands across her chest, Gray shuddered. Dark images spiraled through her, images that she sensed were something more. *Memories*, they were, welling up from some long-forgotten part of her.

Just as the parade of ghostly figures she'd seen by the moat had been memories, not daydreams.

Suddenly Gray knew she wanted this man in any way she could have him. She wanted him fast and mindless, reckless and blinding.

She wanted him slow and hard and endlessly patient . . .

She even wanted him angry and unrepentant. Slaking the heat of a body too long denied. For that, too, was part of him, just as it was part of her. A part of her she'd tried too long to ignore.

Like her drawing, the only question was where she was going to start.

Her eyes began to glisten, to shimmer in the moonlight. It was madness. It was rankest folly. But somehow Gray didn't care. She cast logic to the farthest winds.

Her lips met the hard angle of his jaw, and she felt him shudder, heard him groan.

Danger. Bliss. Endless wanting . . .

"See what you do to me. Do I act like a man repelled, uninterested? Dear God, were I any *more* attracted, I'd . . ."

Gray smiled softly, staring at the moonbeams dancing over his face and neck.

And then she touched him. His chest was hot beneath her fingers. She could feel the racing pulse at his neck, as wild as her own.

And in that instant Gray knew for certain that nothing else mattered, not the fear, not the regret.

He gave her a crooked and utterly devastating smile. "Well? So bad as that? It's been a while for me, but—"

"Rather—too right, I think." Her fingers slid to his shirt. The last two buttons sprang free.

Adrian's breath caught. "Gray. Sweeting. You really don't have to—"

Thoughtfully Gray continued. She spread the soft dark fabric and eased it from his shoulders, while moonlight spilled across them.

Her eyes darkened, locked on the broad, muscled torso revealed beneath his shirt. A wild churning invaded her blood and sent her pulse tripping double-time.

Her hands went absolutely still, poised just above his waist.

Not a sound, not the slightest motion came from Adrian's rigid body.

Slowly Gray looked up. In his dark eyes, she saw something she'd never expected to see.

Honor. Perfect candor.

The look said he wouldn't push her, even now. It was all up to her.

And suddenly, as Gray stared into his eyes, she saw other images, felt a bewildering flood of sound and color and emotion.

Of *memory*.

Memories of a steel-clad warrior who sat a pawing charger, pennants flying as he raced against the wind into battle. Memories of a wheeling falcon that screamed, then shot low to perch on a mail-covered arm.

And then Gray saw herself, long hair unbound as she waited and watched for a warrior long from home, fighting at Richard's side for ideals as inchoate and shifting as the desert sands where he watched his comrades fall, one by one.

Week after week she had waited, month after month. Until seasons changed and months stretched into years.

And still he had not come.

True, she thought blindly, her eyes blurred with tears. All of it true. The sensations were too tangible, too intensely *real* to be an illusion.

And somehow in his raw, sensitized state Adrian read the same images, images he had never seen before.

Images that were memories for him as well.

He went utterly still. "Good sweet God Almighty. It— it cannot be." The realization left him reeling. "You— you were there. We—" A groan rocked through him.

Gray touched his chest gently, understanding exactly what he was feeling. "All that sadness . . . now I think I understand. All those long years . . ." She brushed furtively at her cheeks, looking back down dark, twisting corridors of time to another woman who'd lain against the soft green grass, shedding tears for the man who was beside her now.

"Eight hundred years . . ." Adrian's voice was raw. "It's too long, far too long to grieve, sweeting." He touched her cheek, cursing when he felt the telltale moisture touch his fingers. "What a fool I was. And all from pride, I can see that now. It's always been my damnable pride that's led me astray. But you, my sweet—how could I have let *you* bear the price of it?"

Adrian caught her cheeks and raised her face to him. "When I came back—they said you'd drowned by the pool." His gaze was fierce, as if he were awaiting a killing blow. "It was a lie, wasn't it?"

Gray shivered in his arms as bleak memories poured over her. And suddenly she was powerless to hold back the tears, to hold back the years.

She could only nod silently, while tears ran silver down her cheeks.

Adrian's fingers dug into her shoulders. With a groan he crushed her close, so close that Gray could feel the anger wrack him.

"Lies . . . all lies. Dear God, what was it? They didn't—sweet Lord, I couldn't bear it if they hurt you—"

Gray swallowed. "No, not that. It—it was poison, I think. I remember the first pains, the convulsions. And after that nothing, just darkness. They must have made up that other story about the drowning to protect themselves."

Adrian's head slanted down until his forehead rested against the top of her head. "I always wondered . . . it never made sense to me . . ."

Gray felt the shudder that rocked him then, felt the hot salty rain of tears that fell against her hair and slid onto her neck. "Don't, Adrian," she whispered. "Please— don't."

"*Don't?* Dear God, you *died* because of me! I might just as well have signed the death warrant myself! I should have known what would happen if I left you here, unprotected."

Her hands sank into his hair, holding him close. "It . . . it doesn't matter. Not now. All that matters is that we're here again. That we're together."

"It *does* matter! I betrayed you! And when I finally did return, I was stupid enough to believe you'd forgotten. I even began to think it might have happened just as they'd told me. That you'd lost your reason, snapped—"

"Hush." Gray silenced him with a fierce kiss. She felt him tense, felt him strain against her. "It's—it's over, Adrian. Done and gone for eight centuries now. Just . . . just love me. Give me your joy and . . . yes, your pride. The way it should have been all those years ago."

She moved her open lips over his, hungry, searching. *Remembering* . . .

Dear God, she remembered all of it now. All the pain and joy of those few sweet months they'd had together.

And the force of those memories nearly snapped her heart in two.

"Love me, Adrian," she whispered. "*Now.* Let me feel what it should have been then. I've waited so long . . ."

He cut her off with a raw groan, arching her back against him as his mouth spread hers to receive his hot invasion.

Suddenly pain and sadness were gone. All that was left was the joy and the hot sweetness of homecoming.

Now neither minded that it had come eight centuries too late.

Gray slowly combed her fingers through the long black hair at Adrian's shoulder. "It's—it's all still here, isn't it? You and I . . . all we felt. Dear God, it never ends, does it? It only changes. Only grows . . ."

Adrian's eyes glittered. "And trust? What of that, my heart? Have the ages dimmed your trust? Have my pride and stupidity lost me the only thing I truly need?" His voice fell to a hoarse whisper. "I can see how very much I hurt you then."

Gray touched his cheek gently. "Whatever you did, I've long since forgiven you for."

Adrian's breath slid free in a hiss. "Gray—sweeting, how long I've waited, wanted . . ." His voice caught, low and raw. "I swear it will be magic. One night full of sweet, silver magic."

Her head fell back as his lips worked dizzying patterns along her neck, her shoulder, her collarbone. She shivered, opening to his touch, flowering like the perfect petals of the centifolia rose he swept against her skin.

Like the love-mark she carried on her cheek.

"A-Adrian?" She shifted restlessly as heat swirled through her. Until her heart was full enough to break.

"Soon," he whispered, coaxing a moan from her as his lips worshipped the pale swell of her breast, eased from beneath her lacy gown.

Gray shuddered as she felt his lips close around the velvet bud of her nipple. Her fingers tensed, buried deep in his dark hair, holding him close while pleasure unfolded inside her, petal by exquisite petal.

On and on the pleasure grew. On and on his mouth coaxed, circled, never giving her time to think, to prepare for the next drugging onslaught of ecstasy. She felt the mist cling to her face, felt the air shimmer, supercharged with the raw fury of their primal need.

Slowly, powerfully, he laid her back against the grass and eased the wisp of lace from her skin. And then for long moments Adrian did nothing but look at her. He memorized the pale supple beauty of her body, the dusky seduction of her pebbled nipples and the auburn curls at her thighs.

The wind sighed. The damp ferns whispered.

Then with a harsh groan he found her silken heat and brought their long years of separation to a breathless end.

"A-Adrian—"

"Hush, woman. I've years—*centuries* to make up for."

"But I—"

Gray gasped as he tongued a path of fire across her belly and teased the auburn triangle just below. "Adrian, I don't—you can't—"

And then only raw pleasure, only burning silver joy

as he bared her and gave her all the sweetness of his soul. She arched mindlessly, drowning in unimaginable pleasure.

He caught her close, whispering hot love words on her hungry skin. "Open to me, my love. Open to me while I touch you, taste you. Ah, God, I've heat enough to sweep away all the fear, all the darkness."

And then no more words. Only the sweet, sleek parting of skin. Only the restless, velvet probing.

And with each movement Gray opened farther, fell deeper. Light drifted around them, cast off the gleaming currents, little flashes and pinpoints of energy that danced over their hot, urgent skin.

And always the roses, filling the air with sweetness, with rich, ineffable memories of all the other times they'd strained and yearned and loved this way.

Like a circle never broken. A circle ever widening, forged of joy and tears.

A circle that never died, only grew brighter and expanded.

Gray felt herself bud, felt her heart open in splendor as she reached to catch every perfect, silver ray. "Adrian!"

The night flashed before her, light poured in radiant columns before her eyes. And then she was falling, down through heaven, down through time, down through dark, forgotten centuries until she once again rested on the damp soil, with his hard, beloved body there to protect her.

Fierce and hungry, his eyes searched her face. "God, how I love you, woman. When I think of all those years . . . all those bloody wasted years . . ."

Gray pressed upwards and cut him off. Her hips shifted, searching for his heat, yearning to feel him drive deep inside her.

An odd glimmer rose from their heated skin and hung like a veil of bright mist across the glade. Fury raged between them, an equal thing now, a wild flow of male might and pliant velvet strength as Gray moved to meet him, sheathe him, welcome him.

With his first hot thrust she gasped, feeling the sheer size and force of him.

Swiftly, he drove home, filling her in one fierce, perfect slide. Then slowly he drew back, prolonging her exquisite pleasure until she cried out in breathless abandon.

Adrian threw back his head, shuddering. His eyes closed as passion swirled between them. "Dear God, *again*, Gray. Flower for me once more. Flower around me—give me all your sweetness, for it's my only home, the only hope I'll ever know!"

Gray's heart lurched and took flight.

And when it did she found his waiting.

Dimly she felt his thighs lock, felt tension grip his powerful, braced forearms.

And realized even now he denied himself for fear of hurting her.

She slid her feet over his clenched calves, smiling when she felt him shudder.

"No, by all the saints! I'll not be gainsaid, woman. Our first time will be *my* way—"

But Adrian Draycott, lord of ten thousand men, sovereign power of Draycott Abbey and all its lands, had not counted on the willfulness of a single, stubborn, twentieth-century female.

His eyes blazed as he fought her pull, fought her knowing movements. Velvet muscles rippled and then closed around the part of him buried deep inside her.

He gasped and was lost. "Gray! Sweet God, Gray, don't! I can't—"

"Then *don't*. Oh, God, don't wait!"

At the first savage, unbridled thrust Gray realized just how much he'd been holding back. Even then she welcomed his hot, crushing possession, her thighs locked to his as she rose and caught his shoulder, planting a love-mark of her own against his skin.

With a roar Adrian dragged her close, then twisted them together until she sprawled atop his chest.

His eyes shone black as he caught her straining hips and guided her down to meet each silken thrust. Gray shuddered, feeling his fingers shift, driving her to blindness, to frenzy.

To heaven.

"Again, love." His voice was dark, raw, a seduction in itself. "*Again.*"

She shattered against him, blood thundering, breath flown, mind and body aflame in the dark, lush night.

His laughter broke over her in soft waves amid the violence of her release. Amid the breathless churning storm where he carried her.

Just as her tremors reached their peak and began to fade, he raised her high and pulled her down once more, groaning when he felt her clutch his hot, aching flesh anew.

In joyous abandon he filled her, again and again, while her soul leaped free and his own joined hers, two comets flaming through the star-flung sky.

"A-Adrian! Oh, I can't—it's too—"

"Here, love. I'm right here. Ah, God, so sweet you are—take me with you, Gray. Take me now!"

He gripped her tensely, head thrown back as pleasure found its stunning climax, as the softness of moss and ferns cushioned their wild, driving movements.

Together they spun and tumbled through boundless space, watching stars flash past, hearing the darkness sing around them.

Home again at last. Together. Just where they were always meant to be.

And neither time nor fate, Adrian swore, would ever separate them again.

8

SOFT and dark, his laughter welcomed her back, cushioned her fall into flesh and weight and earthbound gravity. Gray opened her eyes.

"Adrian, I—"

But before the first doubts could intrude, before the first fears could rear their ugly heads, he pulled her beneath him and loosed the joy anew.

Silver ripples of pleasure lapped and surged and broke over Gray's exquisitely sensitized body.

"A-again?" She shivered, her eyes smoky, dazed, luminous with love and inquiry. "You—you can't!"

Smiling darkly, he brushed the crown of one upswept, silken breast, delighting in her instant tremor of response. "Eight hundred years is a long time to wait, sweeting. I'm afraid you'll have to forgive my intemperance . . ."

Fire burst from the dusky crest where his clever lips foraged and suckled. "Forgive?" Gray shuddered, arching mindlessly as the wild pleasure grew. "Sweet heaven, for *t-this?*"

His laughter rumbled over the glade and suddenly it was as if night had fled and light gleamed silver over vine and bough and wave. It was the same world, the same night, Gray thought dimly, and yet both were entirely different now.

Somewhere in the dark woods beyond the glade, distant bells began to peal, low and faint.

Adrian stiffened, flinging back his head, feeling the first raw pangs of despair.

No! Not so soon!

"Not yet," Adrian breathed hoarsely, struggling to hold back the transformation. "Not bloody yet . . ."

But already he felt it. Even without looking, he knew his body had the faint glow that signaled the coming change.

No, not yet! By heaven and all the saints, it was too soon!

He shuddered, clenching his hands and holding her close, letting the sweet tide of her passion wash over him. He watched her gasp, felt her long legs wrap around him as she rode down into ecstasy.

"Ah, Gray, so good . . ." He caught a strand of hair and eased it from her cheek, drinking in the beauty of her wild response.

And then Adrian saw his fingers begin to gleam where bone and tendon shifted and strained.

More time. Please—just a little more time.

But words would change nothing. The high clear music was in his ears, resonating through his shifting body.

Calling him home.

No! he screamed in desperate silence. *This is home. Where she is will always be my home!*

The tones sharpened, vibration turning to a low thunder.

And as Adrian stared down at Gray's beautiful features, he saw his hand begin to glow, saw right through his skin to the rapidly fading outline of his bone.

Sweat dripped from his brow. He caught her fiercely, drinking in her last, breathless cries, memorizing the rhythm of her wild tremors.

Desperately he fought the call, strained to hold his slipping atoms tight-packed, dense, earthbound.

But it was impossible. The ringing grew, plunging into his blood, turning liquid into shimmering networks of light.

"Gray—" His voice was raw. "Gray, I—must go."

She only shivered, tightening her grip on his shoulders.

Gritting his teeth, Adrian pulled from her sweet heat, struggling against the transformation that threatened to come any second. "You—you, too, must go, sweeting. There is danger growing, and I want you safe until it's over."

At that, her eyes finally opened, dark with sated passion.

And then those azure eyes widened. Gray tensed, seeing the light that gleamed over Adrian's face and chest and shoulders. Wildly she reached out for him, only to stare disbelievingly as her fingers slid right through the shimmering mass that only seconds before had been his arm and chest.

"*N-no!*" It was a ragged cry of shock.

Grim-faced, Adrian fell to his knees beside her. By a savage force of will, he drove the blinding radiance back to a dim phosphorescence. "I—love you, Gray Mackenzie. Never—never doubt that. And by all the heavens above, I'll—come back to you. This . . . I swear."

Gray stifled a sob, pressing her fingers to her mouth as she watched him sway and waver before her. "You can't be—dear God, this can't be real!"

But it was. Even the brightness of his body was fading. She could see a glowing outline at his shoulders and head.

"The . . . the boat's moored by the far bank." His voice was barely a whisper now. "Gideon . . . waiting . . ."

"Adrian! No, don't go!" Gray's trembling hands locked across her chest as she watched him shimmer, then swirl apart into waves of purest light.

For a moment his eyes darkened, fixed on her terrified face. "Wait for me," he whispered. "I'll—*find*—you . . ."

And then he simply blinked out, like a candle caught in a wayward gust of wind. Where bone and flesh had once stood, haloed in light, there were now only leaden shadows.

Gray stumbled to her feet, staring blindly at the dark, empty ground where moments before Adrian had stood. "It's just a trick! You—you're just trying to frighten me! Aren't you, Adrian? Tell me, damn you!"

But no voice rose in answer. The glade was silent, chill, all light fled.

And somewhere, far away in the distance, Gray heard the faint peal of bells.

Blindly she stumbled to her feet and crossed the moss-covered bank, her shawl clutched to her chest. Through a blur of tears she made out Gideon's dark form, waiting for her beside the little boat.

For a moment hysteria surged up through her. *It was all a dream, wasn't it? Or some great, elaborate joke?*

But the faint soreness at her thighs told her that the night had been far more a heated fantasy. She would have to begin to face that—along with all the rest of the night's discoveries.

Including the fact that the man you love is the ghost of Draycott Abbey? Gray bit back a hysterical laugh.

Where had it gone, all the magic and splendor? Now the night was cold and all her dreams had fled.

Glittering amber eyes stared up as Gray tugged at the pole and stumbled into the shallow boat. Scrubbing at her tears, she glared at the regal gray form on the bank. "Well, are you coming or not? If I can t-talk to ghosts, I suppose I can talk to a cat!"

The long gray tail arched and twitched. Gideon's sleek head turned, staring off into the restless, rustling woods beyond the glade, where Adrian had vanished moments before.

The cat gave a long, low cry.

Only silence met him, along with the faint hiss of the wind.

A moment later Gideon turned and jumped into the boat, his black paws clearing the wooden side effortlessly.

Shivering, Gray turned and shoved off.

"There's something about you, my friend. Something that's less—and a great deal more—than I've ever seen in any other cat."

Gray shook her head and turned to focus on the lapping waters. Mist dragged at the boat in spiraling fingers, denser now that the night air had grown colder. At the center of the moat Gray slowed her movements, barely able to see through the swirling bank of mist.

At her feet Gideon meowed, gliding up to a perch on the wooden seat as he stared out into the drifting whiteness.

And then they were through the worst of it, only yards from shore.

"There, that wasn't so bad. I only wish I could feel the same about all the other bizarre things I've seen tonight," Gray muttered, clutching her shawl closer about her shoulders.

Slowly she poled to the bank, studying the French doors beyond the terrace.

They were open.

Fear worked up her neck. She could have sworn she'd left them closed.

Her hands clenched on the worn wooden pole as the boat hissed to a halt in the mud and sand at the bank. Gray stared up at the gleaming glass panes, feeling panic well up inside her.

And the fear was with her again, as blind and wrenching

as it had been *then*, when she first realized Matt was trying to kill her. Because she knew too much.

A dark shape glided up the bank and Gray realized that Gideon was making for the open door.

"Gideon, come back!"

She heard the faint *whoosh* of a curtain, then nothing but silence. She tried to move, and felt the fear seize her, hold her helpless, paralyzed.

But because she had to prove that she was not the same woman she had been, that she had learned to conquer her fear, Gray flung down her pole, jumped to the bank, and plunged up to the gate house.

The chill darkness hit her like a fist. Nothing moved in the shadows. "Gideon?"

She moved forward blindly, hands outstretched.

Her knee grazed the leg of a chair. Frowning, she turned toward the wall. There was a mustiness to the room that hadn't been there before, along with a faint, acrid sweetness.

Her neck prickled with fear.

Her hand met the silk-covered wall. She found the welcome outline of the light switch and flipped it down.

The first thing she saw was Gideon, tense as an Egyptian marble statue, hissing softly as he stared at the door of the bathroom. His head cocked; his tail arched.

Slowly, as if in a dream, Gray moved forward.

And then she froze, seized by horror that drove the breath from her lungs.

The dead bird lay on the floor of the bathroom, its dark feathers matted with blood. And on the wall above was scrawled a warning, traced in blood.

Silly, stupid bitch. Did you really think you could escape me?

Out in the darkness, the man waited and watched, fury a poison in his mind and blood.

She could not be allowed to escape him, not again!

The beautiful bitch had betrayed him once, but for that, too, she would pay. And for all the rest of her perfidy, he thought furiously, watching her slim shadow cross through the gate house.

The bitch had always valued her silly little scrawls more than she valued him, right from the very beginning. He swore foully, madness seizing him.

But not much longer, he thought. First he would strip away her pride, and then he'd seize her very sanity.

Just the way they'd seized his, during those hellish months in prison. He laughed softly.

Soon you'll be begging again, Moira. On your knees the way you're supposed to be.

Crying. Pleading for me to touch you. Just the way you used to plead.

And if you don't, I'll do to you the same thing I'm going to do to that damned cat of yours.

9

GRAY stumbled backwards, her hands to her nerveless lips. With a wild cry, she caught up her trailing hem and plunged toward the outer door.

Only inches from the frame she froze, watching the knob turn silently.

All her worst nightmares came to life.

"Adrian—dear God, *Adrian!*"

Gray spun about, one hand crushed to her mouth. She called his name without knowing it, then saw a tall shadow fall across the terrace. Relief exploded through her. "Adrian, I—"

But the cry was cut off stillborn.

Gray saw that it was a different face outside the opened doors. A stranger's face.

A man with darkly tanned skin and sun-bleached hair low on his brow. The man from the florist shop in London?

And then Gray's throat twisted in a knot of fear as she recognized the furtive movements, the hardened sneer— so familiar, even after five years.

No, not a stranger at all.

Just her ex-husband.

Come to kill her, as he'd promised when they'd pulled him cursing from the crowded courtroom.

Gray turned and ran for the front door, stumbling against a mahogany side table.

Adrian! Dear God, come to me now, if you can hear me!

There was a rustling in the air around her, a tingling at her neck.

The next moment the glass doors from the terrace gave way with an explosive crash. "Moira? Where are you, damn it? Where are you, my sweet, lying wife?"

White-faced, Gray inched backwards into the darkness of the front alcove, praying that he wouldn't hear her.

Behind her, thick shoes crunched over shattered glass. "Clever, weren't you? Changing your face, your eye color. Taking a new name and a new identity. But I was even more clever, because I did the same—changed my hair, darkened my skin. You see, the thought of finding you was the only thing that kept me alive in that stinking cell."

Closer the steps came, ever closer. Any second now he would see her!

"And you can forget about running, my sweet. There's no one here to help you now, no one here but the two of us. Now it will be just the way it always used to be. And we're going to do things the same way we did then. You remember, don't you? How it felt?"

Gray shoved her fist to her lips to keep from gagging, to keep from screaming. Dear God, the door had to be close now!

Behind her the flat voice droned on. "I saw the butler drive off hours ago. Even that damned gray cat's gone. I would have killed him first, but the big devil was too smart, I'll say that much for him."

Her ex-husband's eyes narrowed, hazed with madness. "*You'll* be much easier to kill, my sweet."

And then Gray found the cold metal knob. Her heart pounding, she wrenched open the door and plunged into the darkness as an angry growl erupted behind her.

Where, Adrian? Where are you?

Steady, sweeting. The words were a mere murmur in her head, a faint warmth at her shoulders.

But they were there, a lifeline to sanity. Where— where are you? Gray cried raggedly.

I can't—be with you, sweeting. Not yet. But circle around to the glade and cross to the south tower. There's a door there, a very old door. I'll show you how to find it.

She obeyed without question or hesitation, trying to shut out the angry curses that followed her as she ran through the moonlit night.

She made her way past the stables, past the maze, and around to the far side of the little glade, guided by Adrian's silent directions every step of the way. The man behind her crashed on more slowly, having no such guidance.

And with every step his rage grew. Gray knew the pattern all too well.

She forced back a sob, stopping at the bank of the moat to listen to the soft night wind, waiting for Adrian's silent prompting.

But none came.

And then on the far bank where the abbey walls rose up straight and sheer from the moat, she saw a sleek gray shadow detach from the night.

Burning amber eyes rose to greet her.

"Gideon!"

Plunging into the water, she swam toward the cat who waited on the bank like a marble sentinel. At that moment a shot rang out, shrieking past her ear and slamming into the water only inches from her head.

Wildly Gray churned on, hearing more shots hiss past. Half-blind with fear, she struggled from the water to find Gideon pacing before the tower's weathered stone base.

In her terror, Gray had no time to wonder how the great cat came to be there or why she should find the sight of him so comforting.

Behind her came the splash of a large body hitting water. Gray gritted her teeth against the terror that threatened to shatter her reason. "He—he said there was a door. But *where*, Gideon?"

She ran tense fingers over the rough stone, finding no sign of an opening. Abruptly Gideon darted past her feet.

"Where is it, Adrian? I—I can't find it!"

The voice came from the lapping of the waves, the sigh of the wind. *Close your eyes, sweeting. Look with your heart, not your eyes. See my abbey the way it was then, in my picture.*

Desperately Gray scanned the stone base, calling up the image of Adrian's sketch. And then she remembered that the tower had been slightly off, more rounded than its mate to the north. She ran to the center of the curve, fingers pressed to the rough granite.

And as she did, she stumbled on a half-hidden vine and pitched to her knees. She cried out as her arm struck the wall with a dull, ringing echo.

The next moment stone grated against stone. Gray felt the bank beneath her begin to heave.

And then she was sliding down into a black hole that gaped where once the foundation had stood.

Warm fur brushed her face as she clawed through the loose, damp earth and stumbled to her feet. "Gideon?" she rasped.

A faint meow rose in answer.

Shivering, Gray studied the tunnel that stretched before her, dark and damp. She saw glowing amber pinpoints drift through the shadows at her side and move upward.

Gray followed blindly, feeling loose dirt give way to hard-packed clay and finally to rough stone steps.

Up Gray went, her gaze riveted on the amber eyes that gleamed beside her. Ten steps, twenty . . . until she began to lose count.

Behind her an angry curse exploded up the tunnel. "Damn it, Moira, you can't hope to get away! Not *this* time. And this time, by God, you're going to pay! You're going to beg and beg!"

Shuddering, Gray blocked off the sound of that hated voice, the threats she knew too well. Her hands to the cool stone, she circled round and round, climbing ever higher with Gideon right beside her.

Abruptly the steps came to an end. Her hands met stone, nothing but cold stone on three sides. "—Sweet heaven, what now?"

The cat meowed softly, sliding past her ankles, while angry curses filtered up the narrow stairway.

And then Gray felt the familiar tingling at her spine, the soft kiss of an unseen wind.

Lower, my heart. Down by Gideon . . .

Awkwardly, Gray bent down and searched the wall, crying out in triumph when she felt a narrow gap in the stone. But could she manage to fit?

Ah, we were all a bit smaller then, my heart. But you'll fit, never fear. And when you're through, I'll be there waiting.

Wildly Gray pushed through the narrow opening, clawing her way across a layer of rough, damp stones. Something dug into her wrist and she flinched as a small, sharp object pricked her skin. As she crawled forward, she felt it snag in the folds of her lace gown.

But she paid it no thought, all too aware of the curses that were growing closer every second. Before her she could make out a faint gleam, and she realized it was the star-flung sky.

"I'm . . . coming . . . Adrian!"

And then she was through, out into the chill night. Before her on the abbey's high parapet stars gleamed like cold diamonds flung across a lapis sky.

Best of all, a tall shadow paced the windswept battlements.

His arms opened. Gray flung herself inside.

"Well done. Oh, well done, my heart."

Joy welled up as Gray felt the hard muscles flex, tense, crush her close.

Real again. As real in bone and muscle as she ever needed a man to be. And no matter who—or *what*—he was, being held like this was all Gray wanted or needed from life.

Adrian's lips brushed her hair, soft as the sweep of filtered moonlight. Warm as the kiss of the summer wind.

The shot rang out before she knew it, cracking off the stone walls. Cursing, Adrian shoved her behind him and lunged toward the narrow opening that led from the stairs.

Suddenly moonlight glinted off cold steel and the night exploded into sound. White-faced, Gray saw Adrian sway.

Again and again the gun coughed. This time Adrian stumbled back against the wall.

"Run," he ordered. "Door to the house—beyond the far tower—"

"Dear God, no!" Frozen, Gray watched Adrian's tall form sway. His eyes were wide, raw with desperation and pain.

"Go . . . now . . . sweeting. So d-damned s-sorry—"

Oblivious to the stocky figure crawling out from the inner stairway, oblivious to everything but Adrian's growing pallor, Gray plunged forward to catch him.

But it was too late. Her hands slid through warm blood.

For a moment his fingers dug into her wrists. "R-run!" he cried.

Then with a gasp he stiffened and fell back onto the cold stone roof.

Gray barely heard the muffled snarl, the squish of soft soles on stone. Even Gideon's angry hiss seemed far, far away.

"You're next, Moira my sweet. After we finish our business, of course."

Wild eyed, Gray stared down at the cold slabs where Adrian's body lay unmoving, blood pooling in a dark ring about his chest.

Harsh laughter hammered over the parapets, but even then she did not move, unable to stop crying, unable to tear her eyes from Adrian's pale features.

How young he looks, she thought. His features were calm, perfectly chiseled, almost as if he were sleeping.

Instead of dead.

Dead a second time.

Behind Gray came low cursing. "Did you really think you could escape me?"

Suddenly a gun clinked against stone. "Now, Moira, turn around. I want to see your face when I pull the trigger. By God, I want to hear you beg."

Gray hugged her chest, biting down a sob as she watched the wind riffle Adrian's long hair. *Someday, my love. Maybe . . . someday . . .*

And then she turned to face her nightmare, knowing

this was what Adrian would have wanted most.

He was smaller than she remembered, his face unremarkable, his eyes flat and unintelligent. He was altogether forgettable—not the great menacing figure she had imagined.

He was just a man, Gray realized, just a sick twisted man who needed a victim. She shook her head, feeling the fear and hatred slide away until she was free of her past at last.

"But I'm not begging, Matt. And I'm not afraid of you at all. It's over. You've come too late."

He bellowed a curse and raised a shaking arm to strike her, but the next moment a hissing gray cloud of fur exploded through the darkness and landed on his shoulders.

His gun flashed, erupting in a pinpoint of flame. Gray felt something whine past her cheek. A second shot followed, searing along her wrist.

She barely flinched. "You're too late, Matt. I'll never run again. And that was all you wanted anyway, wasn't it? To see me run."

Every word stoked her pursuer's fury. Cursing, he started toward her. "No, you'll never be free of me! *Never*, do you hear?"

Gray inched back, sickened by his hatred, wanting only to be done with him and all that reminded her of him. But she was not going to give him the pleasure of seeing her run—not when she had no hope of succeeding.

Her fingers dug into the granite wall. She looked away, out over the sleeping countryside, over the wooded hills and shimmering moat.

A low singing rose through her head. Far away there came a distant peal of bells.

Something about the sound made Gray think of home, the home she'd never known.

Once again the gun blazed in the darkness. Dimly she realized she must be in shock, because she barely registered the impact of the third bullet.

She swayed, catching at the stone wall for support. She felt a brief burning, then the hot, thick rush of blood at her breast.

But the pain was far away, blurred, as if it belonged to someone else.

Behind her Matt cursed, then stumbled about in furious surprise. "What in the devil—"

He never finished. A low, harsh voice cut him off.

A voice Gray found achingly familiar.

Her breath caught. She spun around.

Faint spirals of light glinted off the windswept walls, growing brighter every second. And at the center of the strange, swirling radiance stood a man, broad-shouldered and long-limbed, his form growing brighter and more solid every second.

"You! But—you're *dead!* I—I saw you die!" Gray's ex-husband stumbled backwards, his face locked in a grimace of fear and disbelief.

His ghostly pursuer threw back his head and laughed, filling the stone walls with a dark rumble of sound. And then he started forward, his face as hard as marble, his eyes glowing like blood-red coals.

"Get—get away, damn you! It's all a t-trick. You don't frighten m-me, do you hear?" But the man before Adrian trembled, his breath coming jerky and fast. He staggered backwards in a desperate effort to escape.

"No? Then perhaps *this* will frighten you." With an unearthly laugh, Adrian Draycott leveled gleaming, outstretched fingers.

And dragged them right through his terrified killer's body.

"But—you c-can't—damn it! I won't—"

With a shrill cry, the man turned and shoved wildly through the gap into the stairway, his gun clattering forgotten behind him. Dark laughter and wild, dancing light followed him every step of the way as he crashed down the stairwell and threw himself desperately into the moat.

Adrian laughed softly. "Gideon? I believe it's your turn."

Hissing angrily, the big gray cat flicked his tail, then turned and glided off into the night.

Only then did Adrian turn, a smile on his face. Slowly the fury faded from his eyes and was replaced with a look of crushing pain. "Dear God, if only I'd known— if only I could have spared you this."

Gray swayed, suddenly weak. She reached out for Adrian as the parapet seemed to sway and the stars to dance a dizzy jig overhead.

Far away she heard the first low moan of approaching sirens.

"Adrian, I don't feel—"

"Here, love. Right here." Hard hands caught her close, pressed her to his chest.

And then Gray saw the faint silver glow that trickled from her own hands, lapping about her arms and chest.

She stared down, speechless, as the glow grew to dancing sparks, and the sparks to solid swirls of light.

Her eyes sought Adrian's, hazy with pain and shock.

His hands tightened convulsively. Protectively. Infinitely gentle. "I love you, Gray Mackenzie. Will that love be enough for you? Enough for you to trust me? Now and forever?"

She caught a ragged breath, feeling the dizziness grow. Around her the ancient stone walls gleamed, bathed in shimmering columns of light.

She managed a nod and let her eyes finish the answer, shining with a love she'd never hoped to find again.

He caught her up, secure in his arms, his long fingers buried in her silken hair. His smile then was just for her, full of love, full of light, full of joy and promise.

Beneath her ear Gray heard his heart race and felt

the heat of his love surround her, part of the same shimmering glow that lit the night.

Adrian's fingers twined tenderly through hers. "Then . . .then let's go home, my heart. These old stone walls have missed you far too long."

A whirring filled Gray's ears, echoed inside her head. Light and sound swirled up, cascading together into exquisite, luminous melodies. Her fingers tightened.

Into the music they went.

Into the light.

Gray was still smiling when the music spilled out and the abbey walls shimmered away to nothing behind her.

Epilogue

T HE midday sun poured down from a cloudless sky onto a green lawn full of mail-clad knights and giggling, wimple-clad maidens.

High above, in one of Draycott Abbey's mullioned windows, Kacey Mallory Draycott, the wife of the twelfth Viscount, watched the festivities of the abbey's first "Medieval Faire," a faint frown tightening her beautiful brow.

"It doesn't seem right, Nicholas. So much gaiety and life when . . ."

Behind her Nicholas Draycott frowned. She was still too pale, still too quiet. And he'd so bloody hoped this idea of hers would cheer her up, help her forget.

Long, gentle fingers circled Kacey's shoulders and

swept aside her silky blonde hair. Warm lips skimmed her neck. "It was *your* idea, remember? You've put Draycott Abbey back on the map." He slanted an ironic glance at the laughing figures below. "Although I'm not sure I'm entirely thrilled at the idea." His hands tightened. "But it's what Gray would have wanted, I think. Certainly that's what matters most."

Kacey sighed, staring out at the billowing tents and colorful stalls. Slowly she nodded. "You're right, of course. You're always right, you insufferable man." Her hands reached up to clasp her husband close. "It *is* what Gray would have wanted. But do you know, sometimes I almost feel as if she's still here, that I hear her soft laughter drifting over the moat. It's crazy, I know, but—"

Abruptly she stopped, staring down at the milling figures.

"Look, Nicholas!"

"At what, my love? The dancing bear or the monk who's rapidly losing his sandals?"

"No, *there*, just beyond the moat. The woman with the auburn hair. It's—I could swear it's Gray!"

Nicholas's lips tightened. His hands locked about Kacey's shoulders.

"Oh, I know it can't be. I know it's crazy and impossible. But just the same, I—"

This time it was Nicholas who gasped, seeing a tall figure in armor and black velvet stride across the green lawns. "It *can't* be!"

"Can't be what, Nicholas?"

"Adrian!" He shook his head soundly. "No, of course, it isn't." Slowly his mouth curved in a dark smile as he watched the two figures fall laughing into each other's arms, watched the tall, bearded man lift the woman with auburn hair up and spin her around in circles.

A long sleek cat inched from one of the nearby stalls and stood studying the laughing pair.

"By God! Yes, he just might . . ." Nicholas's smile grew to a wolfish grin.

"Nicholas?" Kacey turned to stare at her grinning husband. "What are you muttering about? *Who* can't it be—"

And then she sputtered as her husband cut her off with a fierce kiss planted fiercely against her still-parted lips.

With a soft sigh Kacey slid closer, twining her hands about her husband's neck. Abruptly she pulled back, her eyes wide with worry. "Nicholas, you can't. *We* can't! The mayor and his wife will be here any minute to judge the costume parade. And then there will be a joust and fortune-telling and—"

His hands eased over her silk-clad chest. "I don't need my fortune told, sweet one. I'm doomed to a life of utter bliss in the arms of my beautiful wife." He angled her a besotted smile. "And Marston will manage all of those things splendidly. He always does. Sometimes I even wonder why I bother to appear at all." His fingers slid the fragile silk straps from his wife's shoulders. "And Marston will certainly see to it that the mayor and his wife are kept suitably entertained for another hour or so while we—"

"But Nicholas, I—"

His hands eased the wisp of apricot satin lower. "You're impossibly beautiful, do you know that?"

Kacey's eyes darkened as his fingers slid over the warm skin he had just bared. "But those two—they were—"

Nicholas tongued the pebbled crest that spilled into his fingers. "Come, love, can't you leave a pair of lovers to enjoy a moment's rest?"

"But they weren't resting, they were—" Her eyes closed as her husband's lips slid over her aching skin. "Oh, Nicholas."

In the soft, erotic rustle of silk and heated skin that followed, the laughing pair below were entirely forgotten.

*   *   *

Out in the home wood, where the green leaves whispered and the pool bubbled up crystal from the little glade, two shadows drifted, then shimmered to luminous reality.

Sunlight glinted off auburn hair, spilling forward onto gleaming black.

"Adrian! They saw us, I'm sure of it!"

"Of course they saw us, woman. As guardian spirits, we *must* make ourselves visible to the owners of the abbey now and again. Just to keep them on their toes, of course. There, I think I've finally mastered the business. First you fix your gaze. Then you draw a slow, steady breath and count backwards from twenty." His body swirled, then took on solid form, sunlight gleaming off polished armor.

"Wonderfully done! Twenty, you say?" Gray's eyes narrowed as she began to count.

A moment later she too shimmered into full form, her long golden gown gleaming about her ankles. "I *did* it!"

She looked down and studied the brooch pinned to her dress. "I'm so glad I found your brooch. It must have fallen there in the tunnel all those years ago."

Warm fingers slid beneath her long hair. She sighed, easing back against the hard body behind her. "But Adrian, surely not—not *here?* Anyone might come across us!"

"Ah, that's the beauty of it, love. Only Kacey and Nicholas can see us. And they, I assure you, are far too busy to go out searching for ghosts right now, guardian or any other sort."

His fingers slid lovingly over the sweet curves barely covered by Gray's tissue silk gown. "Ah, God, Gray, you task me sorely! From morning to night you set me working with no reward. Had I known our partnership would be like this—"

"You had a kiss at dawn and rather more than a kiss at noon, stubborn man."

Adrian's lips slid hungrily over her neck. "Bloody less than I wanted," he grumbled.

"Well, there was that kitten to be rescued from the moat. And those wretched men from London were going to chop down that ancient oak beside the road. You couldn't allow that, could you?"

The man beside her gave a long-suffering sigh and mumbled something about letting the whole damned home woods be hewn down to twigs.

Gray turned and twined her arms about Adrian's neck, nibbling a path across his hard jaw. "And there were the roses. Only you seem to be able to work such magic with them." Her tongue teased his ear.

"Stop that! Damn and blast, woman, that's unfair! Not when I can't—"

Adrian's breath caught as he watched her silken gown skim to the ground in an erotic *whoosh*. "Sweet God almighty! Gray—"

"Now who's too busy to—"

Laughter rang out over the glade, a soft sound formed of birdsong and the sighing of the wind.

And the soft moans that only lovers know.

There beneath the shadows of a giant rowan, one might have sworn two lovers pressed close, eyes like smoke, hands urgent and hungry.

And there in the quiet glade, while the moat bubbled happily and lazy bees droned from rose to rose, the two shadows met and became one.

And the long years of sadness were banished from Draycott Abbey forever.

Christina Skye

A descendant of Revolutionary War hero Adam Helmer, CHRISTINA SKYE was born in Dayton, Ohio. She holds a doctorate in classical Chinese literature, has traveled back and forth ten times to the Orient, and is the author of four acclaimed books on Chinese art and theater. She speaks fluent Chinese, along with French and Japanese.

But her first love is England, especially the glittering Regency era. "While researching my first novel, *Defiant Captive*, I visited the fog-swept English coast near Rye and spent the night at a medieval, timber-framed inn on charming, cobbled Mermaid Street.

"Talk about magic! That hypnotic visit plunged me headlong into *The Black Rose*, my second novel.

"Did I forget to mention the dashing ghost?

"I hope not because one thing led to another and somehow I found myself staring up at an imposing oil portrait of a proud, but sad-faced aristocrat. Just beneath the painting sat a huge gray cat, whose amber eyes studied me with disconcerting force.

"I soon discovered that Adrian Draycott and his cat were not to be trifled with. Night and day they plagued me, as relentless as only guardian spirits can be.

"They made it quite clear. Adrian was to be given a love of his own.

"The result? You guessed it.

"The story you're holding in your hands.

"Now maybe the ghosts will disappear and I'll have some peace and quiet at last. But something tells me not to count on it . . .

"I'd love to hear your comments about Adrian and Gray's story.
You can write me at:

111 East 14th Street, #277-A
New York, New York 10003.

Please enclose a stamped, self-addressed envelope for reply."

With best wishes,
Christina Skye

Avon Romances—
the best in exceptional authors and unforgettable novels!

Avon Romantic Treasures

Unforgettable, enthralling love stories,
sparkling with passion and adventure
from Romance's bestselling authors